TRANSFORMING US INTELLIGENCE FOR IRREGULAR WAR

TRANSFORMING US INTELLIGENCE FOR IRREGULAR WAR

TASK FORCE 714 IN IRAQ

RICHARD H. SHULTZ JR.

Georgetown University Press / Washington, DC

The publisher is not responsible for third-party websites or their content. URL links were active at time of publication.

Library of Congress Cataloging-in-Publication Data

Names: Shultz, Richard H., 1947– author.
Title: Transforming US Intelligence for Irregular War : Task Force 714 in Iraq / Richard H. Shultz.
Other titles: Transforming United States intelligence for irregular war
Description: Washington, DC : Georgetown University Press, 2020. | Includes bibliographical references and index.
Identifiers: LCCN 2019023968 (print) | LCCN 2019023969 (ebook) | ISBN 9781626167643 (hardcover) | ISBN 9781626167650 (paperback) | ISBN 9781626167667 (ebook)
Subjects: LCSH: United States. Joint Special Operations Command. | Qaida (Organization) | Intelligence service—United States. | Military intelligence—United States. | Irregular warfare. | Iraq War, 2003–2011—Military intelligence—United States. | Terrorism—Prevention.
Classification: LCC UB251.U6 S48 2020 (print) | LCC UB251.U6 (ebook) | DDC 956.7044/38—dc23
LC record available at https://lccn.loc.gov/2019023968
LC ebook record available at https://lccn.loc.gov/2019023969

♾ This book is printed on acid-free paper meeting the requirements of the American National Standard for Permanence in Paper for Printed Library Materials.

21 20   9 8 7 6 5 4 3 2 First printing

Printed in the United States of America.

Cover design by Jeremy John Parker.

CONTENTS

List of Figures   vii

Foreword by Gen. Joseph L. Votel, USA (Ret.)   ix

Acknowledgments   xi

List of Abbreviations   xv

Introduction: War unlike Yesterday's   1

1   Adapting Intelligence for Twenty-First-Century Irregular Warfare   12

2   Transforming from Hierarchy to Networks to Empower Armed Groups   32

3   Transforming Intelligence Collection for Irregular War   49

4   Transforming Intelligence Analysis for Irregular War   93

5   Transforming Covert Paramilitary Operations for Irregular War   132

6   Task Force 714 and the Sources of Transformation   175

Epilogue: More Irregular War and the Challenge of Revisionist State Powers   201

Notes   215

Index   273

About the Author   287

FIGURES

1.1 Time frames, types of products, and desired outcomes of three
    intelligence levels   26
1.2 Differences between state targets and nonstate armed group targets   28
2.1 Three basic types of networks   46
3.1 The F3EAD process   72
4.1 The intelligence cycle   97
4.2 Support for an insurgency   108
4.3 The persistent surveillance concept   113
4.4 The analysis domains   114

FOREWORD

I FIRST MET DICK SHULTZ SHORTLY AFTER BECOMING COMMANDER OF US Special Operations Command (SOCOM) in 2014. One of the distinct advantages of this position was that it often opened access to our nation's very best academic institutions specializing in security studies. One of these was the Fletcher School of Law and Diplomacy at Tufts University in Boston, where Dick is the Lee E. Dirks Professor of International Politics and director of the International Security Studies Program. Over the course of nearly five years as a combatant commander at SOCOM and later at US Central Command (CENTCOM), I visited Dick multiple times to talk with him and interact with the impressive students in the master of arts in law and diplomacy program—the flagship program of the Fletcher School. While these sessions inevitably turned into question-and-answer sessions about current events in the Middle East, the Levant, and Central and South Asia, they were also an exclusive opportunity for me to use this unique platform to think through the pressing military and security issues present in these troubled but vitally important areas. This was a welcome respite from the normal churn and turbulence of day-to-day activities in the region, and Dick soon became a trusted friend and colleague.

For nearly four decades, Dick has been a respected leader, expert, and educator in international security studies. In addition to his responsibilities at the Fletcher School, he has held several academic chairs and advisory positions throughout the Department of Defense and the academic world. From these positions, Dick has directly taught and influenced countless national and international senior government and defense leaders. He has written extensively on security-related issues ranging from Soviet policy to low-intensity conflict to defense innovation. His impact reaches far beyond Fletcher and its prestigious programs, and he is widely recognized as one of our great security thinkers, possessing the rare ability to see beyond the horizon and identify emerging trends in security studies.

Transforming US Intelligence for Irregular War: Task Force 714 in Iraq is his latest contribution to an extraordinary lifelong body of work. This book traces the transformation of our premier counterterrorism organization in Iraq from the nascent and often unproductive operations of 2003 to the networked machine of 2008 and beyond that "ripped the guts" out of al-Qaeda in Iraq (AQI), changed the course of the war, and forever altered how we approach our counterterrorism and interagency collaboration efforts. Over six tightly scoped chapters, he contrasts the intelligence challenges posed by nonstate armed groups, describes their significant empowerment and emergence since the end of the Cold War as complex networked threats, traces how intelligence functions adapted from their original focus on the Soviet threat to the irregular challenges that emerged in the post-9/11 period, and concludes with a discussion of *how* paramilitary operations changed against the rapidly expanding threat of AQI and, most importantly, *why* this transformation worked. In all this are the lessons for today's national security community as it continues to confront these and other threats.

This work is extensively researched. Dick's unparalleled reputation within the special operations community afforded him unprecedented access and ensured this work included many firsthand observations and insights from the primary actors involved in this remarkable transformation. The names will be familiar to every reader.

Within the security and intelligence communities, Task Force 714 occupies an iconic role and stands as the gold standard for adaptation, innovation, and interagency cooperation. It was initially led by Gen. Stan McChrystal and later by Adm. Bill McRaven; it was my great fortune to follow in their footsteps. For those who were part of TF 714, this book traces the evolution and the monumental achievement it attained. For those not part of this organization, it offers an excellent example of how change occurs—only if something actually changes.

The last chapter of this book makes a particularly compelling case for why transformation and innovation succeeded with TF 714. Touching on the importance of culture, organization, leadership, and trust, it offers a blueprint for future leaders to follow. I believe that the principles, practices, and hard-won success of TF 714 are applicable in virtually every sector: business, nonprofit, science, and government.

With this book, Dick Shultz does a service for all of us by clearly documenting how we must approach security challenges of the future. While this work focuses on the irregular warfare challenge that emerged in the post-9/11 period and that continues to threaten our national interests today, the application is much broader—not just for our security but for anyone interested in changing the modus operandi of routine yet increasingly ineffective approaches to problem solving. The main lesson is simple: engaged leadership, purpose-built organization, flat communication, and concerted teamwork can truly make the difference.

I hope that you enjoy this book and learn from it as much as I have.

Gen. Joseph L. Votel, USA (Ret.)
former commander of US Central Command and
US Special Operations Command

ACKNOWLEDGMENTS

THIS BOOK NEVER COULD HAVE BEEN COMPLETED WITHOUT the encouragement and support of the leadership of the US Special Operations Command (SOCOM) and the assistance of members of the command's Joint Special Operations University (JSOU). However, my initial inspiration to conduct this research on the US counterterrorism forces of the Joint Special Operations Command (JSOC) that deployed to Iraq in 2003 as Task Force 714 came from my longtime friend Col. Bill Ostlund, USA.

I first met Bill when he studied at the Fletcher School of Law and Diplomacy at Tufts University in the latter half of the 1990s to prepare to teach in the Social Sciences Department of the US Military Academy. Then the attacks of 9/11 took place, and for the next twelve years Bill served in a number of combat assignments that put him at the center of the fight. These included serving as deputy commander of the Seventy-Fifth Ranger Regiment, with whom he commanded a counterterrorism task force in Afghanistan on two occasions. During the 2011–12 academic year, Bill returned to Fletcher to complete an Army War College Fellowship. With that fellowship, he produced an exceptional study on his experiences as a counterterrorism task force commander, which was subsequently published by the Institute of Land Warfare under the title *Irregular Warfare: Counterterrorism Forces in Support of Counterinsurgency Operations*.[1] As I had served as his academic adviser for the study, it was my introduction to the evolution of JSOC's counterterrorism forces. I was quite familiar with those counterterrorism forces, having completed a study for the Office of the Undersecretary of Defense for Policy in the early 2000s that addressed the question of why those specialized counterterrorism forces, including the army's Delta Force and the navy's SEAL Team 6, were not employed even once prior to 9/11 to hunt down al-Qaeda terrorists who had taken American lives on several occasions.[2]

In 2014, I approached JSOU, where I am a senior fellow, with the idea of conducting a study focused on TF 714. I had become fascinated with two questions about it. One, *how* did these counterterrorism forces transform from a pre-9/11, highly specialized, and compartmentalized unit designed for executing infrequent missions into an organization capable of shattering AQI? Two, *why* was TF 714 able to achieve this remarkable organizational, technological, and operational sea change in wartime? By this time, Colonel Ostlund was serving on the staff of the SOCOM commander, Gen. Joseph L. Votel, and he played an instrumental role in my being able to undertake the initial research. For all of his help, I am extremely grateful. I am fortunate to have a friend like Bill Ostlund.

Dr. Ken Poole, then JSOU's director of Studies and Research, was central to the production of my initial publication. This report, titled *Military Innovation in War: It Takes a Learning Organization: A Case Study of Task Force 714 in Iraq*, would never have seen the light of day without Ken's guidance and assistance. He helped open doors to those who were part of TF 714 and also was a marvelous editor of the monograph. I am also lucky to have a friend like Ken Poole.

At JSOU, I also had outstanding help during the production process from Robert Nalepa, editor in chief for the Joint Special Operations University Press. Always encouraging and friendly, no one is easier to work with than Rob.

To carry out both the initial and later research on TF 714, I was very fortunate to be able to conduct in-depth interviews with several of its senior leaders. To gain access to these individuals, I drew on my long-standing and close association with the special operations community. Since the mid-1980s, I have maintained a professional working relationship with various elements of that community. I want to thank, in particular, Gen. Stan McChrystal, USA (Ret.), and Adm. Bill McRaven, USN (Ret.), who were instrumental in helping me answer the *how* and *why* questions noted above.

What is rewarding about doing such research for JSOU is that it not only publishes and circulates it widely but teaches about it through courses offered in Tampa and abroad. JSOU's director of academic operations, George "Hal" McNair, encouraged me to turn the study into a presentation that could be taught to US and foreign military officers as part of JSOU's Special Operations Forces Integration Course. I did so, and over the last several years I have deployed as a member of JSOU mobile education teams to Saudi Arabia, Tunisia, Morocco, Estonia, Germany, and elsewhere. I cannot thank Hal enough for providing me with opportunities to give practical application to my research. We have traveled to many parts of the world together, and Hal has become a great friend. And through him I have had the opportunity to work with an array of former operators from the United States, the United Kingdom, Germany, the Netherlands, and Poland. Thank you, Hal.

Even as I was completing the JSOU study, I had determined that TF 714 was part of a larger story about twenty-first-century irregular warfare and the extent to which intelligence had to adapt to help meet the challenges posed by it.

Specifically, to what extent were transformational changes needed in the intelligence disciplines of collection, analysis, and covert paramilitary operations? During the Cold War and in its 1990s aftermath, US intelligence was constructed to contend with challenges triggered by nation states. But now it faced a very different adversary—armed groups—and an irregular warfare context. These differences, I believed, had necessitated major changes in the operational methods, practices, and procedures of intelligence. However, no study had uncovered the extent to which such adaptations took place or evaluated the effectiveness and contributions those changes made in helping TF 714 successfully fight twenty-first-century irregular war against al-Qaeda in Iraq and elsewhere.

To undertake this study, I approached the Smith Richardson Foundation and submitted a proposal for research support. At the foundation, Dr. Marin Strmecki, vice president and director of programs, and Dr. Nadia Schadlow, senior program officer for the international security and foreign policy program, were instrumental in helping me submit a successful proposal. Marin and Nadia also took great interest in the substance of the study and encouraged my efforts throughout the research and writing of this book. Their professional advice and friendship have been invaluable. I also want to thank the Lynde and Harry Bradley Foundation for its support of this project and especially Dianne J. Sehler, former director of Academic, International, and Cultural Programs. Dianne likewise was extremely encouraging and helped me successfully submit a proposal.

Two very talented graduate students at the Fletcher School assisted me with the research and drafting of two chapters. I want to thank Namsai Wongsaeree, a wonderfully talented student from Thailand, whose assistance on chapter 1 was invaluable. Since graduating from Fletcher, Namsai has joined Thailand's foreign service, which is fortunate to have her. For chapter 2, I had the outstanding assistance of Polina Beliakova, who joined Fletcher's doctoral program after completing a master of arts degree in government, diplomacy, and strategy from the Lauder School at IDC Herzliya in Israel. From Ukraine, Polina is a truly outstanding student with a bright future ahead of her in academia.

I would like to say a special thank you to Kathy Spagnoli, grants/staff assistant for the International Security Studies Program at the Fletcher School. We refer to Kathy as the "holder of the purse string," but, for this project, she was the manager of the editing process. As our professional editor—Nigel Quinney—returned each marked-up chapter to us, Kathy worked closely with me to answer all his many queries and to make all appropriate changes. She did an outstanding job in helping me finalize the manuscript for Georgetown University Press. I am very fortunate to have had Kathy's marvelous assistance.

Finally, I want to thank and extend my warmest and best wishes to Don Jacobs, senior acquisitions editor for Georgetown University Press. From the very beginning when I submitted the initial proposal, Don has been a delight to work with. He is a real pro, and it shows in all he does with an author. Thank you, Don. It is my good fortune to have found you.

ABBREVIATIONS

ABI	activity-based intelligence
AFSA	Armed Forces Security Agency
AQAP	al-Qaeda in the Arabian Peninsula
AQC	al-Qaeda core
AQI	al-Qaeda in Iraq
AQN Exord	al Qaeda Network Execute Order
AQY	al-Qaeda in Yemen
AUSA	Association of the United States Army
CBRNE	chemical, biological, radiological, nuclear, and explosive
CC&D	camouflage, concealment, and deception
CENTCOM	Central Command
CIA	Central Intelligence Agency
CIG	Central Intelligence Group
CNC	Counternarcotics Center
COI	Office of Coordinator of Information
COIN	counterinsurgency
COMINT	communications intelligence
CRS	Congressional Research Service
CSS	Central Security Service
CT	counterterrorism
CTC	Counterterrorism Center
CTIC	counterterrorism intelligence center
DCGS	Distributed Common Ground System
DI	Directorate of Intelligence
DIA	Defense Intelligence Agency
DO	Directorate of Operations
DOD	Department of Defense
ELINT	electronic intelligence
EM	electromagnetic
F3	find, fix, and finish

F3EAD	find, fix, finish, exploit, analyze, and disseminate
FARC	Revolutionary Armed Forces of Colombia
FBI	Federal Bureau of Investigation
FBIS	Foreign Broadcast Intelligence [or Information] Service
FBMS	Foreign Broadcast Monitoring Service
FISINT	foreign instrumentation and signals
GID	General Intelligence Department
HPSCI	House Permanent Select Committee on Intelligence
HUMINT	human intelligence
HVT	high-value target
I&W	indications and warning
IC	intelligence community
ICBM	intercontinental ballistic missile
IDF	Israel Defense Forces
IED	improvised explosive device
IMINT	imagery intelligence
INT	intelligence
IS	Islamic State
ISAF	International Security Assistance Force
ISI	Islamic State of Iraq
ISIL	Islamic State of Iraq and the Levant
ISIS	Islamic State in Iraq and Syria
ISOF	Iraqi Special Operations Force
ISR	intelligence, surveillance, and reconnaissance
IT	information technology
IW	irregular warfare
J2	intelligence chief/directorate
JIATF	joint interagency task force
JSOC	Joint Special Operations Command
JSOU	Joint Special Operations University
JWR	Joint War Room
LNO	liaison officer
MASINT	measurements and signatures intelligence
NASA	National Aeronautics and Space Administration
NDS	National Defense Strategy
NGA	National Geospatial-Intelligence Agency
NIE	national intelligence estimate
NIMA	National Imagery and Mapping Agency
NMEC	National Media Exploitation Center

NPC	Nonproliferation Center
NRO	National Reconnaissance Office
NSA	National Security Agency
NSC-68	National Security Council Directive 68
O&I	operations and intelligence
OCI	Office of Current Intelligence
ONE	Office of National Estimates
ORR	Office of Research and Reports
OSINT	open-source intelligence
OSS	Office of Strategic Services
PDD	presidential decision directive
PDB	President's Daily Brief
PHOTINT	photographic intelligence
PRIO	Peace Research Institute
QDR	Quadrennial Defense Review
RMA	revolution in military affairs
RTRG	Real Time Regional Gateway
SAS	Special Air Service
SBS	Special Boat Service
SCS	Special Collection Service
SIGINT	signals intelligence
SMO	support to military operations
SNA	social network analysis
SOCOM	Special Operations Command
SOF	special operations forces
SOP	standard operating procedure
SSCI	Senate Select Committee on Intelligence
SWCS	Special Warfare Center and School
TAG	Technical Advisory Group
TF	task force
TMA	traditional military activities
TTPs	tactics, techniques, and procedures
UAV	unmanned aerial vehicle
VBIED	vehicle-borne improvised explosive device
VTC	video teleconferencing
WAPS	wide-area persistent surveillance
WMD	weapon of mass destruction

INTRODUCTION: WAR UNLIKE YESTERDAY'S

IN A 1997 PRESENTATION AT THE NATIONAL PRESS CLUB IN WASHINGTON, Gen. Charles Krulak, who was then commandant of the US Marine Corps, spoke of new security threats and the challenges of "training Marines for the twenty-first century and for different types of conflict." Those future fights, he warned, would be "not like yesterday."[1] In a subsequent speech and essay, the commandant elaborated: "Our most dangerous enemies will challenge us asymmetrically in ways against which we are least able to bring our strength to bear."[2] He singled out irregular conflicts in Chechnya and Somalia as illustrative. But in 1997, Krulak's warning was premature for US security institutions—military, diplomatic, and intelligence—that had responsibility to prepare for future conflicts. Their frame of reference was Operation Desert Storm, the 1991 routing of the Iraqi army occupying Kuwait. It was an exemplar of the twentieth-century paradigm of war. In this case, US and allied forces initiated a month of heavy air bombardment followed by a massive Coalition ground offensive that overwhelmed the Iraqi army, forcing it into a chaotic retreat from Kuwait.

However, in the aftermath of the surprise attacks of September 11, 2001, what Krulak anticipated came to pass. US security institutions were now compelled to confront a conflict environment that differed in three critical ways from that which they had faced during the Cold War and the 1990s.

The first difference was that the forty-plus years of the Cold War and the decade thereafter were, for the most part, a period of prolonged peace. With a few important exceptions—most notably, Korea and Vietnam—US security institutions were not operating in a wartime environment. But since 9/11, those institutions have faced a protracted wartime milieu. The United States has been involved in two major irregular wars in Iraq and Afghanistan, has engaged in war in Syria, and has conducted lengthy, albeit intermittent, military operations in Somalia, Yemen, and Pakistan.

The second difference has to do with the kind of wars US security institutions have fought so far in the twenty-first century. They are very different from the major wars fought by the US military in the twentieth century. Those were conventional wars in which the armies of states fought each other on battlefields. Their theoretical origins can be found in Carl von Clausewitz's affirmations that war is entrenched first and foremost in the interactions between states and that war is a continuation of state politics by "other means." Those other means were the armies of states fighting one another. Regular militaries of two or more states engaged in battles, the objective of which was to destroy the opponent's army and then impose the victor's political will to achieve the goals for which the war was initially fought.

The wars the United States has engaged in since 9/11 have been different from what Clausewitz examined. In its twenty-first-century wars, the United States has battled nonstate actors—armed groups—that have employed indirect and asymmetrical tactics, techniques, and procedures. These are best described as forms of irregular warfare. Irregular warfare is an intrastate fight between the government of a state or an intervening state power and internal armed opposition groups that may receive outside support from other states or other nonstate actors.

The third difference lies in the fact that the armed groups that US security institutions have fought in post-9/11 irregular wars are different from their twentieth-century counterparts. This was particularly apparent in the case of al-Qaeda in Iraq (AQI), the case study around which this book is constructed.[3] AQI was unlike any insurgent or terrorist organization that preceded it. AQI, and several of its contemporaries, did not resemble any organizational pattern seen during the Cold War. It was not hierarchical but organized as decentralized units that employed Information Age technologies to form dispersed networks that could escalate attacks across a broad geographic landscape. Moreover, AQI presented complex challenges that proved difficult to deal with because it had many constituent components that operated in unexpected ways, with scores of linkages that could not be easily identified and charted. There was little consistency in its operational activities.

Twenty-first-century armed groups pose complex challenges because they comprise a plethora of decentralized networks that make effective use of two sanctuaries, one old and the other new. The former consists of populated areas where armed groups hide within plain sight. The Information Age provided the latter one, a new electronic sanctuary in which armed group activities are hidden within vast jams of Internet traffic and innumerable cell phone calls.

In the immediate aftermath of 9/11, as peacetime turned into wartime, US security institutions tasked with combating these new enemies faced major new challenges. The post-9/11 developments just described had a debilitating impact on each of those military, diplomatic, and intelligence institutions and on the effectiveness of their standard operating procedures (SOPs) for warfighting. Those procedures were developed for a different age, a different context, a different problem set, and a different kind of enemy.

A sea change was needed in the way each of those institutions responded to post-9/11 irregular warfare challenges. And while each institution had an important role to play, this book focuses on the most pivotal of those roles: the part played by intelligence in irregular warfare campaigns. Following the toppling of the regime in Iraq, a recurring theme found in the doctrines and operational concepts developed by the US military for fighting nonstate armed groups can be summed up in the refrain *intelligence leads the way.*

Consider *Counterinsurgency*, US Army Field Manual FM-24, published in 2006, which received great fanfare during the 2007 "surge" in Iraq, when an additional twenty thousand US troops were deployed into Baghdad and Al Anbar Province.[4] "Counterinsurgency is an intelligence driven endeavor," it declares. "The ultimate success or failure of its mission depends on the effectiveness of the intelligence effort. . . . Intelligence drives operations and successful operations generate additional intelligence."[5] The Pentagon's 2010 *Irregular Warfare Joint Operating Concept (JOC)* concurred, stressing that "intelligence-driven operations will require long-term investments in human, technical, forensic, and cultural intelligence to illuminate the adversaries' networks, support activities, and personalities."[6] And just as intelligence was entrusted with leading the way in counterinsurgency (COIN) efforts, so it was expected to lead the way in counterterrorism operations, whether conducted alone or as part of a COIN campaign. As we shall see in this study, senior US commanders who led counterterrorism operations in Iraq resolved that intelligence was the sine qua non for success in irregular warfare operations.

Transforming Intelligence for Irregular War

The authors of intelligence studies that appeared in the first decade of this century were in no doubt that the kinds of intelligence methods and capabilities required to meet the challenges posed by twenty-first-century armed groups and irregular conflicts are different from those employed against twentieth-century state threats. For example, in his 2009 book *Intelligence in the Age of Terror*, Gregory Treverton, a former vice chair of the National Intelligence Council, asserted that while "change in intelligence targets is widely acknowledged [by intelligence specialists], its implications run far deeper than are usually recognized. The changes needed go to the heart of how intelligence does its business—from collection to analysis to dissemination."[7]

Neal Pollard of the National Counterterrorism Center agreed with Treverton: "The primary targets of intelligence today are non-state actors: terrorist groups and their leaders, suppliers, sponsors, and facilitators." He went on to add that these changes necessitate "a dramatic shift by the U.S. intelligence community, which was built to focus on states." Pollard held that nonstate threats were "more difficult [targets] to manage . . . than those during the Cold War," and he contended that US intelligence agencies "do not have the configuration . . . to observe the multitude of urban settings and globalized infrastructures" through which these clandestine and networked organizations "move money, people, weapons and plans."[8] Other specialists in intelligence concurred.[9]

According to a growing chorus of such specialists, meeting new challenges necessitated that each of the four primary instruments, or functions, of intelligence —collection, analysis, counterintelligence, and covert action—undergo major adaptations to their operating procedures. Configured for working against state targets, the tools of the intelligence craft were judged deficient for managing twenty-first-century irregular threats. A few examples from books and articles published at this time illustrate the larger argument about the need for adaptation.

Several specialists argued that the collection disciplines demanded significant change. Consider technical intelligence collection, "a group of techniques using advanced technology . . . to collect information."[10] Jeffrey Richelson called for a reexamination of "the value of technical collection against the full range of targets that exist in the post-September 11 world." He challenged the argument that armed groups necessitate that "more attention and resources be devoted to HUMINT [human intelligence] and less to technical collection." Richelson conceded that "America's terrorist adversaries are small and fleet" and that "a satellite that passes briefly overhead during its orbit may not be able to catch a convoy in the desert." But, he pointed out, that does not mean there is no role for imagery. Just the opposite! Other platforms—manned and unmanned—have an important role to play. Richelson provided an interesting analysis of those alternative systems.[11] Other specialists likewise stressed the applicability of unmanned aerial vehicles (UAVs) for intelligence collection against nontraditional collection targets.[12]

Signals collection also received a good deal of scrutiny. Specialists noted that decentralized and networked armed groups must communicate to execute operations through modern information tools, and that makes those groups vulnerable to signals interception. Signals intelligence is a powerful tool, they stressed, that intelligence agencies can wield to penetrate a terrorist group's communications and learn about its plans, hideouts, and much more. But to do so, those tasked with signals collection had to adapt to this new target, and US capabilities required considerable modernization and expansion.[13]

In the aftermath of 9/11, other intelligence specialists began to call for a change in the processes and practices of analysis.[14] For example, Richards Heuer, one of the leading innovators in the field, proposed the need to harness new information technologies with rigorous analytic techniques to boost the capabilities of intelligence analysts to address more complex challenges.[15] The emergence of different kinds of armed groups and the unconventional security challenges they posed fostered recognition of the need for new analytic tools for assessing how nonstate actors organize and operate.[16]

The 9/11 attacks and their aftermath also changed the terms of reference with respect to covert action and whether it should be used at all.[17] This was particularly true of covert action's paramilitary variant, its use in responding to violent extremism, and whether the Central Intelligence Agency (CIA) or the US Special Operations Command (SOCOM) should have major responsibility for executing these missions. While this was not a new issue, the debate was renewed by the 9/11 Commission, which recommended that the Department of Defense (DOD) take over responsibility for paramilitary operations.[18] This proposal not only generated considerable attention in the intelligence-related literature but also attracted serious congressional scrutiny.[19]

This discourse over intelligence reform underscored the need for a critical reconsideration of the state-centric approach to intelligence theory and practice that dominated during the Cold War and the 1990s. Each of the four primary instruments of intelligence would have to undergo major changes to its operating tactics, techniques, and procedures to be able to engage effectively against twenty-first-century irregular threats. This realization followed on the heels of major governmental investigations, critiques, and reassessments of US intelligence that began with congressional hearings in 2002 and culminated in the *9/11 Commission Report*.[20]

What these postmortems all emphasized was the need for change in the structure and functions of post-9/11 US intelligence. But no study to date has determined the extent to which revisions actually took place in the operational methods, practices, or procedures of US intelligence and whether they were effective. *Transforming US Intelligence for Irregular War: Task Force 714 in Iraq* seeks to fill that gap by examining whether, and to what extent, the intelligence disciplines of collection, analysis, and the paramilitary variant of covert action were adapted and restructured during the 2000s for fighting an irregular war against al-Qaeda and its associated movements in Iraq.

This book explores a major counterterrorism campaign in that war, the 2003–10 fight against AQI. Within that campaign it is possible to isolate, delve deeply into, and assess the extent to which intelligence changed its Cold War, state-centric methods in order to fight a new, decentralized, and networked enemy. Through an examination of this case study, we can determine whether, and to what extent, three of the elements of intelligence—collection, analysis, and the paramilitary variation of covert action—were transformed for the fight against a twenty-first-century nonstate armed group.

Counterterrorism Task Force 714

TF 714's commander, Maj. Gen. Stanley McChrystal, has said that it "brought an Industrial Age force to an Information Age war. But in this fight, we are not facing an organized army. If we're going to win, we need to become a network."[21] SOCOM's counterterrorism forces deployed to Iraq in 2003 as Task Force 714. Once in Iraq, TF 714 quickly came face to face with an ugly surprise. Tasked to find, degrade, and dismantle the burgeoning al-Qaeda–dominated insurgent apparatus, TF 714 soon realized that it could not achieve that mission. To do so, TF 714 would have to reinvent itself in the midst of war. Its leadership concluded that the task force faced an enemy that it had never envisaged and that it could not dismantle that foe through TF 714's preexisting ways of conducting counterterrorism operations. TF 714 had to change from a highly specialized and compartmentalized unit customized to execute infrequent counterterrorism missions in peacetime to a wartime, intelligence-led organization if it was to stand a chance of dismantling AQI's clandestine networks that operated across Iraq. TF 714 had to achieve intelligence dominance by developing new methods to battle AQI's secret apparatus.

To change a highly compartmentalized counterterrorism force with a culture of secrecy and semiautonomy—a force that was considered the best in the world at its job—would not be easy. But in 2004, it was clear to General McChrystal that, as constituted, his counterterrorism forces could not keep pace with, let alone reduce, AQI's accelerating operational tempo. He concluded that TF 714 had to "adapt to a new, more ominous threat." It "needed to become a more complex organization with unprecedented capability, and needed to be able to employ that capability on a daily basis."[22] Over the next two years, TF 714 did just that, transforming into a highly effective interagency organization described by one knowledgeable observer as "a precision-killing machine unprecedented in the history of modern warfare."[23] Consider the following acceleration in its capacity to conduct operations against AQI's networks. In August 2004, TF 714 executed eighteen raids against those secret networks. And "as great as those eighteen raids were," explained McChrystal, "they couldn't make a dent in the exploding insurgency."[24] In August 2006, TF 714 executed three hundred raids against AQI targets.[25] And those raids did much more than decapitate AQI's top leadership. They began to eviscerate AQI's extensive network of midlevel operational commanders and the managers of its financial units, communications and media centers, intelligence services, bomb and improvised explosive device (IED) production facilities, and arms acquisitions. From 2006 to late 2009, the task force maintained that operational tempo of three hundred raids a month. In doing so, it severely degraded AQI's capacity to carry out violent attacks. By developing the capacity to operate inside networks, TF 714 was able, in the words of McChrystal, to "claw the guts out of AQI."[26] According to Adm. William McRaven, TF 714's commander in 2008, those results were demonstrable. "We could see our impact on particular parts of their networks," he said.[27] He elaborated: "What we saw in the intelligence being collected during our raids, and from the interrogations of the many members of AQI that we captured on those raids, was that a major decline was taking place in the capacity of different parts of their networks to carry out operations. Our kill/capture raids were considerably driving down their operational capacity. We were able to gauge and evaluate that decline."[28]

As this book will demonstrate, AQI had been significantly dismantled by the end of 2009, as reflected in the decline in its ability to function and carry out attacks. In the words of McRaven, "We were able, through raid after raid, to shatter it."[29]

Research Puzzle and Study Structure

To decipher the puzzle of TF 714's transformation, two interrelated research questions are examined. First, *how* did SOCOM's counterterrorism forces, deployed as TF 714, transform from a pre-9/11 highly specialized and compartmentalized unit designed for executing infrequent counterterrorism missions into an organization capable of shattering the operational capacity of AQI? And to what extent were changes in the methods and practices of the intelligence disciplines of collection, analysis, and the paramilitary variant of covert action important contributors to TF 714's success? Second, *why* was TF 714 able to achieve this remarkable makeover in wartime? To what extent can its success in Iraq be explained as the result of having adopted the practices of a learning organization, which involved turning traditional approaches to military leadership on their heads and learning from the experiences of others?[30]

The book is divided into six chapters. Chapter 1, "Adapting Intelligence for Twenty-First-Century Irregular Warfare," begins by setting the scene for the remarkable transformation of TF 714 into an intelligence-led counterterrorism machine by describing the conflict environment in which US security institutions have operated since 9/11. That context is described as one in which irregular warfare became the predominant form of armed struggle. US security institutions engaged in those conflicts faced violent nonstate armed groups that employed indirect, networked, and asymmetrical strategies. Next, the chapter provides an overview of the four key functions of intelligence—collection, analysis, counterintelligence, and covert action—and explains why this book focuses on only collection, analysis, and the paramilitary variant of covert action techniques. Chapter 1 concludes by contrasting the intelligence challenges posed by states with those presented by nonstate armed groups.

Chapter 2, "From Hierarchy to Networks to Empower Armed Groups," describes how armed groups have experienced significant empowerment since the end of the Cold War, enhancing their capabilities and capacity to conduct irregular war. Distinguishing twentieth-century hierarchical and centralized armed groups from their twenty-first-century decentralized and networked counterparts was critical if TF 714 was to figure out the challenges it faced in Iraq. Chapter 2 illuminates how this evolution of armed groups manifested itself in the emergence of complex networked threats and new operational challenges, of which the Iraq insurgency offered a striking example. AQI consisted of a network of networks spread across Iraq. For US intelligence and counterterrorism forces, this constituted a new kind of adversary.

The next three chapters assess the extent to which the three elements of intelligence noted above—collection, analysis, and the paramilitary variation of covert action—were able to adapt and change from their Cold War modus operandi, which had been routinized over several decades.

Chapter 3, "Transforming Intelligence Collection for Irregular War," begins with a description of the methods of intelligence collection. These include signals, imagery, and measurements and signatures collected by highly technical machines; the acquisition of secrets through human sources; and publicly available open-source information in either electronic or printed form. The development of those collection capabilities was largely shaped by the challenge of penetrating the United States' Cold War foe, the Soviet Union. Finding the USSR's strategic military forces and defense infrastructure drove the development of US intelligence-collection systems for more than four decades. Collection requirements focused on an Industrial Age enemy that was a skilled practitioner of denial-and-deception methods and had a closed political system. Chapter 3 examines the extent to which signals, imagery, measurements and signatures, and human and open-source collection were adapted to support the counterterrorism forces fighting AQI. The extent to which each collection discipline was able to shed its Cold War roles and missions is the central concern of the chapter. It focuses on whether and to what extent changes in these intelligence-collection methods supported TF 714's mission of attacking and dismantling AQI's secret and networked underground.

Chapter 4, "Transforming Intelligence Analysis for Irregular War," likewise begins by briefly looking back to describe the origins of US intelligence analysis and its evolution during the Cold War and the post–Cold War 1990s. Next, the chapter discusses the challenges faced in assessing the changing context of twenty-first-century irregular war and explains why Cold War methods of analysis were no longer sufficient. With this as prologue, the requirements of post-9/11 wartime intelligence analysis are identified, along with the ordeals analysts faced operating in a new and unfamiliar "human warfighting domain," one in which they had to search for unknown or vaguely understood subjects and objects. Analysts had to learn to employ new tools and techniques to discover insurgent and terrorist networks whose signatures or identifiable characteristics and locations were unknown. To do so, analysts sought to exploit changes in post-9/11 collection systems and the vast amounts of data those systems generated to discover secret networks and identify individuals and activities within them. Chapter 4 describes the "new analysis" that emerged during the Iraq War to manage the massive increase in operational-level data and to employ new analytic tools for investigating, unearthing, and connecting key developments and individuals hidden within the AQI network. Only then could the clandestine networks of Iraqi insurgents be uncovered, illustrated graphically, and assessed. Intelligence analysts had to be able to drill down into that data to locate well-hidden insurgent networks. The extent to which these changes allowed analysts assigned to TF 714 to discover and map an enemy hidden in two types of sanctuary is the central concern of chapter 4.

Chapter 5, "Transforming Covert Paramilitary Operations for Irregular War," begins by setting the terms of reference for covert action and describing its different subdisciplines. Scholars of intelligence have divided covert action into specific modes of nonviolent and violent activities. This chapter begins by describing the three traditional covert action variants: propaganda, political action, and paramilitary operations. Next, the US use of covert action is divided into three post–World War II periods. The first two—the Cold War and the post–Cold War 1990s—are variations of peacetime, although important differences exist between them with respect to covert action programs. The chapter briefly highlights how US presidents employed covert action in each period. It also describes how, in the last decade of the Cold War and in the 1990s, presidential use of covert action was constrained by moral concerns manifested in an oversight architecture enacted by Congress to curb the use of covert action. That architecture is described, and its impact on presidential authorities is discussed. With this as prelude, the central concern of chapter 5—the extent to which the 9/11 attacks led to a dramatic rise in the employment of the paramilitary variant of covert action by TF 714—is addressed. After 9/11, al-Qaeda constituted a clear and present danger, and the fight against it rose to the level of war, said President George W. Bush.[31] In 2003, Iraq became the central front for al-Qaeda, the forward edge of the global battle, from which it sought to attack US forces and interests. Chapter 5 examines how AQI escalated its use of violence from 2004 to 2006 in Iraq and how TF 714 recreated itself as an intelligence-led paramilitary force to counteract that unprecedented challenge. Most notably, TF 714 greatly increased the operational tempo of its direct-action night raids against AQI's secret networks. Chapter 5 assesses what impact that had on the conduct of war in Iraq.

Up to this point, this book explains *how* TF 714 was able to accomplish its mission to dismantle AQI's secret networks in Iraq from 2006 to 2010—how it transformed from a stand-alone, highly specialized, peacetime counterterrorism force constructed for occasional hostage-rescue and direct-action missions to a wartime machine capable of sustaining an operational tempo that overwhelmed AQI. What remains to be deciphered is *why* the task force was able, in the midst of war, to accomplish this mission. Why was TF 714 able to achieve this organizational, technological, and operational transformation? The literature on military innovation has found several factors that should have prevented adaptation and change. But those obstacles did not stand in the way of TF 714. Why? What accounts for its capacity to change?

To explain why it was able to innovate, transforming itself during the darkest days of the Iraq War, chapter 6, "Task Force 714 and the Sources of Transformation," identifies three factors that enabled this evolution to occur. Each is an outgrowth of organizational learning. First, TF 714 adopted characteristics that allow an organization facing a crisis in practice to learn through self-reflection and to transform itself based on such reassessments. It employed features of a learning organization that foster introspection, adaptation, and change. Second, the task force's leadership facilitated learning and innovation by acting against the instincts of traditional military commanders. In other words, the leadership decentralized authority to nurture initiative at the operating level that did not have to wait for direction from the top of the chain of command to attack a new target. Third, TF 714 expanded its network to establish liaison relationships with other nations fighting terrorism. It did so to learn from the experiences of allies who faced related challenges and innovated. Of these, Israel was the most prominent. The organizational, technological, and operational adaptations made by Israeli security institutions to overcome the challenge of the Second Intifada held important lessons for TF 714, and through a close liaison with Israeli counterparts the Americans were able to learn the details of those developments.

The chapters in this book give a full account of the remarkable evolution of TF 714 from a highly specialized unit designed for executing infrequent counterterrorism missions into an organization that from 2006 to 2009 shattered the operational capacity of AQI's networks. The war in Iraq was "not like yesterday," as TF 714's commander, General McChrystal, quickly discovered. As he subsequently stated, "Task Force 714 brought an Industrial Age force to an Information Age war." But the task force adapted and innovated to prevail in that irregular fight. What follows is the story of how and why it was able to do so.

CHAPTER 1

ADAPTING INTELLIGENCE FOR TWENTY-FIRST-CENTURY IRREGULAR WARFARE

SINCE THE END OF THE COLD WAR, the predominant form of armed conflict has been generated by armed groups utilizing irregular warfare methods to pursue their objectives against state actors. This form of armed violence, especially following 9/11, has had a significant impact on those US institutions—military, diplomatic, and intelligence—that have been employed to manage irregular warfare operations in Iraq, Afghanistan, and elsewhere.

While each of these institutions is needed to manage a complex twenty-first-century international security environment in which armed groups employing irregular warfare methods are a major source of instability, it is the argument of this book that *intelligence must lead the way.* But it must be a different form of intelligence than the United States relied on in the Cold War and the 1990s. The kinds of intelligence capabilities needed to meet irregular challenges posed by armed groups in an irregular wartime environment are different from those employed against nation-states in peacetime. This chapter provides an overview of the essential differences between the challenges that state and nonstate armed groups pose for the security services of the United States and other nation-states tasked with managing irregular conflict in the twenty-first century.

Armed Groups and Irregular Warfare: Post–Cold War Security Challenges

In 1991, as the Cold War was coming to an end, a US-led coalition of thirty-four countries executed Operation Desert Storm, a massive display of conventional military power that ousted the occupying Iraqi army from Kuwait in a matter of days. For many defense specialists, conventional warfare carried out in this way was the blueprint that "set the stage for future military operations." Operation Desert Storm and the military doctrine upon which it was based were proclaimed the "cornerstones for contemporary military operations."[1]

Also in 1991, the military historian Martin van Creveld published *The Transformation of War*.[2] His central argument was radical and the converse of those who viewed Operation Desert Storm as defining the boundaries of future conflict and war. Further, van Creveld asserted that conventional war between nation-states, like that of Desert Storm and so many wars that preceded it in the twentieth century, was declining. "We are standing today . . . at a historic turning point," he asserted, in which "conventional war appears to be in the final stages."[3] Low-intensity conflicts, in which state and nonstate armed groups engage in irregular warfare, would replace it in short order, he predicted:

> As war between states exits through one side of history's revolving doors, low-intensity conflict . . . will enter through the other. Present-day low-intensity conflict is overwhelmingly confined to the so-called developing world. However, to think this will be so forever or even for very long is almost certainly a great illusion. . . . As the last decade of the century dawns, entire regions whose stability appeared assured since 1945 . . . are beginning to go up in flames.[4]

In all, van Creveld envisaged fundamental changes in terms of who fights, how they fight, where they fight, and why they fight. To begin with, he proposed that states no longer had a monopoly over the use of organized violence and the conduct of war. They were being challenged by nonstate war-making groups and organizations, including terrorists, insurgents, tribes, armed commercial organizations (e.g., criminal cartels), and militias. These nonstate entities would fight in "protracted, bloody, and horrible" ways through "skirmishes, bombings, assassinations and massacres." And they would do so in complex "environments intermingled with civilians," not on open battlefields where armies traditionally faced off. Finally, armed groups would fight not for "reasons of state" but for other objectives, including religion and ethnicity. Plunder would also be a motivation for organized violence.[5]

In the 1990s, only a small number of specialists agreed with van Creveld's audacious forecast. Many military and defense specialists challenged his arguments as without foundation in reviews in professional security journals. For example, the *Naval War College Review* found his hypothesis that future wars would take the form of low-intensity conflicts "vulnerable." Those low-intensity conflicts then taking place were occurring because of a "historically specific set of circumstances" having to do with the "weakness of contemporary states." But the Cold War's aftermath "suggests a new pattern," the reviewer proposed. "States of the 21st century . . . are likely to be more stable and confident" with a "firmer moral basis," making them less vulnerable to "threats posed by low-intensity conflict."[6] *Military Review* was even more critical: "While much of what van Creveld says is thought-provoking, his arguments are often jumbled by bold and sometimes unsupportable assertions." Rather than discovering an "audacious searching examination of the nature of war," the reviewer found van Creveld's "disparate thoughts" to be "preposterous."[7] A review in the *RUSI Journal*, the oldest defense and military affairs journal, concluded that while van Creveld's book "might be useful for academic debate," it was of no use "for practical military planning" and "will not find its way into a soldier's backpack."[8]

But in 2007, less than twenty years later, a former deputy supreme allied commander Europe, Gen. Rupert Smith, intimated that van Creveld had been largely correct. In *The Utility of Force: The Art of War in the Modern World*, Smith asserted, "A paradigm shift in war has undoubtedly occurred from armies with comparable forces doing battle to a confrontation between a range of combatants [state and nonstate] . . . using different types of weapons, often improvised. The old paradigm was that of interstate industrialized war. The new one is the paradigm of war amongst the people. . . . [It] can take place anywhere: in the presence of civilians, against civilians, in defense of civilians."[9] Smith argued that this pattern of conflict had dominated the post–Cold War years and was here to stay for the foreseeable future. It constituted the prevalent pattern of instability taking place in different regions of the world. The nature of war had not changed. It remained "a violent clash of interests between or among organized groups characterized by the use of military force."[10] But what had changed were those doing the fighting. No longer were they only the armies of nation-states. Nonstate armed groups were now central actors. A significant number of scholars and analysts came to the same conclusion.[11]

To what extent were they right? Had the nature of instability evolved since the end of the Cold War and in the shadows of 9/11 in the ways proposed by van Creveld and Smith? In the 1990s, did a shift in the patterns of conflict begin, with interstate war declining while intrastate conflicts were increasing? And has the twenty-first-century security landscape likewise been dominated by intrastate wars that involve nonstate armed groups employing asymmetrical and unconventional tactics, techniques, and procedures (TTPs) to pursue their objectives against nation-states? It is to these issues that we now turn.

Trends in Twenty-First-Century Intrastate Conflict

General Smith's contention that a "paradigm shift in war has undoubtedly oc-curred" is corroborated by what has transpired since the end of the Cold War in 1991. Conflict and instability have appreciably changed, and the predominant form of armed violence taking place over the past twenty-five-plus years has been caused by armed groups waging irregular warfare. A rise in the number of weak and fragile states has provided the context in which many of these newly empow-ered nonstate actors have been able, through violent means, to affect stability and security both at the local level and transnationally. Moreover, some armed groups have demonstrated the capacity to execute violent strikes against powerful nation-states. This appears to be the case in particular for armed groups that can operate transnationally. As is explained below, armed groups today have access to power-enhancing capabilities that were not available to their Cold War counterparts.

Studies of the patterns of armed violence deduced from several conflict data sets, including that of the Peace Research Institute (PRIO) and the University of Uppsala's Conflict Data Program, confirm Smith's assertion.[12] For example, a study by Lotta Harbom, Stina Högbladh, and Peter Wallensteen found that of the 121 conflicts that took place from 1989 to 2005, 90 were intrastate, 24 were internationalized intrastate, and only 7 were interstate. In other words, of the 121 conflicts that took place during that period, 114 involved internal armed groups challenging the legitimacy and authority of nation-states.[13] The *Human Security Report 2009/2010* came to the same conclusion: "The overwhelming majority of armed conflicts today are fought within states" and involve "the government of a state and one or more non-state armed groups." Moreover, intrastate conflicts not infrequently include an international dimension in that "another state may sup-port one of the warring parties."[14]

It was also the case, according to those analyzing conflict trends taking place during the post–Cold War 1990s and first few years of the twenty-first century, that there was cause for optimism. For example, a 2003 study by Mikael Eriksson, Peter Wallensteen, and Margareta Sollenberg found that while "most of the con-flicts . . . were internal," which is consistent with the findings above, conflicts were declining in number. "In 2002, there were 31 conflicts active in 24 places . . . the lowest year for the occurrence of intrastate conflict since the collapse of commu-nism." Additionally, conflicts were killing fewer people.[15]

Subsequently, other assessments of global and regional trends in organized violence came to similar conclusions. For example, the Human Security Report Project, funded by the development ministries of the United Kingdom, Canada,

Sweden, Norway, and Switzerland, observed that by the early 2000s "a dramatic . . . decline in the number of wars, genocides and human rights abuse" had taken place. Moreover, these conflicts were "not only far less frequent today, but also far less deadly."[16]

But these reasons for optimism in the first few years of the new century proved fleeting. As Jack Snyder warned, the data employed to show declining violence was too short-term to generalize. He contended that "it is inappropriate to extrapolate from [such] short-term trends."[17]

Snyder's caution was warranted. Between 2003 and 2017, major intrastate wars escalated. According to Barbara Walter in an article published in 2017, the number of those conflicts "has significantly increased," with "large-scale civil wars . . . occurring in Iraq, Syria, Libya, Yemen, Chad, the DRC, Nigeria, Pakistan, Rwanda, Somalia, Sri Lanka, South Sudan, Chad, Mali, CAR, and Ukraine, with new civil wars threatening to break out in Turkey and Egypt."[18] Each of these conflicts experienced more than one thousand battle deaths of combatants per year. The number of minor intrastate wars, which suffered casualties below that threshold, also rose. According to Sebastian von Einsiedel, 2015 witnessed thirty-eight minor intrastate wars, the highest number since 1994. This sharp uptick, he explained, "has been largely driven by the expansion of the Islamic State and its affiliates, which by 2015 were involved in conflicts in Iraq, Lebanon, Syria, Egypt, Saudi Arabia, Afghanistan, Libya, Russia, and Yemen."[19]

The number of fatalities incurred in intrastate organized violence similarly grew in the 2003–15 period, as documented by Erik Melander, Thérése Pettersson, and Lotta Themnér in "Organized Violence, 1989–2015."[20] They included both battle deaths of combatants and civilian casualties. In 2014, more than 130,000 people were killed; in 2015, this figure was 118,000, according to the Uppsala Conflict Data Program. This means that 2014 was the second-worst year in the post–Cold War period in terms of fatalities, while 2015 was third. Only 1994 was bloodier, due to the Rwandan genocide, which is estimated to have taken 500,000 lives.[21]

The fatalities for the period reported are based on three subcategories of intrastate organized violence. One subcategory is fatalities in a conflict between a state and one or more armed groups. By 2015, many such conflicts had become internationalized—in other words, "at least one of the parties is supported with troops from an external state. . . . Since 2012, this subtype . . . has witnessed an unprecedented increase. In 2015, 40% of all armed conflicts (20 out of 50) were internationalized, the highest share recorded to date."[22]

The second subcategory contributing to this escalation in casualties is intrastate conflicts in which two or more armed groups fight each other. Since 2010, "there has been a clear upward trend in the number of active non-state conflicts," according to Melander, Pettersson, and Themnér. "This is largely driven by conflicts between drug cartels in Mexico as well as fighting between different rebel groups in Syria. The last three years have seen the highest number of non-state conflicts since . . . 1989. In 2015, the Uppsala Conflict Data Program recorded 70 non-state conflicts, the highest ever and up from 61 in 2014."[23]

The final subcategory is one-sided violence in which civilians are directly targeted by both governments and armed groups. This is different from civilian casualties that result from the fighting that takes place in the previous two categories. For the period 2000–2012, there were relatively low levels of one-sided violence. However, in 2013, the number of civilians killed in one-sided violence started to increase again.

What the data on civilian casualties reported by Melander, Pettersson, and Themnér overlook, however, are civilian deaths that resulted from the health consequences of forced displacement. This subcategory includes deaths resulting from malnutrition, disease, and other illnesses. Such indirect deaths would considerably add to the reported rise in conflict casualties.

The context in which post–Cold War intrastate conflicts have taken place has been largely within weak and fragile states. To varying degrees, these states are characterized by an inability to control their territory, maintain a monopoly over the legitimate use of force, and perform core functions of governance, beginning with providing security to their populations. Moreover, they are plagued by widespread corruption. When these conditions become severe, a state's legitimacy with its citizens seriously erodes and may even vanish.[24] Furthermore, these conditions, which contribute to state weakness, can and often do serve as incubators for armed groups, enabling them not only to take root but also to flourish.[25]

Alyson Bailes, Keith Krause, and Theodor Winkler, reflecting on developments since the end of the Cold War, observed that armed nonstate actors engaged in irregular conflicts had become more diverse: "If in the past [during the Cold War] guerrilla groups and national liberation movements largely dominated the picture," the authors found that many "different sub-state actors" were now present. These included "ethnically-based militias, guerrilla or terrorist organizations, clans, tribes, warlords, organized communal groups and criminal gangs," the latter capable of trafficking in "human beings as easily as in small arms, drugs, blood diamonds, tropical woods, and any other commodity that sells."[26]

Other specialists have adopted the term "armed groups" to describe an array of post–Cold War nonstate actors who employ irregular warfare tactics to attack states as well as one another. For example, a book by myself, Roy Godson, and Querine Hanlon proposed an "armed groups taxonomy consisting of four subtypes: insurgents, terrorists, militias, and criminal organizations" but cautioned that in "the real world these distinctions are not so static or long lasting." Rather, we found that "the opposite is more likely. At one point an armed group may be classified as a terrorist organization based on its operational and organizational profile, while at another point it morphs into a militia or criminal enterprise. In other instances, an armed group can simultaneously be described as fitting into more than one of the four subtypes. In other words, at the same time it can correspond to a terrorist organization and a criminal enterprise or some other combination."[27]

Nonstate armed groups since the Cold War's end have not only diversified—they have also grown in number, as can be seen in several armed group databases. Since the late 1990s, these have included the Armed Conflict Database of the International Institute for Strategic Studies, which tracks the activities of hundreds of armed groups in regional and internal conflict zones, "whether active, subject to a ceasefire, or halted by a peace accord."[28] Jane's Information Group's Sentinel Security Assessments, which are divided into seventeen geographic areas across the globe, contain assessments of armed groups active in each of those territories. For example, the assessment focused on North Africa contains facts and figures on thirteen different armed groups active in Libya.[29] And the Mapping Militants Project, which was initiated at Stanford University in 2010, "identifies patterns in the evolution of militant organizations in specified conflict theatres." Currently, it includes more than one hundred in-depth profiles of armed groups, with visual representations of how relationships within these organizations can change over time.[30]

Developments in the international system since the end of the Cold War have offered armed groups new enablers that have enhanced their capacity to challenge both weak and strong states. Over the last twenty-five-plus years, armed groups have gained access to capabilities that were not available to their Cold War counterparts. Most important, three interrelated developments have magnified armed group power: globalization, Information Age technology, and network-based organization.

Each of these can increase the degree of mobility and connectivity for all actors in the international system, including armed groups. Globalization reduces international barriers and, as Peter Thompson points out, can increase "the scale, scope, and speed of interactions occurring today." For armed groups, this provides "the ability to move and adapt quickly to a changing strategic environment [and] provides small, clandestine groups with agility not previously enjoyed."[31] In terms of conducting operations, these developments enhance the capacity of an armed group to maneuver from training and planning sites in one geographic area, to a staging location in another region, to the target in yet another place.

Information Age technologies provide armed groups with the capacity to decentralize into webs of dispersed, complex, and interconnected networks. According to Michael Flynn, Rich Juergens, and Thomas Cantrell, "the global communications revolution" has provided armed groups with "an electronic sanctuary in which actions can be hidden among the innumerable civilian signals that constitute daily cell phone and Internet traffic." From this electronic sanctuary, they can "coordinate activities from dispersed networks in order to self-synchronize, pass information, and transfer funds. In this way, insurgents have become networked coalitions . . . that come together temporarily and are thus difficult to observe and destroy. Drawing support from their networks, they remain low contrast until time to strike and then quickly blend back into the population."[32]

The al-Qaeda–dominated insurgency that mushroomed in Iraq in 2004 exhibited this network-based organizational structure. It consisted of a plethora of decentralized groupings that made effective use of information technologies to form into an array of dispersed, dynamic, and interconnected networks able to conduct violent attacks across Iraq. One informed observer described it as follows: "The insurgency was primarily made up of clandestine cellular networks, applying excellent intelligence tradecraft [methods] to remain hidden and to hide the connections between the individuals in the movement." In other words, the linkages among all the cells that were part of the insurgent networks constituted the organizational system. To keep those networks secret or disguised and hidden, the insurgents employed special intelligence methods so that their "cellular networks were not readily visible."[33]

Irregular War and US Security Capabilities

The historical record illustrates that militaries mired in wars for which they are not prepared, in particular irregular ones, do not adapt easily to reverse the misfortunes they encounter.[34] The same can be said of civilian agencies, including intelligence services, engaged in war. The challenge posed by the insurgency in Iraq beginning in the summer of 2003 illustrates this point. US military, diplomatic, and intelligence institutions did not adapt quickly to a type of war that they did not anticipate and did not understand.

Consider the Department of Defense. It was not until the 2006 edition of the *Quadrennial Defense Review* (*QDR*)—the Pentagon's study conducted every four years that identifies existing and potential military threats and the means to meet those challenges—that initial steps were taken to begin revising military strategy for irregular warfare.[35] On the heels of the 2006 *QDR* came other military initiatives focused on the irregular warfare missions of counterinsurgency and counterterrorism, among them the US Army and US Marine Corps's Field Manual 3-24, titled *Counterinsurgency*, and the DOD's *National Military Strategic Plan for the War on Terrorism*.[36] Both stressed the need to adopt unconventional military methods and to coordinate these activities with civilian government counterparts.

Several other military manuals, directives, and related documents—including the 2007 *Irregular Warfare (IW) Joint Operating Concept (JOC)*, prepared by the US Special Operations Command—addressed operational-level challenges that the US military faced when engaged in protracted irregular warfare against non-state armed groups. The *JOC* defined irregular warfare as a "form of warfare" that involves "'a violent struggle among state and non-state actors for legitimacy and influence over the relevant population.' . . . As such, it encompasses insurgency, counterinsurgency, terrorism, and counterterrorism, raising them above the perception that they are somehow a lesser form of conflict below the threshold of warfare."[37] Additionally, the *JOC* noted that irregular warfare demanded military forces that could "work closely with interagency . . . counterparts at all stages of planning and execution." Unified action was seen as "essential to integrating the application of all available instruments of power to address . . . irregular threats."[38]

Then, in 2008, DOD Directive 3000.07, *Irregular Warfare*, raised irregular warfare to the status of being "as strategically important as traditional warfare," noting that "it is essential to maintain capabilities so that DOD is as effective in IW [irregular warfare] as it is in traditional warfare."[39] Concurrently, Defense Secretary Robert Gates, in several speeches and published articles, expressed this view that irregular warfare posed strategic challenges to the United States and that the Pentagon needed to reorient military forces to effectively meet those challenges.[40]

Beyond the Pentagon, other US government institutions, including the State Department, asserted that managing irregular threats required a deeper understanding of armed groups and of the special kinds of capabilities needed to meet the threats they posed. This was reflected in the Department of State's 2009 *Quadrennial Diplomacy and Development Review*. It highlighted the need to enhance the capacity of existing diplomatic and development personnel, while adding a new cadre of planners, managers, and operators for future irregular challenges.[41]

The 2009 *National Intelligence Strategy* contained the same assessment of the contemporary conflict environment. And it identified similar challenges that demanded attention, resources, and commitment if the intelligence agencies were to be "agile in adapting to emerging threats" from "non-state and sub-state actors increasingly impacting our national security."[42]

Military, diplomatic, and development instruments of US policy all have roles to play in managing a complex security environment in which armed groups and irregular wars are a major source of instability, but intelligence has the pivotal role to play. Indeed, the adversity that can result from a lack of intelligence is a recurring theme found in the doctrines and operational concepts developed for managing these challenges in the years following 9/11. Consider Field Manual 3-24, *Counterinsurgency*, the 2006 manual that received such fanfare during the surge in Iraq. "Counterinsurgency is an intelligence driven endeavor," it declared. "The ultimate success or failure of the mission depends on the effectiveness of the intelligence effort. . . . Intelligence drives operations and successful operations generate additional intelligence." The *JOC* concurred, stressing that "intelligence-driven operations will require long-term investments in human, technical, forensic, and cultural intelligence to illuminate the adversaries' networks, support activities, and personalities."[43]

The centrality of intelligence, and the consequences resulting from a lack of it, was also stressed by senior US commanders who were engaged in irregular warfare operations. For example, Lt. Gen. Michael Flynn, USA (Ret.), during the time he served as deputy chief of staff for intelligence for the International Security Assistance Force [ISAF], lamented, "Eight years into the war in Afghanistan, the US intelligence community . . . is unable to answer fundamental questions about the environment in which U.S. forces operate and the people they seek to persuade."[44]

General McChrystal, in discussing how he established TF 714, likewise highlighted how intelligence must lead the way. In his memoir, *My Share of the Task*, he explains that to locate AQI's midlevel commanders and managers, not just its top leadership, signals and imagery tools were fused together with other sources of intelligence (including interrogation and human-source collection) to drive operations.[45]

Military commanders were not alone in assigning an indispensable role to intelligence for managing irregular threats. Beginning with the *9/11 Commission Report*, there was an emerging line of reasoning among security specialists that not only were the tools or elements of intelligence—whether collection, analysis, counterintelligence, or covert action—indispensable, but that they also needed to undergo important changes to cope with twenty-first-century irregular adversaries.[46] Consequently, the post-9/11 intelligence discourse came to underscore the need for a critical reconsideration of the state-centric focus that had dominated both intelligence theory and practice. However, before we examine why the post-9/11 context demanded this reconsideration to manage the challenges posed by twenty-first-century armed groups, it is necessary to describe what intelligence has traditionally entailed in terms of its methods and activities.

What Is Intelligence?

Intelligence texts all begin by addressing three basic questions. One, what is intelligence? Two, how should its different elements be described? Three, in what ways does it support decision-makers and those who implement decisions?

For Abram Shulsky, intelligence is concerned with "information, activities, and organizations." Information includes data and knowledge that help government decision-makers in the "formulation and implementation of policy to further . . . national security interests and to deal with threats from actual or potential adversaries." Activities, Shulsky explains, are those different methods employed by a state for the "collection and analysis of that information" as well as measures taken by the state to "counter the intelligence activities of adversaries" that seek to gain access to sensitive information. Beyond these collection and analysis functions, intelligence agencies "also may be given . . . the responsibility of undertaking secret activities to advance their government's foreign policy objectives" through various "covert action" operations.[47]

Mark Lowenthal describes intelligence as a process, a product, and an organization:

- *Intelligence as process:* "The means by which certain kinds of information are required and requested, collected, analyzed, and disseminated, and as the ways in which certain types of covert action are conceived and carried out."
- *Intelligence as product:* "The tangible products that contain the results of these processes, that is, the analyses and intelligence operations themselves."
- *Intelligence as organization:* "The units and agencies that carry out these various functions and activities."[48]

Jeffrey Richelson writes that "strictly speaking, intelligence activities involve only the collection and analysis of information" that is turned into intelligence products for use by government officials. However, he notes that "counterintelligence and covert action are also intertwined" within a broader definition of intelligence.[49]

Finally, Roy Godson describes intelligence as "information that is acquired, exploited, and protected by the activities of organizations specifically established for that purpose." He proposes that there are four distinct elements of intelligence, each of which is defined as follows:

- *Collection* is the gathering of valued information, much of it by clandestine means. . . . Broadly speaking, intelligence is gathered from three sources: open, technical, and human sources.

- *Analysis* is the processing of information, and its end products. . . . Analysis entails sifting, screening, [and] comparing information with other data, and, ultimately, including it within a larger intelligence context.
- *Counterintelligence*, as practiced by most states, is the effort to protect secrets, to prevent themselves from being manipulated, and (sometimes) to exploit the intelligence activities of others for their own benefit.
- *Covert action* is the attempt . . . to influence events in another state or territory without revealing [one's] own involvement. . . . Generally, covert action falls into one of four areas: propaganda, political action, paramilitary operations, and intelligence assistance.[50]

Each of these elements of intelligence is important in and of itself, but they are also interconnected. Moreover, one or more specialized organizations are needed to employ each element.

This book focuses on three elements of intelligence: collection, analysis, and the paramilitary variant of covert action.

Collection is understood to mean the collection of information, whether by technical, human, or open-source methods, on both state and nonstate actors. The actor or target, as well as the context of peacetime or wartime, will affect how the collection disciplines are employed.

Analysis takes intelligence that is collected and utilizes it to generate analytic products. Analysts evaluate the information obtained from collection to provide decision-makers and operational commanders with a competitive advantage. This is of critical importance during both peacetime and wartime, but how analysis is conducted is affected by these two different contexts. This book focuses on the changing role of analysis from Cold War peacetime to post-9/11 wartime when key consumers were commanders at the operational level.

The paramilitary variation of covert action examined in this book was conducted by special operations forces (SOF). Direct-action missions by such forces are short-duration strikes and other small-scale offensive actions that are executed secretly. In this book, they are a subset of covert action and involve paramilitary attacks by secret units on networks of armed groups. These operations may be clandestine until the mission is carried out but may also remain secret in a mission's aftermath. Covert action in the form of paramilitary operations executed by SOF has played a crucial role in the fight against nonstate armed groups. The intelligence and special operations communities become essential operational instruments for conducting irregular warfare.

The book does not pay attention to counterintelligence but recognizes its central importance in protecting a state's sensitive information from an adversary's espionage operations. Counterintelligence, at a minimum, denies adversarial states the advantages they would gain if they were able to obtain those secrets. Moreover, when the actor involved is not a state but is a nonstate armed group, the scope and extent of counterintelligence challenges broaden.

William Rosenau describes these challenges in his study of how the instruments of espionage were "organized and practiced" by Hezbollah, the Provisional Irish Republican Army, and al-Qaeda.[51] Several other scholars have shown that other armed groups also have placed a high premium on intelligence and counterintelligence operations as part of their irregular warfare strategies.[52]

The United States has faced such challenges from armed groups since 9/11. Consider al-Qaeda's double-agent penetration and suicide attack against a CIA base located on the Afghanistan-Pakistan border in December 2009. Humam al-Balawi had become a trusted agent of Jordanian intelligence and then of the CIA. He was believed to have access to senior al-Qaeda leaders, was judged reliable, and therefore was permitted to enter the CIA base without being searched. This allowed al-Balawi to kill seven CIA officers as well as his Jordanian handler.[53] The attack demonstrated that his true handlers were al-Qaeda intelligence specialists, who in this operation proved capable of running sophisticated double-agent operations against a high-value US target.

While recognizing that the employment of such espionage methods is part of the modus operandi of many armed groups, the story told in the following chapters concentrates on what US forces did to degrade AQI's secret networks, not on if and how AQI employed espionage to counter the US efforts. That is an important subject but beyond the scope of this book.

It is important to note that each of the elements of intelligence does not exist independently of the others. Indeed, intelligence specialists such as Roy Godson believe there are important synergies among them that should be understood and embraced if intelligence is to be employed effectively. He writes that collection, analysis, counterintelligence, and covert action "exist in a symbiotic relationship with one another. If one is weakened or eliminated, the others are likely to be affected adversely."[54] Consider collection: It "depends heavily on counterintelligence and is also linked to covert action. History is replete with examples of intelligence collectors deceived by rival intelligence services. Counterintelligence can and should forestall this. Collection is also enhanced by covert action programs. . . . Covert action channels are often unique sources of highly prized information."[55]

In the case of TF 714, a reciprocal relationship developed among the intelligence disciplines of collection, analysis, and covert paramilitary operations. Only by employing these three elements of intelligence in an integrated and interdependent manner could TF 714 accomplish its mission to find, degrade, and dismantle the burgeoning al-Qaeda–dominated insurgent networks. This is illustrated in the case study threaded through the chapters of this volume, which assess the effectiveness of counterterrorism task force of Joint Special Operations Command (JSOC) in accomplishing its mission.

Explicit in each of the above definitions is the relationship of intelligence to policy and operations. Intelligence exists to assist policymakers and operators function more effectively at the strategic, operational, and tactical levels. At the *strategic level*, intelligence is critical in the crafting of national security policy and military strategy for senior civilian and military officials. At the *operational level*, intelligence contributes to the preparation and implementation by planners and midlevel officials of contingency and campaign plans. Finally, at the *tactical level*, intelligence supports military forces, diplomats, negotiators, and others tasked with carrying out policies and operational plans.[56]

Each of these levels has different time frames, types of intelligence products, and desired outcomes, as shown in figure 1.1. At the strategic level, the timeline is longer, the types of products include intelligence estimates, and the desired outcome is to prevent policy failure from taking place. At the operational level, the timeline is shorter, the product is actionable intelligence, and the desired outcome is to deter or preempt an action. At the tactical level, the timeline is immediate and time sensitive, the intelligence products include indications and warning (usually referred to as "I&W") and current intelligence (i.e., intelligence that has been recently collected), and the desired outcome is to counter or respond to an opponent.[57]

Of course, intelligence does not always function in such a proscribed manner, and it can fail for numerous of reasons. What follows are three examples of failures that relate to the challenges posed by twenty-first-century armed groups.

One, a key factor that contributed to the success of the 9/11 attacks was the unwillingness of US intelligence agencies to share vital information that could have prevented those attacks.

Two, even when available, intelligence may not be analyzed in a timely fashion, and tragedy can result. Consider the insurgency that followed the US invasion of Iraq. It was predictable that in the aftermath of the US overthrow of the Baathist regime, Iraq would attract radical Islamists who saw themselves as a part of al-Qaeda's global jihad. Iraq, like Afghanistan in the 1980s, turned into a magnet for those warriors. But for a variety of reasons, no such analysis was provided to those drawing up the plans for the invasion and its aftermath.

Three, intelligence can also fail when decision-makers and commanders do not act on timely intelligence that *is* provided to them. In 2001, US SOF achieved an

	Strategic Intelligence	Operational Intelligence	Tactical Intelligence
Time Period	Long term	Short term	Immediate
Type of Intelligence Product	Intelligence estimate	Actionable intelligence that drives operations	Current intelligence for a direct action
Outcome Sought	Prevention of an attack	Prevention of an attack	Reaction to an attack

Figure 1.1 Time frames, types of products, and desired outcomes of three intelligence levels

extraordinary victory in Afghanistan against the Taliban and were closing in on Osama bin Laden and other top-level members of al-Qaeda's leadership at the cave complex of Tora Bora. But they got away. The forces needed to block their escape, which had been requested by local commanders as part of their intelligence assessment of the situation, were not deployed, even though they were available. The failure to prevent this escape was due to the catastrophic mistake of not acting on actionable intelligence.[58]

The intelligence disciplines are also all impacted when the actor changes from a state to a nonstate armed group or groups and when the context changes from peacetime to wartime. This will be made clear in the chapters that follow. Because of the kinds of irregular threats posed by armed groups, intelligence had to be used in a different way from how it had been employed against state threats. This is because attacks from armed groups can come from anywhere at any time. Therefore, intelligence becomes imperative in an attempt to preempt or prevent such attacks by disrupting and degrading an armed group's organization or networks. Intelligence must discover the insurgent and terrorist apparatus that is hidden within urban and electronic sanctuaries. When working against complex twenty-first-century armed groups, intelligence must be tasked to find their underground organizations and secret networks so that specialized units can remove their mid-level commanders and managers from the battlespace.

A Different Kind of Intelligence Challenge

Throughout the Cold War, the US intelligence community (IC) naturally focused on the challenges posed by the Soviet Union. The Cold War gave the IC a clear point of reference: the bipolar competition with the USSR. However, in the post–Cold War 1990s, even after the USSR imploded, state challenges continued to be the focus of US intelligence. This was also true for leading intelligence texts. Revised editions of those volumes appearing in the 1990s, and the first years of the new century continued to emphasize a state-centric approach.

Consider the third edition, published in 2000, of Lowenthal's *Intelligence: From Secrets to Policy*. While the book noted that the US intelligence agenda had expanded beyond state threats to include the challenges of international terrorism, narcotics, and crime, the author's lengthy examination of collection, counterintelligence, covert action, and analysis paid little attention to the need to adapt each of these tools to meet these emerging nonstate armed group challenges.[59]

Shulsky also mentions new "transnational threats" in his revised editions of *Silent Warfare*, published in 1995 and 2001. But this did not alter the volume's central thesis. Intelligence remained state-centric and "inherently connected to the competition among nations."[60]

Richelson, in the 1995 edition of *The U.S. Intelligence Community*, saw post–Cold War intelligence challenges still emanating mainly from nation-states, especially those pursuing nuclear weapons. Additionally, China was considered a "significant intelligence target."[61]

Of course, one could argue that the enduring adherence to a state-centric focus for US intelligence services in the 1990s was reasonable given the fact that nonstate challenges were only just beginning to emerge as serious security threats. However, in the aftermath of 9/11, as specialists woke up to the dangers posed by armed groups, in particular transnational terrorists, they began to realize that intelligence did not merely need to change its targets but to change how it tackled those targets. Irregular threats, the specialists pointed out, were different from those posed by nation-states. And for the intelligence services in particular, armed groups constituted an operationally different kind of challenge.[62]

Recall that in *Intelligence in the Age of Terror*, Treverton asserted that while the "change in intelligence targets is widely acknowledged, its implications run far deeper than are usually recognized."[63] During the Cold War, the most important targets for US intelligence were states, primarily the Soviet Union. In the new century, while states are still important, nonstate actors and particularly transnational armed groups have become primary intelligence targets. Figure 1.2 captures the essential differences between the characteristics of state-based intelligence challenges and those posed by their nonstate armed group counterparts.

As figure 1.2 denotes, armed groups present intelligence organizations with challenges that differ considerably from those of nation-states. The differences begin with the characteristic of *visibility*. Armed groups are underground organizations, clandestine by their very nature, with most of their apparatus hidden in

	States	Armed Groups
Visibility	Observable	Hidden
Shape	Borders	No Defined Territory
Size	Large	Small
Structure	Centralized	Decentralized and/or Network
Location	Over There	Here and There
Strategy	Slow to change	Often Unknown
Intentions	Always Adapting	Often Knowable

Figure 1.2 Differences between state targets and nonstate armed group targets

Source: Adapted from a figure in Gregory Treverton, *Intelligence for an Age of Terror* (Cambridge: Cambridge University Press, 2009), 15.

secret units that can be difficult to discover and disrupt. Therefore, considerable intelligence-collection capabilities must be devoted to uncovering their underground networks. But if uncovered, the apparatus can easily be destroyed. In the Cold War, the intelligence-to-force ratio was low: enemy forces could more readily be found and observed, but if war occurred they would be difficult to neutralize. Intelligence on armed groups is almost completely the opposite: their forces are relatively easy to neutralize once found; it is uncovering and observing them that is the problem.[64] Armed groups are low-contrast in that they can hide within civilian populations, unlike high-contrast targets such as airbases, warships, and armored land forces. One of the primary advantages of armed groups has always been their ability to hide in plain sight. This includes, today, within highly populated urban environments.[65]

The *invisibility* of twenty-first-century armed groups has been considerably enhanced by the virtual sanctuary of the Internet. As a result of their invisibility, terrorist and insurgent groups are for all practical purposes unseen until they strike. In the twentieth century, by way of contrast, threats emerged slowly, often visibly, as new weapons were forged, armies mobilized, and units moved into place. These developments often proved difficult to conceal. Today threats can emerge quickly and seemingly strike out of the blue, as al-Qaeda did on September 11, 2001.[66]

The invisibility of an armed group is enhanced by the characteristic of *shape*. Unlike states, armed groups have no clearly defined territory, are small and organizationally decentralized, and are increasingly networked. Unless there is disputed territory, it is straightforward to identify the fixed shape or boundaries of state actors. Simply opening an atlas, looking at satellite images, or clicking on Google Maps can reveal the shape, or physical silhouette, of every state. In contrast, the fact that armed groups do not have a clearly defined territory makes it harder for intelligence forces to locate and focus attention on specific geographic areas in which an armed group can be found. An armed group may take shape in one location, but as intelligence forces seek to fix it in time and space, the armed group repositions itself and its shape changes.

Size and *structure* also distinguish states from armed groups. States are larger in size and centralized in terms of structure, making them easier to observe. A state's bureaucratic system usually has a hierarchical structure that is quite rigid and discernible, whereas armed groups have much more complicated structures that can transform or morph frequently. One can, in the case of open or democratic states, gain access to a government's website and access information on bureaucratic and organizational structure. Such knowledge is more difficult to acquire when a state is closed and authoritarian. Still, an intelligence service can gain some knowledge of these matters through espionage.

Understanding an armed group's structure has been further complicated by the global communications and information revolution. This has given armed groups a new and complex electronic sanctuary in which to conceal their organizational networks among the numerous civilian signals that constitute daily cell phone and Internet traffic. Within this new sanctuary, armed groups can coordinate activities from concealed networks to self-synchronize, share information, transfer money, and carry out many other activities. In this space, made possible by Information Age technology, armed groups have become "networked coalitions of the willing" that can come together temporarily, making them difficult to visualize in terms of their size and structure.[67]

According to the 2003 *National Intelligence Strategy of the United States*, an armed group network can operate across three geographic levels—global, regional, and state. This is illustrated in the challenges of *visibility*, *shape*, *size*, and *structure* that are posed by al-Qaeda's transnational terrorist network.[68] At the lowest level, al-Qaeda elements operate mostly within a single country. While their operating area is limited, new technology can nevertheless enable their actions to have an international impact. At the middle level, they operate across a region, as can be seen in the Middle East and North Africa. Finally, at the highest level, al-Qaeda has demonstrated a global reach. Al-Qaeda elements at these three levels are connected both directly and indirectly. They cooperate directly by sharing intelligence, personnel, expertise, resources, and hiding places, according to the *National Intelligence Strategy*. They also support each other in less direct ways—for example, by promoting the same ideological agenda or favorable international image.[69]

Beyond visibility, shape, size, and structure, armed groups differ from nation-states with respect to the characteristic of *location*. While the *location* of state targets is clearly abroad—they are "over there"—armed groups can be transnational actors, as figure 1.2 shows. Consequently, an armed group at war with a state may be attacking it locally (here) and transnationally (over there). This causes states to reconsider what has been regarded as domestic intelligence. During the Cold War, US intelligence challenges could be divided more or less clearly into foreign intelligence abroad and counterintelligence at home. The domestic task chiefly involved tracking white-collar spymasters from communist countries as they attempted to recruit spies in the United States. Today, however, targets are to be found both "here" and "there," requiring a rethinking of boundaries and the drawing of new distinctions with respect to location.

Nonstate armed groups differ from their nation-state counterparts in terms of their approach to *strategy*. This creates yet another challenge for intelligence services that have to deal with armed group threats. To survive and grow, armed groups depend on their capacity to adapt their strategy. And when compared with states, they appear to be more able to do so expeditiously. Armed groups are the ultimate asymmetrical warrior that shapes and reshapes its capability to attack a state's vulnerabilities. Consider how leading jihadist strategic thinkers have adjusted and modified their warfighting strategy.[70] The 9/11 suicide bombers did not come up with their attack plan because they were pilots. They had done enough research to find the vulnerabilities of fuel-filled jets in flight and of passenger-clearance procedures, and they trained themselves to fly airplanes for the attacks.[71] In a further adaptation in 2006, al-Qaeda–linked plotters planned to blow up airplanes over the Atlantic with liquid explosives smuggled onto planes as sports drinks or other permitted carry-ons. They sought to adapt to post-9/11 airport security procedures.[72]

Finally, state and nonstate armed groups differ in terms of the extent to which their *intentions* are knowable. Consider democratic states. They consist of various agencies and departments that do not necessarily have the same objectives. The interaction of these actors makes it difficult to estimate intentions. It is also difficult to identify the intentions of countries with authoritarian political systems, where one party rules the country over a long period of time and secrecy is a core regime feature. Armed group intentions, in contrast, are often knowable to intelligence services because such groups need to appeal for support from among the population. Al-Qaeda, for example, has been straightforward about its intentions; as stated on its various Twitter feeds, it is "working to expel the infidels from the lands of the Faithful, unite Muslims and create a new Islamic caliphate."[73] The Islamic State of Iraq and Syria (ISIS) also actively communicates its intentions and recruitment messages on various online platforms, including YouTube and Twitter.[74]

The characteristics of nonstate armed groups highlighted here present a range of operational challenges to US intelligence services that are significantly different from those posed by nation-states during the Cold War. These challenges, according to Neal Pollard, have necessitated "a dramatic shift by the U.S. IC, which was built to focus on states." Pollard argues that nonstate threats are "more difficult to manage" and that meeting these new challenges requires a "re-configuration of the functions of intelligence."[75]

This volume examines three elements of intelligence—collection, analysis, and the paramilitary variation of covert action—and the adaptations each had to undergo in the fight against AQI. The US counterterrorism task force faced an enemy it never envisaged fighting and could not dismantle through its existing ways of operating. It could not keep pace with, let alone slow down, AQI's escalating operational tempo. The task force had to transform from a highly compartmentalized force with a culture of secrecy and semiautonomy to one partnered with and supported by a joint interagency task force (JIATF) comprising principally members of the IC's three-letter agencies (CIA, NSA, NGA, DIA, and FBI). However, for that partnership to work, those intelligence agencies also had to transform to understand the unprecedented irregular challenge faced in Iraq.

AQI was a new problem set. It constituted a strategic surprise for TF 714. It was unlike any insurgent organization that preceded it. Its capabilities and the scale of the challenges it posed were far bigger. AQI was a web of networks. It did not resemble any organizational pattern TF 714 or its interagency IC partners had seen before. It was not hierarchical. There was little consistency to its operational patterns.

The next chapter takes a closer look at post-9/11 armed groups and how they evolved. Today's armed groups are different from their Cold War counterparts in a number of significant ways. Several developments since the end of the Cold War have empowered armed groups in ways that were reflected in the complex challenge AQI posed. Chapter 2 describes how AQI came to consist of a plethora of decentralized units that employed Information Age technologies to form into dispersed networks to escalate its attacks across Iraq beginning in 2004.

CHAPTER 2

TRANSFORMING FROM HIERARCHY TO NETWORKS TO EMPOWER ARMED GROUPS

SUN TZU STATED IN *The Art of War* that it is essential to know one's enemy. For governments facing twenty-first-century irregular threats associated with ideologically driven armed groups, Sun Tzu's enduring maxim could not be more apposite. Over the past two decades, armed groups have experienced significant empowerment, and understanding the ways in which this has enhanced their capabilities and capacity to conduct irregular war is essential. Compared with their Cold War counterparts, today's armed groups have undergone paradigmatic changes in their strategic, operational, and tactical dimensions.

But the nature of these changes, as Task Force 714 discovered in Iraq, can be difficult to pin down or even, at first, discern. The task force did not initially realize it was facing an enemy in AQI that it had never envisaged and could not dismantle through its existing ways of operating.

From an operational and tactical standpoint, understanding the type of organizational structure and the command-and-control system that armed groups employ is essential if effective methods to counter and dismantle them are to be formulated. Therefore, this chapter begins by discussing the evolution of armed groups from hierarchical ones, where leadership exercises close control at the strategic, operational, and tactical levels, to networks that are decentralized and where top leadership exercises influence and inspiration but not operational command and control. The chapter next identifies those enabling factors that fostered the evolution of armed groups from hierarchies to networks. Finally, it addresses the new operational challenges that this radical restructuring poses to the security services of governments that must tackle networked adversaries.

Hierarchical Armed Groups: Yesterday's Adversary

During the Cold War, armed groups employed hierarchical command-and-control structures. A few examples include Germany's Red Army Faction, Italy's Red Brigades, the Kurdish Workers' Party, Basque Homeland and Liberty (better known as ETA), and the Irish Republican Army. Senior leadership in hierarchical organizations like these is dominant both in formulating strategy and in guiding its implementation at the operational and tactical levels. This is achieved through top-down control, which requires constant communication with all levels of the organization.[1]

Robust operational control, coordination, and training translate in tactical terms into the group's ability to perform violent and spectacular attacks.[2] The inherent feature of hierarchical organizations that contributes to this ability is a tight principal-agent relationship—that is, one in which the agents (the rank-and-file members of the armed group) act on behalf of the principals (the armed group's senior leadership) and have no discord with them in carrying out their missions. Hierarchical organizations involve a clear division of responsibilities and therefore create an environment conducive for delivering rewards and punishment to the operatives based on their performance. Centralized command and control allow the leadership to organize and direct individuals who lack practical knowledge or training and cannot be trusted to improvise or operate independently.[3] Therefore, the leaders of centralized armed groups divide their militants into units that execute clearly formulated tasks decided at the top of the hierarchy.

Seth Jones provides an example of a hierarchically commanded insurgent organization: the Algerian National Liberation Front (FLN), which fought against French colonial control from 1954 through 1962. The FLN had an elaborate hierarchical structure with a separate political wing (the National Council of the Algerian Revolution) and a separate military wing (the Algerian Army of National Liberation). However, the political leadership executed control over the military wing, dividing it into two commands—Eastern and Western—with three administrative provinces (*wilayas*) in each. Several committees and bureaus oversaw the military units to prevent shirking and defection, which allowed the FLN to overcome these challenges.[4]

The FLN's centralized structure of top-down control suffered, however, from the disadvantage of slow information transmission and processing: every message had to travel up and down a chain of command.[5] A hierarchical approach is also vulnerable to being disabled through decapitation of its senior leadership.[6] For instance, in 2010–11, when the Revolutionary Armed Forces of Colombia (FARC) lost several senior commanders, including its top leader Alfonso Cano, the organization experienced a breakdown in regional commanders' subordination to the chain of command, resulting in the conduct of autonomous operations in pursuit of personal rather than organizational goals.[7] This shift undermined the spirit of the organization, increased corruption within it, encouraged profit-oriented commanders to involve themselves in drug trafficking, and atomized FARC's organizational structure.[8]

Another example of this vulnerability can be seen in the destructive effect of the targeting of the leadership of Palestinian hierarchical organizations by Israeli forces. For instance, the targeted killing in 1995 of the Palestinian Islamic Jihad leader Fathi Shikaki disrupted the organization's activities for several years because he had no clear successor and the organization proved to be dysfunctional in the absence of guidance from above.[9] Similar dynamics of deterioration in organization capabilities and morale became evident after Israel eliminated Hamas's ideological leader, Sheik Ahmed Yassin, in 2004.[10]

Despite these vulnerabilities of centralized command and control, hierarchical armed groups have been able to achieve political objectives by engaging governments through spectacular and highly coordinated attacks that have involved tactics ranging from subversion and terrorism to positional warfare. For example, consider Chechen militants in the First Chechen War against Russia, who were organized hierarchically. Vertical subordination proceeded from the president of the self-proclaimed Chechen Republic of Ichkeria, Dzhokhar Dudayev, down through trusted senior commanders such as Shamil Basayev and Salman Raduyev to lower-level battalion leaders. Dudayev insisted that every action taking place in the war against the Russian Federation be under his tight control.[11] With Dudayev's approval, Basayev was responsible for shaping the cause of the struggle against the Russian government by gradually transforming it from ethnonational striving for independence to a holy jihad waged against what he characterized in the Second Chechen War as an apostate regime.[12]

In the mid-1990s, Basayev made critical strategic decisions about the means to be employed in the struggle for Chechen independence. For instance, he was responsible for the decision to "bring the war to Russia."[13] He did so by adopting unconventional tactics that involved hostage taking, airplane hijacking, and even the use of weapons of mass destruction (WMDs) by planting a radioactive container in a public park in Moscow in November 1995.[14] Moreover, Basayev did not just inspire and design the attacks against Russian targets—he also took part in directing the execution of those operations. For example, he personally commanded a battalion of two hundred Chechen militants who took two thousand hostages in the Russian city of Budennovsk in 1995, which turned the strategic balance in favor of the Chechen separatists and forced the Russian government to negotiate with the leadership of the self-proclaimed republic. It was also the case that when a Chechen battalion led by the field commander Salman Raduyev took more than two thousand hostages in the city of Kizlyar in Dagestan in late 1995, Dudayev personally managed the operation, including directing Raduyev's execution of hostages.[15] These events exemplify how leadership functions in hierarchically structured armed groups.

Predictably, the reliance on a hierarchical organization and centralized system of command and control made Dudayev and his military commanders priority targets—or "high-value targets" (HVTs)—in Russia's fight against Chechen militants. To eliminate Dudayev's field commanders and their fighters, the Russian government was even willing to risk the lives of hostages. For example, when on January 10, 1996, after the attack on Kizlyar, Raduyev and his fighters together with 160 hostages sought to retreat into Chechnya, Russian special forces engaged them in a battle that lasted for eight days and involved indiscriminately firing Grad rockets into the village of Pervomaysk in an attempt to wipe out the Chechens. To relieve the siege at Pervomaysk, Dudayev sent a diversionary force from Grozny that attacked the Russian forces from the rear, allowing Raduyev, his militants, and the remaining hostages to escape to Chechnya. The hostages held by Raduyev's militants were released and left Chechnya in February 1996.

A centralized and hierarchical form of organization, it should be noted, was foreign to the Chechen culture of combat. Its adoption in the earlier stages of the conflict can be explained by the military background of Chechen leaders who had served in the Soviet Army.[16] For example, Dudayev was an officer in the Soviet Air Forces and became the first Chechen to be promoted to flag rank, attaining the grade of major general. He served in a strategic bomber unit and participated in the war in Afghanistan against the mujahideen, for which he was highly decorated.

However, once the Russian government demonstrated the ability to target the Chechen leaders—Dudayev, for instance, was killed in 1996—Chechen militants decentralized their command-and-control structure. They reorganized to fight in small, flexible units that resembled the traditional Chechen clan-based organization for warfighting.[17] This model of command and control can be characterized as centralization of strategic planning and decentralization of operational and tactical actions.

Decentralization and Networked Organizations

Distinguishing centralized from decentralized organizations is critical to understanding the evolution of armed groups from a hierarchically structured system of command and control to a complex and loosely organized network. Whereas the former is distinguished by the control of senior leadership over strategy and operations, the latter is characterized by the ability of the network's key structural elements—its "nodes"—to exercise autonomy in decision-making, operational planning, and tactical control.

As explained by John Arquilla and David Ronfeldt in their early work on networks and netwar, each node can be an organization, a group, or an individual actor; nodes can be tightly or loosely connected; and nodes can be open to recruitment or closed to new members.[18] Such networks may appear leaderless, guided by several leaders, or with leadership changing over time.[19] In other words, a loose network can demonstrate fluctuation in its constituent elements, which makes it extremely challenging for a government to understand and counter the threat the network presents. In addition, the policy of high-value targeting, a tactic that has been employed successfully by several governments to decapitate a hierarchical armed group's senior leadership, loses its effectiveness when an armed group restructures and adopts a networked apparatus.[20]

To overcome governments' use of these countermeasures, armed groups not only adopt decentralized command-and-control systems but also engage in networked types of cooperation. For example, a recent typology of networked cooperation by jihadist actors includes formal terrorist organizations, loose informal networks, and individual terrorist entrepreneurs that can engage in various types of cooperative relations. These different types of cooperation include mergers and strategic alliances ("high-end cooperation") and tactical cooperation or transactional collaboration ("low-end cooperation").[21] Mergers constitute the highest type of cooperation and feature the full integration of the actors' command-and-control, human, and material resources for an indefinite period. Hezbollah, for instance, was formed by the merger of several smaller Shia militant groups in Lebanon.[22]

Strategic alliances and partnerships, in contrast, do not require the unification of command-and-control systems. However, they presume a long-term commitment to sharing resources and skills as well as strategic coordination among the actors involved.[23] A significant degree of strategic interest overlap is a crucial precondition for forming a successful strategic alliance. The relationship between the al-Qaeda core and its affiliates in various regions can be seen as an example of a strategic partnership.[24]

Low-end cooperation is far more limited, involving short-term pragmatic arrangements over a limited set of objectives. Such tactical cooperation can be based on a common interest and does not generally involve a convergence of strategic goals.[25] For example, after the US-led Iraq invasion, former members of the Baath regime along with tribal sheiks engaged in tactical cooperation with jihadists, both local and foreign, in an attempt to end the occupation of Iraq despite the fact that the long-term strategic interests of these factions diverged considerably.[26] Transactional relationships can be expressed through bartering material goods, such as weapons, or in symbolic arrangements from a pledge of allegiance that does not involve any change in an actor's structure but allows it to use the brand of a more powerful actor.[27] The multiplicity of actors involved in this type of "network of networks," the variety of ways in which they cooperate, and the transnational nature of their activities constitute a complex challenge for governments seeking to disrupt the violent operations of contemporary armed group networks.[28]

One early example of a networked armed group—al-Qaeda—was from its inception designed with the objective of establishing linkages with other Islamist factions.[29] But depending on the period of time, al-Qaeda may be referred to as (1) the original network of the al-Qaeda core (AQC); (2) the AQC and its franchise organizations; (3) the AQC, franchise organizations, and other like-minded organizations; or, finally, (4) all the previously mentioned groupings plus al-Qaeda–inspired independent actors.[30] The al-Qaeda network is sometimes described as a "tree," with AQC as the trunk and its affiliates and associates as branches.[31] The formation of this treelike structure is discussed below.

Before the 9/11 attacks, al-Qaeda maintained a more traditional hierarchical structure in Afghanistan while also engaging in cooperation with other armed groups and individuals that shared its ideological vision.[32] Al-Qaeda also used its camps in Afghanistan to indoctrinate and train jihadist fighters from many different armed groups. From 1996 to the attacks on September 11, 2001, Salafi-oriented Muslims from around the world traveled to Afghanistan to receive irregular warfare training and indoctrination in these facilities. How many did so is hard to determine, as estimates vary widely. The *9/11 Commission Report* noted that "U.S. intelligence estimates put the total number of fighters who underwent instruction in bin Laden-supported camps in Afghanistan from 1996 through 9/11 at 10,000 to 20,000."[33] Others put the number much higher.[34]

Whatever the number, a considerable corps of second-generation Salafi jihadist warriors traveled to Afghanistan from some fifty or more countries. Later, al-Qaeda established connections through them necessary to engage in network-based cooperation.[35] This led to the establishment of the local jihadist groups that subsequently became al-Qaeda franchise organizations.

Osama bin Laden's initial focus was on exporting al-Qaeda's ideology and best practices from the war against the Red Army in Afghanistan to other Muslim countries to overthrow what were described as Western-backed apostate states. These regimes were referred to as "near enemies" in al-Qaeda's vernacular at that time. However, during the latter half of the 1990s, bin Laden broadened al-Qaeda's warfighting doctrine and called for targeting the United States. In a 1998 fatwa, after specifying the American crime of occupation of the holy places in Saudi Arabia, the war America was waging through sanctions against the Iraqi people, and America's support of Jewish aggression in Palestine, bin Laden asserted that the United States had declared war on God. Therefore, it was the duty of every Muslim to "kill the Americans . . . wherever and whenever they find them."[36] In al-Qaeda's idiom, the United States was dubbed the "far enemy." The attacks of 9/11 were an outgrowth of this refocusing of al-Qaeda's targeting doctrine.[37]

However, the attacks on the World Trade Center and the Pentagon resulted in the destruction of al-Qaeda's organizational and operational facilities in Afghanistan and their need to adopt a new organizational structure. The connections with other Salafi jihadist organizations allowed al-Qaeda to adapt to the new reality by morphing into a movement that structurally resembled a network, with formal affiliation between its branches and the center and rather loose connections with individuals and organizations inspired by the al-Qaeda cause on the network's edges.[38]

After bin Laden became the number-one target in the US-led "War on Terror," his control over operational and tactical aspects of organizational activities decreased, although he maintained an influence on the ideological and strategic aspects of the network's functioning through issuing guidance and inspirational statements.[39] The Salafi jihadist ideology promoted by al-Qaeda constitutes the underlying unifying mechanism that drove the actions of the al-Qaeda–associated nodes. Dissemination of strategic guidance and the exchange of operational experience and tactical skills were critical for maintaining the network, and these tasks were accomplished within the virtual sanctuary that al-Qaeda and its associated jihadist groups sought to establish on the Internet. In effect, the Internet was used as a substitute sanctuary for the one lost in Afghanistan.[40]

Despite their formal affiliation with the AQC, the regional nodes of the organization adopted various approaches to the struggle and formed their own networks of support. For instance, the organization al-Qaeda in the Arabian Peninsula (AQAP) tended to rely on support from Yemeni tribes and demonstrated sensitivity to local needs and grievances to strengthen its position in the region.[41] In contrast, AQI, led by Abu Musab al-Zarqawi, lacked the support of the secular Iraqi Sunnis. However, al-Zarqawi decided not to moderate his strategy to match the needs of his potential constituencies. Instead, he chose to ignite Shia violence against Sunnis in order to radicalize the moderates and make them adhere to his vision of the Iraqi future.[42] Although this approach proved to be only partially successful, al-Zarqawi skillfully exploited Internet communication to inspire foreign jihadist fighters to join the insurgency in Iraq. Even though many of them did not formally join AQI, foreign jihadists galvanized by al-Zarqawi's appeal were responsible for the massive wave of suicide bombings against the Coalition troops in Iraq that began in 2004 and escalated in subsequent years.[43] In addition to foreign jihadist fighters and some supportive Sunni tribes, AQI's networks included organizations not affiliated with the AQC, such as Ansar al-Sunna (later Ansar al-Islam) and the Mujahideen Shura Council, which served as an umbrella organization for several Sunni insurgent groups and later morphed into the Islamic State of Iraq (ISI).[44]

Although numerous sources reported that AQI's strategy was at odds with the strategic vision of the AQC and bin Laden, especially with respect to the use of indiscriminate violence, the networks built by al-Zarqawi in Iraq and through its international linkages became the flagship of the Salafi jihadist movement and succeeded in engaging the US forces in Iraq in a prolonged and bloody fight.[45] AQI's network of networks in Iraq became an exceedingly complex challenge for TF 714. The network consisted of many decentralized units that employed Information Age technologies to form into dispersed networks to escalate attacks across Iraq. There were scores of linkages among the nodes that AQI networks comprised, and the linkages did not take the form of static patterns that could be easily mapped and delineated. Rather than a hierarchical organization, AQI consisted of continually shifting, dispersed, decentralized, and interconnected networks.

AQI posed a complex challenge to TF 714. Understanding it, recalled General McChrystal, was "not an easy insight to come by. It was only . . . with considerable difficulty that we came to understand how the emerging networks of Islamist insurgents and terrorists were fundamentally different from any enemy the United States had previously known or faced."[46] Those differences were most apparent, network specialist David Knoke observed, in AQI's "organizational structures and strategies. In place of vertically integrated hierarchies, today's jihadis assemble in continually shifting networks." Their organization did not mirror a hierarchical organizational structure. Their strategy was "to drive out foreign occupying forces by inflicting such high levels of injury and death that a democratic government would be forced to withdraw."[47] This was AQI's method of fighting. It was made up of a plethora of decentralized networks that made effective use of information technologies to conduct operations across Iraq.[48]

For al-Qaeda, Iraq became the central front in the global battle against the far enemy. Al-Qaeda hoped to inflict a defeat with strategic consequences for the United States. Iraq afforded al-Qaeda an opportunity to spawn a new generation of skilled fighters who, after they left Iraq, could carry the fight elsewhere. In the first decades of the twenty-first century, these "Iraqi Arabs" would become a mirror image of the "Afghan Arabs" that at the close of the twentieth century formed al-Qaeda's first generation.[49]

To summarize, the way in which armed groups influence and control their strategic, operational, and tactical activities has a significant impact on the conduct of operations and on the challenges those operations pose for the governments that are trying to disrupt the armed groups' violent activities. In the twentieth century, hierarchical organizations allowed armed group leaders to exercise both influence and control over many, if not all, aspects of the groups' operations. But those leaders were also vulnerable, and their elimination could, and in many cases did, undermine organizational cohesion. By contrast, in the twenty-first century, decentralized networks attained organizational fluidity and proved much less susceptible to disruption through the elimination of the organizations' top leadership. As we shall see, TF 714 eliminated AQI chieftain al-Zarqawi, but that did not affect AQI's operational tempo. Networked armed groups presented a new problem set that necessitated drastic changes in how counterterrorism forces organized and operated.

Why and How Armed Groups Have Moved to Networks

When considering the reasons that explain the adoption of a networked organizational structure by armed groups, it is important to distinguish between objectives and enabling factors. Discussion of the purposes can shed light on the expected benefits of the networked organization, which include compensating for asymmetry in assets through increasing operational mobility and adaptability, minimizing signatures and increasing stealth, and intensifying recruitment. In turn, considering enabling factors would answer the question, what made this change possible and fostered its implementation? Among the factors addressed below are communication technology, common ideological base, and accumulation of operational experience on multiple battlefields in the preceding decades.

Objectives of Organizational Restructuring

Classical counterinsurgency theory suggests several inherent power asymmetries between government forces and the violent challengers that seek to overthrow those authorities. One of the most striking is the asymmetry in tangible assets. When compared with armed groups, governments often have better-equipped and better-trained armies, maintain extensive weapon arsenals, and possess sophisticated intelligence capabilities—and even if one of these conditions is not fulfilled, governments usually have resources to fill the gaps. In contrast, insurgents tend to be inferior in material assets but hope to exploit the galvanizing power of their cause.[50] The involvement of major powers in intrastate conflicts of the post–Cold War period (e.g., conflicts in the former Yugoslavia, Afghanistan, Iraq, and Syria) put insurgents in fights with much better-equipped enemies.[51]

Armed groups employ various measures to overcome these asymmetries. Itai Brun suggests that violent nonstate actors faced with more militarily advanced state adversaries have undergone a revolution in military affairs (RMA) of their own kind—a revolution that Brun refers to as "the Other RMA."[52] Armed groups can undertake adaptations in order to compensate for inherent inferiority in capabilities to increase their capacity to sustain the damages inflicted by governmental forces and to gain the upper hand by turning the states' military superiority into a disadvantage. Adaptation has resulted from the learning process that armed groups such as Hezbollah, Hamas, and al-Qaeda first conducted during the late 1990s and early 2000s through the observation and interpretation of the conduct of government military operations, primarily those of the United States and Israel.[53]

Among the key adjustments made by armed groups were making more use of protective means (e.g., bunkers, tunnels, civilian infrastructure) to enhance survivability; employing low-cost, high-trajectory weapons such as the Qassam rockets used by Hamas that can penetrate enemy territory; using weapons and tactics that cause a high number of casualties among enemy forces and civilians (e.g., IEDs); exploiting information capabilities to build international and domestic pressure on an enemy's government; and engaging in up-close fighting to offset technological superiority of the opponent.[54]

A striking example of the successful utilization of these lessons against a militarily superior adversary can be seen in the 2006 Israeli war with Hezbollah, known in Israel as the Second Lebanon War. Due to advanced intelligence capabilities and superior air power, Israel successfully eliminated Hezbollah's long-range rocket launchers and targeted the organization's main headquarters in the first days of the military operation.[55] However, Hezbollah was capable not only of withstanding that damage but also of disrupting daily life and paralyzing the economy of northern Israel through a nearly constant barrage of short-range Katyusha missiles.

Israel had no choice but to launch a ground operation that involved up-close fighting between Israel Defense Forces (IDF) soldiers and Hezbollah's militiamen, who were more familiar with the terrain than the Israelis, had an elaborate system of bunkers, and relied on hit-and-run guerrilla tactics.[56] Israeli attempts to disrupt Hezbollah's command-and-control system proved ineffective because the organization had a decentralized structure. The mode of asymmetrical warfare adopted by Hezbollah, together with the decentralization of command and control, offset

Israel's superior military technology, allowing Hezbollah to exploit the Israeli intolerance for high numbers of casualties. This undermined support for the war among Israelis.[57] Israel's Second Lebanon War is widely considered a failure; despite being militarily superior, the IDF failed to defeat Hezbollah on the battlefield and thus also failed to destroy its ability to conduct further attacks.[58]

Increasing operational resilience, stealth, and adaptability by armed groups is one of the principal reasons for employing a decentralized networked organizational structure. It allows armed groups to exploit the ambiguities of their operational environment while minimizing the risks of being exposed. Marc Sageman noted that while hierarchical structures are helpful for maintaining control over operations, their chain of command quickly becomes overloaded and rendered inefficient under conditions of high uncertainty that require swift information processing and communication.[59] Networked structures, in contrast, enable fast communication between the relevant nodes without exposing the entire network.[60] This development increases stealth and improves a network's adaptability and operational mobility. Moreover, due to the fluidity of networks and an ability to centralize and decentralize depending on the environment, detecting the nodes participating in particular operations becomes a daunting intelligence puzzle.

As later chapters describe, AQI demonstrated an escalating capacity to perpetrate attacks against the US military forces at a rate that grew exponentially from 2004 through 2006.[61] The initial response by American military forces was to target the top leadership of AQI. However, as those chapters also describe, the US forces discovered that operational approaches developed in the era of classic COIN and waged against hierarchical armed groups had little effect when applied to AQI.[62] That was because its networks did not rely on the guidance, control, and operational decision-making performed by a top leadership that could be eliminated by HVT operations.

Instead, AQI's structure empowered midlevel commanders and managers and fostered cooperation between the operational and support components of its networked apparatus.[63] The clandestine networks of AQI consisted of numerous nodes that involved financial units, media centers, intelligence branches, IED-production cells, and other nodes capable of independent planning and decision-making as well as coordinated action. Such a fluid organizational structure was not affected by the killing of al-Zarqawi in 2006, which would have had, at a minimum, a disabling effect if AQI had been a hierarchical organization. Rather, his death was followed by an escalation in the number of insurgent attacks during the following year.[64] US forces were not able to keep pace with insurgent activities in Iraq, let alone reduce them.

Another reason armed groups decentralize is to secure their recruitment process against government countermeasures. In the past, hierarchical structures institutionalized the recruitment process to a degree that would allow them to fulfill the primary task of the organizational hierarchy—to exercise control over the process. For example, in the 1980s, Sheikh Abdullah Yusuf Azzam created an organization called Mekhtab al-Khidemat (the Service Bureau), which later evolved into al-Qaeda. It sought to control the recruitment campaign by insisting that it alone could enlist foreign mujahideen for the fight against the Soviet troops in Afghanistan.[65] Today such formalization of organizational outreach would make the top-down recruitment efforts visible and susceptible to governmental countermeasures and therefore extremely dangerous for the recruiters and potential recruits.

A decentralized, networked approach, however, allows organizations to benefit from bottom-up channels of radicalization without exposing themselves. They can accomplish this by exporting their cause but not exposing their organizational capabilities, through an array of social media tools. For instance, Sageman notes that social affiliations (friendship, kinship, worship, and discipleship) of the sympathizers of al-Qaeda's cause led to the emergence of closely tied groupings of like-minded individuals in multiple geographic locations.[66] Forming a cohesive group was a necessary precondition for later establishing bonds with jihadist networks through which the group members could join the global jihad.[67] Decreasing the degree of control and instead relying on the projection of influence creates a situation in which radicalization happens in closed and tight-knit groups of individuals (friends, families, student groups, etc.) whose interaction does not raise suspicion and often flies below the radar of the government.

Enablers of Organizational Restructuring

As the preceding discussion makes clear, armed groups have several excellent reasons for restructuring from a hierarchical to a networked organization. But what are the key enabling factors that have made such a transformation possible?

The first and most frequently identified enabler of networked armed groups is the increase in communication capabilities through Information Age technology. There is nothing new about changes in communication technology contributing to significant shifts in warfare. For instance, in the latter half of the nineteenth century, the ability to send telegrams allowed governments to mobilize troops, move armies, and communicate with generals in the field.[68] Similarly, the spread of mobile communication devices fostered information exchange and coordination on the battlefield. This technology not only contributed to the flexibility of military operations conducted by the armies of nation-states but also enabled armed groups to delegate authority to lower-level operatives.

The development of Internet-based communications took this phenomenon further by creating an environment conducive to the adoption of networked organizational structures that do not require leadership oversight and instead enable geographically distant units and individuals to engage directly with the enemy.[69] The Internet provided platforms for spreading and gathering information, recruiting members and supporters, training fighters, and coordinating efforts among multiple units.[70] Information technology made many informal channels of communication—email, chat rooms, forums, message boards, Facebook, YouTube, Twitter—available to terrorist and insurgent groups.[71] These developments, in turn, allowed armed groups to project their ideology-based influence on wider audiences while using one of the main benefits of the Internet—anonymity—to conceal their identities and geographic locations.

Because Web 2.0 technology allows for two-way communication through wikis, microblogging, social networking, and other collaborative Web applications, it has provided potential recruits an opportunity to respond to an ideological appeal and engage in dialogue with the armed group without leaving their homes.[72] In this way, information technology has extended the reach of violent networks to a global scale and engendered the phenomenon of online radicalization.[73] Besides the expanded reach, the speed of information sharing and exchange through Internet-based communication channels plays an important role in the coordination of attacks. To be fully operational, networked organizations have to be able to continually process dense information flows.[74] Advanced communication technology reduces the costs of communication between multiple nodes and allows clandestine networks to exploit their competitive advantage over hierarchically structured adversaries.[75]

A second factor that contributed to networked transformation is the accumulation of experience and the cultivation of shared values by like-minded groups and individuals around the globe, starting in the 1980s in the Afghan war against the Soviet Union. As Arquilla and Ronfeldt note, "The capacity of this [networked] design for effective performance over time may depend on the existence of shared principles, interests, and goals—perhaps an overarching doctrine or ideology— which spans all nodes and to which the members subscribe in a deep way."[76] This shared cause is significant for networked groups to acquire a common strategic vision that serves as a substitute for the centralized control over the group's strategy in hierarchical organizations. Common experiences and a shared narrative define the beliefs and behavior that are reflected in an organization's strategic culture,[77] which allows the networked structures to maintain strategic consistency in terms of commitment to its ideological principles. Illustrative of this is the relationship between the al-Qaeda leadership and its associated movements during the years after the loss of sanctuary in Afghanistan in late 2001. Those associated movements operated independently but still conformed with al-Qaeda's ideology.

The origins of the ideational component of the al-Qaeda strategic culture is rooted in writings of an Egyptian Salafi intellectual, Sayyed Qutb, who called for the overthrow of secular Muslim governments through the means of violent jihad.[78] Adopted by the founder of al-Qaeda, Abdullah Yusuf Azzam, Qutb's ideas of reviving Islam through Salafi jihad, and of an inevitable clash between the Western and Islamic worlds, became the key narrative underlying the jihadist strategic culture that was further developed and tested during the Soviet invasion of Afghanistan. The Soviet-Afghan War and the mobilization of foreign fighters to wage jihad against the Red Army was a crucial step in developing the jihadist ideology. That ideology would inspire later fighters to join the struggle in Bosnia, Chechnya, Somalia, and throughout the Middle East. It spawned a "common language" that enabled the clandestine jihadist networks to inspire global operations.[79]

Participation in these conflicts provided a platform for exchange and accumulation of operational knowledge, ideological socialization of jihadist fighters, development of the culture of martyrdom, and establishment of network connections.[80] This period also produced a new generation of jihadist leaders such as bin Laden and al-Zarqawi who later on, each in his own way, deployed skills and connections to form the global networks that project influence by galvanizing both close and distant audiences with the appeal of a transnational ideology.

Complex Threat and New Operational Challenges

Networked armed groups present governments with an array of new operational challenges. The nature of those challenges varies, at least in part, according to the type of network that an armed group develops.

Variations of networked structures, as described by Arquilla and Ronfeldt in their seminal study, include the chain, the star or hub, and the all-channel versions (see figure 2.1).[81] In the chain structure, information, goods, and other resources move sequentially from one end to another through the intermediary nodes. In the star or hub structure, communication and coordination proceeds through the central node, which is not hierarchically distinct from those connected to it. In the all-channel network, which is the most complex structure, every node is connected to all the other nodes.[82] The last type, while difficult to organize, is an effective operational system for running a complex all-channel network.[83] Furthermore,

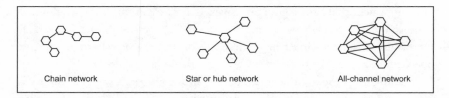

Figure 2.1 Three basic types of networks

Source: John Arquilla and David Ronfeldt, *Networks and Netwars* (Santa Monica, CA: RAND Corporation, 2001), 8.

the all-channel type is the most suitable for providing the benefits associated with organizational restructuring: flexibility, stealth, and operational advantage over a hierarchical adversary. These networked systems pose a new type of challenge to governmental actors engaged in counterterrorism and COIN efforts. Below are prototype illustrations of these descriptions of networks.

Networks consist of nodes that communicate and coordinate with one another along certain paths. Although nodes included in a network might share certain characteristics, networks do not have fixed boundaries in the sense that regular groups do because networks can expand their reach to individuals not formally affiliated with any network component.[84] How networks behave and expand depends on their goals and functions. For instance, covert insurgent networks prioritize survivability and therefore do not grow randomly. However, in order to ensure their survival and remain clandestine, they need to gather intelligence and adopt operational innovations, which require engaging in ad hoc interaction with external actors.[85] To avoid the disruption of their operations, covert networks seek to be unpredictable, which is attained through constantly changing the patterns of interaction between the nodes. This results in another important characteristic of modern insurgent networks—complexity.

According to specialists in modern communications technology, *complex* networks are understood as different from *complicated* ones in that the latter operate in patterned and predictable ways. In contrast, in complex networks, the interactions between their components are constantly changing.[86] The key features of complex networks are the multiplicity of actors involved, their diversity, and their interdependence. Multiplicity pertains to the high number of actors that can potentially engage in a networked interaction. Diversity relates to the heterogeneity of actors involved. Interdependence points to the degree of interconnectedness between the nodes.[87] Each of these features contributes to the two main challenges that complex networks pose to those trying to understand them. First is the unpredictability of outcomes, because similar starting positions can yield different results due to the changing interactions between multiple components of the system. Second, due to cognitive limits and lack of up-to-date information, it is close to impossible for an individual decision-maker to grasp the whole scope of a complex network's operation.[88] Below is a summarization of the characteristics David Snowden and Mary Boone identify with a complex context:

- a large number of intersecting elements
- nonlinear interactions in which minor changes can produce disproportionately major consequences
- a dynamic context in which solutions cannot be imposed but arise from the circumstances frequently referred to as emergence
- elements that evolve irreversibly with one another and with the environment
- in complex systems, agents and context that constrain each, preventing the prediction of outcomes in advance[89]

When it comes to armed groups, a complex threat encompasses high numbers of diverse nodes that may include insurgent and terrorist groups, criminal organizations, terrorist entrepreneurs, self-radicalized lone wolves, tight-knit local cells, foreign fighters, and even state actors that are involved in permanent or ad hoc interactions.[90] In light of the fact that challenges posed by complex networks are an outcome of a dynamic nonlinear interaction between the diverse nodes, the nature of the threat is fluid, always evolving, and context dependent and therefore not discernible by the governmental agencies involved in counterterrorism and COIN. That same unpredictability makes it hard to design templates for COIN efforts. No predesigned template can be identified as sufficient for informing the problem-solving task when it comes to countering a networked adversary.[91] This circumstance limits the utility of previous operational experience in counterterrorism or COIN.

Furthermore, the strategic objective of knowing one's enemy requires an understanding of a multitude of diverse actors involved in networked interaction at a given point in time and, most important, awareness of the current channels of their communications and interactions. In other words, there is no definitive knowledge of the nature of the threat when one fights a complex networked armed group. The speed of information processing is a critical component of the overall success in responding to networked enemies. Actors involved in clandestine networks are not restricted by any formal rules, ranks, or bureaucratic regulations, which gives them a good chance of gathering intelligence from the local population and passing the information through network channels of communication while remaining undetected.[92]

Therefore, when dealing with a networked adversary, identifying these intangible and constantly changing links becomes more important than capturing and neutralizing an individual actor. The Iraq insurgency offers a striking example of a clandestine and extremely fluid networked organization that involved a multitude of actors with various forms of command and control, sometimes overlapping but often decentralized.[93] As TF 714 discovered, AQI constituted a network of networks spread across Iraq under the authority of midlevel commanders and managers.

To conclude, adoption by an armed group of a networked organizational structure serves multiple purposes. It increases operational mobility and adaptability, minimizes signatures and increases stealth, and provides new avenues for recruitment through Web 2.0 social media platforms. Adoption is enabled by various factors: availability of communication technology, common ideological base, and accumulation of operational experience on multiple battlefields. Through the high number of diverse actors involved in dynamic nonlinear interaction, clandestine complex networks pose a constantly evolving challenge that necessitates a reconsideration of the strategic, operational, and tactical dimensions of governmental efforts aimed at tackling this new complex threat. Military commanders and intelligence managers faced with complex challenges have to think and act in ways that are different from the past, when they could assume that they faced a hierarchically organized enemy. The underlying characteristic of complexity is the presence of continuous change facilitated by innovative technologies.[94] In Iraq, AQI posed such a complex challenge.

CHAPTER 3

TRANSFORMING INTELLIGENCE COLLECTION FOR IRREGULAR WAR

By the time President Barack Obama authorized Operation Neptune Spear, the top-secret night raid by the Pentagon's elite counterterrorism force that killed Osama bin Laden, a great deal of intelligence had been amassed about bin Laden's hideout—a walled-in villa—through what this chapter describes as the "disciplines of intelligence collection."[1] These collection tools contributed greatly to the determination that it was highly likely that bin Laden was hiding out in the compound in Abbottabad, a city in the east of Pakistan. However, the intelligence trail leading to it was circuitous and involved, most importantly, the tracking of bin Laden's most trusted courier.

During bin Laden's decade in hiding, US intelligence learned that he greatly feared using any means of electronic communication because it could be intercepted by the National Security Agency (NSA). Consequently, tracking him down was a major intelligence challenge until it was learned from detainees held at Guantanamo that a Kuwaiti national—Abu Ahmed al-Kuwaiti—was not only a member of bin Laden's inner circle but also a trusted courier. He was also said to be a subordinate of Khalid Sheikh Mohammed, the architect of the 9/11 attacks. However, for several years after learning this tantalizing bit of intelligence, US agencies remained in the dark about the real identity of al-Kuwaiti and his whereabouts.

From 2007 to 2009, American intelligence agencies were able to determine that the courier was born in Pakistan but ethnically was an Afghan Pashtun. He grew up in Kuwait after his family migrated there. Then, in 2009, thanks to NSA intercepts of cell phone and email communications, al-Kuwaiti was found in Pakistan. Once his whereabouts were pinpointed, the full gamut of US intelligence-collection capabilities were brought to bear to track his pattern of life, movements, communications, and associations. Al-Kuwaiti was, in effect, put under a 24/7 stakeout, which eventually led to the villa in Abbottabad where he resided with his family. He was followed there by an overhead intelligence, surveillance, and re-connaissance platform as he drove from the provincial capital of Peshawar, located in northwestern Pakistan. For the next several months, the villa was monitored through all the intelligence means available to the US government. Eventually US analysts concluded that there was a strong possibility bin Laden was residing inside. Operation Neptune Spear followed shortly thereafter.

This chapter examines the different intelligence-collection tools used to find bin Laden. As the chapter explains, those collection capabilities have undergone considerable adaptation since 9/11 to deal with new and different targets. In his widely used text *Intelligence: From Secrets to Policy*, Mark Lowenthal observes that "collection is the bedrock of intelligence. . . . Without collection, intelligence is little more than guesswork."[2] This truism, and the onset of the Cold War, drove the US government to develop "multiple means of collecting the intelligence" it required. In the lexicon of intelligence, these are sometimes known as "INTs."[3]

The development of those collection capabilities was largely shaped by the challenge of "penetrating the Soviet target," as Lowenthal observes. The USSR was "a closed society with a vast land mass, frequent bad weather, and a long-standing tradition of secrecy and deception."[4] It also was heavily armed. Its modern arsenal of conventional and nuclear weapons was aimed at what Soviet security services called *glavnyy vrag* (the "main enemy")—the United States.[5] Consequently, Moscow's military capabilities became the single most important concern of US intelligence collection during the Cold War.

The chapter highlights how Soviet military forces drove the development of US intelligence-collection capabilities for more than four decades. Collection requirements were focused on an Industrial Age enemy that was a skilled practitioner of denial-and-deception methods. According to a former US Air Force deputy chief of staff for intelligence, surveillance, and reconnaissance, Lt. Gen. David Deptula, "In that industrial-age . . . intelligence was a massive, personnel-intensive operation aimed at supporting national and military decision making."[6] The intelligence community gathered intelligence largely through an array of highly technical means, produced periodic reports, and provided them to policy-makers to inform national security policy and strategy.

However, in the aftermath of 9/11, those collection disciplines, assembled to work against the Soviet target, had to undergo a sea change in how they functioned. No longer was the United States confronted only by threats posed by nation-states; now it was also in the crosshairs of nonstate armed groups empowered by Information Age capabilities. And no longer was it a peacetime environment. The United States was at war. Moreover, as noted in previous chapters, this wartime milieu was "irregular in its nature."[7] The principal threats to the United States now were posed by clandestine, decentralized, and networked nonstate actors that operated transnationally. These developments necessitated that the United States adopt unconventional methods of fighting, which, in turn, demanded that the intelligence-collection tools be reconfigured to support operations against the new and different enemy.

Deptula characterizes this change in intelligence collection as the difference between "gathering and hunting." He equates Cold War intelligence collection with farmers who gather the harvest and periodically deliver products to market.[8] That was the Cold War approach to intelligence collection. It involved gathering massive amounts of technical information that, periodically, was turned into intelligence reports and delivered to policymaker consumers. Collection systems worked within a peacetime security environment.

The irregular wartime context in which intelligence collection took place after 9/11 was very different, explains Deptula. Consequently, it had to "undergo a cultural transformation and trade the farmer's [approach] of . . . methodically gathering and producing information" for a new approach that was more akin to hunting. Hunters needed intelligence that drove the targeting cycle. For hunters, intelligence focused on "anticipating, finding, and fixing on elusive and often dangerous prey."[9] The relationship between intelligence and operations, in an irregular wartime context, had to become symbiotically connected. This necessitated "closing the gap that existed in the past" between those who collected intelligence and those who "operated on that intelligence."[10]

This chapter begins by examining the emergence of the US intelligence-collection disciplines in the aftermath of World War II and their maturation during the Cold War. Next, the impact of the end of the Cold War on those collection disciplines is appraised. The central part of the chapter focuses on the challenges that intelligence collection faced as the threat evolved from state to nonstate actors and the context from peacetime to wartime. Embedded within this examination is an assessment of the extent to which the collection disciplines were able to adapt to support operations carried out by Task Force 714 in Iraq.

However, before turning to these matters, a brief sidebar is necessary to set the terms of reference with respect to what constitutes the disciplines of intelligence collection.

The Disciplines of Intelligence Collection

Scholars have divided the collection of intelligence into categories. Jeffrey Richelson, in the sixth edition of his formative volume *The US Intelligence Community*, divides collection into five categories.[11] Mark Lowenthal and Robert Clark do the same in *The Five Disciplines of Intelligence Collection*.[12] This quintet includes the collection by highly specialized machines of (1) signals, (2) images, (3) measurements and signatures, (4) the acquisition of secrets from human sources or spies, and (5) the mining of publicly available open sources that are in electronic or printed form.[13] Each is briefly described below and will serve as the framework for examining the evolution of US intelligence collection from a Cold War to a post-9/11 context and from peacetime to wartime.

Signals Intelligence

Signals intelligence (SIGINT) encompasses both communications intelligence (COMINT) and electronic intelligence (ELINT) collection methods. COMINT comprises information gathered through intercepting the communications of individuals transmitted by "voice (telephone, standard cell-phone, satellite phone, walkie-talkie), the Internet, Morse code, or facsimile."[14] The Information Revolution has had an extraordinary impact on this category of SIGINT. Because of the many sophisticated ways armed groups exploit those burgeoning technologies, US intelligence has faced serious challenges. However, these developments have also provided the IC with opportunities. COMINT can be collected through space, airborne, and ground systems.

ELINT intercepts "non-communications signals from military and civilian hardware." Richelson notes that this practice began in World War II by identifying the "location and operating characteristics of radars."[15] During the Cold War, the number of ELINT targets multiplied and included not only data about the electromagnetic radiation of radars but also the instrumentation signals of different military platforms transmitted "back to organizations controlling the exercise" of them. Examples include "altitude, speed, and trajectory" of new aircraft.[16] "Missile detection, space tracking, and ballistic missile early warning" are other examples.[17]

During the Cold War, a third component of SIGINT emerged that focused on the interception of foreign instrumentation and signals (FISINT). This category includes the instrumentation readings of different components of Soviet missiles, aircraft, and other platforms that were transmitted during testing and evaluation. The interception of these data was critical to understanding the challenges those systems posed and how to counter them.[18]

Imagery Intelligence

Imagery intelligence (IMINT) focuses on gathering pictorial representations of places and objects from a distance. IMINT was gathered initially by conventional photography. Later, images were obtained through complex infrared, electro-optical, and radar sensors. IMINT made great advances during the Cold War through the "development, production, and employment" of a number of different specialized aircraft, such as the U-2, and "spacecraft that permitted U.S. intelligence to closely monitor developments in the Soviet Union and other nations through overhead imagery."[19] Today platforms include unmanned aerial vehicles (UAVs) such as the Predator, Reaper, and Global Hawk. As this chapter describes, UAVs played a critical role when intelligence-collection requirements expanded following 9/11 to put an emphasis on operational targets.

Measurement and Signatures Intelligence

Measurements and signatures intelligence (MASINT) is perhaps the most complex of the technical intelligence methods. The Department of Defense's *Dictionary of Military Terms* describes MASINT as information derived from the "quantitative and qualitative analysis of the physical attributes of targets and events to characterize, locate, and identify" them. MASINT employs various sensors to collect highly "specialized, technically derived measurements of physical phenomenon intrinsic to an object or event."[20] MASINT methods are also employed to investigate intelligence amassed by other collection disciplines.

Richelson notes that because the technical methods of collection employed have little in common with one another, MASINT is "more a description of the product, stemming from a particular type of analysis of the data produced by a variety of collection activities."[21] Abram Shulsky and Gary Schmitt give the following well-known example of MASINT: "Special sensors have been developed to detect and characterize nuclear detonations. These include seismometers, which measure shock waves associated with underground nuclear tests; devices to detect the radioactivity associated with nuclear materials or the fallout of above-ground nuclear tests; and sensors for the remote detection of the flashes of light produced by above-ground nuclear tests."[22] MASINT sensors can also be employed to discover the development, testing, and proliferation of other types of weapon systems (both WMDs and conventional weapons), to verify arms control agreements, and to detect narcotics-production facilities.

Human Intelligence

Human intelligence (HUMINT) is the original collection discipline, writes Michael Althoff: "Throughout most of recorded history, the gathering of intelligence has been accomplished by human agents rather than the technical means that became dominant during the twentieth century."[23] HUMINT can take several forms, including the recruitment of foreign nationals as agents with the objective of directing them "to collect information in their home country or in a third nation." For the United States, "during the Cold War, the primary target was . . . the Soviet Union."[24] In the Cold War's aftermath, the HUMINT mission refocused on other state actors as well as on nonstate armed groups.

Beyond this classic mission, HUMINT can also be acquired from defectors and émigrés. Defectors often hold important official positions in adversarial states but decide to change sides, leave their homeland, and share what they know with the intelligence services of their new home. During the Cold War, defectors from the USSR and other communist states were valuable sources of intelligence. Émigrés leave their home countries for various reasons. They may have valuable information that is of interest to the intelligence services of the state to which they relocate. For example, notes Richelson, "the Iranian émigré community in Los Angeles has long been of interest to U.S. intelligence." The CIA has sought to "cultivate contacts with members of that community, seeking information from Iranians who have traveled to Iran or communicated with relatives."[25]

In the aftermath of 9/11, a new category of HUMINT—detainees—became a critical source of information in the irregular war waged against al-Qaeda and its associated movements. The detainee issue became highly charged because of the interrogation methods initially employed to compel them to provide intelligence. However, interrogation underwent a transformation in Iraq, and members of AQI captured by TF 714 became important sources of operational intelligence.

Open-Source Intelligence

The fifth collection discipline, open-source intelligence (OSINT), is defined by Eliot Jardines as "information that is publicly available to anyone through legal means, including request, observation, or purchase, that is subsequently acquired, vetted, and analyzed to fulfill an intelligence requirement."[26] The sources that are the targets of this category of intelligence collection include those found on television and radio as well as in publicly available printed materials such as government documents and commercially published books and magazines.

In the aftermath of 9/11 and with the evolution of Web 2.0 technologies, the Internet became an important area of operations for armed groups. They not only established websites to propagate their ideologies, explain their goals, and discuss their activities in chatrooms but also employed a wide range of social media tools such as Twitter, Facebook, Flickr, and YouTube to conduct a wide range of virtual activities. In response, US OSINT devoted considerable attention to the Internet and social media.

Intelligence Collection: World War II and Its Aftermath

Through most of its history, the United States did not have an established system for intelligence collection. The reasons for this were twofold. First, as Lowenthal explains, US presidents did not see a need for it. The nation "did not have strong foreign policy interests" and "faced no threat to its security from its neighbors or from powers outside the Western Hemisphere."[27] This was the primary reason. However, it is also the case that there was a distaste for the spy business among US policymakers.[28]

This ended abruptly with the Japanese surprise attack on Pearl Harbor on December 7, 1941. Prior to the attack, President Franklin D. Roosevelt, at the urging of his close adviser William Donovan, considered establishing a centralized intelligence organization. The onset of the war brought Donovan's efforts to fruition. Roosevelt acted swiftly and instituted the Office of Coordinator of Information (COI) in the summer of 1941, with Donovan as its director. Its mission was to collect information and use it as the basis for analysis to be given to senior policymakers. However, as the United States became enmeshed in war with Germany and Japan, COI morphed into the Office of Strategic Services (OSS), and its mission expanded to include an array of secret intelligence activities.[29]

World War II also saw signals intelligence—intercepting and decoding German and Japanese communications—established and quickly become one of the most important intelligence tools. During the war, the United States achieved great success employing SIGINT. It was vital in the fight against the Empire of Japan, as the outcome of the naval battle of Midway in June 1942 illustrates. That story, told in several volumes, including Stephen Budiansky's *Battle of Wits: The Complete Story of Codebreaking in World War II*, is a tale of how signals intelligence led to a great US naval victory.[30] SIGINT allowed Washington to know Tokyo's operational plan for the battle and as a result to cripple its navy for the rest of the war. Another notable development during World War II was an exponential increase in imagery collection, with the United States making "extensive use of airplane photography."[31]

With the war's end, US intelligence capabilities were reduced considerably as part of America's general demobilization. However, in 1946, the need for intelligence began to be reconsidered by the Harry Truman administration, and a Central Intelligence Group (CIG) was established. While the Departments of State, War, and Navy retained their independent intelligence capabilities, the CIG was tasked to "evaluate intelligence from all parts of the government, and to absorb the remnants of OSS's espionage and counterintelligence operations." As the Soviet threat burgeoned, the CIG "accrued new missions and capabilities," evolving into a "fledgling national intelligence service authorized to perform strategic analysis and to conduct . . . clandestine activities abroad."[32]

The turning point for post–World War II US intelligence was the passage of the National Security Act of 1947. It signaled a profound change in how Washington viewed the role of intelligence in national security and foreign policy. No longer was intelligence only a wartime necessity. Rather, as Lowenthal observes, the 1947 law "gave a legal basis to the intelligence community. . . as well as to the position of director of central intelligence, and created the CIA under the director." It "signaled the new importance of intelligence in the nascent Cold War."[33]

In terms of the intelligence-collection disciplines, growing Soviet military power and the threat it posed to the survival of the United States shaped the way each of the disciplines evolved. At the time of the 1947 act, the IC was still in its fledgling stages. It consisted of the newly created CIA, the Federal Bureau of Investigation (FBI), the State Department's Office of Intelligence Research, the Office of Naval Intelligence, the Intelligence Division of the Army, and the Air Force Directorate of Intelligence. Missing were two agencies that became core Cold War intelligence-collection bastions: the NSA and the National Reconnaissance Office (NRO).

Soviet Military Power and Cold War Intelligence Collection

The Soviet Union presented the nascent IC with a unique challenge. It constituted what came to be described as a "denied area."[34] What this meant was that the vast expanse of territory that made up the USSR was extremely difficult to access by traditional HUMINT operations. This made the Soviet Union a hard target for collecting HUMINT because, as Matthew Aid writes, it was "hermetically sealed from the outside world" by its security services.[35] The seriousness of this situation struck home for the United States in August 1949 with the surprise of the first Soviet atomic bomb test, five years ahead of when it was expected.[36] The United States had no agents embedded in the Soviet Union to warn of its nuclear progress. The detonation of a Soviet bomb shattered the illusion of a comfortable American lead and revealed just how little was known in Washington about the USSR's commitment to developing an atomic bomb. In reality, that program, explained Oleg Bukharin, was "the crown jewel of Soviet military power" and "a closely guarded secret." To keep Washington from knowing about it, Moscow "built an elaborate, multi-layered system of deception . . . to thwart all foreign intelligence operations."[37]

Secrecy also shrouded the development of the long-range systems the Soviets intended to employ to deliver nuclear strikes. Consider the US uncertainty over whether Moscow would commit to developing long-range bombers or intercontinental ballistic missiles (ICBMs). Washington assumed the Kremlin had selected the former, based in part on the public display of new strategic bombers in the mid-1950s. However, later in the decade, it became apparent that the Soviets had opted to concentrate on missile development. This surprise again revealed how little the United States knew about Soviet strategic military programs.

This ignorance was due, in part, to the fact that the newly established CIA found it extremely difficult to establish agent networks inside the USSR to uncover the details of the Soviet military-industrial system. The paucity of HUMINT meant the United States would have to rely on an array of technical collection systems to penetrate the Soviet edifice. What follows highlights the development of those signals, imagery, and measurement and signatures capabilities that were able to observe Soviet conventional and nuclear military forces, to measure and assess them, and to listen to how they were managed.

Signals Intelligence Leads the Way

As the United States became increasing troubled by Soviet expansion in Eastern Europe in the aftermath of World War II, but before the shock delivered by the Soviet atomic weapons test in August 1949, Washington turned to signals intelligence. It was the one collection tool that could penetrate the Iron Curtain to intercept communications in order to try to learn the "strengths and capabilities of the Soviet armed forces, the production capacity of Soviet industry, and . . . Soviet work in the field of atomic energy."[38] However, to achieve this objective, the United States had to rejuvenate its SIGINT capabilities.[39]

To address this paucity of SIGINT, a new organization—the Armed Forces Security Agency (AFSA)—was created. But it had a brief and troubled existence,[40] and President Truman decided to appoint a special committee in December 1951 to examine US communications intelligence. Based on its findings, Truman in 1952 replaced AFSA with the NSA. The secretary of defense was designated executive branch authority overall for SIGINT.[41]

SIGINT came to play a central role in assessing the strengths and capabilities of the Soviet military, according to Adm. John Michael McConnell, former NSA director. He equated the impact of the NSA during the Cold War with SIGINT accomplishments in World War II: "*SIGINT* successes [in the Cold War] . . . were no less significant in terms of gravity and magnitude for changing world history and for protecting the interests of the United States, our allies, and democracy."

Signals intelligence, he judged, contributed significantly to "winning the Cold War."[42]

The specific contributions that each of SIGINT's subdisciplines made to understanding Soviet military power remain classified. What we do know, according to William Nolte, is that COMINT was a "core sub-discipline" because of its capacity to intercept Soviet day-to-day communications of both tactical and strategic importance, "depending on whether the communications were taking place between the heads of state or platoon leaders."[43] At the tactical level, Aid explains, COMINT "generated vitally important intelligence" that included "information on the movements and activities of Russian Army combat units . . . and logistics and transportation activities." Tactical COMINT also helped the United States map parts of the Soviet defense system.[44]

At the strategic level, COMINT likewise had some spectacular successes against the Kremlin leadership. "In the 1960s, the NSA successfully intercepted the car phones used by Soviet leaders driving around Moscow in their Zil limousines."[45] Later, US satellites developed the capacity to "intercept Soviet and Chinese telephone and radio communications across the UHF, VHF, and microwave frequency bands."[46] The NSA made important contributions during the Cuban Missile Crisis, as several accounts have noted.[47] In the 1970s, through a "breakthrough in Soviet ciphers . . . signals intelligence detected advanced warning of the Soviet invasion of Afghanistan."[48] COMINT was also important outside the Soviet context.[49]

While these achievements were important, they pale in comparison with what the other SIGINT subdisciplines contributed to US understanding of Soviet military power. Beginning in the 1950s, Nolte explains, ELINT played a "vital role" in electronically mapping the Soviet radar system, and continued to do so throughout the Cold War.[50] In the 1960s, the NSA and the CIA began to exploit Soviet telemetry, the "instrumentation readings transmitted from a missile or aircraft undergoing testing."[51] Intercepted telemetry allowed US analysts to "estimate the number of warheads carried by a given missile, . . . the probable size of its warheads, and the accuracy with which the warheads are guided . . . to their targets."[52]

The third subdiscipline of SIGINT, FISINT, provided the United States with the capacity to collect electronic signals in addition to Soviet missile telemetry. These included "emissions associated with the testing and operations of aerospace, surface, and subsurface systems that have military or civilian applications."[53] FISINT and telemetry data were important for monitoring arms control agreements.

To collect signals intelligence, the United States employed an array of systems, or platforms. Early on, this entailed constructing "a multi-layered network of 70 strategic intercept stations and an equal number of tactical units" around the perimeter of the USSR.[54] Planes were employed to collect signals intelligence from along the borders of the Soviet Union.[55]

In the 1960s, signals collection experienced a major transformation with the launch of Ferret satellites. These gave the United States the capacity "to intercept signals emitted by Soviet, Chinese, and other nations' air defense, ABM, and early-warning radars." During the Cold War, Ferret satellites would go through several renovations.[56] Also during the 1960s and 1970s, two other satellite systems—Canyon and Rhyolite—were developed for high-altitude electronic and communications intelligence collection. According to Richelson, the "primary function" of Rhyolite satellites "was intercepting the telemetry signals of Soviet and Chinese offensive and defensive missiles, ASAT tests, and space launches." New versions of Rhyolite, as well as follow-on systems, added additional capabilities.[57]

All of these developments and many that remain secret in the SIGINT collection programs of the NSA and the platforms on which they were deployed, especially NRO satellites, enabled the United States to penetrate the closed Soviet system to learn about its military programs. SIGINT was the first leg of a troika of technical collection tools developed for monitoring a unique enemy.

The Strategic Importance of Imagery

During the 1950s, the United States also began allocating considerable resources to developing aircraft and satellites that could safely overfly the Soviet Union to photograph strategic military forces and defense infrastructure. In the forefront was the Lockheed U-2, an ultra-high-altitude reconnaissance aircraft that first flew over Soviet territory in July 1956. From an altitude of nearly 70,000 feet, the U-2, in a four-year period, produced "more than 1,285,000 feet of film," photographing "approximately 15 percent of [the USSR's] total area." Those photographs were used to prepare "5,425 separate photo-analytical reports."[58] According to Allen Dulles, CIA director at that time, the U-2 program revealed "four critical aspects of Soviet military power: its bomber force, its missile force, its atomic energy program, and its air defense system."[59] U-2 overflights abruptly came to an end in May 1960, following the downing of one of the planes by a Soviet surface-to-air missile over west-central Russia.[60]

At the time of the U-2 shootdown, the US overhead reconnaissance program had already developed a safer alternative with the launch in August 1960 of a camera-carrying satellite. Code-named Corona, its mission was to photograph from space. Photos taken from the satellite were retrieved monthly by way of a capsule returned to earth.[61] The Corona program was the beginning of space-borne imagery-collection systems developed under the auspices of the NRO. They

were tailored to peer deep inside the Soviet Union. Several increasingly sophisticated satellite systems followed over the next three decades. The devices carried by
those satellites to collect images also experienced one trailblazing innovation after
another, overcoming limitations caused by night, clouds, and bad weather and
continually improving the resolution of the photos taken.

Initially the means employed on Corona satellites for photographing were traditional cameras, albeit sophisticated ones, that produced optical images of objects
on the ground visible only in daylight. In technical terminology, they were in the
visible part of the electromagnetic spectrum.[62] In the lexicon of intelligence, they
were categorized as photographic intelligence, or PHOTINT. However, by the late
1960s, the NRO's satellite reconnaissance program included other types of sensors, and photographic intelligence was officially redesignated as IMINT.

Imagery collected by different sensors can be divided into three categories: optical and electro-optical, radiometric and spectral, and radar and synthetic-aperture
radar.[63] As noted above, conventional cameras were the first devices used for optical imagery collection. Corona satellites, from 1960 to 1972, carried a succession
of ever-improving cameras that produced remarkable results. By the late 1960s,
the United States had "photographed all 25 Soviet ICBM complexes . . . cataloged
Soviet air defense and anti-ballistic missile sites, nuclear weapons related facilities,
submarine bases, and IRBM [intermediate-range ballistic missile] sites."[64]

Once specific targets were identified, another satellite system was employed to
produce higher-resolution pictures. Code-named Gambit, it was a "close-look"
satellite that produced "high-resolution imagery on specific targets (rather than of
general areas)." This allowed for the production of more detailed intelligence, particularly of weapon systems.[65] Cameras underwent groundbreaking change with
the development of systems that "transformed a picture image to a digital image
that could be transmitted electronically to distant points. The signal was then
reconstructed and . . . transformed [back] into a photograph."[66] This innovation
enabled real-time coverage "of a site or activity."[67]

While optical systems constituted the mainstay, imagery was also gathered by
reconnaissance satellites from nonvisible parts of the electromagnetic spectrum.
To do so required special sensors, including those that could derive thermal images from ultraviolet and infrared releases. Sensors that detect and measure such
radiation are called radiometers.[68] This capability has been particularly valuable
for the detection of concealed tanks, trucks, and aircraft.[69] For example, during
Operation Desert Storm in 1991, the United States made use of it to locate and
track the nighttime movement of Iraqi armored forces.

More sophisticated radiometric-measuring devices create "many simultaneous
images of a scene" to produce a more accurate composite representation of the

target, including a description of the materials of which it is composed.[70] Multi-spectral imagers are used to overcome an opponent's deception tactics by identifying, for instance, underground facilities.[71] Against the USSR, this capability was important because Moscow was a skilled practitioner of deception.[72] For example, the Soviets sought to conceal intermediate-range nuclear missiles in deep underground bunkers in Warsaw Pact countries.[73]

Yet another form of imagery collected during the Cold War was that derived from remote-sensing instruments that projected their own energy, then recorded the reflections of that energy using radar. Because they sense energy directly provided by the sensor itself, such instruments can work at night and through rain and cloud cover. Richelson explains that "radar imagery is produced by bouncing radio waves off an area or an object and using the reflected returns to produce an image of the target."[74] Radars are optimized for a number of different collection missions.[75]

The management of imagery-collection systems was based on an agreement between the DOD and the CIA, the two parts of the US government involved in overhead reconnaissance intelligence. In 1961, the air force and the CIA together created the NRO, which was given responsibility for "overseeing and funding the research and development of reconnaissance spacecraft and their sensors, procuring the space systems and their associated ground stations, determining launch vehicle requirements, operating space systems after they attain orbit, and disseminating the data collected."[76] The NRO also managed airborne platforms. Responsibility for assessing imagery collected by NRO systems was assigned in 1961 to the National Photographic Interpretation Center, which was also a joint CIA-DOD project.[77] Darryl Murdock and Robert Clark note that the explosion in imagery collected necessitated the creation in 1967 of the Committee on Imagery Requirements and Exploitation and subsequently the National Imagery and Mapping Agency, which in 2003 became the National Geospatial-Intelligence Agency (NGA).[78]

While SIGINT led the way in the early 1950s, it was imagery that provided the big picture of the strategic military systems that the Soviets developed and deployed, even as Moscow sought to hide them. In conjunction with SIGINT, imagery was the second leg of the troika of technical collection tools developed to monitor Soviet strategic forces and the military-industrial infrastructure that produced them. The third leg was MASINT.

MASINT: Filling in the Gaps

Signals and imagery-collection platforms were continually modernized during the Cold War through very expensive research-and-development programs to improve their capacity to penetrate the closed Soviet system. But as effective as they were, gaps existed in what they could collect. MASINT methods were developed to address those gaps. MASINT concentrated on tracking acoustic signals from submarines, analyzing seismic signals from nuclear detonations, detecting the construction of underground facilities, monitoring missile tests, and scrutinizing activities at potential chemical and biological warfare sites. How successful MASINT proved to be in collecting data on these and other Soviet activities remains highly classified. However, the extent to which MASINT was strategically important can be inferred from what has been written about it in the open literature.[79]

MASINT improved the IC's capacity to penetrate the Soviet state to uncover important details about its strategic forces and military-industrial infrastructure. But what made it distinctive was not only these collection activities but also the analytic techniques used to identify signatures and to associate those signatures with objects or activities. Signatures are the characteristics or dimensions of specific objects. An example can be seen in the collection and analysis of the performance characteristics from a Soviet ICBM test. When compared with the known features of known Soviet ICBMs, MASINT would enable US intelligence to detect and differentiate specific signatures that could reveal a new generation of Soviet ICBMs. In another example, uranium being enriched for use in nuclear weapons could be detected by MASINT, which also developed the capacity to detect underground facilities, industrial pollutants, anthrax and nerve gas production, various types of explosives, and concealed armored forces.

MASINT completed the troika of technical intelligence tools developed to uncover the USSR's vast array of deployed nuclear and conventional military forces and the scientific and industrial infrastructure that produced them. The acquisition of that knowledge necessitated harnessing unprecedented twentieth-century advances in technology. Taken as a package, this troika of technical intelligence tools was able to penetrate the closed Soviet system to find out the size of its arsenal as well as the operational dimensions of Soviet weapon systems. Their contributions cannot be underestimated.

HUMINT: A Valuable Intelligence-Collection Complement

HUMINT collection can take several forms, including the classic mission of recruiting foreign nationals with access to secret information. That mission, explained Ted Shackley, a highly decorated member of the CIA's clandestine service, is essential for revealing what "neither the eye in the sky [imagery] nor the big ear [signals] can tell us." While technical collection can reveal much "about another countries [*sic*] capability . . . this isn't enough. We also need to know . . . [their] intentions." And for that you must "rely on a . . . human source."[80]

But acquiring that kind of insider knowledge from recruited agents posed a monumental challenge for a fledgling CIA as the Cold War unfolded in the late 1940s. The reasons for this were twofold. First, the closed Soviet political system had established a counterintelligence superstructure that dominated daily life.[81] Second, the CIA was a young and inexperienced intelligence service. Recruiting the kind of agents identified by Shackley was a daunting task, especially inside the Soviet state. According to Michael Sulick, a career CIA intelligence officer who served as director of the US National Clandestine Service from 2007 to 2010, "the Soviets guarded their secrets by pervasive monitoring of foreigners in the USSR, restricting contact with its citizens, especially those with access to secrets."[82]

To collect HUMINT in the initial period of the Cold War, the CIA could not rely on the classic method of identifying and recruiting Soviet officials. Doing so against the control system established by the KGB in Moscow was, observed former director of central intelligence Richard Helms, "as improbable as placing resident spies on the planet Mars."[83] Instead, the agency relied on what an earlier CIA director, Allen Dulles, called "volunteers."[84] These were individuals who worked for Soviet officialdom but decided for various reasons to switch sides and secretly provide the United States with highly sensitive information they had access to because of the positions they held.[85]

Volunteers took two forms. First, there were those who, after initiating contact, would provide information only if granted asylum in the United States. The second type also initiated contact but agreed to stay in place, continuing to appear to serve as loyal Soviet officials, but secretly they would provide intelligence purloined from their work stations. Of the two types, the latter was more valuable because such individuals were continually adding to the CIA's knowledge of developments in that part of the Soviet system where they worked. The number of volunteers who stayed in place is not knowable outside the CIA. However, the small number whose activities are now public knowledge suggest volunteers could provide valuable intelligence. Here are two cases.

The first is Oleg Penkovsky, a colonel in Soviet military intelligence who in the mid-1950s was assigned to the Soviet Committee for Scientific Research in Moscow. That office nominally managed scientific exchanges with the West, but many of its delegations were fronts for intelligence operations that sought to secretly acquire technologies for Soviet weapons development. During the summer of 1960, Penkovsky contacted the CIA station in Moscow.[86] This led to a meeting in London in April 1961 with American and British intelligence officers when

Penkovsky was part of a Soviet trade delegation. He agreed during the meeting to work against the USSR.

For eighteen months, Penkovsky "passed more than 5,000 photographs of classified military, political, and economic documents to British and U.S. intelligence." This included information revealing "the Soviets' relatively weak capability in long-range missiles."[87] He also made available "copies of the Soviet General Staff publication *Military Thought* . . . in which Soviet generals debated war in the nuclear age."[88] During the Cuban Missile Crisis, information provided by Penkovsky was said to be a "key ingredient in U.S. decision making as President Kennedy stood up to Khrushchev."[89] Shortly after the crisis, Penkovsky was arrested, tried, and, on May 16, 1963, executed in Moscow.[90]

The second example, Adolf Tolkachev, was an electronics engineer and military aviation specialist who worked as a senior designer at the Scientific Research Institute for Radio Engineering in Moscow.[91] The institute specialized in designing radars for Soviet military aircraft. He approached US officials in Moscow in 1977 and 1978 and agreed to serve as an agent for the CIA. From then until 1985, when he was exposed, Tolkachev "provided plans, specifications and test results on existing and planned Soviet aircraft and missiles."[92]

In US intelligence circles, Tolkachev is considered by many to be the most important Soviet official, after Penkovsky, to serve as an agent in place during the Cold War. Barry Royden, a former CIA director of counterintelligence, has written that Tolkachev's information was "so voluminous and so valuable" that even after his arrest in 1985, intelligence analysts "continued to exploit his information until approximately 1990."[93] However, as was often the case with such operations, not everyone agrees with this assessment.[94]

The number of agents of Penkovsky and Tolkachev's caliber that the CIA ran during the Cold War is a deeply held secret. So, too, is how much the intelligence derived from such operations contributed to US knowledge of Soviet strategic and conventional military power. However, given the size of the Soviet military industrial complex and force structure, the contribution would likely be judged complementary to the massive amounts collected by the technical intelligence disciplines.

OSINT: Monitoring International Broadcasts and News Outlets

In the twenty-first century, the strategic importance of open-source intelligence information has increased exponentially. It now includes sources of communication that could not have been imagined when the United States first began to collect the shortwave radio transmissions of the Axis powers during World War II. According to Eliot Jardines, open-source intelligence "came about . . . with the establishment of the Foreign Broadcast Monitoring Service (FBMS) in February 1941. FBMS was instituted when Secretary of State Cordell Hull prevailed upon President Franklin Roosevelt to do so. The president agreed and directed the U.S. Treasury to allocate $150,000 from his emergency fund for recording, transcribing, translating, and analyzing . . . the Axis powers' shortwave propaganda broadcasts."[95]

Once established, FBMS's initial focus was Japan. It "published its first *Daily Report* of translations on 18 November 1941. Its first analytic report, released on 6 December, warned of Tokyo's increasingly belligerent tone." The report further noted that Tokyo's "commentary on the United States is bitter and increased." One day later, Japan attacked Pearl Harbor.[96] With America now at war, FBMS became the Foreign Broadcast Intelligence Service (FBIS), and its focus expanded to encompass all the Axis powers and their broadcasts in different regions of the world. By the end of 1942, FBIS was "translating 500,000 words a day from 25 broadcasting stations in 15 languages."[97]

When the war ended, FBIS became a casualty of the general demobilization initiated by the Truman administration. The Federal Communications Commission shut it down on December 4, 1945. However, shortly thereafter, FBIS was reestablished within the Military Intelligence Division of the War Department. From there, it moved to the Central Intelligence Group. Jardine writes that "what saved FBIS from extinction was that its . . . analysts were already casting a concerned eye toward Moscow and warning of a possible threat from an emboldened Soviet Union."[98]

With the creation of the CIA in 1947, FBIS was moved under its auspices and stayed there throughout the Cold War to become, as the Foreign Broadcast Information Service, the predominant unit for collecting and analyzing open-source information. To do so, FBIS "established a global network of foreign bureaus that both monitored and translated foreign broadcasts." In locations where it could not do so, it "established agreements with the monitoring services of . . . over a dozen countries."[99]

The Post–Cold War 1990s: US Intelligence Collection Faces a Paradigm Shift

The end of the Cold War precipitated a rush by Congress to reassess the necessity of maintaining the IC and its collection disciplines as they were constituted. That community had developed over four decades with the principal task of collecting information on and "monitoring a well-catalogued array of fixed targets in Soviet territory."[100] Given the closed and highly secretive nature of the Soviet system, the technical collection disciplines had blossomed into sophisticated and resource-intensive endeavors.

In the aftermath of the USSR's implosion, the future of those collection disciplines and of the IC as a whole became the subject of considerable public discussion that continued through much of the 1990s. The debate took several forms, beginning in February 1992—two months after the USSR was officially dissolved—with the introduction of reorganization proposals by the Senate and House intelligence committees. Each started with the premise that with the end of the Soviet threat, the time was right to cut the budget and reorganize the IC.

To that end, Sen. David Boren and Rep. David McCurdy, the chairs of each chamber's intelligence committee, proposed an array of structural changes with the goal of achieving greater IC efficiency. As for the budget, it was to be slashed, and the workforce reduced considerably. With respect to intelligence collection, consolidation was the watchword, with national agencies established for all human, signals, and imagery collection. While neither proposal found its way into law, they nonetheless set the agenda for the debate over intelligence reform that ensued through the 1990s. The substance of that agenda focused on reorganization, budget and workforce reduction, and strengthening congressional authority with respect to IC oversight. Subsequent reform initiatives followed this agenda.

Consider the findings of the Commission on Roles and Capabilities of the US Intelligence Community, chartered by Congress in 1994 as a bipartisan panel to assess the relevance of US intelligence activities in a post–Cold War era. The commission's report, released in March 1996, focused on streamlining the IC by reducing the civilian workforce an additional 10 percent over already significant cuts.[101] With respect to structure, the report recommended streamlining and called for the Office of the Director of Central Intelligence to be given the authority to make the IC a more integrated interagency body. What the commission did not identify, with any specificity, were the post–Cold War collection targets that a reformed IC was to tackle.

A similar prescription was presented in a 1996 report by the House Permanent Select Committee on Intelligence (HPSCI), which also focused on reorganization issues. The mission of the CIA, the report recommended, should be reduced to intelligence analysis, with its operational arm becoming a separate organization. The NSA and the NRO would merge. The Office of the Director of Central Intelligence would be given more power to manage the numerous agencies that constituted the IC.[102]

But this vision of a streamlined IC began to change as the twentieth century neared its end. Several developments prompted that change, including US military engagements in several UN-sponsored peace operations in the Balkans and

Africa; attacks by terrorist groups on US targets; the expanding threats posed by other nonstate armed groups, including drug cartels; the challenges emerging from weak and failing states; and the proliferation of weapons of mass destruction.

As a result, an argument gained traction that to address this changing international security environment, a refocusing of the intelligence-collection disciplines was required. No longer should the collection targets be confined to nation-states. Collection systems would now have to "cover a much broader universe of threats, [that were] harder to find and often mobile."[103] What this signified, proposed John Diamond, was movement "away from the national strategic mission of the Cold War and toward a real-time battlefield information role" for US intelligence.[104] US military forces deployed in conflicts in the Balkans and elsewhere were requesting real-time tactical intelligence. Diamond notes the impact of this on imagery collection: "The reliance of U.S. combat forces on spy satellites for at least part of their tactical intelligence has grown to the point where deployment scenarios are eclipsing strategic scenarios in the imagery intelligence world."[105]

The post–Cold War switch from the centrality of strategic intelligence to the burgeoning importance of its tactical counterpart was under way. This shift would affect not only what was collected but also how quickly it was analyzed and sent to military consumers. Again, consider imagery. Those many images collected, collated, and transmitted by the NRO had to be analyzed by a new organization—the National Imagery and Mapping Agency (NIMA)—and forwarded expeditiously to warfighters. According to the NIMA director in the late 1990s, Lt. Gen. James C. King, his "agency now measured its imagery analysis and forwarding timelines in days and was moving toward technologies that will compress that timeline into minutes and hours."[106]

Although King would prove prescient, the 1990s was a decade of transition for the collection disciplines. New challenges from nonstate actors were emerging but were not yet seen as tier-one security threats in Washington.[107] Recall that during the Bill Clinton presidency al-Qaeda was not viewed as a clear and present danger, and its attacks certainly were not assessed as rising to the level of war. Even when US embassies in East Africa were bombed and the USS *Cole* was nearly sunk—acts of war if they had been carried out by a nation-state—the perpetrators of those attacks were not treated as a major national security threat. This had an impact on collection priorities.

Consequently, while the Cold War context that shaped collection requirements had disappeared, it was not clear how those requirements should be revised to meet twenty-first-century threats. The need to do so was underscored in reviews initiated by Congress of specific collection agencies—among them the NRO and the NSA—and their post–Cold War requirements.

The National Commission for the Review of the National Reconnaissance Office found that "the clarity of mission and sense of urgency that led past Presidents and Congresses to invest in the future of space reconnaissance had dissipated," resulting in "a lack of policy direction from senior officials."[108] The report found that the NRO's space-based reconnaissance mission was in transition, and the "array of new threats facing the United States has never been more complex and the demands on the NRO from new customers have never more intense."[109] This finding generated an internal debate within the NRO over which customers should have higher priority and how to balance strategic with tactical collection requirements.[110]

A broadening of collection targets to include armed groups was also an emergent concern at the NSA. Empowered by the Information Revolution, armed groups now had access to new communication and encryption systems, which had the potential of making the NSA's tasks far more difficult. This was underscored by Congress in the Intelligence Authorization Act for fiscal year 2001. Congress cautioned that the NSA was entering the twenty-first century deficient in the technological infrastructure and human capital necessary to maintain the status quo, much less to contend with emerging new threats.[111]

Others characterized new challenges to the NSA as more ominous. For example, the Technical Advisory Group (TAG) was established in 1997 by the Senate Select Committee on Intelligence (SSCI) "to review the U.S. SIGINT efforts. . . . Composed of leading scientists and experts in technology and intelligence," it completed "two classified reports on NSA's capabilities." According to the Congressional Research Service (CRS), "the TAG identified serious deficiencies."[112] Without going into the classified specifics, the CRS concluded that to manage this "changing geopolitical and technological environment . . . requires that NSA's organization and operations be substantially altered" to include "significant budgetary increases."[113]

The warnings sounded by the TAG found their way into the media. David Ensor of CNN reported that the NSA was "in crisis, overwhelmed by too many targets, too much information and the challenges created by increasingly sophisticated technologies." No longer was its "eavesdropping equipment . . . enough to handle the current load of information."[114] Investigative journalist Seymour Hersh added that the NSA had "failed to prepare fully for today's high-volume flow of E-mail and fiber-optic transmissions" and to keep pace with "signals [that] are becoming more complex and difficult to process" because they are "more and more encrypted." Unless the NSA changed, it "will go deaf." Hersh reported that the TAG "urged the agency to immediately begin a major reorganization and start planning for the recruitment of several thousand skilled computer scientists . . . to devise software and write information-retrieval programs that would enable the agency to make sense of the data routinely sucked up by satellite and other interception devices."[115]

Despite the alarm bells rung by groups such as the TAG, there was generally no sense of urgency or US government consensus over how and on which targets the collection disciplines should be refocused. Numerous government studies were conducted about the future of US intelligence, but they tended to concentrate on the reorganization and reduction of budgets and workforces for a peacetime environment in which the United States would reap the benefits of the post–Cold War peace dividend.

To be sure, new challenges were identified as arising. These included the proliferation of WMDs, terrorism, nationalist and ethnic conflicts, failing states, religious extremism, and international crime syndicates. But there was no consensus in Washington that any of these posed a clear and present danger.

US Intelligence Collection in the Aftermath of 9/11: Refocusing for Irregular War

On August 7, 1998, the US embassies in Dar es Salaam, Tanzania, and Nairobi, Kenya, were hit nearly simultaneously by trucks laden with explosives. More than two hundred people were killed, and more than five thousand were wounded. The Clinton administration accused Osama bin Laden of masterminding the attacks. Less than two weeks later, Washington launched cruise missiles against al-Qaeda training camps in Afghanistan, but bin Laden and his associates were gone. In November, the administration turned the matter over to the Department of Justice, which brought indictments against bin Laden and twenty-one members of al-Qaeda, charging them with terrorist attacks against Americans abroad. The missile strikes were a one-off. As far as the White House was concerned, the chief tool for combating terrorism was to be law enforcement.[116]

The CIA director, George Tenet, saw the attacks differently. In December, he "issued a directive to several CIA officials and the Deputy Director of Central Intelligence for Community Management stating: 'We are at war. I want no resources or people spared in this effort, either inside CIA or the intelligence community.'" The memo had little impact. According to the 9/11 Commission: "Almost all our interviewees had never seen the memo or only learned of it after 9/11. The NSA Director . . . believed the memo applied only to CIA. . . . CIA officials thought the memorandum was intended for the rest of the Community given the fact they were already doing all they could."[117]

Tenet hoped to use the embassy bombings as a catalyst to establish a unified IC strategy for fighting al-Qaeda. But the 9/11 Commission found that he did not have the clout to do so.[118] One starting point for such a strategy would have been to refocus the collection disciplines tactically on al-Qaeda's apparatus and activities.[119] But there was no mechanism that could "pull together human sources, imagery, signals intelligence, and open source into a comprehensive collection strategy."[120] Even if this barrier could have been overcome, traditional collection methods geared for use against state targets were inadequate for collecting data on twenty-first-century armed groups such as al-Qaeda. Consider SIGINT. It was challenged by al-Qaeda's use of Information Age technologies and operational security practices. HUMINT collection, too, proved limited against terrorist groups in general and al-Qaeda in particular. Neither of these collection tools, nor other ones, had been adapted to address this new danger.

In sum, while the 9/11 Commission found that parts of the IC worked hard to understand the threat posed by al-Qaeda in the late 1990s, in particular the Counterterrorism Center (CTC) at the CIA, there was no comprehensive effort to do so by the IC that yielded warning of the possibility of 9/11-type attacks. This, concluded the commission, was because there was no consensus within the IC over the need "to collect intelligence on and analyze the phenomenon of transnational terrorism. The combination of an overwhelming number of priorities, flat budgets, an outmoded collection structure, and bureaucratic rivalries resulted in an insufficient response to this new challenge."[121]

Post-9/11 Wartime and Intelligence Collection

President George W. Bush, in his State of the Union address on January 29, 2002, began as follows: "As we gather tonight, our nation is at war."[122] At the 2002 graduation ceremony of the US Military Academy in June, the president told the cadets, "You graduate from this Academy in a time of war [in which] we face a threat with no precedent." To prevail against it will "require new thinking [and] . . . transforming the military."[123] In effect, President Bush was echoing General Krulak's declaration in 1997: this war against terrorism would be "not like yesterday."[124] The armed group the Bush administration was going to war against—al-Qaeda and its associated movements—presented a more complex challenge than its twentieth-century counterparts because it had access to capabilities not available during the Cold War. As chapter 2 explained, new enablers and power enhancers considerably increased al-Qaeda's operational capacity.

To meet this challenge, the intelligence-collection disciplines had to undergo considerable refocusing. The remainder of this chapter examines the extent to which imagery, signals, measurements and signatures, human, and open-source collection adapted to support hunters instead of gatherers (to borrow Deptula's characterization). To be of service to those hunters, the collection disciplines had to shed the roles and missions they had embraced in the Cold War.[125]

Fixing on al-Qaeda Targets: The Central Role of Imagery

In the aftermath of 9/11 and the overthrow of the Taliban regime, which sent al-Qaeda fleeing into Pakistan, national imagery collection entered a new period in which support for military operations moved to center stage. Dennis Fitzgerald, at that time the deputy director of the NRO, wrote that this period would be marked by "a new operational environment and associated expectations regarding assured space reconnaissance capabilities. Current expectations are that there can be no coverage gaps in overhead intelligence collection capabilities because the military is heavily dependent upon NRO systems and products for planning and operations."[126]

This shift was not entirely new. The transition from imagery principally collected to support national intelligence agencies focused on the military capabilities of the USSR to time-sensitive collection of tactical imagery intelligence for military commanders began with Operation Desert Storm in 1991. But the post-9/11 warfighting context was not an offspring of that twentieth-century conventional war.

For twenty-first-century irregular wars, imagery collection had to undergo further change. The new enemy was not the conventional military forces of a state adversary but clandestine armed groups. Al-Qaeda presented a new problem set consisting of many decentralized units employing Information Age technologies to form into dispersed networks. Such challenges are difficult to collect imagery on because they have many dispersed units that interact in secret ways. Scores of linkages between those networks cannot be easily identified and mapped.

In response to this challenge, tactical imagery collection burgeoned and came to play a central role in the "fix" phase of the F3EAD targeting cycle (find, fix, finish, exploit, analyze, and disseminate; see figure 3.1) employed by TF 714 for fighting AQI. In that phase, once an enemy target was identified, fixing on it meant persistently watching its location, developing a comprehensive understanding of what it was doing, tracking members of the target if they began to move, and mapping the linkages between it and other parts of an al-Qaeda network. Although imagery collection could do this alone, the rapid development of state-of-the-art overhead intelligence, surveillance, and reconnaissance (ISR) systems played a vital role in the fix phase.

One way to understand ISR, writes Stephen Price, is to break it down into its component parts: "Specifically, *intelligence* is defined as the product that results

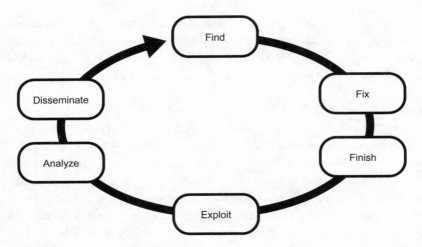

Figure 3.1 The F3EAD process

Source: Richard Shultz, *Military Innovation in War: It Takes a Learning Organization* (Tampa, FL: JSOU Press, 2016), 40.

from ISR operations. It is the information that fuels the decision maker's understanding of his operational environment. *Surveillance* provides the information to be refined into intelligence through persistent observation via long dwell times with a continuous collection capability" focused on a specific area, such as a city neighborhood. Finally, *reconnaissance* provides focused "coverage of a specific target at a specific time in a more active collection operation." Taken together, the three components of ISR provide "specific, analyzed information, gathered through persistent and focused coverage" of an enemy.[127]

The collection platforms for executing ISR missions include satellites in space, manned aircraft such as U-2 spyplanes, and UAVs. The imagery each collects goes digitally to the Distributed Common Ground System (DCGS) of five core sites that process, evaluate, and disseminate imagery products to military commanders and operators. What follows is a closer look at each of these constituent parts, which collectively have amounted to what one observer has dubbed an "ISR Revolution."[128]

The most expensive of the imagery platforms are the surveillance satellites. They constituted one of the greatest technological achievements of the Cold War, but they were not easily adapted to the war against al-Qaeda and associated movements for the following reasons. First, the satellites in service at the time of 9/11 were Cold War–era systems, developed to find and monitor the strategic forces and military-industrial infrastructure of the Soviet Union. They were not designed for the operational tempo of an irregular war or for the underground or subterranean nature of nonstate armed group targets. Additionally, collection priorities for NRO satellites still concentrated on the testing and deployment of the strategic and conventional forces of adversarial states. After 9/11, the DOD did seek to acquire smaller satellites that could meet new tactical requirements, but this effort progressed slowly, and the first of the smaller satellites was not launched until June 2011.[129]

Aside from satellites, manned aircraft, primarily from the US Air Force, were assigned ISR missions.[130] Following 9/11, the U-2 was adapted for irregular warfare missions in Iraq and Afghanistan. For example, U-2s were used to detect ground sites where IEDs were planted to kill American soldiers. Other types of manned aircraft were also employed by the air force for ISR missions.[131] These provided support to ground forces deployed in war zones. The MC-12W Liberty, for instance, was used, not least because its "operational system includes . . . sensors capable of providing full-motion video" to forces engaged in irregular operations.[132] Naval aircraft (principally, the P-3C Orion) have also flown ISR missions in Iraq, Afghanistan, and elsewhere.

The most important platform providing ISR support for post-9/11 warfighting operations was the UAV. According to Rebecca Grant, UAVs came "a long way, and fast. When the U.S.-led coalition launched ground operations in Iraq in March 2003, it did so with just nine MQ-1 Predator UAVs in theater."[133] In 2002, the inventory was 167 Predators and Reapers. By 2008, there were 246 Predators, 126 Reapers, 491 Shadows, and 33 Global Hawks. The fiscal year budget grew from $2.5 billion in 2008 to $4.1 billion in 2011.[134]

The MQ-1 Predator, developed in the 1990s, had an initial range of 454 miles and a flight time of twenty hours and flew at twenty-five thousand feet. The Predator was designed "to provide warfighters with persistent ISR" and "precision weapons."[135] Predators employ a wide range of sensors to collect imagery, including full-motion video. The Predator was quickly followed by the MQ-9 Reaper, which has a longer range (1,150 miles), flies higher (fifty thousand feet), and can be deployed for twenty-four-hour missions. It carries "an infrared sensor, color/monochrome daylight TV camera, image-intensified TV camera, laser designator, and laser illuminator" as well as "full-motion video from each of the imaging sensors which can be viewed as separate video streams or fused."[136]

The RQ-7 Shadow is an unmanned aircraft system developed specifically for the US Army and US Marine Corps. Its mission is to "locate, recognize and identify targets up to 125 km from a brigade tactical operations center. The system recognizes tactical vehicles by day and night from an altitude of 8,000 feet. . . . Imagery and telemetry data is transmitted in near-real-time from the Shadow ground control station to joint stars common ground station, all-sources analysis system and to the army field artillery targeting and direction system."[137] This system was extensively employed in the wars in Afghanistan and Iraq.

Finally, the RQ-4 Global Hawk flies higher (sixty thousand feet), longer (twenty-eight hours), and farther (eighty-seven hundred miles) than its UAV counterparts. Its integrated sensor suite provides a worldwide ISR capability, providing persistent near-real-time coverage. The Global Hawk does so through a "multi-intelligence platform that simultaneously carries electro-optical, infrared, synthetic aperture radar (SAR), and high and low band SIGINT sensors."[138] The Global Hawk provides a wide range of ISR collection capabilities for wartime operations.

From the beginning of the Iraqi insurgency in late 2003, ISR played an increasingly important role in meeting the intelligence demands of operational forces and, in particular, those of counterterrorism forces, notably TF 714. The task force faced the complex challenge of finding insurgents and terrorists who were embedded across Iraq. For the counterterrorism forces, their mission of dismantling al-Qaeda's clandestine underground meant employing the F3EAD targeting process against midlevel commanders and managers of those networks. These network components included a large number of al-Qaeda's financial units, communications and media centers, intelligence services, bomb and IED production facilities, and arms acquisition specialists that fostered the enormous rise in attacks across Iraq from 2004 to 2006.

It quickly became apparent that the demand for ISR by US counterterrorism forces was insatiable. ISR platforms scanned for individuals, tracking midlevel commanders and managers on a near-constant basis to provide actionable intelligence as they moved across urban and rural terrain. ISR assets then identified additional individuals, their hideouts and safe houses, and other suspicious locations they visited. In doing so, the intelligence collected by UAVs played a central role in mapping AQI networks, enabling TF 714 raiding teams to conduct strikes to capture AQI commanders and managers and those with them.

According to Michael Flynn, who served as TF 714's intelligence chief in Iraq, "Airborne ISR has become critical to this war because it offers persistent and low-visibility observation of the enemy, as well as an ability to detect, identify, and track him in this low-contrast environment." This was "the key to defeating a foe whose primary strength was denying US forces a target." "Persistent collection," Flynn explained, "requires long dwell times and must be focused using multiple sensors on discrete parts of the network in order to achieve the fidelity of information required for targeting."[139]

As UAV sensors became increasingly advanced, they could provide on the same platform the capacity both to conduct broad coverage of large geographic areas and to provide detailed and high-resolution views of a specific target within that broader territory. Known as wide-area persistent surveillance (WAPS), this dual capacity meant that "context is maintained even as particular subjects of interest (individuals, vehicles, buildings, etc.) are examined in detail and over time." This capability, notes Daniel Gouré, is important for "stringing together a number of specific data points . . . to develop a more comprehensive picture of an adversary's forces, command and control system, and networks." And by doing so, it "allows intelligence analysts to identify the network that provided the homicide bomber with his orders, funding, training and device."[140]

As the wars in Iraq and Afghanistan continued into the second decade of the twenty-first century, new programs provided sensors and processing technologies to conduct WAPS to support counterterrorism and counterinsurgency missions. One of these technologies was the Gorgon Stare system. According to one description, it consists of a "sensor package capable of viewing entire cities or battlefields." Mounted on a Reaper, it is "equipped with both electro-optical cameras for daylight operations and infrared cameras for operations after dark. Gorgon Stare's spherical array enables warfighters to track enemy movements, even dismounted individuals, across an area measuring four kilometers in diameter."[141]

Two Reapers deployed with this ISR capacity over a contested area "continuously for many days" could "discern patterns in the behavior of insurgents—where they hid, how they operated, who they interacted with."[142] Advances in Gorgon Stare made it possible to watch between thirty and sixty targets in a small city. Gorgon Stare could provide

> direct line-of-sight transmission to warfighters in combat . . . [or] wide-area imagery and full-motion video to operations centers for detailed analysis. Either way, the day-or-night, synoptic versatility of the system affords unprecedented situational awareness to U.S. warfighters. U.S. commanders can routinely tag and track particular vehicles or individuals on the ground that they suspect of being enemy operatives, and understand the recurrent patterns underpinning their tactics. This is something genuinely new in combat that greatly enhances the survivability and success of friendly forces.[143]

To summarize, imagery gathered through UAVs became one of the foundations for intelligence collection in the irregular wars that the United States engaged in following 9/11. It provided an important means for conducting persistent surveillance to fix on enemy targets and carry out continuous collection across geographic locations, gathering real-time operational data.

In Iraq, "ISR assets" were trained on "a different target set and demanded much longer dwell time." The search for AQI networks, including "their safe houses, routes, and strongpoints, demanded a high degree of positive identification. It also took more time and assets to ferret out targets. . . . Often, missions required repeated, sequential sweeps of key target areas."[144] According to Flynn, by doing so, ISR provided TF 714 with the opportunity to discern how a specific part of an AQI network was carrying out activities through direct and persistent surveillance. He characterized this overhead shadowing as a "24/7 airborne stakeout."[145] General McChrystal explained that ISR made an important contribution to TF 714's ability to work inside AQI networks to distinguish central from peripheral figures, discern patterns of life and behavior, and identify clusters of associations.[146]

Beyond Iraq and Afghanistan, ISR was equally important in what have been termed "small-footprint" counterterrorism operations against affiliates of al-Qaeda—for example, in Yemen and Somalia. For the counterterrorism task forces operating in those regions, ISR collected actionable intelligence on al-Qaeda in the Arabian Peninsula and al-Shabaab, making positive identifications and fixing on targets.

Cell Phones, Email, and Web 2.0 Mediums: A SIGINT Nirvana

Signals intelligence during the Cold War relied heavily on ELINT and FISINT variants, which garnered a major portion of the available resources because of the collection demands surrounding Soviet military power. COMINT was of lesser standing and received less funding. In terms of targeting, Robert Clark writes that COMINT focused on the Soviet "leadership, research and development organizations, and test facilities." Against those objectives, it "seldom provided much detail because it dealt primarily with brief conversations."[147]

During the post–Cold War 1990s, COMINT began to diversify as "narcotics trafficking, money laundering, and organized crime became important targets."[148] And after the 1998 bombings of the US embassies in Tanzania and Kenya, the NSA boosted collection of the communications of terrorist groups, particularly al-Qaeda. However, at that time, writes Matthew Aid, the NSA was "reluctant to become more actively involved in counterterrorism" operations due to its "traditional culture as an intelligence collector. . . . NSA officials took the position that it was more important to collect intelligence on the targets being monitored than to disrupt or destroy them."[149] In other words, the NSA was a gatherer of intelligence, not a supporter of what General Deptula termed "hunters," who needed intelligence that focused on "anticipating, finding, and fixing on elusive and often dangerous prey."[150] TF 714, as chapter 5 makes clear, was an irregular counterterrorism force of hunters, who needed this kind of intelligence.

The NSA was also constrained in its capacity to take on new missions focused on nonstate armed groups by the drastic reduction in its personnel and budgets during the 1990s. The extent of those cutbacks was summarized by the NSA director, Lt. Gen. Michael Hayden, in his testimony before the Joint Inquiry of the Senate Select and House Permanent Select Committees on Intelligence in October 2002: "NSA downsized about one third of its manpower and about the same proportion of its budget in the decade of the 1990s. . . . And with a budget that was fixed or falling . . . demands from our customers were unrelenting."[151] Hayden then contrasted those cuts with the revolutionary changes in communication and information technologies during those same years:

> That is the same decade when mobile cell phones increased from 16 million to 741 million—an increase of nearly 50 times. That is the same decade when Internet users went from about 4 million to 361 million—an increase of over 90 times. Half as many landlines were laid in the last six years of the 1990s as in the whole previous history of the world. In that same decade of the 1990s, international telephone traffic went from 38 billion minutes to over 100 billion. This year, the world's population will spend over 180 billion minutes on the phone in international calls alone.[152]

Since the Cold War, explains Clark, COMINT had changed: "Telephone surveillance in the past relied on identifying the telephone of intelligence interest and placing a wiretap on it. Most telephone surveillance today focuses on cell phone traffic because it is the preferred communications medium." And the volume of that traffic seems to have no upper limit.[153] Moreover, in the Information Age, cell phones are not the only target for the NSA. In addition to voice, its targets now include "data communications, facsimile, video and any other deliberate transmission of information" through various Internet platforms.[154]

Gaining access to and collecting information from these sources is only the starting point. Next, that information must be processed, which means converting it "into a form suitable for analysis" by "narrowing the incoming volume to a manageable size."[155] To do so, various filtering techniques such as "word spotting" and "speech recognition" are employed. If the message is encrypted, "powerful computers that process the encrypted text" are utilized to decipher and make sense out of it. Furthermore, "in most cases" processing includes "language translation."[156]

The final stage before dissemination is analysis. This includes assessing the material "for content and context." In addition, it may involve techniques known as traffic and signature analysis. The former is "used to identify key stations in a network, and the pattern of network communications," which "can sometimes provide intelligence about pending operations." Signature analysis involves the capacity to "identify and track a target" by identifying a unique communication pattern.[157]

These groundbreaking changes in communications and the requirements for managing their collection, processing, analysis, and dissemination had serious consequences for an NSA degraded by the drawdown of the 1990s. General Hayden told the intelligence committees that the NSA was on a path along which it "would cease to be an industrial strength source of American intelligence. It would . . . begin to resemble an intelligence boutique: limited product line, limited customer set, and very high unit prices."[158] According to Aid, as 9/11 approached, the NSA, with "an annual budget of less than $4 billion per annum, was struggling mightily to transform and modernize itself with only mixed success to show for all of its efforts . . . promoting its modernization and reform agenda."[159]

However, in the aftermath of the attacks on 9/11, the importance of the NSA skyrocketed, with COMINT dominating signals collection. The NSA's budget, approximately $4 billion in 2001, would by 2009 more than double to $9 billion, reaching $10.8 billion in 2013.[160] The agency would also acquire "new hardware and software designed to improve NSA's ability to collect, process, and analyze the ever-increasing volume of material being intercepted every day."[161]

As a result of these developments, the NSA became "the single most important intelligence agency in finding al-Qaeda and other enemies overseas, according to current and former counterterrorism officials and experts."[162] But to do so, it had to change its culture. As Director Hayden told Congress in 2002, the agency had to "become hunters rather than gatherers."[163] That is to say, the NSA had to provide actionable intelligence to those tasked with stalking al-Qaeda. It would need to turn into a vital contributor to the F3EAD targeting cycle in the war zones of Iraq, Afghanistan, and beyond.

Collecting SIGINT on counterterrorism targets is different, writes Daniel Byman, "than *SIGINT* against traditional targets. . . . Simply deciding who to monitor and narrowing down their locations can be exceptionally difficult. There is no equivalent of the Soviet embassy in plain sight that presents itself as an obvious target" for collection tools.[164] Despite such obstacles, the NSA rose to the challenge of helping the hunters. Its broad capacity to vacuum up and assess different forms of modern electronic communications and data activities from cell phones, email, social media messaging, and Internet surfing to carry out collection against the cyber sanctuary of AQI provided the kinds of intelligence TF 714 needed in Iraq. The NSA provided the means for tracking AQI in real time.

Within the NSA, the Central Security Service (CSS) functions as a combat-support agency, providing SIGINT to deployed warfighting forces. According to DOD Directive 5100.20, the CSS "provides *SIGINT* support for the conduct of military operations, pursuant to tasking, priorities, and standards of timeliness assigned by the Secretary of Defense. If provision of such support requires use of national collection systems, these systems will be tasked within existing guidance."[165] The CSS has four centers outside of its headquarters in Maryland: in Georgia, Texas, Hawaii, and Colorado. It also has offices around the world, principally in US embassies.

With respect to providing actionable intelligence to warfighters, NSA/CSS Georgia has been the major provider. According to its mission statement, NSA/CSS Georgia "specializes in working closely with military customers to understand their operations, their requirements and their culture to ensure that signals intelligence is tailored and responsive to the needs of the warfighter."[166] In 2012, NSA/CSS Georgia opened a $286 million facility at its Fort Gordon location that provides its workforce "with the latest state-of-the-art tools to conduct signals intelligence operations."[167] Aid reports that

> senior U.S. military officers . . . voiced amazement at both the quality and quantity of the intelligence they received from NSA's huge listening post at Fort Gordon. . . . One senior U.S. Navy officer who toured the Fort Gordon station in 2006 was stunned by the breadth of the intelligence being produced by the site's intercept operators, linguists, and analysts, including hundreds of linguists speaking ten different dialects of Arabic, as well as Hebrew, Farsi, Pashto and Dari (used in Afghanistan), and the Kurdish dialect spoken in northern Iraq.[168]

Within the Fort Gordon complex are several geographically targeted operations centers, including "Cobra Focus, where many of NSA's best Arabic linguists were producing vitally important intelligence on Iraqi insurgent activities from intercepted cell phone calls relayed to the station via satellite from inside Iraq."[169] Another center concentrates on Afghanistan. NSA/CSS Georgia also has a "highly sophisticated intelligence fusion center . . . where agency analysts pull together all of the *SIGINT* being collected by the station and other NSA listening posts into finely tuned written products for the agency's ravenous customers." According to one military consumer, the Geospatial Cell "was producing some of the best intelligence available on what the bad guys were up to."[170]

In addition to targeting cell phones, the NSA developed sophisticated systems to access emails, text messaging, and Internet surfing as well as the capacity to penetrate computer systems and networks. However, because these systems are all highly classified, information about specific examples in the open literature is limited. One exception, discussed by Aid, describes two NSA units, Tailored Access

Operations and the Remote Operations Center. Among the targets of each were al-Qaeda communications:

> Monitoring this traffic is managed by a super-secret NSA office at Fort Meade called Tailored Access Operations (TAO). Working closely with the CIA and other branches of the U.S. intelligence community, TAO identifies computer systems and networks being utilized by foreign terrorists to pass messages. Once these computers have been identified and located, a small group of computer hackers . . . who call themselves computer network exploitation operators, assigned to yet another NSA intercept unit at Fort Meade called Remote Operations Center (ROC), break into the systems electronically to steal information contained on their hard drives, as well as monitor the email traffic coming in and out of the computers.[171]

Information on other NSA systems can be gleaned from news coverage by the print and electronic media. For example, according to a news report on NBC, one system, known as "XKeyscore, gives analysts a tool by which they can pluck individual data points out of a massive indexed database. Collecting a wealth of Web activity from unencrypted Web traffic . . . it serves as a first stop in a larger data collection and mining process that can then serve to pinpoint subjects (say, suspected terrorists) for further inquiry."[172]

The *Guardian* newspaper described this program as providing electronic surveillance tools "to search . . . through vast databases" to collect "nearly everything a typical user does on the internet, including the content of emails, websites visited and searches, as well as their metadata." Analysts can search in real time by "name, telephone number, IP address, keywords, and the language in which the internet activity was conducted or the type of browser used."[173] The XKeyscore system also provided NSA analysts with the capacity to assess how individuals collaborate and share information online. According to the *Guardian* report, "an NSA tool called DNI Presenter, used to read the content of stored emails, also enables an analyst to read the content of Facebook chats or private messages."[174] In effect, this advanced electronic surveillance system makes available a set of tools to search the activity of an individual, revealing what he or she "does on the internet." It can also target a specific website "to learn the IP addresses of every person who visits it."[175]

To collect this kind of COMINT, several different platforms have been employed. According to Richelson, these include "space and airborne collectors, ground stations, covert listening posts, surface ships and submarines."[176] The space and airborne systems are similar to, and not infrequently the same as, those used to collect imagery. UAVs, for instance, carry both kinds of sensors, as do the manned aircraft employed by the US Air Force for ISR missions. US embassies also serve as facilities for signals collection. They "target the internal political, military, police, and economic communications of the nation in which the embassy is located."[177] The NSA and the CIA, through a joint covert program—the Special Collection Service (SCS)—plant and operate eavesdropping devices in various foreign locations. A well-known example is the SCS team that set up near bin Laden's compound in Abbottabad. Yet another source of SIGINT is small, mobile SIGINT teams maintained by the US Special Operations Command; in Iraq, these supported counterterrorism operations against AQI commanders and managers.

Prior to the 2003 invasion, COMINT played a limited role in Iraq because Saddam Hussein had prevented the establishment of commercial cellular networks. However, in the aftermath of the invasion, the cellular industry quickly established itself across the country. As a result, "Iraqi insurgents and their allied foreign fighters quickly began using cellular networks to communicate with one another, allowing American *SIGINT* operators . . . to begin exploiting insurgent communications."[178] Starting in 2004, COMINT became an important part of TF 714's operations against AQI and a major contributor to the F3EAD targeting cycle. The NSA supported TF 714's raiding teams that targeted AQI's mid-level commanders and managers. A large number of NSA specialists deployed to the TF 714's headquarters in Balad, fifty miles north of Baghdad. Like IMINT, COMINT played an important role in finding and fixing insurgents to gain an understanding of the inner workings of their networks.

To enhance TF 714's operational capacity, the NSA developed a special data processing and mining system called Real Time Regional Gateway (RTRG) that was introduced in Iraq in 2007. RTRG has been the subject of special reports by ABC News and Fox News and is also described in *@War: The Rise of the Military-Internet Complex* by Shane Harris, senior correspondent for the *Daily Beast*.[179]

RTRG played an important role in the full-court press TF 714 put on AQI's networked organization. It was an outgrowth of the way in which the NSA director, Gen. Keith B. Alexander, reshaped his agency for irregular warfighting. He believed that in order to defeat Information Age armed groups such as AQI, those doing the fighting had to be empowered by an "unprecedented data collection plan." A *Washington Post* profile described his goal as seeking to collect "everything: Every Iraqi text message, phone call and e-mail that could be vacuumed up by the agency's powerful computers. Rather than looking for a single needle in the haystack, his mantra was, 'Let's collect the whole haystack.'"[180] Alexander was "a leading apostle for harnessing technology's awesome power," and he "quietly presided over a revolution in the government's ability to scoop up information in the name of national security," pushing hard for "tools, resources and the legal authority to collect and store vast quantities of raw information."[181]

RTRG was one such tool. Like McChrystal, the NSA director judged that to defeat an enemy like AQI, it was essential to operate inside its clandestine networks. To do so, the NSA had to develop a mechanism to "bring high-level national intelligence directly to the warfighter" by "fusing all the data coming in from raids, intercepted communications, interrogation reports, drone footage, and surveillance cameras into a single, searchable system."[182] Essentially, Alexander proposed creating a Google for warfighters. What RTRG did was pull all those "disparate pieces of data" together and provide analysts with the means to "look for patterns" of behavior within a searchable system to identify how AQI networks operated in different parts of Iraq. Moreover, "as RTRG grew," explains Harris, "its regional scope expanded too." AQI had a transnational footprint, which led NSA analysts to "start looking outside of Iraq in a hunt for the insurgents' and terrorists' financial backers." For example, they identified a financier in "Syria who was funneling money to bomber cells and helping to provide safe passage for replacement fighters through Iran."[183]

In sum, the NSA played a major role in the new way of fighting irregular and networked armed groups. The intelligence collected by the NSA and the other agencies, when combined with that obtained from TF 714's raids, made powerful contributions to the F3EAD cycle. Fighting an enemy like AQI was different, explained TF 714's intelligence chief, then Colonel Michael Flynn: "For the task force to get inside al Qaeda in Iraq's decision cycle, it needed to drastically increase both its intake of all sources of data and the speed with which it molded that information into actionable intelligence."[184] The NSA contributed significantly to the accomplishment of those tasks.

MASINT: Again, Augmenting Imagery and Signals Intelligence

As noted above, MASINT emerged during the middle years of the Cold War as a highly technical collection discipline to expose aspects of Soviet strategic programs that signals and imagery collection could not uncover. MASINT concentrated on tracking acoustic signals from Soviet submarines, analyzing seismic indicators from nuclear detonations, detecting the construction of underground facilities, monitoring missile tests, and scrutinizing activities at potential chemical and biological warfare facilities. Secrecy, however, continues to obscure the technical details—and the degree of success—of these and other MASINT actions during the Cold War.

The same is true of the details of intelligence gained through the "qualitative and quantitative analysis of data derived from specific technical *MASINT* sensors" employed to identify unique features associated with the irregular warfare activities of those armed groups that the United States has been fighting since 9/11.

Only limited insights can be gleaned. For example, Clark notes that MASINT "material analysis is an important part of countering IEDs and the explosives used by suicide bombers."[185] MASINT was employed to locate IED factories, including those producing massive devices carried by cars and trucks known as VBIEDs (vehicle-borne IEDs). These factories were a part of the AQI networks that TF 714 worked to dismantle.

MASINT has been utilized to detect attempts by armed groups to produce chemical weapons by identifying the unique signatures such facilities give off. During Operation Enduring Freedom in 2001, US intelligence reported detecting "a crude chemical weapons research laboratory in Derunta, a small village near the eastern Afghan city of Jalalabad." Intelligence officials noted that other evidence led them to believe that al-Qaeda had "primitive capabilities" in terms of developing chemical weapons but could not weaponize what had been produced.[186] In Iraq, insurgents launched several chemical attacks, including, in the period from October 2006 to June 2007, no fewer than fifteen car- and truck-borne IEDs carrying chlorine tanks that killed more than one hundred civilians and wounded nearly one thousand more. The location of VBIED production facilities became a MASINT collection objective.[187]

Another discovery by US forces during Operation Enduring Freedom was of a "partially built biological weapons laboratory near Kandahar." US forces found no definitive evidence that al-Qaeda had "succeeded in obtaining a biological weapon," but what the "discovery demonstrated [was] a concerted effort on the part of al Qaeda to acquire a biological weapons capability."[188] A report in the journal *Homeland Security* titled "Biological Terrorist Attack on US an 'Urgent and Serious Threat'" identified a number of signs pointing to the interest of terrorist organizations in producing biological weapons. For example, "a laptop belonging to a Tunisian jihadist reportedly recovered from an ISIL [Islamic State of Iraq and the Levant] hideout in Syria contained a trove of secret plans, including instructions for weaponizing bubonic plague and a document discussing the advantages of a biological attack."[189] Such discoveries explain why facilities for the production of biological weapons by armed groups have become another MASINT collection objective. John Morris and Robert Clark note that the United States has "developed [MASINT] sensors and methodologies for . . . detection of chemical, biological, radiological, nuclear, and explosive (CBRNE) materials. The threat of using these materials in terrorist attacks has spurred much of this development."[190]

MASINT was used in the Balkan wars of the 1990s to detect and provide forensic evidence of war crimes by locating mass graves. It does so through hyperspectral remote imaging.[191] In Iraq, too, this MASINT tool has been employed to detect mass graves.[192]

Like state actors, nonstate armed groups employ camouflage, concealment, and deception measures to avoid detection by the imagery-collection platforms of their state opponents. Al-Qaeda and the Islamic State, as well as other armed groups, have gone underground to conceal themselves, either using existing cave complexes or building tunnel networks. Among twenty-first-century armed groups, Hamas is in the forefront in terms of the use of tunnel networks. Arthur Herman describes the Hamas tunnels as "lined with concrete, and iron rails were installed down the middle to facilitate the transportation of soldiers, missiles, and weapons in—and kidnapped Israeli victims out. Some of Hamas' tunnels were large enough to drive a truck through, and nearly all were booby-trapped."[193]

Underground facilities are a major concern for US intelligence. The NRO has a "Hard and Buried Targets Working Group, while the National Geospatial Intelligence Agency had as of 2005 an Information and Underground Issues Division in its analysis directorate, and by 2008 the Defense Threat Reduction Agency had a Hard Target Research and Analysis Center."[194] MASINT has increasingly been used to detect the underground facilities of insurgents, terrorists, and criminal groups. For example, airborne MASINT sensors can be used to detect warmth coming out of cave and tunnel entrances. Other sensors focus on magnetic emissions given off by metal equipment such as weapons or wiring used to provide electricity in tunnels. MASINT also includes gravity-measuring instruments, seismic-testing technologies, and ground-penetrating radar that scan areas for underground facilities.

How successful MASINT has been in detecting and collecting information on these and other armed group materials and activities in Iraq remains a highly classified secret. But there is no doubt that MASINT is seen as a strategically important intelligence-collection tool in the fight against irregular warfare enemies.

HUMINT: Still Needed but Different Methods

In the years immediately following the 9/11 attacks, HUMINT, which is primarily the CIA's mission, received considerable scrutiny. As noted above, classic HUMINT involves case officers recruiting agents in foreign governments who become sources that remain in official positions and provide sensitive information. But as also noted earlier, HUMINT targets began to change with the emergence of nonstate actors—most important, terrorist groups—as threats to US security. They constituted a new challenge for the CIA.

Nonstate actors are different from state targets, and traditional intelligence methods are not easily employed against them. In the case of al-Qaeda, as Éric Denécé explains, US intelligence agencies confront a "virtual organization that has no land or physical headquarters to protect and operates without a central command."[195] Moreover, such "jihadist groups are closed societies. . . . Their very strongly-held, radical Islamic beliefs make them resistant to conventional methods of recruitment as double agents. . . . Consequently, gathering secret intelligence via human assets (HUMINT) has become increasingly difficult and dangerous."[196]

These post–Cold War challenges, which 9/11 magnified, led intelligence experts to call for reform of HUMINT-collection methods. Those methods had performed poorly against al-Qaeda, the experts averred, and change was essential. However, no consensus emerged over how to go about reform and the extent to which it was possible. Indeed, some specialists doubted that the CIA could ever penetrate such organizations with any degree of success.[197]

Others argued that it was possible but would require major changes in the CIA's tradecraft, personnel system, and culture. Among those voicing this view were former senior CIA officers. For example, Sam Faddis, a former Directorate of Operations (DO) officer, proposed that rather than recruiting young US citizens who can be cleared for the CIA's clandestine service and training them in languages, the agency should focus on selecting individuals at the midcareer level with ethnic roots and practical experience in those regions where extremists hole up.[198] Gary Berntsen, another DO career officer, likewise agreed that the culture and personnel system of the CIA's clandestine service had to change.[199] And in his essay in an edited volume titled *The Future of American Intelligence*, Reuel Marc Gerecht outlined a potentially innovative approach for operating against radical Muslim organizations—an approach that would require structural changes in how clandestine intelligence officers are selected, trained, and deployed.[200]

The George W. Bush administration directed the CIA after the 9/11 attacks "to increase the number of clandestine case officers by 50 percent, to some 1,800 operatives," according to a 2006 *U.S. News & World Report* exposé. However, the extent to which this directive actually sharpened the CIA's HUMINT-collection capacity is uncertain.[201]

Irrespective of President Bush's effort to boost the number of CIA case officers, the United States relied on three other HUMINT methods to attain intelligence on irregular threats. The first involved liaison arrangements with foreign intelligence services, which, explains Byman, is "classified as a type of HUMINT, having long been important for [addressing] a range of intelligence issues" and gaps.[202] Jennifer Sims describes it "as a form of subcontracted intelligence collection." She noted in a 2006 study that liaison was becoming "an increasingly important source of U.S. intelligence collection against the mercurial terrorist threat."[203] This was certainly true of efforts to combat al-Qaeda and its transnational network. Members of that network were often well beyond the reach of CIA case officers but not of those local intelligence services with which liaison arrangements could be formed. This potential existed in North Africa, the Middle East, and the Arabian Peninsula, where several countries were fighting al-Qaeda and its associated movements.

Intelligence services in those states, which often have elite status and broad authority because of their place in the power structure, had collection capabilities that the CIA found in short supply. They knew the local culture intimately, of course; were fluent in the language or languages and dialects spoken; and could move freely, fitting into the local scene.

Illustrative was the CIA's liaison with Pakistan. According to Sims, "collaboration with Pakistan's intelligence service ([Inter-Services Intelligence])" from 2001 to 2006 resulted in Pakistan "handing over 300 suspected militants, including many senior ones."[204] The latter included Khalid Sheikh Mohammed, who was captured by Inter-Services Intelligence in Rawalpindi in March 2003 and extradited to the United States. In return, US military assistance to Pakistan rose from a few million dollars in the 1990s to more than $13 billion from 2002 to 2010.[205]

To facilitate liaison, the CIA established counterterrorism intelligence centers (CTICs) "where U.S. and foreign intelligence officers worked side by side to track and capture suspected terrorists and to destroy or penetrate their networks." Orchestrated by CIA director George Tenet, the CTICs constituted "a fundamental shift in the CIA's mission that began shortly after the 2001 attacks. No longer was the agency's primary goal to recruit military attachés, diplomats and intelligence operatives to steal secrets from their own countries." Now the focus was on "seeking ways to join forces with other governments it once reproached or ignored to undo a common enemy." The intelligence services in these countries had "much more intimate knowledge of local terrorist groups and their supporters" than CIA officers operating out of embassies in the capitals.[206]

One of the most important CTICs was established in Jordan. In the decade following 9/11, Jordan's General Intelligence Department (GID) and the CIA worked closely together in the fight against al-Qaeda. A glimpse into that association became public with the death of a GID officer in Afghanistan in December 2009, when (as described in chapter 1) Humam al-Balawi, a trusted agent of Jordanian intelligence, turned out to be an al-Qaeda double agent and killed seven CIA officers as well as the GID officer.

This illustrated but one of the dangers that reliance on foreign liaison could engender. Others included the unreliability of liaison partners such as Pakistan, which opposed some key US policies, and the appalling human rights records of some of the intelligence services with which the CIA was liaising.[207]

A second alternative for gaining HUMINT was through detainees. In the years following 9/11, interrogation of captured members of al-Qaeda generated great controversy because of the coercive methods, including waterboarding, employed by the CIA to extract intelligence. With the release in December 2014 of the SSIC's "Study of the CIA's Detention and Interrogation Program," the controversy reached a new level of intensity. Sen. Dianne Feinstein, chair of the committee, characterized the program as "a stain on our values and our history." With respect to effectiveness, the report asserted that these extreme methods played no role in disrupting terrorist plots or capturing terrorist leaders.[208] Three former CIA directors and deputy directors argued to the contrary on the pages of the *Wall Street Journal*. The program was invaluable, they countered, taking members of al-Qaeda off the battlefield, disrupting their plots, and saving lives.[209]

In Iraq, a different approach to interrogation was employed to gain intelligence from AQI members captured on TF 714 night raids.[210] Those individuals had extensive knowledge of the AQI networks in which they were ensconced. The challenge was getting them to divulge that information. TF 714 interrogators found that to do so they needed intimate knowledge about their prisoners. The way to acquire it was with the assistance of intelligence analysts they worked side by side with in Iraq. Those analysts were mining intelligence collected by ISR and extracted from electronic devices and documents gathered on TF 714's raids. That information was vital to how interrogators questioned detainees.

Michael Flynn, TF 714's intelligence chief, explains that as an interrogator, he "wanted to know more about that guy being interrogated than he knew about himself. And that was . . . our goal for our interrogation officers. I want the detainee to think that I know more about him than he knows about himself."[211] The master Israeli interrogator Michael Koubi described this as convincing a detainee that he "cannot hide anything" because the interrogator knows "everything about his background. You know about his family, his wife, his children, his friends, and his neighborhood." With such knowledge, Koubi asserted, "people who talk tough in public will often submit in interrogation."[212]

This knowledge empowered an interrogator to employ subtle and clever methods. But to employ this capability effectively required interrogation capacity. In Iraq, this had to be constructed from the ground up, explained General McChrystal in an interview in July 2014: "When we started, we had—I don't know—ten people handling the detainees. By the time this was cranking, in the facility at our headquarters [in Balad] the task force had approximately three hundred personnel focused on detainee interrogation."[213] These included analysts, who often took part in interrogations.

Integrating analysts into the interrogation process had been employed by other intelligence services operating against armed groups. Here is how a highly experienced Israeli analyst describes how she interacted, on a daily basis, with her interrogator counterpart:

> She explained she could request that a specific suspect be detained for interrogation if, based on other sources, she knew he was potentially a valuable source for a critical piece of information. She could request the interrogation take place quickly, especially if the intelligence sought was perishable. She could provide an interrogator with specific questions and detailed knowledge that he could use when interrogating the suspect. . . .
>
> She could even listen into an interrogation and say to the interrogator, "Ask him about this" or "Get him to clarify that." By being able to do so, she could get the specific details needed to guide the police and military commanders.[214]

These procedures, developed by other intelligence services, were fully employed in Iraq by TF 714. Admiral McRaven has affirmed that these methods were so successful that detainees became "the single best source of knowledge on AQI networks. Detainees would tell you literally everything they knew about their place in a network. And you did not have to use force to get them to do so."[215]

Matthew Alexander was one of those skilled interrogators. He subsequently published examples of how this process worked. One technique was to build trust and affinity with a detainee. This approach helped US forces find Abu Musab al-Zarqawi, who, as the leader of AQI, was responsible for many violent and deadly attacks in Iraq from 2003 to 2006. Information from a detainee led to al-Zarqawi's spiritual adviser, Sheikh Abdul-Rahman, who led them to a safe house where he and al-Zarqawi were meeting. They were both killed by an air strike.[216]

The third alternative for gaining HUMINT was through the exploitation of various items collected on TF 714 raids. According to Byman, these could include "pocket litter, hard copy documents, hard drives, cell phones, and other important electronic items with significant intelligence value."[217] Their exploitation could yield valuable HUMINT, as was the case with Khalid Sheikh Mohammed. "His computer . . . contained the names of over 100 Al Qaeda operatives, a list of wounded and killed terrorists, passport photos of members, and other vital information."[218]

In the intelligence lexicon, this is known as site exploitation. It is described as actions taken to "ensure that documents, material, electronics and personnel are identified, collected, protected, and evaluated to facilitate follow-on actions." It provides "intelligence for future operations, answers information requirements, and provides evidence to keep detainees in prison."[219] The following example illustrates how site exploitation can connect several disparate pieces of intelligence:

> The documents or equipment found in a cache produce fingerprints. A follow-up cordon and knock operation in the vicinity of the cache and the proper use of biometric equipment produce a matching set of fingerprints from a detainee. Thorough [tactical questioning] of the detainee produces a name and a meeting location. A surveillance operation of the meeting location produces further intelligence and a subsequent raid, which produces more intelligence and evidence. Without proper site exploitation of the cache, the fingerprints would have been destroyed, and no subsequent operations would have been identified through the targeting process.[220]

In Iraq in 2004, McChrystal found that such items, collected on TF 714 raids, were not being exploited in this manner for intelligence purposes. He later explained that "human error, insufficient technology, and organizational strictures all limited our ability to use that intelligence to mount the next raid." Instead of exploiting it, the teams "filled emptied sandbags, burlap sacks, or clear plastic trash bags with scooped-up piles of documents, CDs, computers, and cell phones, and then sent them to our base." Once the bags arrived, they were placed in storage. McChrystal found little to suggest that their contents were being methodically mined for intelligence.[221]

He was determined to remedy this. McChrystal described how the items were eventually mined at his headquarters by intelligence specialists:

> We went from . . . bags of captured items sitting there and we'll read them when we get time, which was weeks later, to analysts sitting in a series of rooms doing so as soon as it arrived from the raid. And this room was the cell phone room. Detainee phones were taken there immediately after a raid, and they had these machines that as soon as we capture someone with a phone, we hook the phone up, and we have computers that suck the guts out of the phone, they see who he's called . . . who he's talked to. Has anybody else that we captured talked to these people?[222]

A similar capability existed for captured computers, he explained: "Specialists laid everything out in the computer room. . . . They start triangulating what they found, they start translating it. . . . They're doing a scan for information which we could use for target identification."[223]

In sum, operators carrying out raids against al-Qaeda targets morphed into HUMINT collectors through site exploitation. But to do so effectively, explains Flynn, operators had to become collectors and accept the fact that they were going to have to do things differently and that their operations had more in common with techniques used by the law enforcement community. For example, they had to carefully collect details on the detainees at the site of the raid. He gave the example of pocket litter:

> In the past, three guys would be captured on a mission, and a bag of items collected. A bag of stuff would be captured, and we might ask the operators, "Where did you get this particular item?" And they would say, "We don't remember." We wanted to know whose pocket it was in, who was in possession of it. This kind of detail was important because we found over time that guys who were holding documents were not actually the guys we wanted. It was somebody else who was in the room. And that somebody else would play dumb because they knew we didn't always keep everybody detained. We needed to know that kind of detail.[224]

This could lead to an interrogation that revealed information on another target in the same neighborhood on the same night where the initial operation took place.

Open-Source Intelligence

OSINT collection has received considerable attention since the Open Source Center was established in Reston, Virginia, in 2004. Eliot Jardines defines open-source collection "as the process of finding, selecting, and acquiring information from publicly available sources . . . and analyzing it to produce actionable intelligence."[225] Before the Information Revolution, OSINT consisted of published materials such as books, magazines, and newspapers as well as radio and television broadcasts. The advent of the World Wide Web expanded open-source information exponentially. The Internet now is "the largest single repository" of open-source intelligence, and "almost any subject of intelligence interest has extensive coverage in it."[226]

Armed groups' online activities constitute a critical open-source collection target because the Internet serves as a platform from which to propagate ideology, explain goals, and discuss activities in chat rooms and through social media tools such as Twitter, Facebook, Flickr, and YouTube. The Internet has proven to be a transformational capability for armed groups. As Hanna Rogan observes, it can "fulfill different objectives, most importantly of a communicative character."[227] This is accomplished through the posting of information, news, and other materials.

Open-source collection has contributed importantly in the post-9/11 period to an understanding of terrorist and other types of extremist groups. To be sure, these are underground organizations that strive to maintain secrecy about their operational activities and whereabouts. But they also project a public narrative, and the collection and analysis of that public persona can provide important insights into various aspects of the organizations' modus operandi. Through their Internet platforms, groups such as al-Qaeda and its associated movements seek to inspire and recruit members, spread their storyline, and carry out a host of other, more specialized tasks.

For example, several Western specialists began to discover in al-Qaeda's Internet activities a category of postings on various websites that they characterized as conforming with the subject matter of Western strategic studies. The first experts to notice this were Brynjar Lia and Thomas Hegghammer, specialists on terrorism with the Norwegian Defense Research Establishment's Transnational Radical Islamism Project.[228] Their 2004 study explained that an al-Qaeda document, *Jihadi Iraq*, described how force was to be used by al-Qaeda to split the US-led coalition in Iraq. The first step was the terrorist strikes on Madrid passenger trains on March 11, 2004, which were intended to induce Spain to withdraw from the coalition, according to the authors of *Jihadi Iraq*. Lia and Hegghammer contended that this "text, which is secular in style, analytical in approach, and pragmatic in objectives, displays a level of political awareness and strategic calculus that breaks with most preconceptions" about how groups such as al-Qaeda function.[229] The detailed strategic maneuvers described in the document were illustrative of what one would find in the strategic gambits of modern states.

Lia and Hegghammer proposed that *Jihadi Iraq* was illustrative of a "growing online literature" that should be characterized as "jihadi strategic studies."[230] In a later assessment, Hegghammer advanced this proposition by demonstrating that within al-Qaeda's expanding use of the Internet, attention was being paid not only to the question of *why* to fight jihad but also *how* to fight it.[231] These initial studies led other researchers to explore whether additional topics discussed on al-Qaeda websites could likewise be grouped within the subject matter of strategic studies. Mark Stout found that "written works of an intellectually vigorous group of thinkers within AQ showed that strategic thought grounded in mainstream global thinking on revolutionary warfare exists within this community."[232] And Lia discovered considerable dialogue among al-Qaeda thinkers "over issues such as how training should be defined, its ultimate purpose, and where and how to prepare jihadi fighters."[233]

To summarize, open-source collection revealed how at the strategic, operational, and tactical levels after 9/11, members and supporters of al-Qaeda engaged in a sophisticated and innovative dialogue about how to carry on the fight in Iraq, elsewhere in the region surrounding the "land between the two rivers," and beyond to the homeland of what al-Qaeda called "the far enemy." This intelligence revealed that the United States was facing not only a powerful nonstate adversary with staying power but also one that consisted of strategic thinkers engaged in a complex dialogue over how to adapt and evolve in order to continue to escalate their war against the far enemy.[234]

Such information contributed to the knowledge TF 714 derived from the intelligence gathered on night raids or the SIGINT that told of the importance of those night raid targets and their place in one of AQI's networks in Iraq. The knowledge underscored by Lia, Hegghammer, and others put the intelligence being gathered by TF 714 into a broader understanding of the strategic calculus that drove its enemy's operations in Iraq. And in doing so, TF 714 networked its campaign into the larger global war against al-Qaeda and its affiliates with a similar jihadist agenda.

CHAPTER 4

TRANSFORMING INTELLIGENCE ANALYSIS FOR IRREGULAR WAR

It was not initially evident following the 9/11 attacks and subsequent Iraq invasion that the practices of US intelligence analysis would need to undergo important changes to provide actionable intelligence in a complex irregular warfare environment against networked nonstate enemies. Assessments of 9/11 following the attack reflected on the failure by the IC to connect the dots. This view is captured in the executive summary of the *9/11 Commission Report*: "While there were many reports on Bin Laden and his growing Al-Qaeda organization, there was no comprehensive review of what the IC knew and what it did not know, and what that meant. There was no National Intelligence Estimate on terrorism between 1995 and 9/11."[1]

As a result, the new watchword for the IC was reform. But those appraisals were looking backward to fix what had gone wrong. They did not consider the applicability of Cold War methods of intelligence analysis for assessing new threats emerging in twenty-first-century irregular conflicts. Just a few years later, however, those engaged in the Iraq War realized that the disciplines of US intelligence, including the methods of analysis, that had been established during the Cold War and had focused on the Soviet threat were no longer sufficient to meet America's needs.

In her 2008 essay "The New Analysis," Carmen Medina, the director of the CIA's Center for the Study of Intelligence, called for change. She asserted that "analysis is at a historic turning point" and "needs to be completely different" from Cold War methods. "What is most wrong with intelligence analysis," she explained, was "its essential design, which over the years has failed to adapt to new threats, to new understandings of human and social dynamics, and . . . to new technologies."[2] Medina's critique was sweeping. Nevertheless, her central point regarding the need to adopt new techniques and tools so that intelligence analysts could adapt to new and different twenty-first-century security challenges was spot-on.

Among those post-9/11 challenges, Medina asserted, "the most significant driver changing analysis is the revolutionary explosion in data." During the Cold War, analysts "for the most part dealt with fairly limited amounts of data," and they could "assemble and read all relevant information, usually in a matter of weeks."[3] Now, she observed, consider the intelligence that British analysts had to assess during the investigation into a 2006 al-Qaeda "plot to bring down as many as a dozen transatlantic jets." According to Peter Clark, chief of Scotland Yard's Anti-Terrorist Branch, during that inquiry the police collected from site exploitations "more than 400 computers, 200 mobile telephones and 8,000 . . . memory sticks, CDs, and DVDs, which he estimated contained some 6,000 gigabytes of data."[4] Traditional methods of analysis could not exploit such a vast mass of data. Automation-enabled tools were needed.

As this chapter describes, new analytic tools and technologies were needed for processing, investigating, unearthing, and connecting key developments and individuals hidden from view within the sheer volume of data. Only then could the secret networks of insurgents and terrorists be uncovered and illustrated graphically. Intelligence analysts had to be able to drill down into that data to locate well-hidden insurgent and terrorist networks

Letitia Long, who served as the director of the National Geospatial-Intelligence Agency from 2010 to 2014, notes that during the initial years of the Iraq War, it became apparent there was a need for "the analytic community to re-think the analytic environment. "To analyze big data," which was being collected and fused into massive multi-intelligence (multi-INT) databases, Long described how analysts began to "apply advanced automated tools and techniques to visualize and comprehend that data to identify patterns of activity and trends within it over time."[5] This was the starting point for discovering and mapping insurgent networks that in Iraq were hidden in two havens, one within the population and the other in the virtual world. New analytic tools were needed to empower analysts to discover and grab diverse targets hidden in an overwhelming mass of data.

The pages that follow describe what this "new analysis" came to entail, the changes it encompassed, and how it was employed in Iraq to support those given the mission of attacking and dismantling AQI's secret and networked underground. But before doing so, the chapter briefly looks back to describe US intelligence analysis, recount its evolution during the Cold War, and explain why it had to adapt to twenty-first-century irregular war.[6]

Cold War Intelligence Analysis

The National Security Act of 1947 legislated a major restructuring of US foreign policy, military, and intelligence institutions for formulating and implementing Cold War policy. With respect to intelligence, it established the Central Intelligence Agency "to correlate and evaluate intelligence and provide for its appropriate dissemination." But the CIA initially focused on the production of current intelligence (i.e., real-time intelligence information) rather than national intelligence estimates (NIEs), which addressed major policy issues.[7] The reason for this was that the new agency sought bureaucratic visibility and "quick recognition." But this emphasis "frustrated successive efforts to encourage the production of estimates." Consequently, "as CIA developed between 1947 and 1950, it never fulfilled its estimates function."[8]

This caught up with the agency on June 25, 1950. The outbreak of the Korean War was a devastating surprise attack, seen by officials in Washington as a strategic intelligence failure. It occurred shortly before Walter Bedell Smith took over as CIA director. Once in charge and much to his chagrin, Smith found that even in the shadow of the Korea failure, the CIA was not producing a "coordinated estimate of the situation in Korea."[9] As a result, he acted on the recommendations of a 1949 National Security Council study and transformed the CIA's Office of Reports and Estimates into three functional divisions: "The Office of National Estimates (ONE), whose sole task was the production of coordinated national estimates; the Office of Research and Reports (ORR), to support ONE and conduct basic research; and the Office of Current Intelligence (OCI), to write . . . daily reports for policymakers."[10]

Next, Smith established a separate directorate at the CIA tasked with concentrating all analytic activities in one place: the Directorate of Intelligence (DI).[11] The DI became the central location for Cold War intelligence analysis, which was designed for assessing the Soviet threat. What follows highlights how the DI carried out its mission, the types of intelligence products generated, the methods or tradecraft employed, and the focus on the Soviet target.

Analysis and Estimates

For the US IC that matured during the Cold War, the key mission was to provide senior officials with assessments they could rely on to formulate and implement policy. In his 1949 book *Strategic Intelligence*, Sherman Kent, the first director of the DI's ONE, stressed the importance of this role.[12] He asserted that the Cold

War presented policymakers with complicated challenges and that it was the duty of intelligence analysts to help them navigate that complex terrain by "producing assessments timed to their decision cycle and focused on their learning curve. This included providing actionable intelligence that can help with curbing threats and seizing policy opportunities." Kent judged that informed intelligence analysis could provide policymakers with a competitive advantage over foreign adversaries.[13]

The Intelligence Cycle

As the DI began to take shape, the production of analysis was assigned a key place in the intelligence cycle. The conceptual origins of the cycle can be found in Kent's 1949 volume, which provided a framework for collecting intelligence and turning it into finished analytic products to help policymakers navigate the decision-making process.[14] The production of analysis came to play an integral part in the intelligence cycle. It was one in a series of five steps, as depicted in figure 4.1.

The intelligence cycle has been described by Arthur Hulnick, a CIA career analyst, as the "gospel of how intelligence functions. . . . No concept is more deeply enshrined."[15] Robert Clark, also an experienced intelligence officer, adds that "over the years, the intelligence cycle has become somewhat of a theological concept: No one questions its validity."[16] As both explain, this static and linear model often does not represent reality. Nevertheless, it is a useful starting point for understanding the role of analysis in the Cold War practices of US intelligence.

As figure 4.1 illustrates, the cycle begins with "requirements," which, Clark explains, "amounts to a definition [or identification] of an intelligence problem."[17] This can take the form of a question that a policymaker wants answered—for example, "Is the Soviet Union seeking nuclear weapons superiority through the buildup of those forces and, if it is and if it accomplishes that goal, what will the consequences be for the balance of power between Washington and Moscow?" In its idealized form, requirements are generated by policymakers. However, Hulnick finds that requirements are often advanced by the members of the IC based on their interaction with policymakers.[18]

The second step in the cycle gathers intelligence to address the policy requirements. This involves directing one or more of the collection agencies described in the previous chapter to gather it. In the case of the above question concerning Soviet nuclear forces, gathering the required intelligence would likely have involved a major collection effort by all relevant agencies. Hulnick notes that intelligence managers are "the real drivers of the intelligence collection process." They identify gaps that exist in current intelligence databases and specify what needs to be collected.[19]

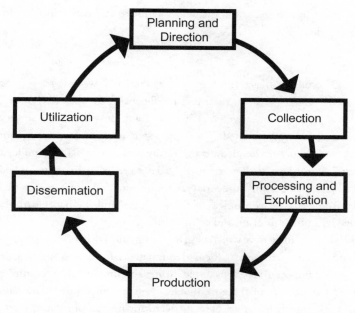

Figure 4.1 The intelligence cycle

Source: US Marine Corps, *Marine Air-Ground Task Force Intelligence Dissemination* (Quantico, VA: Marine Corps Combat Development Command, 2003), 12.

Once intelligence is collected, the third step prepares it for analysis. "Foreign language material is translated. Encrypted signals decrypted. Film translated into visible imagery. Responses from HUMINT sources are validated in a report format." These data are brought together with other "relevant historical material" related to the problem under consideration.[20] They are now ready for analysis, step four in the cycle.[21]

The initial assessment, once completed, goes through a review by peers and supervisors of the analyst who drafted it. Based on this appraisal, a finished piece of analysis is ready for dissemination to policymakers. It can take the form of a written product or an oral briefing.[22]

For the intelligence cycle to function in this manner, certain contextual conditions are necessary. First, time must exist for the cycle to move through its stages. In a fast-moving and time-sensitive crisis situation, decision-makers may not have sufficient time to complete the cycle. Second, the kind of analysis produced by the intelligence cycle may not be applicable in wartime, which is also characterized by fast-moving events and the need for actionable intelligence. Nevertheless, the Cold War, although it had its share of crises and wars, was generally an environment in which the intelligence cycle and the analysis process embedded in it could function as intended.

Analytic Products

The key DI products that were developed as the Cold War progressed included NIEs, current intelligence, and warning intelligence.[23] Of these, NIEs were considered "the most authoritative."[24] They typically dealt with critical Soviet strategic challenges facing the United States. NIEs sought to "project existing military, political, and economic trends into the future and to estimate for policymakers the likely implications of those trends."[25] They were termed *national* intelligence estimates for three reasons: the strategic implications of the issues covered, the high-level policymaker consumers of the products, and the participation of the collective IC in their drafting and coordination.

NIEs were divided into two types: recurring and ad hoc. The latter—called special intelligence estimates—focused on potentially dangerous situations of critical policy importance. An example during the Jimmy Carter administration concerned the stability of the government of Shah Mohammad Reza Pahlavi in Iran. Was this US ally in danger of being overthrown by revolutionary forces? This issue was of great concern to the White House. In terms of recurring NIEs, the most important, as noted above, focused on the Soviet Union and its strategic nuclear forces.[26]

While NIEs were considered the premier analytic product during the Cold War, other types of reports were sometimes also greatly valued by policymakers, especially current intelligence information. Current intelligence helped policymakers address "pressing problems," whereas NIEs were concerned with "more distant issues."[27] Current intelligence took different forms, the best known of which was the President's Daily Brief (PDB). While different presidents have tailored the size and organization of the PDB to meet their requirements, the PDB has been described as "a compilation of current intelligence items of high significance to national policy concerns," containing "information from the most sensitive U.S. sources." After 9/11, with the United States at war, President George W. Bush elevated the PDB "to unprecedented levels of importance," spending "as much as an hour on the briefing" each day.[28]

In addition to NIEs and current intelligence, a third important category concerned warning and focused on "developments that could have sudden and deleterious effects on U.S. security." Warning intelligence comes in two categories—strategic and tactical. Tactical warning deals with the more immediate context and seeks to "detect and deter specific threats . . . such as military attack, terrorism, WMD developments, illicit transactions, and political crises abroad." Tactical warning analysts search for and evaluate "information about incident, perpetrator, target, timing, and modalities. The goal is to deter and limit damage by identifying in advance when, where, and how a declared or potential adversary will forcefully strike."[29] Strategic warning, in contrast, seeks to "help policy officials decide—in advance of specific indicators of danger—which of the many plausible general threats to US security interests deserve concerted defensive and preemptive preparations."[30]

The Primacy of Soviet National Intelligence Estimates

The evolution of US intelligence analysis was shaped by the Soviet threat, which was seen as the central strategic challenge facing the IC. According to Richard Kerr, former deputy director of intelligence at the CIA, the major effort of the DI during the Cold War "was to assess Soviet strategic and conventional military forces and to provide judgments about Soviet doctrine . . . and intentions."[31]

Initially, the DI's focus was more narrowly fixed on the Soviet economy because Kremlin military power was considered to be the domain of the intelligence arms of the Department of Defense.[32] However, demands by US policymakers to gain a deeper understanding of Soviet capabilities and the threats they posed resulted in the CIA developing its own corps of experts. Those experts focused on coordinating NIEs on all the key dimensions of Soviet military power. The most crucial of these NIEs, according to Donald Steury, was "*Soviet Forces for Intercontinental Conflict*, which considered Moscow's capabilities to wage nuclear war as an organic whole, comprising both offensive and defensive elements." Other NIEs examined Soviet conventional forces, including those of Warsaw Pact nations.[33]

According to Kay Oliver, former CIA chief historian, the scope of the work on Soviet military power was "without parallel in the Intelligence Community in terms of . . . the commitment of resources, consensus of priority requirements, and high-level support."[34] NIEs of Soviet military power dominated the IC's analytic enterprise, according to Harold Ford, who served in the 1980s as vice chairman and acting chairman of the National Intelligence Council.[35] And, as the previous chapter illustrates, this was also true of the requirements for the collection of intelligence.

The process for drafting and coordinating intelligence estimates began in the early 1950s under the auspices of the CIA's ONE. The methodology adopted for evaluating Soviet military capabilities and potential was prognostic. It developed special "analytic approaches for assessing weapons production, analyzing weapons testing and, by the early 1960s, estimating military manpower and effectiveness."[36] Buttressing this process was the availability of large amounts of data gathered by advanced technical collection systems.

NIEs concerned with Soviet strategic nuclear forces paid attention to their complex and interrelated economic, industrial, and technological underpinnings. These issues required highly specialized knowledge: "NIEs drew fully upon the resources available from the many intelligence organizations in the U.S. government." While this made them "national documents that reflected the judgments of those intelligence organizations" that were part of the NIE process, "the participation of so much CIA analytical talent in the preparation of these estimates . . . guaranteed the Agency a kind of hegemony over the process."[37]

Nevertheless, and not infrequently, agreement among analysts was often not possible, and NIEs contained dissenting views. Beginning in the 1970s, the accuracy of NIEs of Soviet military power generated considerable controversy as a public policy issue. The larger US community of think tanks and academic specialists focused on the size of Soviet nuclear forces and the purposes for which they were produced, challenging NIE key findings. Illustrative was the A Team–B Team exercise of the mid-1970s called for by President Gerald Ford. This involved a competitive evaluation of NIE 11-3/8, which focused on inferring from an examination of Soviet nuclear forces their strategic purpose.

The CIA analysts who produced the NIE—the A Team—judged the purpose of Soviet nuclear forces to be deterrence only, achieved by rough parity with US nuclear forces. The B Team, composed of outside experts who were vocal critics of past Soviet NIEs, demurred. They argued that based on evidence of new Soviet ICBMs, of a major program to build underground shelters to secure them, and of expanded air-defense capabilities, Moscow was developing a first-strike capability. The A Team–B Team experiment generated a great deal of controversy. The accuracy of other Soviet estimates—such as those dealing with Soviet defense spending the Soviet economy—likewise attracted outside criticism.[38]

Other Cold War Intelligence Estimates

Although the Soviet threat shaped the IC's processes for producing NIEs, the methods "had application to other emerging [nation-state] challenges such as Communist China."[39] North Korea, too, remained an analytic preoccupation after the 1950 surprise attack. Beyond those states, other areas of concern included the Middle East, with the continuous Arab-Israeli confrontation and periodic wars. Also, beginning with the 1979 fall of the shah, Iran and the rise of Islamic extremism fostered by it became an important topic of intelligence analysis. "During the Kennedy and Reagan administrations . . . first Fidel Castro's Cuba in the 1960s and later Nicaragua and the Contras in the 1980s" were seen as posing "direct challenges to U.S. regional policies" and consequently generated considerable analytic attention.[40]

During the Vietnam War, intelligence analysis looked beyond state-centric challenges to those posed by nonstate armed groups. The DI was involved in an incendiary debate with the DOD and its military command in South Vietnam—MACV—over the strength of communist guerrilla forces fighting there and the will of their North Vietnamese patrons to continue fighting against American military power. Unlike their DOD counterparts, the analysts at DI did not underestimate the strength and determination of the enemy.[41]

In the 1980s, transnational challenges posed by armed nonstate actors started to receive attention within the DI with the establishment of special centers devoted to analyzing those actors. The first such center was the Counterterrorism Center (CTC), launched in 1986. It subsequently became the model for the 1989 Counternarcotics Center (CNC), which focused on criminal organizations as transnational threats. However, at least during the remainder of the Cold War, transnational dangers were not the subject of great policy concern, and therefore the centers were DI backwaters.

Analytic Tradecraft

The "mission of an analyst" has been described by James B. Bruce and Roger Z. George as "applying in-depth substantive expertise, all-source information, and tough-minded tradecraft [methodology] to produce assessments that provide distinctive value-added [insights and judgments] to policy clients' efforts to protect and advance U.S. security interests."[42] How analysts go about these tasks, however, has changed considerably in the transition from Cold War, state-centric peacetime to post-9/11 wartime, in which nonstate armed groups are the main adversary.

The analytic approach developed by the DI for producing finished intelligence has been described by Medina as the "lone wolf model," in which analysts "could reasonably have expected to read relevant information in a defined period of time after which he or she would write a paper that conveyed his or her views on a particular situation or development."[43] Richards Heuer, one of the CIA's leading analytic tradecraft innovators, has described the analysis process in similar terms. Cold War analysis was a "mental activity done primarily by a sole analyst."[44]

In this model, intelligence analysts became subject-matter experts in a particular issue area. Their knowledge and critical thinking about specific issues yielded "expert judgements." The analytic process was "an activity that takes place largely in the individual analyst's head," writes Heuer. The piece of analysis is "the product of a single analyst and the analyst tends to feel ownership of his or her analytic product."[45] The outcome of the process—expert judgments—combines "subject matter expertise with critical thinking. Evidentiary reasoning, historical method, case study method, and reasoning by analogy" are employed to produce a finished piece of intelligence.[46]

Given the overriding importance of Soviet estimates, early in the Cold War the DI began to develop what turned into a legion of specially trained analysts and customized tradecraft methods to provide the ways and means for assessing the closed and highly secretive state that constituted the Soviet Union. As an intelligence challenge, the USSR was unique in many ways, and this necessitated the development of a specialized type of analyst—the Sovietologist—who was schooled to understand and assess the USSR. Sovietology was a method of exploration and evaluation developed by necessity to meet this challenge. Special analytic competency based on an understanding of Soviet culture was formulated to decipher what intelligence data could be mustered through human and technical means of collection. That required analysts with a deep understanding not only of the Russian language but also of the cultural dimensions of a closed system dominated by a counterintelligence state of mind.

As the Cold War forged ahead, a small group of individuals associated with the DI also sought to professionalize the methods of analysis, proposing various innovative initiatives.[47] These efforts resulted, during the 1970s, in the establishment of analytic standards that sought to achieve greater rigor, objectivity, and excellence. They were to be applied during the crafting of analytic products, serving as the foundation for finished intelligence products. Jim Marchio, in his review of declassified national intelligence assessments, identified eight such standards.[48]

In the 1980s, attention focused on the epistemology of intelligence analysis and, in particular, on issues of method, validity, and scope. Efforts were made to introduce alternative analytic techniques for use in conducting intelligence assessments so as to overcome what came to be considered a major shortcoming in the traditional approach to analytic production: reliance on expert judgments by individual analysts.

Broadly cast, these new techniques addressed what Heuer has described as "mental model or mind-set" challenges that all analysts face. In his 1999 book *The Psychology of Intelligence Analysis*, he explained that analysts "construct their own version of 'reality' on the basis of information provided by the senses, but this sensory input is mediated by complex mental processes that determine which information is attended to, how it is organized, and the meaning attributed to it." As a result, what people perceive, how readily they perceive it, and how they process this information after receiving it are all strongly influenced by past experience, education, cultural values, role requirements, and organizational norms, as well as by the specifics of the information received. This process may be visualized as perceiving the world through a lens or screen that channels and focuses and thereby may distort the images that are seen. To achieve the clearest possible image . . . analysts need more than information. . . . They also need to understand the lenses through which this information passes. These lenses are known by many terms—mental models, mind-sets, biases, or analytic assumptions.[49]

Such mind-sets can put analysts in a position in which they are not equipped to assess complex problems with partial and ambiguous data that may also have been manipulated by the subject of the assessment's denial-and-deception actions. In *The Psychology of Intelligence Analysis*, Heuer exposed the potential weaknesses in expert judgments found in finished analysis produced by individual analysts.[50] His solution was to organize analysts into teams to overcome "the wide range of cognitive pitfalls" described in his volume.[51]

Teams of analysts would be introduced to new analytic procedures that could help them "challenge judgments, identify mental mind-sets, stimulate creativity, and manage uncertainty. Incorporating regular use of techniques such as these would enable one to structure thinking for wrestling with difficult questions," exposing analysts to different and opposing viewpoints.[52] In doing so, analysts could mitigate the cognitive traps noted above. Methods for alternative analysis were seen as particularly needed for complex challenges. However, it was only in the late 1990s that "the term 'alternative analysis' came to be used" in the IC.[53]

Intelligence Analysis in Transition: The Post–Cold War 1990s

As highlighted above, the Soviet challenge was the predominant issue facing US intelligence during the Cold War. An analytic expertise was constructed to assess all aspects of Soviet military power. By what means the "DI developed the capability to produce analytic intelligence on the Soviet Union," writes Douglas Garthoff, a Soviet analyst for three decades, is "the story of how the DI came to fulfill its most fundamental responsibility . . . [against] America's chief adversary in a worldwide struggle that defined the era of the Cold War."[54] A corps of experts was assembled in the Office of Soviet Analysis.

To be sure, as Kerr notes in his account of the CIA's analytic "track record," a myriad of other intelligence issues were covered during the four decades of the East-West confrontation.[55] Nonetheless, these were fundamentally sideshows—until December 26, 1991, when the Soviet Union was officially dissolved. "Within a week," notes Garthoff, "Soviet [Analysis] was replaced in the DI office name with Slavic and Eurasian [Analysis]."[56] The Cold War was over, and this fostered a reevaluation of the size and focus of intelligence analysis.

The need to downsize the workforce and reduce the budget was a refrain found in all intelligence reform proposals. Domestic priorities demanded a reallocation of government spending, and that included drawing down the intelligence budget. Reform initiatives called for cuts of 10 to 20 percent or higher in appropriations. As with the other intelligence components, the analysis budget and workforce were substantially reduced. By 1996, Allan Goodman notes, "analytical capabilities . . . were atrophying, both qualitatively and quantitatively," reducing the capacity of "the intelligence services to attract, train, and hold outstanding career professionals."[57]

At the same time, new issues were identified that would form a challenging agenda for post–Cold War intelligence analysis. New analytic specialties were needed to "focus on new targets and to support policy-makers and military commanders concerned with [new] areas of instability, transnational issues and other topics."[58] To addresses these, in March 1995 the Clinton administration adopted Presidential Decision Directive 35: Intelligence Requirements (PDD-35). It identified those issues viewed as urgent and less urgent and tasked US intelligence to manage them. PDD-35 defined the importance of national security challenges requiring intelligence support using a 0-to-4 tier system.[59]

Tier 1 priority was "assigned to intelligence Support to Military Operations [SMO]. Tier 2 concerned providing political, economic, and military intelligence on countries hostile to the United States to help to stop crises and conflicts before they start." These were traditional state-centric challenges. Tier 3 was designated "to activities addressing counter-proliferation, as well as international terrorism, crime and drugs." These were new, transnational threats.[60] Tier 4 consisted of countries of little interest to the United States.

The analytical priorities set out in PDD-35 mirrored those identified in the intelligence reform reviews taking place at that time. For example, the growing importance of analytic SMO was the subject of a staff study produced as part of the House Permanent Select Committee on Intelligence study *IC21: The Intelligence Community in the 21st Century*. It identified two reasons for the growing importance of SMO. First, in the aftermath of Operation Desert Storm, many commentators proposed that "a priority for reorganization of our intelligence capabilities should be to plan for capabilities that would support the military requirement to be able to engage in two, near-simultaneous major regional contingencies"—in other words, two Desert Storm–type wars. Second, the expanding role of US military forces in peacekeeping and peace enforcement operations in the 1990s necessitated increased intelligence support.[61]

As a result, the 1990s saw IC analysts "supporting tactical combat situations," shifting from "intelligence as a contributor, to intelligence as a participant."[62] To meet this new requirement, the CIA established the Office of Military Affairs, with DI analysts assigned on rotation and sent "forward to support military operations and exercises" in order to "strengthen ties in peacetime that will be needed in wartime."[63] As described below, intelligence support to military operations burgeoned after 9/11, particularly in the fight against al-Qaeda in Iraq. However, the battlefield no longer resembled Desert Storm; instead, it was an irregular warfare arena in which US forces battled nonstate armed groups.

Those engaged in the intelligence reform debate also identified terrorism, organized crime, and the proliferation of nuclear, biological, and chemical weapons as presenting different intelligence problems than those that dominated during the Cold War. According to Paul Pillar, "transnational threats are not fought against a single arch-enemy, do not have identifiable front lines, and seldom have clear beginnings and ends. The targets for intelligence collection and analysis are shadowy and ill-defined."[64]

Transnational challenges identified in PDD-35 included terrorism and organized crime. Both were singled out as security threats in the last decade of the Cold War. The Reagan administration saw the dangers posed by international terrorism as necessitating the establishment in 1986 of the CIA's CTC, which brought analysts and operations officers together. The CTC was to produce "analytic products and, at the same time," its analysts were to become "closely involved with operational activities." The CTC was to foster a partnership between the DI and the Directorate of Operations. As it evolved, the CTC came to see itself as "one stop shopping . . . for intelligence support to planning and execution of U.S. counterterrorism policy in all its forms."[65]

In 1989, the DI established the CNC to consolidate the DI's work on drug trafficking, which had begun earlier in the decade. Pillar notes that "the nature of the illegal narcotics trade and those who practiced it meant analysis of this subject quickly and inevitably branched into related activities." For example, "the involvement of insurgent groups and other resistance movements in drug trafficking required CNC to look at such groups . . . in addition to its main task of monitoring drug cartels." As CNC's focus broadened to cover other aspects of transnational organized crime, "the Center's name changed in 1994 to the Crime and Narcotics Center."[66]

WMD proliferation activities in several countries were identified as a critical post–Cold War concern, suggesting that they were more important than the tier 3 priority assigned to them by PDD-35. For example, Paula Scalingi, a professional staff member of the HPSCI and a former CIA analyst, wrote in 1995 that US intelligence now faced "the challenge of assessing an increasing and varied proliferation threat that must be monitored globally. At present, US intelligence estimates that there are at least 25 countries, some with hostile intentions, that are developing nuclear, chemical or biological weapons." And in most cases, each of these countries was also either "developing, or seeking to purchase ballistic missiles to deliver these weapons."[67]

Due to the attention generated by the dangers posed by WMD proliferation, the director of central intelligence established the Nonproliferation Center (NPC). The goal was to improve DI expertise and coverage of WMD proliferation and to foster interaction with the policy community on these issues. While it was supposed to be an IC organization, the NPC, like the CTC and CNC, was located at CIA headquarters and was staffed primarily by agency personnel. But because of the complexity of the issues involved, NPC drew on "analytical work . . . performed outside the Center."[68]

Post-9/11 Wartime Intelligence Analysis

As noted, as the 1990s came to an end, the challenges posed by transnational threats including terrorism began receiving added attention by IC analysts. But in the wake of the 9/11 attacks, those issues, which PDD-35 had consigned to tier 3 priority, moved to center stage as the United States found itself at war with violent extremists. With that war came the need to rethink existing approaches to analysis. Carmen Medina was not alone in calling for intelligence analysts to employ new techniques and tools to understand and assess irregular warfare challenges that were taking place in a new warfighting context. Those changing conflict dynamics, in turn, would necessitate a different intelligence cycle.

The Human Warfighting Domains and a Changing Intelligence Cycle

Much intelligence analysis during the Cold War focused on Soviet military capabilities found in what US security specialists referred to as the air, land, and maritime domains.[69] It was within those physical locations, also termed warfighting domains, that American armed forces would fight their Soviet counterparts if war came. It was strategically essential to assess the quality and quantity of Soviet nuclear and conventional capabilities that would be employed within each of those physical spaces. The NIEs, which were concerned with estimating Soviet nuclear and conventional military strength, were the single most important analytic products of the IC.

However, as Thomas Doherty notes, the twenty-first-century international security landscape and the irregular wars that have dominated it have engendered a new "Human Warfighting Domain," which he describes as one "where human factors are the decisive point in winning a war."[70] In his book *The Utility of Force: The Art of War in the Modern World*, British general Rupert Smith makes a similar argument about the context in which irregular war is taking place in the new millennium. He proposes that in the aftermath of the Cold War, the location or domain has changed from armies fighting each other on distant battlefields in industrialized war to "war amongst the people," or population-centric war.[71] In another words, twenty-first-century wars are being fought in the human domain.

Moreover, Doherty goes on to propose, the emergence of the human domain engendered the revival by the US military of counterinsurgency strategy during the Iraq War. According to US Army Field Manual 3-24, *Counterinsurgency*, COIN is a competition with insurgents to gain the support and/or control of the uncommitted middle of the population, as illustrated in figure 4.2.[72]

To be able to operate successfully within the human warfighting domain during the Iraq War, the United States adopted a COIN approach, jettisoning the conventional military methods that were failing badly in the irregular war that followed the defeat of Saddam's army. COIN operations sought to gain the support of the uncommitted middle of the population by first separating them from the insurgents. COIN is population-centric: the goal is to secure the population and then begin to meet their needs through humanitarian relief and economic development assistance. To gain control over contested territory and to provide security to the population requires driving insurgents away through clear-and-hold military operations, securing the cleared territory by keeping military forces in place.[73]

COIN operations in Iraq conducted by US Army and Marine Corps forces, in conjunction with the surge and the Sunni Awakening movement,[74] were able to isolate the population from AQI, establish local security, and then, in conjunction with interagency partners, shift to nonkinetic lines of operations. These included striving to foster governance, reconstruction, economic development, and the rule of law. At its core, COIN is about human security, reconstruction, and development within the human domain.

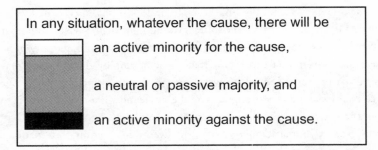

Figure 4.2 Support for an insurgency

Source: *Counterinsurgency,* US Army Field Manual No. 3-24 (Washington, DC: Department of the Army, December 2006), 36, http://usacac.army.mil /cac2/Repository/Materials/COIN-FM3-24.pdf.

However, there was one more component of COIN strategy—counterterrorism—executed by the United States in Iraq. US counterterrorism operations focused on weakening and degrading AQI's secret networks, a complex array of operational, command, and support units. They were beyond the reach of regular army and Marine forces engaged in the COIN operations described above. To degrade AQI's clandestine networks through counterterrorism operations, a special counterterrorism unit—Task Force 714—was needed. Its forte was offensive and highly lethal paramilitary raids targeted to degrade AQI's secret networks. The story of how TF 714 developed a joint interagency intelligence capacity to successfully support counterterrorism operations is the subject of the remainder of this chapter.

For TF 714 to accomplish its mission, it had to transform and be augmented by a robust intelligence capability provided by multiple intelligence agencies that came to support its paramilitary operations in Iraq. Initially, according to the leadership of TF 714, the focus of its operations was on finding, fixing, and finishing targets—the "F3" process. It did not exploit and analyze the intelligence that was being collected during those operations. To do so, F3 had to transform into F3EAD—find, fix, finish, exploit, analyze, and disseminate (depicted in figure 3.1, in chapter 3). According to General McChrystal, innovative task force members in Iraq developed this concept when they "turned their attention from rounding up former Baathists," their initial mission, "to attacking Zarqwai's emergent [insurgent] organization.[75] This, in turn, necessitated change in the methods of intelligence analysis.

Analysis, within the traditional intelligence cycle established during the Cold War, as depicted in figure 4.1, was part of a process that provided policymakers with finished assessments about subjects that were identifiable or known. That cycle, Gregory Treverton explains, was "linear and resembles a production line." As described previously, "it proceeded from requirements, to collection, to processing and analysis, to dissemination."[76] The cycle begins with a request by an intelligence consumer for an assessment about an issue he or she wants to know more about. For example, during the Cold War, such a request often had to do with Soviet military power. The role of analysis in the cycle was to take the information that had been collected and processed, combine it with relevant material that already existed on the topic, and produce a finished assessment for dissemination to relevant intelligence customers.

In today's international security environment, many of the most important intelligence targets are no longer fixed or even known. This is certainly the case with respect to networked nonstate armed groups such as AQI. Consequently, rather than assessing known subjects and objects, analysts often search for unknown or vaguely understood ones. Robert Clark writes in *Intelligence Analysis: A Target-Centric Approach* that this is particularly true of "complex systems in that they are nonlinear, dynamic, and evolving. As a result, they can almost always be represented as dynamic networks . . . that constantly change with time."[77]

Faced with these challenges, the role of intelligence analysis had to change, as did the intelligence cycle. While the Cold War form of analysis remained relevant for traditional state challenges, a different approach was needed for the operational challenges posed by nonstate actors.

Analysis and F3EAD

In the F3EAD cycle that grew out of the early years of the Iraq War and the need to understand a complex, covert, and networked insurgency, the analysis phase no longer involved reporting on the status of things that were already known and could be observed. Rather, the role of analysis was to discover and gain knowledge about the operational activities of insurgents and terrorists that were unknown. Instead of reporting on the identifiable, analysts now had to find the hidden.

In the traditional intelligence cycle, the analyst generated products—pieces of analysis—on known objects such as a missile launcher or a nuclear materials processing facility. In the post-9/11 irregular warfare context, as first experienced in Iraq, analysts supporting counterterrorism TF 714 became sleuths, searching through massive amounts of geospatial, signals, and other intelligence data that were vacuumed up on specific geographic areas, investigating it to uncover anomalies, trends, patterns, and connections among events and individuals. With the shift from the national security focus in the 1990s on proliferation and conventional military forces to terrorism, armed groups, and transnational actors, intelligence analysts swung their attention from the military forces and capabilities of state actors to the operational activities of terrorists and insurgents who hid within the population and on the Internet. Analysts had to learn to employ new tools and methods to enhance their ability to discover, visualize, and map enemy activities and networks.

The area of operations in which terrorist and insurgent activities took place and secret networks formed was now the human domain. That domain was both physical (the urban jungle of cities) and virtual (the computer-based online milieu of the Internet). Analysts looked at data gathered from multiple intelligence-collection methods, including site exploitation of specific geographic locations. In Iraq, data could take the form of intelligence collected on a neighborhood within a city—most likely, Baghdad, Mosul, Ramadi, or Fallujah—where it was thought that an AQI network existed. But the signatures of the members of such networks—their distinctive characteristics—were not easily observable. Just the opposite. Analysts had to forage through multisource intelligence data collected on those urban settings to identify patterns of activity that took the form of recognizable movements that connected individuals to one another and to specific locations.[78] Discovering those connections between individuals in specific geolocations became the starting point of analysis. The transactional contacts among them, once discovered, had to be observed and assessed to determine whether they were merely coincidental or the product of relationships among individuals in a specific insurgent network.

Consequently, within the F3EAD cycle, the analysis process changed from the traditional approach of stitching together scant and often disparate pieces of information to draw transitory conclusions, to mining data to unearth leads about possible linkages among people, places, and activities. The initial find phase of the F3EAD cycle takes place at both the intelligence and the operations levels to establish a starting point for collection targeting. From this exploration of all-source data, targets are generated. Once leads from the find phase are identified, various collection tools fix on those detected individuals or geographic locations 24/7 to identify the patterns of activity taking place that connect people based on their presence at common physical or virtual locations. The objective, in Iraq, was to determine whether uncovered associations were part of an insurgent network. If that was the case, then the full gamut of intelligence-collection tools was directed against it, persistently and repeatedly, to develop an operational picture of a particular AQI network.

Analysis in the F3EAD cycle (as depicted in figure 3.1) does not result in a finished piece of intelligence ready for dissemination to policymakers. Rather, it takes the form of intelligence that leads to focusing (fixing) on an individual or physical location to further determine whether the day-to-day activity being observed (e.g., walking, driving, Internet usage, cell phone calls, text messaging) reveals a specific geolocated network. Such activity patterns, when linked to others, bring the clandestine and low-visibility terrorist or insurgent network into view.

The analyze stage assesses and evaluates information gained from the preceding stages of find, fix, finish, and exploit. The goal of analysis is to turn information into intelligence that can be used both to fix on a specific entity and to help identify the composition of a number of other entities that constitute a specific insurgent network. If the goal of analysis is fixing on a specific entity, the continued and persistent collection process may well reveal the nodes and linkages of a particular network—be it an enemy communications facility, an IED production plant, or a unit of fighters—by observing its daily pattern of life. This can include the day-to-day goings-on at a selected location, an entity movement from that location to other locations, visits by other entities to the location being observed, and identification of key personnel associated with the site. This information may result in a decision to conduct a raid against the geographic site under observation to capture enemy personnel and conduct a site exploitation.

If the goal of analysis is identifying other network elements, the role of the analyst is to perform more in-depth examination of the collected data to identify how a network is organized in a particular geolocation at a particular point in time. Various tools can be used to reveal the details of the network's structure and design, how members carry out activities, where key members reside, and what patterns of interaction are taking place within the specific network under scrutiny.

In sum, according to US Army Field Manual 3-60, *The Targeting Process*, "the bottom line of the analyze step is to examine and evaluate information and rapidly turn it into actionable intelligence that can be applied to defeat an enemy's network. Some information may be immediately actionable, such as that providing the location of another HVI [high-value individual]. Other information may need further analysis and corroboration."[79]

Known, Unknown, and Big Data Opportunities

US intelligence analysts in the past worked in what Patrick Biltgen and Stephen Ryan describe as a "data-poor" environment. "The things we did not know, and the data we could not obtain far outnumbered the things we knew and the data we had. . . . Historical intelligence textbooks describe techniques for reasoning through limited data sets and making informed judgments."[80]

Analysts today face a different context due to the Information Revolution and the technological developments that made it possible. The Information Revolution has opened the possibility of making massive amounts of data available to analysts. The rapid changes in collection systems have made possible the assemblage of vast volumes of information, especially from imagery and signals sensors, that are too large to be dealt with by traditional analysts. New tools are needed to mine the data. This information explosion is often referred to as "big data." The technical disciplines of intelligence collection—geospatial (imagery), signals, and measurement and signatures—have resulted in new and highly sophisticated sensors employed on an array of platforms.

For example, consider the capacity imagery sensors now provide to conduct persistent surveillance of a geographic area to search for and fix on specific objects of interest. According to David Pendall,

> the essence of persistent surveillance is to use collection systems to detect, collect, disseminate, and characterize activity. . . . Persistent surveillance has three core components: multimode and multidimensional continuous collection across all environments (sensing); near-real-time data and knowledge distribution via systems with tailored, user-defined presentation formats (delivery); and horizontal integration of data and advanced, distributed analytics (sense-making and understanding).[81]

This capacity is captured in figure 4.3.

These developments have allowed the IC to adopt the "collect it all" mantra of former NSA director Keith B. Alexander, who, when faced with the post-9/11 irregular challenges posed by transnational armed groups such as al-Qaeda and its associated movements, proposed that the NSA, rather than looking for a single needle in a haystack, should collect the whole haystack. "Tag it, store it," he declared, "and whenever you want, go searching in it."[82] This kind of thinking, when coupled with advancements in collection sensors and platforms, has resulted in the unprecedented collection of data by the collection agencies, as depicted in figure 4.4. And the impact of these developments on intelligence analysts, explains Chandler Atwood, has been transformational: "The increase in sensors and resulting vast amounts of disparate data coupled with the increasing capabilities of IT [information technology] systems to handle the deluge are transforming intelligence analysis. The traditional process of stitching together sparse data to derive conclusions is now evolving to a process of extracting conclusions from aggregation and distillation of big data."[83] Of course, this transformation creates its own set of new challenges because of the difficulty of digesting all the data and correlating them to other relevant information. But collecting them all creates the possibility of connecting the dots to find nuggets in time to act.

"Big data," explain Kenneth Cukier and Viktor Mayer-Schönberger, allow

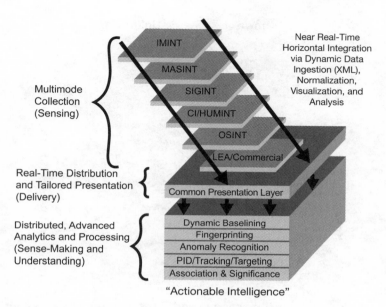

Figure 4.3 The persistent surveillance concept

Note: *CI* means "counterintelligence," *LEA* means "law enforcement agency," and *PID* means "plan identification number."

Source: David Pendall, "Persistent Surveillance and Its Implications for the Common Operation Picture," *Military Review* (November/December 2005): 42.

today's analysts to search, discover, and "learn from a large body of information things that we could not comprehend when we used only smaller amounts."[84] But to do so, Biltgen and Ryan add, analysts must be able to "triage, prioritize, and correlate information from giant volumes of data" using "fundamentally different approaches to storage, ingestion, management, and analysis."[85] Multi-INT aggregated data are searched to find associations between people, events, and activities with the objective of uncovering unknown patterns of behavior to drive more focused collection and investigation. This approach, as explained below, is essential for exposing the secret and dispersed networks of today's armed groups.

To graphically depict this post-9/11 transformation of the methods of intelligence analysis from assessing and reporting on what is known to discovering and then illuminating what is unknown, particularly with respect to "the identity and behavior of individual entities," Biltgen and Ryan divide the analysis function into four domains, as shown in figure 4.4.[86]

The vertical axis of figure 4.4 is concerned with the *behaviors and signatures* of "observable phenomena that can be collected."[87] In the lexicon of intelligence, a signature is "a set of distinctive characteristics of persons, objects, or activities

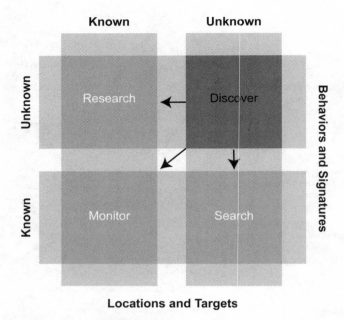

Figure 4.4 The analysis domains

that result from the processing of collected intelligence."[88] The horizontal axis focuses on the *locations and targets* where those "subjects of collection activities" can be found.[89] Of the four analytic domains, traditional analysis, as practiced from the beginning to the end of the Cold War, was concerned with the domains of researching, monitoring, and searching. Each domain dealt with behaviors and signatures and locations and targets that were either known or knowable.

In the lower left quadrant of the graphic, *Monitor*, analysts during the Cold War focused on monitoring *known knowns*. The goal of the analyst was to determine whether there had been any changes in the behavior and signature or location of the target under observation. For example, consider Soviet ICBM bases. The US overhead imagery program sought to provide analysts with the capacity to monitor those Soviet strategic weapons that were deployed and to determine whether any new ones were added to known ICBM sites. The locations and signatures were known. And behavior could be monitored to detect and identify changes.[90]

In the upper left quadrant, *Research*, the geolocation of the target of interest to the intelligence analyst is known. For example, a newly constructed chemical weapons production facility has been identified. But the distinctive characteristics or signatures associated with that facility are unknown to intelligence. This is the analytic domain of the *known unknown*. The role of the analyst is to research the location and, drawing on all available intelligence means, to learn what he or she does not know about that facility. The task is to identify the type of weapons being produced, their composition and lethality, and where they are being deployed. The activities that are taking place and their distinctive signatures must become knowable to the analyst.

In the lower right quadrant, *Search*, the intelligence analyst is "looking for a known signature/behavior in an unknown location."[91] Continuing with the example of the chemical weapons production facility, the analyst knows that short-range missiles have been fitted with warheads laced with sarin gas at the aforementioned facility. He also knows some of those missiles have been surreptitiously transported from the facility, but it is not known to where. To find the answer, the analyst will search intelligence being gathered by various sensors to seek to discover the locations to which the sarin-laced missiles have been deployed.

To summarize thus far, the analysis domains of monitoring, researching, and searching all have one thing in common. Each starts with knowledge of either the signature or the location of the intelligence subject of interest (e.g., an ICBM base or a chemical weapons facility). Part of the equation is known. However, today's networked and subterranean insurgent and terrorist groups and the irregular warfare milieu in which they operate generate a fourth analytic domain where neither the location nor the signature of the object of interest is known. This is the upper right-hand quadrant of *Discover*—the domain of the *unknown unknown*. In this domain, explain Biltgen and Ryan, "you don't know what you're looking for, and you don't know where to find it."[92]

While this domain is not new, a post-9/11 conflict environment dominated by complex, clandestine, and networked nontraditional threats has elevated its strategic significance. And this has caused the IC to rethink traditional practices of intelligence analysis. No longer can analysts only *monitor* what they know, *research* what they know they do not know, or *search* for what they know in locations that are unknown to them. They must now also *discover* insurgent and terrorist networks whose signatures or identifiable characteristics and locations are both unknown. To do so, intelligence analysts have to exploit changes in post-9/11 collection systems and the vast amounts of data they are capable of generating to discover those networks and identify their constituent individuals and activities.

Multi-INT Fusion and Data Preparation

Analysts assigned to TF 714 in Iraq were among the first to encounter the challenge of working with large amounts of intelligence data collected in a war zone.

That intelligence had to be assembled into databases that could be searched to discover AQI patterns of association and activities that were unknown.

Today the process for managing this intelligence is referred to as "multi-INT data fusion." Intelligence gathered by each of the collection methods, explains Atwood, is "spatially and temporally indexed [or 'meta-tagged'] at the time of its collection . . . to a specific point in space and time." This is also described as "georeferencing" the data.[93] It is the first step in being able to uncover information buried in big data about unknown insurgent and terrorist networks. Activity that takes place within a designated geographic space—for example, in an area of a city—can be identified and pegged to a specific location and point in time. Georeferencing the data collected is accomplished through automated systems. Once this is completed, analysts can search geographic areas to connect individuals and activities to specific locations. Analysts employing this approach, explains Biltgen, assume that "everything happens somewhere and if you can visualize that and understand it, then trends and patterns in a network will start to jump out."[94]

Once multi-INT data are georeferenced, analysts can begin to discover low-contrast insurgent and terrorist networks hidden within population and electronic sanctuaries. They do so by focusing on the activities and transactions occurring in a particular area of interest and searching the data that have recorded those activities. Dave Gauthier, who served as chief of strategic capabilities in the Office of Special Programs at the NGA, gives the following example of how something as basic as license plate data could be utilized: "Using wide-area motion imagery to process vehicle tracks . . . the license plate of every vehicle in Baghdad" was georeferenced and stored. "Most of them may be irrelevant, but there's the idea that some of them will be relevant in the future when an event happens."[95]

Multi-INT data that are merged and georeferenced are treated neutrally regardless of the source from which they were obtained and the sequence in which they were collected. What is important is the degree to which a piece of data contributes to "understanding entities and their activities."[96] Any piece, potentially, could be the critical one that links activities to specific actors.

Analysts in Iraq, faced with adversaries who lacked identifiable signatures, sought to exploit multisensor data by employing different tools to search for clues of associations within it. These are leads or tips that provide direction to dig deeper into the existing data or to have collection systems redirected to gain more information on an individual or activity that has been identified. Atwood describes this as "an analysis method which rapidly integrates data from multiple INTs and sources around the interactions of people, events, and activities, to discover relevant patterns, determine and identify change, and characterize those patterns to drive [further] collection." By mining a "large volume of data from a variety of intelligence sources," analysts can foster the "discovery of weak signatures and patterns in a noisy data environment." Having associated "activity data with information about the attributes, relationships, and behavior of known and unknown objects," they can begin to visualize insurgent networks hidden within both population and Internet sanctuaries. And this "knowledge enables the discovery of new facilities, links and nodes, and patterns of activity."[97]

To summarize, multi-INT fusion is a process that amalgamates data amassed by different collection methods into a database before intelligence analysis takes place. In doing so, it makes possible a far-reaching change in the traditional approach to analysis by the IC. "The evolution of data fusion methods," explain Biltgen and Ryan, "recognizes that the fusion of information to improve decision making is a central process in many human endeavors, especially intelligence."[98] But throughout the Cold War, and in the first decade of its aftermath, intelligence gathered by each of the five collection disciplines was not commingled or blended into a congruent whole. Rather, it was kept separate in compartments, or "stovepipes." The only time data would undergo integration was when an analyst, working on a specific intelligence issue or requirement, requested data from the different intelligence disciplines to conduct an all-source intelligence assessment.

Now intelligence data collected by different imagery, signals, measurement and signatures, human, and open-source methods are fused or amalgamated. Multi-INT intelligence data go through a process in which each fragment associated with a person, place, or thing is georeferenced or associated with a specific spatial location, or geographic coordinate, where some activity took place. They are also referenced temporally to specific times. Spatial and temporal cataloging of the data in this way necessitates the use of automated procedures, including complex algorithms, the specifics of which are beyond the scope of this book.[99]

Once data have been reformatted and georeferenced spatially and temporally, analysts can begin to search for what in Iraq were described as "low-contrast" and "easily camouflaged insurgents" unseen "among civilian clutter" and as an "electronic sanctuary in which actions" were "hidden among the innumerable civilian signals that constitute daily cell phone and Internet traffic. It is from this new sanctuary that the enemy coordinates activities from dispersed networks."[100] To exploit such data to uncover insurgent and terrorist networks, analysts have to employ new automated tools.

Exploiting Big Data: Network Analysis

As TF 714 gained greater understanding and experience in Iraq, intelligence analysts sitting in front of computer screens at the unit's headquarters in Balad were able to watch the movements and listen to the communications in real time of members of different AQI networks. The analysts also monitored activities surrounding AQI hideouts through an array of intelligence sensors. In effect, they conducted 24/7 surveillance stakeouts of those targets. In the F3EAD cycle, this is the fix phase. Once a potential target of interest was identified, the full gamut of intelligence-collection sensors could be focused on it to learn details about an individual's or a location's pattern of daily activity to determine its role in a particular network operating in a specific geolocation.

Through the persistent use of ISR capabilities, TF 714 was able to observe specific AQI targets for extended periods of time. The objective was to provide analysts with details of the targets' activities, which could be used to graphically illustrate the elements and interconnections that constituted a particular insurgent network. And once the task force decided to move on that target—the finish phase of the cycle—more network details would result from site exploitation and interrogation.

However, those same collection sensors could also be employed to initiate surveillance of a geographic area where AQI was suspected of operating. The sensors would be pointed by the analysts working the target with operators. Intelligence gathered would become part of an existing database that analysts could investigate to identify potential insurgents and their activities, locations, and associations. But, in doing so, they were delving into the domain of the unknown unknown—a domain where, to quote Biltgen and Ryan, "you don't know what you're looking for, and you don't know where to find it."[101] It was in that human domain where twenty-first-century transnational insurgent and terrorist organizations presented complex challenges to intelligence analysts.

New Analytic Tools

To discover those unknown unknowns, analysts required new analytic tools to investigate the big data contained in multi-INT databases. Only then could they come to understand and graphically depict the complex and nonlinear networks of twenty-first-century armed groups.

In his book *Intelligence Analysis: A Target-Centric Approach*, Robert Clark, who served as an intelligence officer in both the US Air Force and the CIA, describes al-Qaeda and other armed groups as "Threat Networks in which *nodes* can be almost any kind of entity—people, places, things, concepts. Links define relationships among the nodes." It is for this reason that he asserts that a "*Threat Network* is a better concept for intelligence analysis" than a communications or social network, which are more narrowly focused in terms of the nodes that constitute them.[102] Threat networks, Clark elaborates, are "complex systems that are nonlinear, dynamic, and evolving . . . [and] constantly change with time." They have "spatial attributes: They exist somewhere in space at a given time. They also have temporal attributes: They move around or change as time passes."[103]

The puzzle that US intelligence faced in battling irregular and networked adversaries was how to discover their spatial locations and frequent movements. The goal of intelligence was to identify targets of interest—network nodes—and, once they were located, to monitor their activities to learn more about their behavior and the network in which they were nested. To accomplish this goal, intelligence analysts needed to employ methods and tools to search for associations in multi-INT databases that had been prepared or conditioned for exploration. Originally categorized as data-mining and link-analysis techniques, these tools first appeared in the 1980s.

Data mining, in its most general sense, is a method employed to "discover useful, previously unknown knowledge by analyzing large and complex data sets." The term is often used to refer both to actual data mining and to the "application of automated data-analysis tools."[104] As the storage capacity of computers in the 1980s expanded to be able to amass increasing amounts of data, data sets "became too large to be analyzed with traditional statistical approaches."[105] Fortunately, advances in the field of artificial intelligence, including algorithms, made automated exploration possible.

Initially, data-mining tools were "widely used in a variety of business sectors," according to Lei-da Chen, Toru Sakaguchi, and Mark Frolick. The tools proved invaluable to businesses such as credit card companies, financial services, banks, telemarketers, airlines, manufacturers, telephone companies, and insurance companies.[106] The goal of these tools was to "ascertain general knowledge about a group rather than knowledge about specific individuals." In other words, data mining was employed to identify transactional patterns among unrelated individuals to forecast the likelihood of their doing the same thing. Christopher Clifton writes that data mining sought to discover "interesting and useful patterns and relationships in large volumes of data." To do so, it "combines tools from statistics and artificial intelligence with database management to analyze large digital collections."[107]

Link modeling and analysis is one of those tools, although its use predates the emergence of big data. Clark notes that link modeling and analysis "has a long history; the Los Angeles police department reportedly used it first in the 1940s as a tool for assessing organized crime. Its primary purpose was to display relationships among people or between people and events. Link models demonstrated . . . ties between entities."[108] In subsequent decades, link analysis continued to be used by law enforcement to map criminal organizations. It was also used by CIA analysts.

Steve Ressler reports that the CIA employed it "in Thailand in the 1960s to understand family and community relationships." Analysts "conducted a series of open-ended interviews and in a short time were able to map out the clandestine structure of local and regional Communist organizations and associated sympathetic groups."[109] He also notes that a form of link analysis, traffic analysis, was used by intelligence analysts beginning in World War II: "This technique consists of the study of the external characteristics of communication in order to get information about the organization of their communication system. It was not concerned with the content of phone calls but interested in who calls whom and the network members, messengers, and gatekeepers." Traffic analysis was also "used by the British MI5 internal security service to combat the IRA."[110]

Early use of link analysis, notes Clark, "was an arduous and time-consuming endeavor because graphic trees had to be constructed on paper." However, when software tools became available, the process was streamlined "by allowing the storage of data as it comes in and by graphically displaying different types of relationships among the entities." Automation "facilitated the organization and presentation of data to assist the analytic process. . . . Once relationships have been created in database systems, they can be displayed and analyzed quickly in a link analysis program."[111]

Among the initial software tools developed for automated data exploration through link analysis was Analyst's Notebook, which was produced by IBM. Since its first appearance, Analyst's Notebook has gone through frequent updates and new versions.[112] It was among the first pieces of software to provide analysts with a visual analytic tool that could be employed to explore complex data sets comprising large amounts of information to identify connections and patterns of interaction to "build a cohesive intelligence picture." As it was refined, Analyst's Notebook came to provide "a comprehensive range of visual analytic tools which are designed to help users discover key individuals, connections, relationships, events, patterns and trends that may otherwise have been missed . . . within disparate data sets."[113]

Complex Challenges and Networked Organizations

Link modeling and analysis "has been replaced almost completely by network analysis . . . because it offers a number of advantages in dealing with complex networks," writes Clark.[114] Complex challenges and decentralized networked organizations are unlike their complicated and hierarchal counterparts. Over the last twenty-five years, those differences have received considerable attention in business and management studies.[115] Gökçe Sargut and Rita McGrath have observed that coping with accelerating "levels of complexity" has posed an acute challenge for those "managing a business today." Complexity "affects almost everything we touch: the products we design, the jobs we do, and the organizations we oversee. Most of this increase has resulted from the information technology revolution. . . . Systems that used to be separate are now interconnected and interdependent, which means that they are, by definition, more complex."[116]

Several specialists, among them David Snowden and Mary Boone, have concluded that complex challenges are different both in degree and in kind.[117] Three characteristics, according to Sargut and McGrath, illuminate their distinctiveness: multiplicity, interdependence, and diversity. Complex domains have been assessed to have a much larger number or multiplicity of "interacting elements." And there are scores of connections and linkages among those elements, fostering considerable interdependence. But those interactions are nonlinear, making the identification of enduring patterns impossible because they do not exist. Finally, diversity is reflected in the high "degree of heterogeneity" among the elements that compose a complex milieu.[118]

Unlike complicated challenges, the outcome for complex ones cannot be anticipated or estimated beforehand. That becomes known only in retrospect. The consequences of actions are not comprehensible in advance due to the number of nonlinear interactions taking place. Sargut and McGrath observe that "in a complex system, the same starting conditions can produce different outcomes, depending on the interactions of the elements in the system."[119]

In the twenty-first-century security context, states are confronted by terrorist, insurgent, and international criminal organizations that take the form of complex and networked adversaries. Consequently, network analysis has become an indispensable tool utilized by the IC to identify and target these irregular antagonists. It has become indispensable because it not only provides visual depictions of the linkages between different entities but also exposes whether those associations are positive or negative, strong or weak, important or inconsequential. "Analyzing a network" in this way, explains Clark, "involves answering the classic questions—who-what-when-how-why—and placing the answers in a format that the customer can understand and act upon." In the IC, this is known as "actionable intelligence."[120]

More specifically, network analysis provides the diagnostic means to

evaluate the importance of individuals . . . within networks and the assets available to them. Specifically, are they connected to a larger number of other organizations? Who provides them with access to the different resources they require to carry out operations and other activities? What is their role in the network? How close are they on average to other actors in other networks? Do they have the power to easily share information in the network? The answer to such questions [helps intelligence and security specialists] identify the individuals [they] would want to focus on and to determine the nature of the power they hold.[121]

The Key Elements of Network Analysis

To understand threat network analysis, a brief introduction to the basic elements of networks is necessary. Such an introduction can be found in Sudhanshu Chauhan and Nutan Kumar Panda's study *Hacking Web Intelligence: Open Source Intelligence and Web Reconnaissance Concepts and Techniques*.[122] Chauhan and Panda's focus is on social network analysis (SNA), while that of the IC is on a variation of it—what Clark describes as threat network analysis. Although there are important differences between the two, they share the same basic elements.

Chauhan and Panda describe social networks as consisting of "different social elements and the relationship between them. . . . What this means is that by using SNA we can measure and map the relationships between various entities, these entities being people, computers, and a collection of them. . . . SNA utilizes visual representations of the network for the purpose of better understanding it and implements mathematical theories to derive results. There are various tools that can be used to perform SNA."[123]

For SNA, nodes represent people and groups. For threat network analysis, which is best understood as "an extension of SNA used by the intelligence community," nodes "can be anything." For example, if an analyst is charting a threat network design of a terrorist organization, it would be important "to include associated organizations, weapons, locations, and the means for conducting terrorist operations (vehicles, types of explosives)."[124] All these elements should be included in a graphic portrayal of the terrorist organization. The goal of SNA, and threat network analysis, is to understand the entities that make up a network, their activities, and the relationships between and among them.

Nodes are the basic organizing concept of a network, the essential element, and "the whole analysis revolves around them."[125] *Edges* "represent relationships. Relationships are required to establish how one node connects to another. . . . The number of edges [or linkages] connected to a node defines its degree" of activity.[126] Networks are made up of nodes and edges.

Nodes and edges can have different characteristics. These include direction, type, weight, ranking, and betweenness. With respect to direction, two types of edges are identified by Chauhan and Panda: directed and undirected edges. The former "are the edges with a unidirectional or one-way relationship. The best example of a directed edge is X → Y." These are "one-sided [or one-way] relationships." The latter, undirected, constitute "mutual relationships, such as X ← → Y." In a social network, such relationships "can be anything like X and Y are friends or classmates or colleagues."[127] In a terrorist network, they can denote that X and Y are members of an operational unit of a particular terrorist network.

Type refers to the types of relationships that put a node and an edge into a group. Chauhan and Panda explain: "Let's say that there are different nodes and edges but if some of the edges are similar by the type let's say of a group, then we can distinguish them quite easily." In terms of an insurgent network, type could be the members of a component of that network, such as an IED production facility. Type "has a significant role in differentiating different nodes and edges."[128]

Weight has to do with the number of connections or linkages, whether directed or undirected, between two nodes. Chauhan and Panda give this example: Because "X relates [interacts] with Y in five ways then the weight of that edge is 5. We can draw five edges [connections] between those two nodes or we can draw a deeper [or thicker] edge between them to make it easy to understand that these two nodes contain a higher weighted edge." In other words, these two entities—say, members of that part of an insurgent network focused on weapons acquisition—have a very active relationship.

Weight can be either positive or negative. Consider an organized crime network. A positive weight could be the relationship or nexus between a criminal chieftain and a political leader in which both benefit financially from their interaction. A negative weight, in contract, might be characterized by the suborning of the politician to the will of a criminal chieftain through intimidation and death threats. The Colombian cocaine kingpin Pablo Escobar described these two choices for the political leader as "*plata o plomo*"—cooperate and you will receive silver, or do not cooperate and you will receive lead.[129]

Relationships can also be *ranked* to denote "the priorities of the relationship established between two nodes."[130] Finally, *betweenness* denotes "two different groups of nodes connected to each other by an edge." These edges represent "a unique quality" because they "combine two different groups or set of nodes."[131]

To summarize, these are the basic or core elements that are utilized for "mapping and measuring of relationships between different entities." In a social network, the nodes or entities are usually people, while the links represent relationships or flows between the nodes."[132]

Network analysis includes both "mathematical as well as graphical analysis of relationships" to deduce "conclusions such as who is a hub in the network, how different entities connected to each other, and why they connected to each other with a proper logical and data-driven answer."[133] It is important to note that overlaying this sort of traditional network analysis are other value-added inputs, all of which go into identifying how to prioritize the most important nodes of the network to collect on and strike.

Threat Network Analysis

Almost two decades of involvement in post-9/11 irregular wars in Iraq and elsewhere has resulted in the US military and intelligence communities developing the means to gain an operational-level understanding of the threat networks of those insurgent and terrorist groups they have confronted. New tools were developed that analysts could utilize to uncover those networks. According to Clark, "one of the most powerful tools in the analyst's toolkit is network modeling and analysis. . . . The netwar model of multidimensional conflict between opposing networks . . . is more and more applicable to all intelligence." Consequently, it became a key means for identifying and mapping the threat networks of "insurgents, violent global jihadists, and international criminal organizations such as human smugglers and narcotics traffickers."[134] The role of the intelligence analyst was to discover and map the essential components of those networks—the edges and links, direction, types, weights, rankings, and betweenness of their nodes—and then to pinpoint weaknesses.

Insurgent and terrorist networks became the targets for intelligence analysts to work against. Their objective, explains Clark, was "to develop a detailed understanding of how a threat network functions by identifying its constituent elements, learning how its internal processes work to carry out operations, and seeing how all of the network components interact."[135]

Illustrative of these developments is the *Commander's Handbook for Attack the Network*, produced in 2011 by the US Joint Forces Command's Joint Warfighting Center.[136] To understand target networks and how to assess them, the handbook proposes an analytic process in which "pattern analysis, link analysis, social network analysis, and forensics are the foundational methods that enable intelligence analysts to begin templating threat networks . . . providing intelligence support to targeting. Available intelligence is fused and simplified to create a model of how the threat network generally operates."[137]

The initial step in threat network analysis is to begin to develop a profile of the insurgent or terrorist organization's "capabilities and requirements, activities, and operational areas . . . [so as to] enable the staff to begin to identify potential targets and the target area."[138] Once this has taken place, the various collection disciplines can be massed against these initially identified entities to further refine understanding of the insurgent or terrorist network's profile. This will allow "analysts to graphically represent those functions and activities, overlaying what we know and what we don't know in order to . . . create opportunities for learning. Network templating enables the commander and staff to map the network's people and activities on the ground using all-source intelligence in order to 'Fix' the enemy" within the F3EAD cycle.[139]

To summarize, network analysis, when combined with multi-INT fusion and big data preparation, can provide analysts with the tools needed for discovering and charting the inner workings and dynamics of insurgent and terrorist networks. Through target network analysis, intelligence analysts learned how to identify and map the operational profiles of complex, clandestine, and dynamic adversaries to determine how best to degrade them. These techniques began to emerge and develop in the aftermath of 9/11, when the US counterterrorism force in Iraq was assigned the mission of dismantling al-Qaeda's clandestine underground.

Exploit and Analyze: Iraq and Task Force 714

Several of the changes that characterized the transformation in the processes of analysis since 9/11 were first put into practice by the US counterterrorism force that deployed to Iraq in 2003 as TF 714. Once on the ground, it was assigned a new mission for which it was unprepared. Tasked to find, degrade, and dismantle the burgeoning al-Qaeda–dominated insurgent apparatus, the unit quickly realized that it was not able to execute that mission. General McChrystal, the task force commander, explained that, as constituted, the counterterrorism force could not keep pace with, let alone reduce, AQI's burgeoning operational tempo. The unit had to "adapt to a new, more ominous threat."[140]

That adaptation took the form of TF 714 changing from a highly compartmentalized and stand-alone counterterrorism force into one partnered with and supported by a joint interagency task force comprising members of the IC. That partnership was constructed to manage, exploit, and analyze the intelligence needed to uncover and target AQI's secret networks. It established a union of common purpose to do so. And that common purpose, according to Lt. Gen. Michael Flynn, TF 714's senior intelligence officer, meant that "instead of 80 percent of the task force effort being focused on operations and 20 percent on intelligence collection and analysis, the opposite became the case." What this meant, he explained, was that "the days are gone where intelligence was a subordinate component of operations."[141]

Additionally, TF 714's targeting approach also had to change from the F3 cycle to that of F3EAD. In 2003, its approach was the standard F3 construct, explained

General Flynn. That was the "main effort." What was missing was attention to "exploit and analyze. When I got to the task force," he added, "F3 was where we were spending most of our time. I looked at that, and I asked, 'What are we doing in the areas of exploiting and analyzing intelligence?' F3 is where 80 percent, probably more like 90 percent, of the attention of the task force was focused."[142] "The problem with the F3 cycle," added Adm. William McRaven, who commanded TF 714 as a vice admiral after McChrystal, was that "you never understand the scope of the network you are fighting."[143] That was because TF 714 was not able to exploit the intelligence its counterterrorism units were collecting during night raids. As McChrystal recounted in his memoirs, "On each mission they found documents and electronics, as well as people who knew names and plans that we wanted to know. But human error, insufficient technology, and organizational strictures limited our ability to use this intelligence to mount the next raid. And the sole analyst in Mosul or Balad was unable to digest the information brought back. . . . [Additionally,] the teams were ill-equipped to question suspected insurgents they found on the targets."[144]

Once the JIATF was established at TF 714's Iraq headquarters with personnel deployed to it from each of the three-letter intelligence agencies, the amount of information available to analysts began to grow rapidly. The JIATF was not the producer but the consumer of this intelligence data. The data were gathered through an array of collection methods that revolved around the site exploitations that took place during each of TF 714's night raids against AQI targets. According to Byman, as noted above, site exploitation can yield "pocket litter, hard copy documents, hard drives, cell phones, and other important hard copy and electronic items with significant intelligence value."[145] Intelligence was extracted from all those devices and documents, explained McChrystal, by specialists at his Balad headquarters. "There was the cell phone room. Detainee phones were taken there immediately after a raid, and they had these machines [to which], as soon as we capture someone with a phone, we hook the phone up, and we have computers that suck the guts out of the phone. They see who he's called . . . who he's talked to. Has anybody else that we captured talked to these same people?"[146] Captured computers as well as various portable USB-based memory devices used to store data were likewise dissected.

The amount of intelligence gleaned from site exploitation was immense because of the surge in the number of night raids conducted monthly by TF 714 teams. From 2004 to 2006, TF 714 grew into an industrial-strength counterterrorism force whose operational tempo increased from eighteen raids in August 2004 to three hundred raids in August 2006. And from 2006 through 2009, it sustained this tempo. Night raids also yielded detainees, members of an AQI network captured during those operations. Intelligence from site exploitation of documents and electronic devices, as well as from detainee interrogation, would identify new targets against which TF 714 directed airborne ISR platforms. ISR provided it with "long dwell-time [and] persistent surveillance directed against known and suspected terrorist sites or individuals." The goal was "to apply multi-sensor observation 24/7 to achieve a greater understanding of how the enemy's network operates by building a pattern-of-life analysis."[147]

ISR was crucial in the fix phase of the F3EAD targeting process. When focusing on a target, ISR could employ special sensors to watch an AQI member or facility for an extended period of time. This was referred to as "the unblinking eye." ISR also provided important intelligence that was needed to exploit AQI's extensive use of modern communication devices, McChrystal added. Once under video surveillance, a target's cell phone and computer could be monitored from airborne ISR platforms through SIGINT collection, revealing the identities, locations, and activities of other potential key midlevel commanders and managers of AQI's networks.[148] TF 714 also could call on a close-in, on-the-ground SIGINT capability it could deploy to monitor a target's cell phone usage.

As this process matured, the amount of intelligence data amassed burgeoned exponentially. The remainder of this chapter highlights how these intelligence data were used during the exploit and analyze phases of the F3EAD cycle by TF 714 analysts, identifies tools those analysts used to search for associations and linkages, and describes how analysts graphically illustrated the composition of AQI networks at given points in time so that operational teams could degrade them from the inside out.

TF 714 and its IC partners in the JIATF found themselves in 2004 in the domain of the unknown unknowns. Operators and analysts had to discover AQI networks whose signatures or identifiable characteristics and locations were shadowy and surreptitious. To unmask them, TF 714 exploited the data generated through night raids. The size of that data was described "as huge" by one former senior intelligence officer who served in the task force. He noted that it was the result of TF 714's changeover from a stand-alone "persistent strike force to a precision ops-intel team."[149] This allowed TF 714 to achieve the operational tempo noted above, which, in turn, generated the explosion in data collected through an array of technical and human intelligence methods.

Once TF 714 identified a target, it could call on the full gamut of intelligence capabilities of its interagency partners to fix on it in time and space to track its pattern of life, physical movements, and connection within one or more other members of an AQI network. The task force massed intelligence capabilities to collect data on an industrial scale.

Collected data then had to be managed, turning it into exploitable intelligence. This is where multi-INT fusion came into play. Recall that this is described above as a process that amalgamates data gathered by different collection methods into searchable databases that intelligence analysts can delve into. The task force drew on the best IT solutions available to do so because its leadership gave those working on this challenge the latitude and resources to find and acquire the technology they needed. The goal, recalled McRaven, was to acquire data-management systems so that "every bit of intelligence data collected was coded and put into one of those systems." To achieve this goal, he added, "a great deal of money was allocated."[150]

The massive amounts of intelligence collected fed the exploit and analyze phases of the F3EAD cycle. And the partnership between TF 714 and the JIATF brought together the critical ingredients of people, process, and systems to identify, locate, map, and target key nodes within AQI networks. From the three-letter intelligence agencies, as well as from their military counterparts, analysts with an array of specializations were seconded to the JIATF. Several had broad expertise dealing with al-Qaeda both in Iraq and beyond. Others were regional specialists as well as those whose expertise was in the technical analysis of signals, imagery, and measurement and signatures. They all brought not only their own skills and experiences but also those of the agencies they represented, through the capacity to reach back and engage with them. This connected the seconded specialists to a much larger network of civilian and military agencies. The following three examples illustrate how TF 714 was able to integrate diverse elements of the IC back in the United States into a unified effort.

The first example highlights the use of video teleconferencing (VTC) technologies. General Flynn explained how VTC was used to elicit help with problems TF 714 faced in Iraq. An analyst might explain in a VTC reach-back meeting that his unit "needed some help with something. And he might ask NSA specialists linked in through VTC, 'Do you think you guys can do this for us?' And their answer would come back right then and there. . . . In the early days, they usually would say, 'I have to go back and ask my higher officials.' But as time went on, they would immediately say, 'Absolutely, we can do that.'"[151]

In a second example, "cameras were placed in special rooms at 714's HQ where intelligence exploitation teams searched cell phones captured on raids only a few hours earlier. As they pored over that data, intelligence analysts at CIA in Langley, through video links, took part in that exploitation process in real time, contributing their expertise."[152]

Third, the task force learned that the National Media Exploitation Center (NMEC), established as part of the Defense Intelligence Agency (DIA) in 2003, had a powerful capability for assessing captured documents. Given that the task force was collecting massive amounts of AQI documents as part of site exploitation, NMEC seemed a natural partner. But it was located in Northern Virginia. To be able to reach back and send that intelligence to NMEC, TF 714 "augmented the thicket of antennae on its hangar roof with a grove of huge satellite dishes," according to McChrystal.[153] As a result, NMEC became an important contributor to the F3EAD cycle, providing valuable insights from captured documents.

At two points in the F3EAD cycle—exploit and analyze—analysts played key roles in the fight against AQI. In the exploit phase, working side by side with operators, analysts examined, assessed, and processed captured members of enemy networks as well as their computers, cell phones, and other materials, in a real-time context, to identify follow-on targets that often were tackled immediately. An array of specialists at TF 714's headquarters at Balad constituted an "exploitation system," explained the former senior intelligence officer cited earlier, "that was ready for interrogation of captured personnel and for documents and device exploitation."[154] They could quickly identify and triangulate important pieces of information about AQI personnel and activities found in those communication devices, documents, and other materials collected by teams during night raids.

Sometimes what they found identified a new target that would be quickly fixed in time and space to watch, and they would become "intimately familiar with the target's habits and characteristics to the degree that they could easily recognize something unusual and in some cases even detect a visual signature of how the target walked, traveled in groups, or engaged other people."[155] This familiarity often resulted in greater understanding of the place of that individual in a particular network, other members of it, and operational patterns of behavior. At other times, explained the former senior intelligence officer, TF 714 would go straight to the finish phase and "strike because of the danger [the targets] pose" or "because of their potential intelligence value."[156]

Intelligence derived during the exploit phase was integrated into databases so that, explained McChrystal, it could be "studied to better know our enemy and identify opportunities to further attack its networks."[157] This was the goal of the analyze phase of the F3EAD cycle. Here, intelligence specialists seconded to the JIATF focused on deeper examination and exploration, with the goal of representing in a graphic or visual presentation an AQI network in a particular part of Iraq at a particular point in time. Those networks were not orderly, centralized, or hierarchical. Rather, they were decentralized, chaotic, and widely dispersed. They had no single command center or leader. Their members used technology effectively and often had an array of military and other skills.

Still, there were critical nodes within the networks that analysts were constructing. Those nodes were midlevel commanders and managers who had the authority and the capacity to maintain and even escalate AQI's operations. They were a network's center of gravity. They managed and led a wide array of planning and decision-making mechanisms, operational detachments, financial units, communication and media centers, intelligence branches, bomb and IED production facilities, and arms acquisition systems. It was those midlevel leaders and managers who made a network tick. Finding and understanding them was a major analytic challenge.

The goal of analysts working at this stage of the cycle was to discover who these midlevel members were and to determine their role and function in the schemata of a particular AQI network. By doing so, the analysts enabled TF 714's raiding teams to execute operations inside that part of the enemy apparatus. The analysts identified the inner workings of a network, how its units behaved, the connectivity between its members, the degree to which key nodes operated autonomously, where the leadership resided, and how leadership was distributed among members.

In effect, TF 714 was attacking from the inside out. Seeing a network represented on a geospatial graphic display allowed those selecting targets to focus on more important individual actors or nodes and on disrupting the connections or links between them. McChrystal referred to them as "the guts of AQI. I said we will claw the guts out of AQI, and it will collapse."[158] He summarized the process as follows: "The way we dealt with a particular part of their network, once we identified it, was to dominate its operational tempo, to pummel it constantly through raids against it, to drive it down, and make it collapse in upon itself."[159]

To provide this kind of understanding, analysts made use of the new analytic tool kit described above. They employed analytic and automated tools to gain an operational-level understanding of those insurgent and terrorist groups they were fighting. New tools were continually developed, and analysts utilized them to uncover those networks.

TF 714 was in the forefront of both fostering these developments and employing them in the fight against AQI. Their operators and analysts, working together, conducted link and network analysis of conditioned and fused data to identify people, places, and things of interest and the linkages or relationships between them. Once they had been geospatially located, those people's activities were monitored to learn more about the network to which they belonged. The task force, explained a former senior member, became better and better at assessing data and conducting geospatial analysis due to the availability of increasingly effective tools developed by both the government and the commercial sector. However, he added, "what made it work was ops-intel collaboration, that marriage of intelligence and operations." These tools "made our analysis more effective, allowing us to understand AQI networks, who was important in them, who the leaders were, who the specialists were with different skills. This allowed us to have a disruptive effect on their networks. We were able to get inside their cycle and prevent them from doing operations."[160]

Finally, the use of analytic and automated tools provided TF 714 with the capacity to discover and diagram AQI's organizational patterns. At first, it could not do so. This became apparent, recalled the chief of TF 714, when the task force tried in 2004 to portray AQI on a standard map and draw it up on a whiteboard at the Balad headquarters. AQI was not hierarchical or orderly. There was little consistency to its operational behavior. AQI was "fundamentally different from anything we had seen in the past," McChrystal explained. However, eventually, by using the methods and tools described in this chapter, the task force was able to gain an understanding of AQI as "tangled networks that did not resemble any organizational structure or pattern we had ever seen."[161] The picture that emerged was of a complex, adapting system. "We intuitively knew that the day we had that kind of knowledge on AQI . . . it would be over," concluded TF 714's commanding general, "because any time we knew where they were and who they were, we could capture or kill them quickly."[162] Analysts, employing the methods and tools described here, provided TF 714 operators with that knowledge, and the results were as McChrystal described.

From 2006 to 2009, the task force maintained an operational tempo of three hundred raids a month against AQI's networks in Iraq through the intelligence-operations methods described in this chapter. TF 714's commander noted that as this period progressed, the unit was "able to map out different parts of their networks, what they were involved in, who was involved, and how they were linked together."[163] In effect, the task force had developed the capacity to operate inside AQI's networks. By doing so, as the next chapter delineates, TF 714 was able to dismantle AQI's networks to the degree that they could no longer function in a cohesive manner.

CHAPTER 5

TRANSFORMING COVERT PARAMILITARY OPERATIONS FOR IRREGULAR WAR

THE USE OF COVERT OPERATIONS BY AMERICAN PRESIDENTS has been a contentious issue since the late 1970s, when the Senate convened hearings to investigate the activities of the CIA and other intelligence agencies. During that "season of inquiry," as one scholar termed it, the CIA's covert action programs were on full display for public scrutiny.[1] Those revelations generated considerable debate over whether the United States should engage in covert operations at all. As a result, by the end of the 1970s, Washington's covert action capabilities were reduced considerably, leading one former chief of the CIA's Covert Action Staff to lament that "covert action . . . showed all the earmarks of a dying art-form."[2]

However, as this chapter will describe, the attacks of 9/11 moved covert operations from the wings to center stage, especially with respect to covert paramilitary operations carried out by the secretive counterterrorism units of US Special Operations Command. Recall Operation Neptune Spear, mentioned in chapter 3. On April 29, 2011, President Obama authorized a top-secret night raid by elite counterterrorism forces targeted on a compound suspected of housing Osama bin Laden. The residence was located in Abbottabad, sixty-eight miles north of the Pakistani capital, Islamabad. The raiding party took off from eastern Afghanistan, 160 miles west of Abbottabad. The outcome of that operation was sensationalized in the 2012 movie *Zero Dark Thirty*.

But what happened on that night raid in Abbottabad was standard operating procedure for the US military's counterterrorism forces in the Iraq War. They carried out, each month from 2006 to the end of 2009, hundreds of those types of operations—paramilitary night raids—from the shadows against AQI.

Those counterterrorism forces became the tip of the spear in the post-9/11 irregular wars fought by the United States against al-Qaeda, its associated movements, and its Islamic State of Iraq and Syria (ISIS) progeny. The effort constituted a major change in the use of secret paramilitary operations. It also signified a dramatic shift in the roles and missions of those counterterrorism forces tasked with serving as a key weapon system for fighting armed groups. They transformed from pre-9/11 highly specialized and compartmentalized units designed for executing infrequent peacetime counterterrorism missions such as hostage rescue to an organization capable of a wartime operational tempo of hundreds of strikes a month.

This transformation did not occur without controversy. US covert operations during the Cold War generated great debates and disagreements. Should a democracy employ such means? If so, under what conditions and to what extent? Such questions became highly charged public policy issues beginning in the later 1970s. In the post–Cold War 1990s, even more serious reservations were raised about covert operations as an instrument of statecraft. They were viewed as very risky, with more failures than successes, and out of step with democratic values. Those opposed to covert action equated it with morally dubious activities that should be shunned by the United States.[3]

However, 9/11 changed the terms of reference with respect to covert operations because, after those attacks, the United States was at war. That shift from peacetime to wartime had a profound impact on the use of covert operations, specifically their paramilitary variant, which was elevated to a major weapon system for fighting extremists. The military's secret counterterrorism units experienced a meteoric rise in prominence.

This chapter focuses on that transition in the use of covert operations from peacetime to wartime and what it entailed. The chapter examines three security contexts. Those milieus—Cold War, post–Cold War, and post-9/11—differed considerably in terms of how US presidents employed covert operations and how legal and operational architectures were fashioned to oversee and constrain the use of covert operations. The first two are examined as a prelude for assessing the role of covert paramilitary operations in a very different milieu, that of post-9/11 irregular war and the fight against AQI. In examining this transition from peacetime to wartime, the chapter focuses on how counterterrorism forces, highly compartmentalized units designed to execute infrequent special operations missions before 9/11, transformed during the Iraq War.

In conjunction with this operational assessment, the chapter also examines how the oversight architecture for employing covert operations, constructed prior to 9/11, was adapted for a security context that was different from the peacetime milieu for which it was originally established.[4] However, before turning to these matters, a brief description of covert operations and their subdisciplines is necessary.

Definition and Subdisciplines of Covert Action

Roy Godson contends that covert action is "an American term-of-art that came into use after World War II."[5] However, when exactly it began to be used to give precise meaning to an array of secret activities is not clear. Godson also notes that "other states do not use the term" but seek to achieve the same effects: "influencing events in another state or territory without revealing its own involvement."[6]

William Daugherty, a former intelligence officer turned academic, concurs: "In simplest terms covert action is about influence. It is . . . intended to influence a target audience to do something or refrain from doing something." He adds that these operations may "take place in peacetime, between peace and hostilities . . . or in actual war."[7] As recounted in this chapter, prior to 9/11, US post–World War II covert operations took place in a nominally peacetime context that gave specific meaning to what constituted "influence" and how it was pursued covertly.

During the 1990s, the very applicability of covert action as a tool of statecraft was open to question, as serious reservations were raised about its relevance now that the Cold War was over. While the US Congress did not go so far as to end the use of covert action, it did seek through law and oversight to tighten the constraints on when and how covert action could be employed by presidents. This approach was codified in the Intelligence Authorization Act for fiscal year 1991, which defines covert action as "an activity or activities of the United States Government to influence political, economic, or military conditions abroad, where it is intended that the role of the United States Government will not be apparent or acknowledged publicly, but does not include . . . activities the primary purpose of which is to acquire intelligence, traditional counterintelligence activities, . . . traditional diplomatic or military activities or routine support to such activities."[8]

This legal definition describes what a covert action program initiated by a US president intends to accomplish. It also differentiates covert action from other government activities. The act establishes congressional oversight procedures and presidential reporting requirements. However, nowhere does the act identify different covert action tactics, techniques, and procedures.

Scholars of intelligence have divided covert action into specific types of operations. For Godson, they include "propaganda, political action, paramilitary operations, and intelligence assistance."[9] Daugherty concurs with the first three, which he calls the "traditional methods" of covert action. He adds that Information Age technologies will offer new covert action opportunities "for the imaginative intelligence professional."[10] Below, the traditional methods of covert action—political action, propaganda, and paramilitary operations—are briefly described.

Secret Political Action

Perhaps the most diverse subdiscipline of covert action is political action. Godson describes it as employing "political means to influence foreign events."[11] The overall goal, writes Mark Lowenthal, is "to help friends or to impede foes."[12] One often-cited example of the former is British use of a veiled political action campaign to influence President Woodrow Wilson to enter World War I to help turn the tide against Germany. To achieve this objective, the chief British intelligence officer in the United States positioned himself to become a close confidant of the president. While Wilson was aware of British efforts, they were kept secret from other parts of the American government.[13]

When political action aims at influencing policies of an adversarial government, the operational approach is different. A case in point is Soviet attempts, as World War II neared its end, to secretly manipulate Washington to support a postwar policy to keep Germany deindustrialized. To accomplish this, Moscow directed a key member of the Roosevelt administration, Harry Dexter White at the Department of the Treasury, whom Soviet intelligence had recruited, to promote this policy within the upper reaches of FDR's administration.[14]

Covert political action programs may support nongovernmental bodies in friendly or adversarial states as well. These include political parties, labor unions, ethnic or religious groups, civic associations, and social movements. One reason this support is provided secretly is that actors taking such advice or material assistance are politically vulnerable. Their acceptance of foreign assistance can be used against them in the rough-and-tumble of domestic politics. During the 1950s and 1960s, the United States funneled money and advice to political parties in foreign countries to help them win elections and then foster US interests. For example, "a program supporting Japan's rightist Liberal Democratic Party . . . played a fundamental role in U.S. policy toward Japan."[15]

Secret assistance to labor unions also took place in post–World War II Europe. Beginning in the late 1940s, Moscow sought to gain control over labor movements in several European countries. To counter this effort, the CIA worked through American unions to assist their counterparts in Western Europe. By the 1980s, the United States also supported labor organizations inside Soviet-dominated Eastern Europe, most notably Solidarity in Poland.[16] As these examples illustrate, the targets of political action programs include an array of state and nonstate actors.

Covert Propaganda

Propaganda constitutes "any technique or action that attempts to influence . . . attitudes or behavior of a group, in order to benefit the sponsor. It is usually . . . concerned with public opinion and mass attitudes. The purpose is to persuade—either to change or reinforce existing attitudes."[17] Throughout the twentieth century, nations openly sought to sway opinion in other countries through a variety of tools, including "official government pronouncements, books, magazines, radio and television broadcasts."[18] The Information Age expanded this capacity.

Propaganda conducted covertly can take two forms—gray or black. In each case, the source of the information seeks anonymity. Godson differentiates gray from black in terms of the degree of concealment: "Covert propaganda can be black (well hidden) or gray (disseminated with a thin veil)." He adds that the rationale for secrecy is that "the sponsor may judge that anonymous propaganda is more effective, or that at worst it can be disowned."[19] The information communicated in covert propaganda, like its overt counterpart, can be accurate, fabricated, or somewhere in between.

Consider the use of radio broadcasts. During the Vietnam War, a secret unit under the US military command in South Vietnam that was running a large covert action program against North Vietnam created an imaginary resistance movement known as the Sacred Sword of the Patriots League. It was said to comprise men from the north who had fought first against the French and then the Americans but who were now disillusioned with communist rule and were forming a secret organization to fight against it. A radio station was established to broadcast messages from "liberated territory" in the southern part of North Vietnam.[20]

During the Cold War, the Soviet Union also carried out propaganda campaigns through international front groups posing as autonomous entities.[21] One example was the World Peace Council (WPC). Individuals aligned with the USSR dominated its leadership. Among the WPC's primary missions was to organize international symposia, conferences, demonstrations, and related activities to call for a "halt to American nuclear weapons production and deployment, particularly in Western Europe."[22] For informed observers, the Soviet role was understood. For many political activists, this was not the case.

The architect of black propaganda "goes to extraordinary lengths to cover his tracks, making it difficult . . . to identify him with a particular project." For example, black propagandists may use "a secretly controlled journalist to write" a story that attacks a policy or member of an enemy government.[23] Once in print, the article is circulated to begin a chain reaction. Daugherty recounts the claim that the United States created HIV as a biological warfare weapon. The accusation was first published "in India in a pro-Soviet newspaper." The KGB then helped spread the story globally. It "endured for more than four years."[24]

Paramilitary Operations

Covert paramilitary operations can include secret assistance to resistance and guerrilla movements. For Abram Shulsky, this entails extending support to "groups that seek either to influence a government's policy through violent means or to overthrow it."[25] During the Cold War, the Soviet Union assisted a number of armed groups it termed "national liberation movements."[26] The United States, during the Reagan administration, supported resistance struggles being fought by the Afghan Mujahideen and the Nicaraguan Contras.[27]

States have also afforded covert paramilitary assistance to groups that employ terrorism as their principal way of using force. Beginning in the 1970s, sponsorship of international terrorism became a favored tool for a number of states, including Iran, Libya, Syria, and Iraq. That assistance ranged from offering training and a haven to providing money, weapons, communication equipment, intelligence, and other operational enablers.[28]

States have fostered coups and carried out assassinations through covert paramilitary means. During the Cold War, the United States did both. As with the other options in the paramilitary tool kit, however, coups and assassinations were less commonly employed than secret political action and covert propaganda.

A final category of paramilitary operations involves US special operations forces or their CIA counterparts in direct-action operations conducted on a secret basis. These operations can include stand-alone missions such as hostage rescue. They can also take the form of a covert paramilitary campaign to target and dismantle the secret underground apparatus or command-and-control system of an armed group. According to William Rosenau and Austin Long, the goal of such "anti-infrastructure operations" is to dismantle the "subterranean 'ecosystems' that sustain insurgencies" through "intelligence coordination and the integration of intelligence with an action arm."[29] Only through such a dedicated effort is it possible to dismantle "the inner workings . . . of the largely invisible structures that sustain armed insurgent opposition."[30]

During the Cold War, those invisible insurgent structures were largely hierarchical, so anti-infrastructure operations aimed at removing their upper-echelon leaders. Eliminating these key figures had a significant impact on insurgencies such as those waged by the FARC, Peru's Shining Path, the Kurdistan Worker's Party, and the Irish Republican Army, all of them hierarchical organizations. Removing leaders undermined esprit de corps and caused organizational fragmentation. To varying degrees, each armed group was demoralized by such anti-infrastructure operations.[31]

US Covert Operations during the Cold War

The tools employed by presidents to manage violent threats, including covert action, must be tailored to the prevailing context. An important consideration is whether it is wartime or peacetime, and, if it is the latter, what kind of peace exists. As noted above, the US use of covert action since World War II can be divided into three periods. The first two—the Cold War and the post–Cold War 1990s—were variations of peacetime, although there were important differences between them. This can be illustrated by highlighting how US presidents employed covert action in each period and how that presidential use of covert action was increasingly constrained by a legal and oversight architecture enacted by Congress.

Policy and Programs: Political Action Leads the Way, 1947–75

The 1976 final report of the Senate Select Committee to Study Governmental Operations with Respect to Intelligence (hereafter, the Church Committee) observed that "no activity of the Central Intelligence Agency has engendered more controversy and concern than covert action."[32] There were several reasons for this notoriety, including the Church Committee itself, which focused on "major covert action programs" from the late 1940s to the mid-1970s.[33] These included plots to assassinate Fidel Castro, coups in Iran and Guatemala, the Bay of Pigs invasion of Cuba, and paramilitary campaigns in Laos and North Vietnam.[34] But focusing on paramilitary operations gives the impression that the CIA was following in the footsteps of its OSS predecessor, which conducted a substantial program of clandestine subversive and paramilitary operations during World War II.[35] The CIA's post–World War II covert operations were not a replica of the OSS's operations.

The operational focus of the CIA's covert action programs through the first three decades of the Cold War was not paramilitary action. The Church Committee itself noted that its "findings on paramilitary activities suggest that these operations are an anomaly, if not an aberration." Nevertheless, the committee asserted that there were good reasons for focusing on paramilitary operations because they were "among the most costly and controversial forms of covert action."[36]

However, the report noted that for the period scrutinized, of the "900 major or sensitive covert action projects, in addition to thousands of smaller ones," most consisted "of propaganda and political action."[37] Moreover, the initiation of covert operations following World War II was the result of crises generated by Soviet clandestine support to communist parties, unions, and others seeking to come to power through elections. To prevent such electoral victories, Washington turned to covert political action.[38]

The initial focal point was the 1948 Italian election. An Italian Communist Party victory was in the offing, as Moscow poured in secret assistance to help it win. To prevent this outcome, the CIA initiated a covert action program aimed at providing secret financial assistance and advice to noncommunist political parties. The effort was successful and served as a template for the Cold War.[39] Similar political action programs were initiated elsewhere in Europe to help democratic parties turn aside Soviet subversion.[40]

In 1950, National Security Council Directive 68 (NSC-68) set out a road map for the containment of the Soviet Union. The directive's characterization of the USSR reflected George Kennan's depiction of Moscow as ruthless and expansionist.[41] Kennan and NSC-68 were in agreement that an important tool for checking Soviet actions was political warfare fought, in part, through covert political action.[42]

Washington's view of the Soviet threat intensified with the Korean War. The threat was now global. In response, the CIA was directed to "expand its European approach into a worldwide effort to anticipate and meet communist aggression."[43] The passage below captures the scope of this expanded covert action program:

> By 1953, there were major covert operations in 48 countries, consisting primarily of propaganda and political action. . . . The 1950s saw an expansion of Communist interest in the Third World. Attempts to anticipate and meet the Communist threat there proved to be an easier task than carrying out clandestine activities in the closed Soviet and Chinese societies. Political action projects in the Third World increased dramatically. Financial support was provided to parties, candidates, and incumbent leaders of almost every political persuasion. The immediate purpose of these projects was to encourage political stability, and thus prevent Communist incursions; but another important objective of political action was the acquisition of "agents of influence" who could be used at a future date to provide intelligence or to carry out political action. Through such projects, the CIA developed a worldwide infrastructure of individual agents, or networks of agents, engaged in a variety of covert activities. . . . Using the covert action budget as one measure of activity, the scope of political and psychological action during the 1950s was greatest in the Far East, Western Europe, and the Middle East, with steadily increasing activity in the Western Hemisphere.

The international labor, student, and media projects of the International Organizations Division constituted the greatest single concentration of covert political and propaganda activities. [44]

The expansion of covert political action programs to the developing world continued under the Eisenhower administration as part of "larger policies aimed at preventing the spread of communist rule and influence."[45] The rationale for an enduring program of covert political action, noted Daugherty, was twofold. First, it was to counter the "most significant Soviet threat [which] came not from general war but from Soviet subversive measures." Second, it was to employ the most "cost effective tools" to implement US policies.[46] In doing so, while democratic forces were preferable, and while the CIA sought to assist liberal and even left-wing elements, nevertheless, as Richard Best observes, "American interests were often seen as requiring cooperation with authoritarian regimes."[47]

The Eisenhower administration's use of covert action crossed a major threshold to encompass those "costly and controversial" paramilitary operations highlighted by the Church Committee, most notably coups in Iran and Guatemala. Each coup removed leaders seen as threats to American interests.[48] Paramilitary operations during the Eisenhower years also included Operation Zapata, the plan to overthrow the Castro regime.[49] The Kennedy administration also instituted a full array of covert action programs. According to a senior member of that administration, the president "took a great deal of interest" in those activities and "approved around 550 . . . political action, propaganda, and paramilitary operations."[50]

To manage these efforts, the White House established two "special groups" at the National Security Council. One was to oversee the CIA's long-standing political action operations to counter Soviet subversion. According to the Church Committee report, the Kennedy administration "mounted an increasing number of political, propaganda, and economic projects." Expenditures for these projects during the early 1960s "increased by almost 60 percent."[51] The other special group oversaw paramilitary programs in northern Laos and North Vietnam. With respect to the former, the objective was to employ guerrilla operations against North Vietnamese and Pathet Lao forces to prevent Hanoi from taking control of northern Laos.[52] Against Hanoi, the Kennedy administration "wanted guerrillas to operate in the North" and initiated a campaign of covert paramilitary operations that turned into one of the largest of its kind during the Cold War.[53]

A final major paramilitary operation in the 1960s, also in Vietnam, was the controversial Phoenix Program. Undertaken by the CIA, the mission was to employ paramilitary raids to dismantle the clandestine infrastructure of the Viet Cong. Rosenau and Long note that Phoenix provoked extreme views; some saw it as "a massive assassination campaign."[54] Its defenders argued that the Phoenix Program was successful but that its achievements were squandered when the United States withdrew from Vietnam.[55] Whatever the judgment on the Phoenix Program, counterinfrastructure programs in general were deemed a critical component of counterinsurgency theory and practice.[56]

The period from the later 1960s through the mid-1970s began a downturn in covert operation programs. The Church Committee reported a "decline in every functional and geographic category of covert action except for paramilitary operations in the Far East which did not stop until 1973," with the US withdrawal from Vietnam.[57] Several factors contributed to this decline, among them congressional investigations. Also important was the Carter administration's "threshold doctrine," which limited the use of covert action to "extreme circumstances, when absolutely necessary."[58] However, once the administration was under way, the White House found itself turning to covert action to support dissidents in the Soviet Union and to assist the Afghan mujahideen resisting the Soviet invasion. Covert aid also went to those opposing the Sandinista revolution in Nicaragua.[59]

Three issues having to do with covert action played out during the last decade of the Cold War. First, the downturn in covert action programs was reversed under the Reagan administration. Second, as an outgrowth of the 1975–76 congressional investigations of US intelligence, the newly established intelligence committees spent a decade seeking to establish an architecture for intelligence oversight that checked presidential use of covert action. Third, a small number of experts in special operations began arguing that nonstate threats were emerging that necessitated the development of paramilitary capabilities to manage those challenges.

Covert Action Redux: The Reagan Years

During the 1980s, the Reagan administration employed the full range of covert action tools. For example, in 1982, propaganda and political action programs were targeted at the Soviet bloc states of Eastern Europe. The goal was to weaken Moscow's control by assisting opposition elements. Consider Poland: assistance to the trade union Solidarity was provided after it was forced to go underground.[60]

In Afghanistan, paramilitary assistance to the mujahideen resistance fighting Soviet military occupation grew steadily, particularly in terms of providing sophisticated weapons. These included the FIM-92 Stinger, a shoulder-fired antiaircraft missile that leveled the playing field for the resistance against Soviet attack aircraft, especially helicopter gunships.[61] The covert paramilitary program grew from $100 million in 1981 to $700 million in 1988.[62]

While there was executive-legislative consensus over the Afghanistan program, Nicaragua generated intense discord. In 1981, the Reagan administration began providing secret military assistance to a rapidly growing armed resistance known as the Contras. Many of the Contras' early members were from the National Guard forces of the former regime of Anastasio Somoza. Members of Congress condemned the Contras for human rights abuses. This executive-legislative discord was stoked by the disclosure in 1984 that the Reagan administration had mined Nicaraguan ports to further pressure the Sandinista government. As congressional opposition hardened, legislative efforts were made to constrain the covert action program.[63]

In the midst of this wrangling, the Reagan administration sought alternative funding through another covert operation that involved the secret sale of weapons and spare parts to the Iranian government, which was at war with Iraq. In return, the White House sought Iranian help in obtaining the release of American hostages being held by Tehran's surrogates in Lebanon. The link to the Contras came from profits made from the sale of those weapons and spare parts. Apparently they were sold to the Iranians at an inflated price, and the profits went to the Contras. A congressional investigation was launched to determine the extent of the subterfuge and what steps could be taken to strengthen the oversight architecture to prevent further such chicanery.

Revising and Expanding Congressional Oversight

Over the next five years, Congress and the president sparred over changes in congressional authority to monitor the president's use of covert action as established by the Intelligence Oversight Act of 1980.[64] In 1990, the Senate Select Committee on Intelligence proposed a notification process that defined covert action as "[any] activity that satisfied [the following] three conditions." First, "it must be conducted by an element of the U.S. government." Second, "it must be meant to influence political, economic, or military conditions abroad." And third, "the role of the U.S. Government in sponsoring the activity must not be intended to be apparent or acknowledged publicly."[65]

The proposed bill also identified activities that did not constitute covert action. These included "intelligence collection, traditional military activities, and routine support to traditional military activities." However, as Robert Chesney notes, the "SSCI did not . . . define these [exclusionary] categories in the statutory text itself. Rather, the idea was to explain their intended meaning in the accompanying committee report."[66]

Reagan's successor, President George H. W. Bush, demurred over what constituted traditional military activities. The proposed TMA exemptions from the covert-action definition, described in detail in the committee report, were too sweeping, as Chesney notes:

> SSCI explained that it intended that TMA "encompass almost *every* use of uniformed military forces," including not only "actions taken in time of declared war or where hostilities with other countries are imminent or ongoing," but also low-intensity scenarios . . . such as "operations to rescue U.S. hostages held captive in foreign countries, to accomplish other counterterrorist objectives (i.e. the extraterritorial apprehension of a known terrorist), or military actions in support of counternarcotics operations in other countries." . . . The report went on to make clear that SSCI assumed that U.S. government responsibility "would be apparent or acknowledged at the time of the military operation." When that was not the case—i.e., when "military elements *not* identifiable to the United States [are] used to carry out an operation abroad without ever being acknowledged by the United States"—the operation would not constitute TMA.[67]

In effect, the report proposed that initially undetected low-intensity military operations would fall within the TMA category. The exemption did not work, as the definition of covert action already excluded operations in which the US role could eventually be acknowledged.[68] When this definition was included in the proposed bill, President Bush vetoed it and executive-congressional sparring continued over what constituted unacknowledged TMA.

A compromise was eventually reached by which an "unacknowledged military operation" could qualify as TMA if it was "commanded and executed by military personnel" and "took place in a context in which overt hostilities either were (a) ongoing, or (b) anticipated (meaning approval has been given by the National Command Authorities . . . for operational planning for hostilities)."[69]

In sum, unacknowledged TMA, including counterterrorism and other contingency operations were not covert operations if they met these requirements. This was, Chesney concludes, because the president or secretary of defense approved the operation. Therefore, an "unacknowledged military operation [was] covered by this part of the TMA exemption [and] thus would not have to be reported to SSCI and House Permanent Select Committee on Intelligence (HPSCI) or supported by a covert action finding."[70]

The White House ultimately agreed and signed the Intelligence Authorization Act. It had taken a decade, but an agreed-on architecture for congressional oversight of executive branch use of covert action within the context of the Cold War became the law on August 14, 1991.[71] Four months later, Gorbachev resigned and the Soviet Union dissolved. The Cold War was over.

Emerging Nonstate Threats

During the 1980s, a small number of US military professionals and civilian security analysts contended that the international conflict environment was changing with the emergence of nonstate threats. They argued that the United States was not prepared for these violent challenges. Two variants of what at the time was termed "low-intensity conflict" were of particular concern: revolutionary and guerrilla insurgency and international terrorism.[72]

The most senior officer making this argument was the army chief of staff, Gen. Edward Meyer. In her study *Unconventional Warfare*, Susan Marquis notes, "By the mid-1970s it was clear to Meyer that the US defense establishment's single-minded emphasis on the Soviets striking through the Fulda Gap was far removed from the actual world security environment."[73] He asserted that unconventional threats, including international terrorism, were on the rise and that the United States needed to develop new capabilities to respond effectively. Meyer called "for the military to expand its capacity to fight in the shadows—above all through Special Operations Forces."[74] He "conceived of a new organization that would reach beyond the army and bring the counterterrorist forces of each of the military services together in a joint permanent Task Force."[75] No such organization existed at this time.

In the late 1970s, the US Army did establish a counterterrorism unit in response to a rising number of international terrorist incidents. That unit deployed as a part of a mission to rescue US diplomats taken hostage in the US embassy in Tehran in 1979. Designated Operation Eagle Claw, the plan was to covertly enter Iran and free the hostages. The mission, launched in April 1980, had to be aborted due to several problems that turned into a tragedy when, as the forces prepared to leave their forward desert base inside Iran, one of the helicopters collided with a transport aircraft, resulting in the destruction of both aircraft and the deaths of eight servicemen.[76]

The failed mission served as a catalyst for Secretary of Defense Harold Brown to authorize the formation of a counterterrorism joint task force consisting of special operations units from each service. Once in office, the Reagan administration fostered the development of this new force for hostage rescue and direct-action counterterrorism missions. Finally, in April 1987, SOCOM was established. It is beyond the scope of this book to discuss that decision and how the command was organized and led.[77] However, it should be noted that among its subordinate elements was the counterterrorism joint task force, which was designated Joint Special Operations Command. During the later 1980s and the 1990s, JSOC developed an array of army, navy, and air force units for hostage rescue and direct-action missions.[78]

The Post–Cold War 1990s: Downsizing Covert Operations

In the post–Cold War 1990s, many reservations were raised about the value of retaining covert action as an instrument of statecraft. Covert action was increasingly viewed as a very risky enterprise, with more failures than successes and out of step with democratic principles. Those opposed to covert action equated it with morally dubious activities—dirty tricks and dirty wars—that should be eschewed. Others wondered why it was needed at all now that the Cold War was over.

Consider former senior policymakers such as Roger Hilsman, who in the Kennedy administration had played an important role in Vietnam War decision-making and who weighed in against covert action. With the end of the East-West struggle, Hilsman pondered in a *Foreign Affairs* article whether the CIA still had a role. Hilsman argued for a major scaling back of the agency in general, and he found no continuing relevance for covert action. It was, he believed, "overused as an instrument of foreign policy, and the reputation of the United States had suffered. . . . Covert political action is not only something the United States can do without in the post–Cold War world, it is something the United States could have done without during the Cold War as well."[79]

Other assessments were more circumspect about shutting down covert operations. The rationale for not doing so appears to have been the emergence of new threats posed not by states but by international terrorist and criminal groups. The security landscape was evolving away from how the United States had understood and managed security challenges since World War II. Covert action, for some, was a necessary tool to help manage these new challenges. This was true for former CIA director Robert Gates, who saw the need to preserve covert action capabilities but argued that paramilitary missions should become the responsibility of the Department of Defense. He proposed that the Pentagon be "given responsibility for paramilitary operations around the world, most of which in the past have been carried out as covert activities of the CIA."[80] The rationale for this transfer was the state-of-the-art development of JSOC's counterterrorism forces.

In the midst of this public debate, the Clinton administration initiated a program to downsize the IC, including the CIA. The Cold War was over, and there was no need—or so the administration thought—to devote the same amount of resources to intelligence. However, Daugherty notes that while the administration was "intrinsically hostile to covert action," it retained "three transnational covert action programs . . . counter-narcotics, counterterrorism, and operations to . . . thwart weapons proliferation programs." By the mid-1990s, the administration had "added to each of these programs."[81]

This was particularly the case with "the counterterrorism program [which] grew in response to . . . Presidential Decision Directive (PDD) 39."[82] A reading of that directive suggests that the administration had come to regard terrorism as a serious "threat to national security as well as a criminal act." And it intended to "apply all appropriate means to combat it."[83] Three years later, another directive—PDD 62—declared that "offensive measures" would be used against foreign terrorists posing a threat to America.[84]

These directives, explained Richard Clarke, who chaired the National Security Council's Counterterrorism and Security Group during the Clinton administration, "led to the planning of several counterterrorism operations," which he described as providing the White House with more aggressive options, to be carried out by special operations forces.[85] "Snatch operations in Afghanistan were planned to seize bin Laden and his senior lieutenants." After al-Qaeda operatives carried out attacks on US embassies in Kenya and Tanzania, "options for killing bin Laden were entertained, including a gunship assault on his compound in Afghanistan. SOF assaults on al Qaeda's Afghan training camps were planned. . . . And preemptive strikes against al Qaeda cells outside Afghanistan were also planned in North Africa and the Arabian Gulf."[86] But none of those operations were ever carried out.

The following self-imposed restraints prevented those missions from being executed, even as al-Qaeda escalated its attacks.[87] First, during the Clinton presidency, al-Qaeda was not considered a clear and present danger, and its attacks did not rise to the level of war. The former commander of SOCOM in the mid-1990s, Gen. Wayne Downing, explained in a 2002 interview that when he was in command of SOCOM, he stressed that al-Qaeda was "using terrorism as an asymmetrical weapon with which to attack. . . . It was war, he told the Pentagon's senior leadership. But no one wanted to address terrorism as war." And even after "bin Laden declared war on America in a 1996 fatwa, and bombed U.S. embassies . . . the Pentagon still resisted calling terrorism war."[88] The CIA likewise did not consider the fatwa a declaration of war, because only nation-states could declare war. Al-Qaeda's declaration "was only propaganda."[89]

Rather than seeing it as war, the administration regarded terrorism as a crime and terrorists as criminals. "Criminalization" was a second self-imposed restraint, explained Gen. Peter Schoomaker, SOCOM commander from 1997 to 2000. This "had a profound impact on the Pentagon," he explained. Terrorism was "not up to the standard of our definition of war, and not worthy of our attention." Consequently, "Defense Department tools were off the table."[90] The central tool for combating terrorism was not the military. It lacked the statutory authority. So, "whenever the White House proposed using SOF," it was told "the Pentagon lacked authority."[91]

Related to this second restraint was another legal issue. Under the US Code of Federal Regulations, Title 10 outlines the statutory authorities of the armed forces. During the 1990s, DOD lawyers argued that the military did not have the legal authorization to carry out covert paramilitary attacks against al-Qaeda targets under Title 10. That mission was exclusively the CIA's under Title 50. However, it is not the case that only the CIA has that authority. Title 50 leaves it to the president to choose which agency or department to entrust with paramilitary missions. The Pentagon is one option. But at the time, as a former senior DOD official explained, the Pentagon "took the position that it lacked the authority because it did not want the authority."[92] DOD leaders were skeptical about SOF missions, which they saw as very risky. Walter Slocombe, who served as President Clinton's undersecretary of defense for policy, explained, "We certainly looked at . . . the possible use of SOF." But options that put people on the ground to attack al-Qaeda targets were seen as "much too hard. It was much less risky to fire off cruise missiles."[93]

A final obstacle thwarting the use of SOCOM's counterterrorism force was the intimidation of civilian advocates of such operations by senior military officers. A former Pentagon official explained how generals subdued civilian enthusiasts by recounting a briefing on covert counterterrorism options given to the secretary of defense:

> The civilian, a political appointee with no military experience, says, "As your policy adviser, let me tell you what you need to do militarily in this situation." The JCS Chairman sits there, calmly listening. Then it is his turn. He begins by framing his sophisticated PowerPoint briefing in terms of the "experience factor," his own judgment, and those of his four-star associates. The "experience factor" infuses the presentation. Implicitly, it raises a question intended to discredit the civilian: "What makes you qualified? What makes you think that your opinion is more important than mine when you don't have the experience I have?" "Mr. Secretary," concludes the Chairman, "this is my best military advice."[94]

In such situations, the official said, "civilians were often dissuaded from taking on the generals." And in those instances when civilians pushed back, they were discredited as "cowboys."[95]

In the 1990s, the purveyors of "best military advice," when it came to countering terrorism, were always wary of the use of force, especially when it entailed SOF's paramilitary options. This was true even when President Clinton began asking about the applicability of those counterterrorism forces, as one former senior official recounted. "Those options were discussed, but never got anywhere. The Joint Staff would say, 'That's cowboy and Hollywood stuff.' The president was intimidated . . . [and] the White House took the 'stay away from SOF options' advice of the generals."[96]

To summarize, during the post–Cold War 1990s, grave reservations dominated the discourse over the value of covert action, including its paramilitary variant, as an instrument of statecraft. Many equated it with morally dubious activities that could involve the United States in dirty tricks and dirty wars. Such activities, they counseled, should be avoided. Even during the second Clinton administration, as US embassies in East Africa were bombed and the USS *Cole* nearly sank, the employment of SOCOM's counterterrorism forces to conduct covert paramilitary strikes against the perpetrators of those actions—al-Qaeda—was seen as ultra vires.

Post-9/11: Wartime and Covert Paramilitary Operations

The attack on 9/11 transformed how the United States viewed al-Qaeda and the conduct of war. Al-Qaeda now constituted a clear and present danger, and the fight against it rose to the level of war, as President Bush said on many occasions. But the nature of that war diverged from twentieth-century wars. Al-Qaeda was a different kind of antagonist—one that had demonstrated how it could bypass the superior military power of the United States to attack major targets within the American homeland. Moreover, measures based on Cold War strategic concepts of deterrence and containment were not sufficient to meet this new threat. Those measures were inherently defensive, said President Bush, and this "war will not be won on the defensive. We must take the battle to the enemy," he said, to "disrupt their plans, and confront the worst threats before they emerge. . . . Our security will require transforming the military . . . to strike at a moment's notice . . . to be ready for preemptive action."[97]

To fight this new enemy, the United States required new methods for warfighting that were different from those that had kept America secure during the Cold War. But what this meant for counterterrorism strategy and the employment of covert paramilitary operations was not immediately clear.

Operation Enduring Freedom: An Unconventional Warfare Campaign

Operation Enduring Freedom, initiated less than a month after the 9/11 attacks, was illustrative of this new form of warfare. To destroy al-Qaeda's sanctuary and overthrow the Taliban regime that provided refuge to bin Laden and his followers, the Bush administration chose to execute an unconventional warfare campaign.

The administration tasked the CIA and US Army Special Forces with assisting the Northern Alliance, an internal opposition movement made up of former Afghan government officials and tribal leaders, which was judged a viable resistance force with capable leaders. For unconventional warfare to be a feasible option, an indigenous armed group must exist and be capable of developing into an effective resistance. The Northern Alliance, which had been fighting the Taliban since 1996, met those requirements.

Unconventional warfare operations aim to gradually degrade the organizational cohesion and operational effectiveness of the armed forces of an opposing government through guerrilla operations. The DOD defines unconventional warfare thus: "Activities conducted to enable a resistance movement or insurgency to coerce, disrupt or overthrow a government or occupying power by operating through or with an underground or guerrilla force in a denied area."[98] Afghanistan was a denied area in 2001 in that it was under unfriendly control and US forces did not have access. However, by early October 2001, Uzbekistan, which borders Afghanistan, granted airspace clearance to the United States and provided US SOF with a base of operations from which to conduct operations inside Afghanistan.

A small number of special operations troops, supported by extensive US airpower, were assigned the mission of eliminating al-Qaeda's infrastructure and overthrowing the Taliban regime. They were mainly from the Fifth Special Forces Group, which is primarily responsible for operations within US Central Command's (CENTCOM's) area of responsibility. CENTCOM retains a regional expertise that encompasses the Middle East, the Persian Gulf, Central Asia, and the Horn of Africa. For Operation Iraqi Freedom, elements of the Fifth Special Forces Group were designated Joint Special Operations Task Force–North, or Task Force Dagger. Their mission was to coordinate with the Northern Alliance and help it shut down al-Qaeda's sanctuary and topple the Taliban regime.

Unconventional warfare operations in Afghanistan in the fall of 2001 were successful, dislodging both al-Qaeda and the Taliban within sixty days. This speedy victory was achieved by a special operations force of approximately 350 troops combined with considerable US airpower, CIA advisers, and an indigenous irregular force of fifteen thousand members of the Northern Alliance. In October 2001, another SOCOM force deployed to Afghanistan as part of Task Force Dagger. These troops were from JSOC. Designated Task Force Sword, they were to conduct direct-action attacks against al-Qaeda and Taliban high-value targets. Task Force Sword's first target was Mullah Mohammed Omar, the Taliban's leader. In a mission that lasted only a few hours, a force of fewer than one hundred operators raided Omar's residential compound on the outskirts of Kandahar. He was not there.[99]

By December, bin Laden and several hundred al-Qaeda members were cornered by Task Force Dagger in a network of fortified caves in the mountains of Tora Bora. Task Force Sword took part in that operation, which lasted until December 17, when the al-Qaeda leader and many of his followers escaped into Pakistan. CENTCOM's goals in Afghanistan were the toppling of the Taliban regime and the elimination of al-Qaeda's sanctuary. By the end of 2001, those objectives had been achieved, and the unconventional warfare campaign came to an end. US policy now focused on helping the new Afghan government, headed by Hamid Karzai, establish itself. A three- to five-year period of postconflict support was envisioned. As for Task Force Sword, it remained in Afghanistan, was renamed Task Force 11, and continued hunting for members of al-Qaeda hiding in the largely ungoverned Federally Administered Tribal Areas of northwestern Pakistan.[100]

However, Secretary of Defense Donald Rumsfeld had a more expansive mission in mind for JSOC. While al-Qaeda's central leadership was holed up Pakistan, it had affiliates and cells in many parts of the world and was capable of launching attacks against US targets in the American homeland and abroad. During the latter half of the 1990s, when al-Qaeda had a secure sanctuary in Afghanistan under the protection of the Taliban, al-Qaeda had evolved into a transnational organization. According to the *9/11 Commission Report*, "the Taliban seemed to open the door to all who wanted to come to Afghanistan to train in the [al-Qaeda] camps. The alliance with the Taliban provided al Qaeda a sanctuary in which to instruct and indoctrinate new fighters and terrorists, import weapons, forge ties with other Jihad groups and leaders [globally], and plot and staff terrorist schemes." The number of foreign fighters trained during that time was estimated to be between ten thousand and twenty thousand."[101] As a result, al-Qaeda established a global network of linkages with radical Islamist groups in various parts of the world.[102]

In 2002 and 2003, the DOD and IC learned much more about the extent of this network. For Secretary Rumsfeld, new attacks could come from any part of it. He worried that bin Laden could communicate with radical Islamist groups and inspire their operatives to attack through messages sent via couriers or over the Internet. As he expressed in a July 2002 memo to Undersecretary of Defense for Policy Douglas Feith titled "Manhunts," Rumsfeld wanted to know "how do we organize the Department of Defense for manhunts?" According to Robert Andrews, acting assistant secretary of defense for special operations at the time, Rumsfeld had "fastened on the manhunt thing; he looked at that as the silver bullet against terrorism."[103]

The secretary saw JSOC as ideally suited to execute direct-action manhunts worldwide against al-Qaeda and its affiliates. In another memo, dated July 22, 2003, Rumsfeld instructed Gen. Charles Holland, chief of SOCOM, to develop a plan to execute manhunts on a global scale.[104] This became a top priority, according to the JSOC commander at the time, Maj. Gen. Dell Dailey. The result was a new "secret directive," described as "the Al Qaeda Network Executive Order." It "expanded the power of special-operations troops," writes Mark Mazzetti, "to kill, capture, and spy in more than a dozen countries. The order gave [JSOC] . . . broad authority to launch operations across an arc of territory from North Africa all the way to the Philippines."[105] Rumsfeld saw JSOC as tailor-made for "preemptive actions." He pushed to give it the authority to attack al-Qaeda's global network, which was identified by US intelligence as having taken root in fifteen to twenty countries.

Direct-action raids are JSOC's strong suit, a core specialty. According to Joint Publication 3-05, *Special Operations*, they constitute "short-duration strikes . . . to seize, destroy, capture, exploit, recover, or damage designated targets in hostile, denied, or diplomatically and/or politically sensitive environments."[106] During the 1990s, JSOC conducted direct-action manhunts in Colombia, Somalia, and Bosnia. In each of these cases, the target was believed to be within the country. For example, in Colombia, JSOC engaged in the successful hunt for Pablo Escobar, the head of the Medellín drug cartel.[107] During the same period, JSOC forces sought unsuccessfully to capture the Somali warlord Mohammed Aideed.[108] And in Bosnia, they hunted for Ratko Mladić and his subordinates, who as members of the Army of Republika Srpska in the Bosnian War committed war crimes through a campaign of ethnic cleansing targeted against Muslim Bosniaks.[109]

An essential requirement for each of these manhunts was actionable intelligence, which is defined somewhat obliquely in the *Department of Defense Dictionary of Military and Associated Terms* as "intelligence information that is directly useful to customers for immediate exploitation without having to go through the full intelligence production process."[110] In other words, actionable intelligence is intelligence delivered with "speed, accuracy, and timeliness necessary to operate at the highest potential and conduct successful operations."[111] Collecting actionable intelligence, even against targets like those of the 1990s—which were searched for not across the globe but locally in Colombia, Somalia, and Bosnia—proved highly challenging. But when manhunts became a global enterprise, the intelligence challenges increased exponentially.

Operation Iraqi Freedom, the War after the War, and Task Force 714

In the early days of 2003, Washington began final planning for war in Iraq. For the JSOC commander at the time, General Dailey, this meant that in addition to figuring out how to conduct manhunts against al-Qaeda's global network, he now had to prepare his forces to support the US invasion. Deployed as Task Force 20, Dailey's force "was tasked with seizing key targets including airfields deep in Iraq, capturing high value targets, providing long range special reconnaissance, and searching for weapons of mass destruction." Although Task Force 20 gained notoriety when it rescued Pfc. Jessica Lynch, who had been captured when her convoy was ambushed in Nasiriyah, its role in the conventional fight in Iraq was ancillary.[112]

After Baghdad fell and the conventional war ended, Task Force 20 was assigned the manhunting mission of capturing high-level Baathist officials, notably Saddam Hussein and members of his Revolutionary Command Council. To identify them, the Pentagon produced a deck of playing cards, "an idea that dated as far back as the Civil War. . . . The cards were officially named the Personality Identification Playing Cards." Saddam Hussein was designated the Ace of Spades.[113] This was the kind of direct-action mission for which Task Force 20 was thoroughly prepared. And in July 2003, it cornered Saddam's sons Uday and Qusay in a raid in Mosul. Both died in the ensuing shootout.[114] Task Force 20 also participated in Operation Red Dawn, the capture of Saddam in December near his hometown of Tikrit.

In fall 2003, Maj. Gen. Stanley McChrystal became the new JSOC commander and deployed to Iraq. Shortly thereafter, Task Force 20 morphed into Task Force 714, and its mission underwent a radical change.[115] Washington was coming face to face with an "ugly surprise," a war after the war in Iraq—a war that had never been imagined by those who planned Operation Iraqi Freedom.[116] But mounting violence in the fall clearly indicated that an organized insurgency was burgeoning. Then, early in 2004, acts of insurgent violence began to rise precipitously, from two hundred per week in January to over six hundred by the summer months. During 2005, they climbed to over eight hundred,[117] and they almost doubled during 2006, rocketing to more than fourteen hundred per week.[118]

Escalating violence resulted in a new mission for TF 714. It now was directed to uncover and dismantle the secret underground apparatus of AQI that was orchestrating this escalating insurgency across Iraq. Given their counterterrorism and paramilitary specializations, secretive JSOC forces were seen as ideally suited for the assignment.

However, what TF 714 soon discovered was that AQI's clandestine underground apparatus was not like that found in yesterday's insurgencies. Its internal workings and organizational structure were considerably different from those of its twentieth-century counterparts. That realization would have a profound impact on TF 714's targeting strategy, necessitating a redefinition of what constituted an HVT. In the past, insurgencies were viewed as hierarchical organizations, and

HVTs were those in the very top echelon. Taking out a few key leaders significantly undermined the effectiveness of past insurgencies.[119]

But AQI's effectiveness was not determined by a small top echelon. The reason for this, TF 714 would soon learn, had to do with AQI's decentralized and networked structure. What made AQI effective was all those who commanded and managed its midlevel functional components.[120] It comprised a wide array of planning and decision-making mechanisms, operational detachments, financial units, communications and media centers, intelligence branches, bomb and IED production facilities, and arms acquisition entrepreneurs. It was those midlevel commanders and managers who had authority to keep up and escalate operations. They were the new HVTs, and there was a small army of them operating underground across Iraq. TF 714 found itself unprepared for this new mission.

TF 714 was going to war against an enemy that was different from any it had trained to confront in the peacetime environment of the 1990s. Then Colonel Michael Flynn, TF 714's intelligence chief beginning in the spring of 2004, characterized AQI as "a strategic surprise" for the task force because "the capability and scale of the threat it posed was far bigger than any we had ever previously thought about. . . . Clearly, the scale of the terrorist networks that existed in Iraq . . . and the scope of AQI's operations surprised us."[121] Others concurred. Lt. Gen. Bennet Sacolick, USA (Ret.), who commanded TF 714's army units, observed that "the capacity of the insurgency to escalate and to change and to reinvent itself was a big surprise."[122]

Surprise in war is a constant possibility. And modern militaries know it. Thus, they seek to develop know-how to respond to unforeseen challenges. At the tactical level, the operational units of TF 714 were prepared for surprise. They had learned roles, methods, and modes of behavior that primed them to adapt to the unexpected. But the surprise experienced in Iraq was not at the tactical level, and that would prove to be a major challenge for the organization as a whole.

TF 714's initial response was to double down and do more of what it already did extremely well. "The initial response," explained McChrystal, was that "we will just do more of what we are already very good at and then we would have done our part."[123] Maj. Gen. David J. Scott, USAF (Ret.), who from 2003 to 2006 served as one of TF 714's deputy commanders, saw this as resistance to change due to a culture predicated on a self-perception of excellence:

The CT [counterterrorism] force was based on a culture, and that culture was one that the members of the task force believed in. And this was a culture that developed over a long period of time. And so the culture was believed in, and doing more of the same but improving it, . . . refining the standard operating procedures of the CT force—that was the first choice. This was an organization that believed it was the best in the world, and so failure was not something that one expected. There was resistance to changing routines and standard operating procedures.[124]

What became evident to the task force's leadership, however, was that a "more of the same" response was not going to have any meaningful operational impact on AQI. To be sure, those operations that TF 714's teams executed were highly successful. The problem was there were not enough of them. They had little impact on AQI's operational tempo. The task force was facing an enemy it had never envisaged and could not degrade through existing ways of operating.

Still, reaching a consensus among task force members that existing methods were inadequate proved difficult, explained McChrystal, because the individual units were comfortable with what they believed was their effectiveness. Task force units excelled at the tactical level, and that sense of excellence "increased inertia. Why should we change? At the micro-level we could do a lot of things very, very well. From the beginning of the fight [against AQI], we could hit targets, we could capture and kill, and we could do those things exceedingly well."[125]

But TF 714 was operating as a peacetime strategic scalpel, and no matter how expertly it was wielded, it was losing ground in an unfamiliar wartime environment in which the enemy was escalating attacks. Change was demanded, explained McChrystal: "We needed to view the mission differently and that was whether we were winning or losing in Iraq against al-Qaeda, not just whether we captured or killed its members. . . . Winning is what counts. That should be our metric of success."[126]

By late fall 2004, the realization set in that the task force had to change from a strategic scalpel to what later came to be described by one knowledgeable observer as "a precision-killing machine unprecedented in the history of modern warfare."[127] TF 714 had to "capture or kill on an industrial scale, which was not something it had ever been built to do," explained William McRaven, who in 2004 was TF 714's deputy commander.[128] To operate at industrial strength meant TF 714's "basic mission fundamentally had to change," he explained, which was going to "require us to change the way we were organizationally structured, manned, trained, equipped, and everything else."[129]

TF 714 had suffered a strategic surprise, but it was not paralyzed. Rather, it recognized it would have to adapt to overcome an unfamiliar enemy. AQI was, said McChrystal, "much bigger . . . much more dynamic. It had more speed, momentum, and it was benefiting from a very different operating environment than the task force had ever anticipated."[130]

As explained in chapter 2, AQI posed a complex challenge for TF 714. Understanding it, McChrystal recalled, was "not an easy insight to come by. It was only . . . with considerable difficulty that we came to appreciate how the emerging networks of Islamist insurgents and terrorists were fundamentally different from any enemy the United States has previously known or faced."[131] AQI's organization was not modeled on a hierarchical structure. Its strategy was to drive US forces out of Iraq by inflicting casualties at such a high rate that Washington would be compelled to withdraw. Organizationally, it was decentralized and widely dispersed, comprising a plethora of networks and nodes that made extensive use of Information Age technologies to execute attacks across Iraq.

What TF 714 faced in Iraq in 2004 far surpassed early iterations of terrorist networks, McChrystal explained:

> We had studied terrorism and terrorist networks. So, it wasn't this epiphany that this is different than what we thought. . . . But this was much bigger; this was much more dynamic and more complex. It had much more speed, and it was benefiting from a very different operating environment than we had anticipated. . . . And that created the scope and complexity of the problem on a much greater scale than we had ever dealt with before or anticipated we would ever face.[132]

AQI was evolving and transforming expeditiously, said McRaven. "It was a rapid evolution. . . . The insurgents were building their networks very fast. They didn't just come into Iraq with a perfect organization. They had to build it."[133] As AQI evolved in the fight against TF 714, its component parts emerged as a web of dispersed, dynamic, and interconnected networks.

AQI's underground or clandestine apparatus carried out insurgent and terrorist attacks from a new sanctuary within which it was embedded and from which it could rapidly communicate to execute operations across Iraq. TF 714's intelligence chief explained how the "global communications revolution" provided AQI with "a new complex electronic sanctuary in which actions can be hidden among the innumerable civilian signals that constitute daily cell phone and Internet traffic. It is from this new sanctuary that the enemy coordinates activities to self-synchronize, pass information, and transfer funds. . . . Drawing support from their networks, they remained low contrast until it is time to strike and then quickly blend back into the population."[134]

To defeat this complex web of networks, TF 714's chief intelligence officer told McChrystal in early 2004 that TF 714 had to become more of an intelligence organization than an operations organization. "I said, your intelligence operations are a small part of your organization, and they need to be 80 percent of what you do as an organization. It needs to be the majority of what the Task Force does." While TF 714 "was an exquisite capability, they did not have the intelligence that they needed. They weren't even considering it to the degree that they should have."[135] This was an important learning juncture for TF 714—the realization that intelligence had to lead the way in the fight against AQI. But how was it going to gain access to that intelligence, and how was it going to adapt clandestine paramilitary ways of operating?

JIATF: Reorganizing Task Force 714 for War

For a military organization at war, having actionable intelligence is the road to success. It is an essential capability. And this was especially true for TF 714, which was embroiled in a fight with an underground and networked enemy. Intelligence—information and knowledge—had to lead the way. Amassing and disseminating timely and accurate intelligence about AQI was the sine qua non for operational success. In effect, the task force had to achieve intelligence dominance. According to Roy Godson and his associates, intelligence dominance means developing "sufficient local knowledge to map the infrastructure of armed groups, and gather the evidence to arrest and/or neutralize the support structure and leadership of the groups."[136]

Godson and this volume's author first learned of the concept of intelligence dominance in 2004 when we initiated an eighteen-month research project that included interviewing recently retired senior intelligence officers in Israel who had served in Shin Bet (Israel's internal security agency), Aman (the intelligence directorate of the Israel Defense Forces), and Mossad (the foreign intelligence service responsible for intelligence collection, covert operations, and counterterrorism). Those services had reshaped Israeli intelligence to de-escalate the bloody Second Intifada. Begun in 2000, terrorist attacks over the next three years killed more than one thousand Israelis and wounded more than seven thousand. But by 2005, the number of Israeli casualties had dropped precipitously. In 2002, 452 Israelis died. In 2005, that number plunged to 56.[137] How did the Israeli intelligence services do it?

What we learned from our research was that to accomplish this, Israeli counterterrorism operations had to be intelligence-led. One ex-senior officer of Shin Bet explained what that meant: "To defeat terrorists you must know everything about them. Everything! Who are their leaders and how do they plan and carry out operations? How are they organized and what methods are used for recruitment? What are their weaknesses and vulnerabilities. . . . Without systematic profiles of the enemy, operations to neutralize such unconventional adversaries are usually futile."[138] The information for such profiles, a retired general who served in high-level positions in Aman explained, "requires local intelligence that is collected block by block, village by village" to identify an armed group's "strengths, weaknesses, and vulnerabilities and to turn this information into operational opportunities."[139] As we talked with these and many other retired professionals, we realized that intelligence, security, and military services that achieve intelligence dominance do so by seamlessly joining collection, analysis, and direct-action paramilitary operations at the local level.

In 2004, TF 714 was nowhere close to having attained intelligence dominance. McChrystal recalled that his organization was "not even exploiting the intelligence they collected on operations. The process was defective. Across the task force," he explained, "operations should have been conducted to collect and produce more and better intelligence on AQI's networks." They should have generated intelligence, and that intelligence should have been the means for accelerating the tempo of operations.[140] Moreover, the task force should have been finding ways to engage and work with key parts of the US IC.

To achieve intelligence dominance, TF 714 had to restructure itself and develop a new organizational mechanism for fighting AQI, which was itself a new problem set. The task force could not do this by itself. An innovative organizational mechanism was needed to unravel the AQI puzzle. TF 714, however, was the latest incarnation of SOCOM's counterterrorism forces, which had evolved over two decades as a top-down military organization that was compartmentalized and semiautonomous. McChrystal described it as a closed system in which problem solving was the responsibility of the leadership. High-ranking officers were the ones who broke challenges down, thought through puzzles, and selected the most efficient solutions. Those solutions, once identified, were implemented by the organization's rank-and-file teams. Although TF 714 did not completely conform to the top-down model in that there was flexibility in terms of problem solving by its teams at the tactical level, above that level it adhered to a traditional chain of command.[141]

This was TF 714's approach when it deployed to Iraq. But that "organization was designed for a problem set that no longer existed," explained McChrystal. "We brought an industrial-age force to an information-age conflict."[142] This traditional method was too deliberate and hierarchical, and TF 714 was too autonomous and self-contained to decipher the puzzle presented by Iraq's fast-paced and networked insurgency. TF 714 had to be redesigned, and it partnered with several US intelligence agencies to be able to figure out and neutralize the unprecedented operational challenges confronting it in Iraq. The problem of understanding and dismantling AQI could not be accomplished by a highly compartmentalized, stand-alone, and top-down military organization.

The options facing the task force were stark: transform or fail. TF 714 would have to expand and form new partnerships with members of the IC. And all those partners were going to have to learn to work together as a team. The far-reaching scope of that transformation was (albeit, only subsequently) captured in the McChrystal maxim: "To defeat a networked enemy, we had to become a network." By this he meant that TF 714 "had to figure out a way to retain [its] traditional capabilities of professionalism, technology, and, when needed, over-whelming force, while achieving levels of knowledge, speed, precision, and unity of effort that only a network could provide."[143]

A new mechanism for setting such a transformation in motion was not im-mediately apparent to the task force leadership. There was no blueprint for turn-ing TF 714 into the kind of intelligence-driven, problem-solving organization that could achieve the objectives envisaged by its commander. However, there was a little-known organizational concept—the notion of a joint interagency task force—that McRaven was familiar with and that he proposed to McChrystal. If adapted to TF 714's complex Iraqi battlespace, McRaven would recommend, a JIATF could provide a way forward to unravel the AQI puzzle.

According to Evan Munsing and Christopher Lamb, a JIATF is a "model for whole-of-government problem-solving" that, by fostering "cross organizational collaboration," seeks to overcome the "natural tendencies [of many organizations] to seek autonomy rather than collaboration."[144] Such interagency collaboration has frequently been touted since 9/11 as the way to address today's complex secu-rity challenges. McRaven had served in the White House, was knowledgeable of the JIATF construct, and thought it had applicability for addressing the paucity of the actionable intelligence that TF 714 had to overcome to be able to get inside AQI networks to learn how they were operating. At a JSOC commanders' confer-ence in late 2004, he proposed consideration of the JIATF concept to McChrystal: "'We need a joint interagency task force,' I said, and Stan's up at the whiteboard writing that down—'joint interagency task force.' . . . So, we talked it through. I said, 'Look, we need CIA, we need FBI, we need everybody—all the three-letter intelligence agencies. If we don't understand what CIA's doing or what FBI's doing or NSA, then we're missing things. They have information we're not seeing.'"[145] McChrystal was persuaded. But embracing the JIATF approach was the easy part. Operationalizing it would prove very demanding. Deeply rooted cultures of se-crecy, autonomy, and exclusiveness infused not only TF 714 but also all those three-letter intelligence agencies that McRaven proposed partnering with.

During 2005, the JIATF was formed. Instituting among its members col-laborative problem-solving methods able to foster effective diagnoses of AQI's operational practices proved a knotty undertaking. It necessitated forming together members of the IC—those three-letter agencies—and the task force into a union of trust and common purpose. Flynn explained that creating trust meant, for example, that the CIA would give the task force "access to some of their most sensitive human intelligence data" and would do so confident that TF 714 was "going to use it appropriately. We had to constantly work to make sure that the big intelligence community agencies felt that they could trust the task force with their information."[146]

Achieving buy-in by the three-letter intelligence agencies to set this in motion "took quite a while," recalled McChrystal. The key was to convince each agency that "this isn't TF 714's mission that you are supporting—this is our mission that you are a part of." And TF 714 would "share our intelligence completely; we shared things that they would not have otherwise had access to. . . . Suddenly, [they learned] we weren't just consumers—we were providers of intelligence and partners."[147] The keys to persuading each agency to become a partner was to give it access to intelligence it did not have and to make it feel it was part of a mission of the utmost importance in the war against al-Qaeda and its associated movements.

Through that partnership, the JIATF, whose members were colocated at TF 714's headquarters in Balad, was able to help manage and exploit the intelligence utilized to uncover AQI's secret networks. As discussed in earlier chapters, the massive amounts of intelligence collected fed the exploit and analyze phases of the F3EAD cycle. And the partnership between TF 714 and the JIATF members brought together the critical ingredients to identify, locate, map, and target AQI's midlevel managers and commanders. From the three-letter intelligence agencies—including the NSA, the CIA, the DIA, the NGA, and the FBI—came a legion of analysts and other specialists who deployed forward to be part of the JIATF team. They lived and worked with TF 714's operational units but were also connected to their home agencies and could draw on all those competences and resources. To strengthen that connection further, the JIATF was under the leadership of a JSOC operational commander. In his memoir, McChrystal described the impact of the JIATF on TF 714 as transformational, changing TF 714 from "a collection of niche strike forces into a network able to integrate diverse elements of the U.S. Government into a unified effort."[148]

F3EAD: Identifying and Targeting AQI's Critical Nodes

By itself, TF 714 could not employ the F3EAD targeting cycle described previously. It did not have the intelligence capacity and personnel to do so. Therefore, achieving buy-in by the three-letter intelligence agencies was essential to achieve intelligence dominance. Without them, the process of analyzing and exploiting intelligence to foster more operations could never have achieved the tempo needed to dismantle AQI's networked apparatus.

The JIATF brought together three critical ingredients—people, process, and systems—to enable the F3EAD cycle to achieve and exploit intelligence dominance. Charles Faint and Michael Harris describe F3EAD as a "system that allows Special Operations Forces to anticipate and predict enemy operations, to identify, locate, and target enemy forces, and to perform intelligence exploitation and analysis of captured enemy personnel and materiel." F3EAD enabled the task force "to plan and execute operations against the enemy faster than the enemy could react" to those operations. As explained in chapter 4, F3EAD provided a way for the task force to get inside AQI's networks to "simultaneously direct [multiple] operations against several parts of [AQI]."[149] This set in motion a continuous cycle that provided TF 714's paramilitary teams with the capacity to dominate the operational tempo of the battle against AQI.

TF 714 and its JIATF partners were able to achieve and employ intelligence dominance against a modern, networked armed group. All the intelligence that was gathered through the collection disciplines, as described in chapter 3, could be fed into the exploit and analyze phases of the F3EAD cycle to speed up turn-around time to achieve the operational tempo TF 714 teams needed to degrade AQI's networks. However, what this process could not do was produce a grand organizational design showing all al-Qaeda's different elements in Iraq. There was no such fixed structure that the F3EAD process could discern. AQI was a complex system comprising interconnecting networks that were frequently adapting and changing.

What the F3EAD system did allow TF 714 to do was to get inside AQI sub-networks to reveal particular nodes and the interrelationships between them. It could expose an operational unit, an IED production and distribution process, or a financier grouping. And once inside, it could distinguish central from peripheral members, patterns of behavior, and clusters and groupings of nodes in order to disrupt and degrade that particular part of AQI's system from the inside out. If it could do this fast enough, hitting many targets rapidly every night, the task force would outpace AQI's capacity to adapt and renew itself.

At first, explained Lt. Gen. Eric Fiel, USAF (Ret.), who served as a deputy TF 714 commander, "we would not know what a particular element of AQI looked like. All we knew was that a certain geographic location was experiencing a high level of insurgent activity. An initial raid could give the task force pieces of information about it."[150] The starting point would be a piece of intelligence from a phone, computer, or detainee interrogation gathered on a night raid. In that data, the analysts were looking for various things. First, they looked for contacts—who is talking to whom? Second, they looked for information found on phones and computers that could be used to press detainees to outline their network groupings. Who is part of the network, and what does the network do? Third, they looked for clues that could be pieced together to form the outline of a subnetwork for one part of AQI in one part of Iraq. The analysts figured out where it was located, who populated it, what its communication patterns looked like, who was in charge, and what those leaders were planning to do.

All this intelligence, collected and exploited in a very short period of time, was triangulated with information already in data-management systems. This allowed the analysts to fill out a diagram of an AQI subnetwork. There were critical nodes within the network that could be attacked to disrupt and degrade it once the task force was able to operate inside. McChrystal summarized the process as follows: "The way we dealt with a particular part of their network, once we identified it, was to dominate its operational tempo, to pummel it constantly through raids against it, to drive it down and make it collapse in upon itself."[151]

The intelligence gathered through this innovation also had applicability beyond Iraq. It was shared, explained McRaven, with "everybody [in the US government] that was looking for information and intelligence that might affect the al-Qaeda threats they were chasing . . . everywhere from the US to Europe, North Africa, through Southwest Asia."[152] In doing so, the TF 714 leadership fostered development of a much broader network that was connected in several key ways.

First, that network employed the most sophisticated information technologies and transmission systems to connect the IC partners deployed to Balad with their headquarters back in the United States to facilitate intelligence sharing and exploitation. For example, not all the computers captured on night raids by TF 714 teams in Iraq could be handled at Balad; there was not enough capacity there to download the computers' contents, extract important intelligence using advanced software, process that information, and link it to other information. But one of TF 714's partners had that capacity in the United States, and through reach-back networks content could be transmitted there. "This required the Task Force to push large amounts of data back to Washington," explained Collins. "As a result, the Task Force purchased huge satellite dishes and paid for commercial satellite bandwidth to push the data."[153]

A second information technology that the task force employed to facilitate intelligence sharing and exploitation was video teleconferencing. Most notably, VTC was used for TF 714's daily operations and intelligence (O&I) briefings. Each session started with up-to-the-minute details and appraisals of the raids conducted the night before and the intelligence collected on those operations. Key intelligence insights deduced from those missions were delineated, and analysts explained what that information revealed about specific AQI networks in Iraq and beyond.

The daily O&I briefing was transmitted from TF 714's headquarters by VTC to twenty to thirty operational detachments and intelligence units affiliated with TF 714, located across Iraq. It was also transmitted to other units of JSOC fighting in the Levant, the Maghreb, and beyond. The home headquarters and the regional posts for each of the JIATF's IC partners also could take part in the daily O&I briefing. As a result, explained McChrystal, the attendance grew to "7,000 almost daily. . . . The information that was shared in the O&I was so rich, so timely, and so pertinent to the fight in Iraq and beyond, no one wanted to miss it."[154] Knowledge learned about AQI was often highly valuable to others fighting al-Qaeda elsewhere, just as their knowledge could be useful to TF 714. The JIATF made use of VTC in a number of other ways to foster interagency cooperation.[155] To be able to do so, McRaven explained, it "was necessary to overcome a VTC architecture not built for this kind of undertaking and which kept crashing." The task force had to "make the investment to get the old technology changed out and to build a whole new network that created a 90 percent reliability on the VTC."[156]

A third way in which the TF 714 leadership fostered connectivity with the task force's JIATF partners and others in the fight against al-Qaeda was through the use of liaison officers (LNOs). The role of LNOs was to facilitate working relationships with the larger US government counterterrorism network, generating trust and strengthening ties with the array of partner agencies and other organizations that were tasked with combating different aspects of al-Qaeda's global franchises, activities, and operations in and beyond Iraq. The mission of the LNOs, McChrystal wrote, was to foster a reciprocal rapport in which each partner agency shared and benefited. "We hoped that if the liaisons we sent contributed real value to our partners' operations, it would lay a foundation for the trusting relationships we needed to develop between the nodes of our network."[157]

Covert Paramilitary Operations and Presidential Authorities

On September 14, 2001, the United States Congress, in a joint resolution, authorized the president to "use all necessary and appropriate force against . . . [those] he determines planned, authorized, committed, or aided the terrorist attacks that occurred on September 11, 2001, or harbored such organizations or persons, in order to prevent any future acts of international terrorism against the United States." This authorization to use military force was designated by Congress as "consistent with section 8(a) (1) of the War Powers Resolution."[158] It was signed into law by President Bush on September 18, 2001.

The joint resolution, from the perspective of the White House, constituted the equivalent of a declaration of war and granted the president broad legal authority as commander in chief to use force as long as he determined that a particular individual, group, or organization was connected to al-Qaeda and its war against the United States. In signing the resolution, President Bush noted that he did so within the context of "maintaining the longstanding position of the executive branch regarding the President's constitutional authority to use force."[159]

The resolution was unprecedented in that it authorized the use of force, "consistent with section 8(a) (1) of the War Powers Resolution," against an adversary that was not a nation-state. The attacks on September 11, from the perspective of Congress and the president, constituted an act of war by al-Qaeda, a nonstate armed group. As noted previously, bin Laden's declaration of war on America in 1996 had been dismissed by most because only nation-states could declare war on nation-states. Consequently, the attacks on US embassies in East Africa and the USS *Cole* in the port of Aden were not considered acts of war.

But in 2001, the circumstances of war expanded for the Bush administration. A state of war could now be said to exist between the United States and al-Qaeda, even though the latter was not a state. Moreover, because those who carried out the attacks on 9/11 were operating transnationally, the president believed that his authority as commander in chief permitted him to attack al-Qaeda cells and affiliates wherever they had sanctuary or presence. The battlefield was not confined to Afghanistan (and later Iraq) but was global because al-Qaeda was a transnational organization.

This understanding of the post-9/11 context was reflected in the operational directive for fighting the war: the Al Qaeda Network Exord (AQN Exord). This classified execute order, signed in spring 2004 by Secretary Rumsfeld with the assent of President Bush, "gave the military new authority to attack the al Qaeda terrorist network anywhere in the world." It provided a "sweeping mandate to conduct operations in countries not at war with the United States" but where al-Qaeda elements had a sanctuary or presence.[160]

The AQN Exord reflected the White House understanding of the post-9/11 wartime setting. The 2004 order identified fifteen to twenty countries, including Syria, Pakistan, Yemen, Saudi Arabia, and several other Persian Gulf states, where al-Qaeda militants were believed to be operating or to have sanctuary.[161] And, as Chesney notes, the order "streamlined the authorization process as much as possible, tailoring it to the circumstances of specific anticipated locations of operations. . . . The new order specified a way for Pentagon planners to get the green light for a mission far more quickly."[162]

JSOC was assigned the lead role in carrying out the order, its forces being judged best suited for fighting a war that was "irregular in its nature."[163] The decision constituted a major shift in the conduct of paramilitary operations away from the CIA, which had been assigned to manage them during the Cold War. The Bush administration concluded that the CIA did not have the capacity needed for a sustained wartime campaign against al-Qaeda and associated movements. The agency's capacity had been greatly reduced during the 1990s, leaving it with insufficient manpower and support structure to take on al-Qaeda.

Instead, SOCOM's counterterrorism forces—JSOC—were assigned that responsibility. Rumsfeld believed that JSOC had a significant comparative advantage over the CIA, possessing a much more robust capacity to conduct ongoing paramilitary operations in a wartime context against an irregular and dispersed enemy. Since 1980, president after president had invested resources to hone these special units for offensive counterterrorism and other direct-action missions. By the late 1990s, they were touted as the best of their kind in the world.[164]

But did the DOD have the authority to execute an ongoing covert paramilitary campaign? Did it have to comply with the covert action oversight architecture constructed for a peacetime context when employing counterterrorism forces for wartime missions? The Intelligence Authorization Act for fiscal year 1991, which was "the governing legislation on covert action, codified two requirements for any such operations: first, there must be a written presidential finding stating that the action is important to U.S. national security . . . and second, the administration must notify the congressional intelligence committees of the action as soon as possible after the finding has been issued."[165] Congress defined covert action in 1991 legislation as follows:

1. An activity of the U.S. government;
2. To influence political, economic, or military conditions abroad;
3. Where it is intended that the role of the U.S. government will not be apparent or acknowledged openly.[166]

In light of these stipulations, was the Bush administration required to submit findings for its covert paramilitary operations directed against al-Qaeda? There is disagreement over this matter, which has been framed under US law as a Title 10 versus Title 50 issue. According to the US Code of Federal Regulations, missions of the US military fall under Title 10, whereas intelligence activities, including covert action, are Title 50 matters. But in today's irregular wartime context, military and intelligence activities increasingly overlap. Consequently, legal and security specialists have wrangled over whether paramilitary raids by TF 714 units were Title 10 military operations or intelligence operations as defined by Title 50.

Andru Wall, an expert in national security law and former legal adviser to SOCOM, notes that the congressional intelligence committees have worried that "the military is increasingly conducting activities that appear very similar to activities conducted by the CIA . . . yet are not subject to the oversight of the intelligence committees." This is because the White House does not consider "these secret military activities . . . covert action because they are either intended to be acknowledged at some point or they are [considered] traditional military activities." Congress has disagreed with this position taken by the executive branch, arguing "for oversight of the military's secret activities by asserting that these are not actually traditional military activities" but covert actions as understood in the 1991 Intelligence Authorization Act.[167]

This raises the issue of what constitutes traditional military activity in a twenty-first-century irregular warfare context. Where do paramilitary direct-action raids conducted on a secret basis, like those carried out by special task forces such as TF 714, fit in? Wall proposes that these missions, if "conducted under military command and control pursuant to a Secretary of Defense–issued execute order . . . are military operations and not intelligence activities." This is true even for "unacknowledged military operations [that] may be exempt from intelligence committee oversight." Wall finds congressional attempts to "redefine [them] . . . as intelligence activities legally and historically unsupportable."[168] In other words, in the post-9/11 irregular wartime context, covert paramilitary missions directed against al-Qaeda are military and not intelligence operations.

Jennifer Kibbe, who has written extensively on covert action and congressional oversight, argues that "guidelines for the 'traditional military activities' exception need to be updated to tighten what has become a loophole and to enforce the requirements for covert action more stringently." She opines that whether an operation is considered a covert action should be "determined by the action itself, not by whether it is being conducted by the CIA or the military."[169] Moreover, with respect to the issue of wartime and what constitutes the battlefield, she maintains that when "SOF are conducting unacknowledged operations in countries with which the United States is not at war, they are, in fact, acting covertly and should follow the same regulations for presidential findings and congressional notification that the CIA does."[170] These countries presumably would include Syria, Pakistan, Yemen, Saudi Arabia, and others noted in the AQN Exord as places where an al-Qaeda affiliate has sanctuary or presence. Iraq and Afghanistan would be exceptions to Kibbe's interpretation.

The Bush administration had a different view. The United States was at war with al-Qaeda and its affiliates. If they had sanctuary or presence in one of those states, then that location could become part of the battlefield. While the United States was not involved in hostilities with those states, it nevertheless could use SOCOM's counterterrorism forces, as well as other capabilities, to attack al-Qaeda and associated elements in those locations. And the Bush administration interpreted those strikes as traditional military operations, not as covert actions requiring a finding.

However, counterterrorist operations in several of those states—including Yemen, Somalia, and Pakistan—could not go forward without presidential approval. The same was not true for TF 714 in Iraq. Its commanders had the authority to initiate secret paramilitary campaigns on an ongoing basis. Presidential approval was required in those other states where al-Qaeda was active, due to political sensitivity. In those states, where US military forces were not deployed and fighting, operational decisions were not to be left to military commanders in the field. This did not mean that every operation had to be approved by the Oval Office. Rather, a process was established whereby potential missions were discussed with the president in advance so that he could delegate authority to strike specific targets in these sensitive locations.

In sum, the employment of covert action's paramilitary variant crossed a momentous threshold in the aftermath of the 9/11 attacks. The United States was now at war with al-Qaeda and its associated movements. Consequently, covert action was no longer considered a peacetime instrument of policy; now it was seen as a crucial operational capability for conducting irregular war against a complex, transnational, and networked enemy. Because the nature of this war diverged dramatically from twentieth-century conventional warfare and was irregular in its nature, the Bush administration found it needed to employ capabilities that differed considerably from traditional military forces. The battlefield and the enemy were not like yesterday's.

To fight this unconventional and transnational enemy, SOCOM's counterterrorism forces were assigned a key role in that campaign. And when Iraq turned into the central front in al-Qaeda's global war against the United States, the burgeoning AQI-dominated insurgency became that war's main focal point. The remainder of this chapter discusses how TF 714 and its JIATF partners transformed into an intelligence-led direct-action paramilitary force that was able to get inside AQI's networks to dominate their operational tempo, eliminating a large number of the midlevel commanders and managers who made AQI networks work.

The Irreducible Minimum: Winning at the Operational Level

A situation report of US prospects in Iraq from the spring into the early fall of 2006 would have had the following bottom-line assessment: as insurgent violence skyrockets, the prospects for US success plummet.[171] To be sure, such a forecast could easily have been deduced from the escalating "significant acts of violence" reported in the DOD's *Weekly Security Incidents Trends*. By September 2006, those totals had climbed sharply to more than fourteen hundred—nearly double what they had been the previous summer. And in the summer of 2007, they peaked at nearly eighteen hundred incidents weekly.[172] Enemy violence was skyrocketing, while almost every prediction of the possibility of US success in Iraq pointed to a continuing downward spiral.[173]

However, by the end of 2009, significant acts of violence had plummeted to fewer than two hundred per week. And this trend continued into 2010, according to the *Weekly Security Incidents Trends* accounting of enemy attacks against US and coalition partners compiled by the DOD.[174] Another measure of the decline in the insurgency can be seen in the drop in US military fatalities. That number had soared from 486 in 2003 to 904 in 2007. However, in 2009 the number dropped to 149, and in 2010 it fell to 60.[175] In sum, the security situation had dramatically changed at the operational level. The following four interrelated factors contributed to this dramatic change in the Iraq War:

- adoption of a new COIN strategy
- addition of thirty thousand troops through the surge
- Sunni Awakening movement, which opened the door for the remarkable growth of police that, in turn, gave the coalition forces the capacity needed to control the physical and human terrain once cleared of insurgent forces
- operations conducted by TF 714 against AQI's clandestine networks

The introduction of COIN began with the Marine campaign plan initiated in early 2006 in Anbar Province. At that time, Washington believed Anbar was lost.[176] But by the end of 2006, Anbar was reaching a security tipping point. The COIN-based campaign plan—with its interrelated elements of clearing out insurgents through maneuver operations, holding the cleared territory through combat outposts, engaging and aligning with local sheikhs and their tribes, and building local Iraqi police units drawn from those tribes—was shifting the ground in Anbar. The conditions were in place to bring about a sea change in 2007.[177] That occurred in the late spring, when the total of weekly violent incidents for the province dropped from 450 attacks in the first week of January to roughly 150 four months later. By July, the weekly total was less than 100.[178] When Gen. John Kelly took command of the Marine forces in Anbar in 2008, he found a situation that differed dramatically from the one he had left in early 2005, having served at that time as the assistant commander of the First Marine Division. Reflecting back on those days, Kelly recalled that when he left Iraq in early 2005, roughly four hundred violent events were taking place each week in Anbar Province. But when he returned in February 2008, that number was down to fifty attacks.[179]

In February 2007, Gen. David Petraeus replaced Gen. George Casey Jr. as commander of the Multi-National Force–Iraq. Petraeus initiated a similar COIN strategy, enabled by the addition of thirty thousand surge forces and the growth of the Sunni Awakening. The latter, which was critical to success, was a movement that had begun in Anbar, in which Sunni tribesmen who had formerly fought US troops as part of the insurgency had realigned to fight against the insurgency, chiefly AQI and those affiliated with it. As the Marines found in Anbar in 2006, "without the Awakening, the surge would not have stabilized Iraq by the summer of 2008. It was not until the Sons of Iraq stood up," write Stephen Biddle, Jeffrey Friedman, and Jacob Shapiro, "that bloodshed fell fast enough; without them, our findings suggest that Iraq's violence would still have been at mid-2006 levels when the surge ended."[180] The surge first focused on the greater Baghdad region. The results were the same as they had been in Anbar, with violence declining precipitously in the Baghdad area by the end of 2008.[181] In 2009, that decline in fighting spread elsewhere, and, by 2010, insurgent attacks declined to between one hundred and two hundred per month.

But effective COIN requires more than the "clear, hold, build" formula found in the classic COIN literature of the 1960s as well as in its post-9/11 counterpart, US Army Field Manual 3–24, *Counterinsurgency*.[182] It also necessitates the capacity to dismantle the clandestine infrastructure of insurgent organizations. It was AQI's subterranean networked mechanism that gave them the capacity to initiate, rapidly increase, and sustain insurgent operations across Iraq. The mission assigned to Task Force 714, said General McChrystal, was to "learn about the inner workings of that largely invisible ecosystem in order to dismantle it."[183]

To what extent was TF 714 able to accomplish this mission and dismantle AQI's networks? As noted earlier, it was able to raise its monthly operational tempo from eighteen raids in August 2004 to three hundred in August 2006 and to sustain that rate into 2009–10. But how effective were those operations? To what extent were they able to attain McChrystal's goal to "claw the guts out of AQI" so that its networks collapsed?[184]

The key to degrading AQI's operational capacity was to kill or capture its midlevel commanders and managers—those who made its networks run. They were identifiable and potentially vulnerable because they had to move, communicate, and make things happen. This was not the case with AQI's top-level leaders. To try to identify, isolate, and focus on one top individual at a time within an AQI network "was a fool's mission. . . . It was beyond what we could know when we initiated operations against a particular network of AQI," McChrystal recounted. The alternative was to focus on the attrition of those midlevel elements as they were identified through the F3EAD targeting process: "To hit those targets faster than they could replace them, to make them worry about our ability to constantly pummel them, and to make younger and less experienced those who replaced them."[185]

Against those targets, TF 714 took an industrial approach. Month after month, the task force identified and tracked down midlevel managers and commanders through F3EAD targeting. A snapshot of what could be accomplished in a single month—October 2007—is illustrative. During that month, TF 714 captured or killed forty-three commanders and managers, including six emirs (local chiefs or leaders) at the city level or higher, six geographic or functional cell leaders, fourteen foreign terrorist facilitators, three car bomb cell leaders, six logistical support emirs, and eight media/propaganda operatives.[186]

The goal of this relentless targeting was attrition. According to the commander of TF 714's special army units, Bennet Sacolick, "We intended to conduct raids at a rate that they could not withstand. Through those raids, we sought to disrupt, degrade, and dismantle their networks faster than they could reestablish them. Eventually, we concluded, that led to the decline in the capacity of their networks."[187] The results were demonstrable. Once TF 714 reached a tempo of three hundred missions per month, it could see its impact on particular parts of the AQI networks during a given period. McRaven explained, "We measured cycles in different operational elements such as bomb-making facilities and financing elements. We might seriously degrade a bomb-making unit, and we could measure its decline in productivity. The same was true for other parts of their operating systems. We could also see when a unit was able to reestablish itself and how long it would take to do so. Then we would begin hitting it extensively again, driving down its capacity."[188]

From 2006 through 2009, the task force maintained an operational tempo of three hundred raids per month against AQI's networks. During 2008, McRaven recalled, the task force concluded that from "the intelligence being collected during our raids and from the interrogations of the many members of AQI that we captured on those raids, . . . a major decline was taking place in the capacity of different parts of their networks to carry out operations. Our kill/capture raids were considerably driving down their operational capacity. We were able to gauge and evaluate that decline."[189]

McChrystal recalled that the commanders of TF 714's raiding units, as early as late 2006, "began discerning the impact of their operations." They told him that AQI was "cracking, it was not at the same level of proficiency, and its effectiveness was lessening. We can see it." He noted this was "counterintuitive because at that time violence was escalating."[190] But those at the operational level saw AQI weakening. "What they saw and what we heard from many of those who were captured and interrogated was that AQI could not control territory as they had earlier. And that the TF 714 teams were able to attack them in those areas and beat them up badly."[191]

By the late spring of 2007, those same commanders were coming to the conclusion that AQI was in demonstrable decline. And one year later, task force deputy commander Eric Fiel believed that the indicators were even stronger, signifying that "AQI had been seriously degraded."[192] Those indicators included "what AQI was saying about their situation in their own messaging and communications," which TF 714 was collecting through its extensive signals intelligence capacity. This reinforced what "we were learning from detainee interrogations about the impact of our targeting."[193]

AQI's midlevel managers and commanders, according to the commanding general of SOCOM's counterterrorism forces in 2011, Gen. Joseph L. Votel, were the most important targets because they "made the organization function." But "estimating with precision the degree to which the task force was able to degrade those midlevel operational commanders and managers was difficult."[194] This was because there was no "finite target set we could know about," observed McChrystal. That said, TF 714 did "keep a running total of the emirs, commanders, and managers," such as the forty-five in October 2007 "that were taken off the battlefield. And there was real attrition."[195]

From 2006 to 2009, the tally grew considerably as the task force gained extensive knowledge about various parts of the AQI networks. This knowledge included an understanding of who the commanders and managers of various subnetwork components were. McRaven observed that as this period progressed, "we were able to map out different parts of their networks, what they were involved in, who was involved, how they were linked together. With that knowledge, we were able, through raid after raid, to shatter them."[196]

Among those members of TF 714 interviewed for this book, there is a strong consensus that, by the end of 2009, AQI had been seriously degraded by TF 714's operations and that this was reflected in the decline in AQI's ability to function and carry out missions. For example, Sacolick, in asserting this was the case, employed the "continuum of effects" framework—disrupt, degrade, dismantle, and defeat. By 2009, TF 714 had disrupted AQI's clandestine apparatus, operational timetable, and freedom of movement, putting the group on the defensive. It had also disrupted its ability to conduct larger operations and degraded a large number of AQI's operational cells, financial units, communications and media centers, bomb and IED production facilities, and arms acquisition networks. Eventually TF 714 had dismantled networks to the degree that they could no longer function in the cohesive manner they once had.[197] The task force had developed the capacity to operate inside those networks to break up a considerable number of them.

In 2010, in conjunction with its Iraqi counterparts, TF 714 took several of AQI's top leaders out of the fight. "In the space of two weeks, Abu Ayyub Al-Masri, Al-Qaeda's overall leader in Iraq, Abu Abdullah Al-Rashid Al-Baghdadi, the leader of the Islamic State of Iraq, and Ahmed Al-Obeidi, the northern commander of Al-Qaeda in Iraq . . . were killed in two separate operations. . . . In all, twenty-six insurgent leaders were killed or captured between January and June 2010."[198] This partial decapitation, in conjunction with the success TF 714 had had in removing midlevel managers and commanders as well as in degrading and collapsing networks, hurt AQI badly.

But what did it all mean? Was TF 714 winning? "We needed [in 2004] to view the mission differently," McChrystal recalled, "and that was whether we were winning or losing in Iraq against al-Qaeda, not just whether we captured or killed its members. . . . Winning is what counts. That's our metric of success."[199] When it comes to winning in today's irregular wars, remarked Sacolick, a final defeat of the insurgent underground networks is illusive because the remaining elements of such organizations, once they have been seriously disrupted and degraded, can go into a semidormant stage, regroup, and then reappear phoenixlike. Consequently, once AQI was largely degraded, it had to be kept at that stage while the political reconciliation and reconstruction phases that should follow a successful COIN and counterterrorism program had time to be established and take root.[200]

McChrystal echoed this view: "Winning is relative in these kinds of wars. There is no V-E Day. We put AQI on its back, having badly beaten it up. But until the political causes of the conflict are addressed, it could reemerge." Consequently, during the post-conflict period, which can last for many years because political reconciliation and reconstruction are complicated and protracted processes, AQI "had to be kept on its back."[201]

In effect, after three-plus years of industrial-strength counterterrorism operations, TF 714 had reached what Gen. Raymond Odierno, then commander of Multi-National Force–Iraq, referred to as the "irreducible minimum." By this, he meant that even when a COIN and counterterrorism program is able to greatly weaken a group like AQI, that group will still retain a capacity to carry out periodic attacks.[202] At the operational level, this is winning. During 2009, recalled McRaven, the task force was "only carrying out two to three raids a night because AQI's operational tempo was way down." He added, "We were beginning to hand those missions off to our Iraqi CT force counterparts."[203]

That said, the conclusion of those who led TF 714 was that an effective COIN strategy and counterterrorism program can take one only so far. They are necessary parts of the resolution of irregular wars against nonstate armed groups, but they are never sufficient in and of themselves. What COIN and counterterrorism can achieve is to establish the prerequisites for postconflict transition, political reconciliation, and reconstruction. For the COIN forces in Iraq, the goal was to sweep the insurgents from the cities and towns and then to hold that ground. In Iraq, the Sunni Awakening was an important facilitator for holding ground once the insurgents were cleared.

For TF 714, its primary mission was to disrupt, degrade, and dismantle AQI's networked secret underground—to hit AQI's networks every night, killing or capturing a large number of its midlevel managers and operational commanders and undermining its operational tempo.

Once territory was held and the insurgent networks had been degraded to their irreducible minimum, post-conflict transition, political reconciliation, and reconstruction could begin. In Iraq, the transition began in August 2010 and culminated in December 2011 with the completion of the US withdrawal of forces in accord with the 2008 agreement between the United States and Iraq. While withdrawing, the United States continued to train Iraqi security forces to enhance their capacity and professionalism. Beginning in 2011, most US officials involved in the transition process assumed that a follow-on US force would stay in Iraq to continue security capacity-building while other interagency elements facilitated postconflict political reconciliation and reconstruction. A follow-on version of TF 714 would help its Iraqi counterparts maintain the irreducible minimum required to ensure that AQI did not have an opportunity to reconstitute itself and return to the offensive. But that follow-on mission did not take place.

Postscript: The Consequences of Withdrawal

From 2006 through 2009, industrial-strength counterterrorism operations by TF 714 had greatly weakened AQI. The organization appeared to be at the end of the line—on life support. During 2010, TF 714 and its Iraqi partner, the Iraqi Special Operations Force (ISOF), kept the pressure on AQI as the United States began the drawdown of its combat forces. In August 2010, the last brigade combat team withdrew from Iraq, and on August 31, President Obama declared the end to "the American combat mission." Those US forces remaining were to transition to noncombat stability activities as part of Operation New Dawn. The remaining fifty thousand troops would concentrate on training and advising the Iraqi security forces to improve their capacity to maintain the stability established in Iraq during Operation Iraqi Freedom and would complete their withdrawal by the end of 2011.

Operation New Dawn had three principal objectives. The first was to continue to advise, train, and equip the Iraqi security forces to become capable of maintaining internal stability and security. The second was to assist Iraq's defense ministry and other security institutions in developing the capacity to oversee and manage operating forces. Both of these activities fit within the noncombat stability mandate of Operation New Dawn. But the third component called for a continuation of TF 714's warfighting operations, carried out in conjunction with its ISOF counterpart. TF 714 was to persistently attack AQI and keep it "on its back," said McRaven, preventing any resurgence. During 2010, TF 714 did so very effectively, he pointed out.[204] Nevertheless, despite sustaining heavy losses, AQI managed to maintain a small number of network elements run by competent commanders and managers.

Operation New Dawn was to be completed by the end of 2011, reducing US forces to zero and terminating the US military presence in Iraq.[205] But in late 2010 and throughout 2011, there was a great deal of discord and political wrangling, both within the Obama administration and between it and the government of Iraqi prime minister Nuri al-Maliki over a post–Operation New Dawn interagency "residual force" that would help maintain stability, continue to professionalize the Iraqi security forces, and facilitate the longer process of post-conflict political reconciliation and reconstruction. For a complex set of reasons that are beyond the scope of this chapter, reaching an agreement on the residual force proved to be a bridge too far for the Obama and Maliki governments.[206] Consequently, when the United States reduced its forces to zero by the end of 2011, that meant an end to the US military presence.

As these developments were unfolding in 2011, Prime Minister Maliki began to rapidly reverse the gains that had been made by the United States in professionalizing the Iraqi security forces. He consolidated his control over the security institutions, turning them into sectarian tools he could use for the political repression of his opponents. This included "controlling appointments to all senior positions in the ISF [Iraqi security forces] to create a network of officers loyal to him."[207] Of course, this ran counter to what the United States had sought to achieve—a professionalized Iraqi army in which officers were promoted based on merit. Maliki's control of the security institutions extended to ISOF. During the transition period, he used ISOF units against political enemies. As politicization and sectarianism crept into ISOF, operations partnered with TF 714 suffered. When it became clear there would be no residual force, TF 714 began decamping from its base in Balad, and operations ended.

In 2011, as the United States moved down the path to zero troops in Iraq, the Maliki government employed Iraq's security institutions to consolidate power. As it did so, the gains that the Iraqi military and police forces had made, thanks to the tens of billions of dollars invested by the United States to train and equip those forces, began rapidly unraveling. Serious questions emerged about the capacity of the Ministry of Defense and Ministry of Interior forces to execute the full range of their duties.[208]

As a result of these developments, AQI's surviving elements began to revive. AQI's Shura Council selected a new leader, Abu Bakr al-Baghdadi. Rebranding itself as the Islamic State of Iraq, the group began rebuilding. ISI's ranks swelled in 2011 and 2012, as did attacks on police and military facilities. Facilitating these developments were the sectarian policies of the Maliki government and the drawdown of US forces, in particular TF 714. This resurgence culminated in ISI taking control of significant territory in northern Iraq from 2012 to 2014. Baghdadi promoted himself to "Caliph Ibrahim" and declared the creation of the "Islamic Caliphate" on this territory. ISI then morphed into the Islamic State of Iraq and the Levant and seized control of Iraq's second-largest city, Mosul.

The security gains achieved through the four interrelated actions discussed above—a new COIN strategy, the surge, the Sunni Awakening, and operations conducted by TF 714—were lost. Rather than capitalizing on them to keep al-Qaeda on its back at the irreducible minimum while facilitating postconflict political reconciliation and reconstruction through the creation of a residual force, the Maliki government allowed al-Qaeda to rejuvenate itself.

CHAPTER 6

TASK FORCE 714 AND THE SOURCES OF TRANSFORMATION

As previous chapters document, Task Force 714 was able to reinvent itself during the Iraq War. In doing so, it transformed from a highly specialized and compartmentalized counterterrorism force constructed to carry out occasional hostage-rescue and direct-action missions in peacetime to a wartime force that raised its operational tempo to three hundred night raids per month, which enabled it over the course of three years to acutely degrade AQI, dismantling many of its networks across Iraq. TF 714 did so by finding, attacking, and eliminating a large number of al-Qaeda's midlevel commanders and managers. As the preceding chapters illustrate, these commanders and managers were the linchpin of AQI, what General McChrystal described as "the guts of AQI."

This book, thus far, has explained *how* TF 714 accomplished that mission. This chapter deciphers *why* TF 714 was able to achieve this organizational, technological, and operational sea change.

The literature on military innovation, briefly discussed below, finds several roadblocks that should have prevented TF 714's transformation. But those obstacles were overcome. *Why?* What accounted for TF 714's ability to reconstruct itself to eviscerate AQI? To answer this question, this chapter begins by highlighting factors that academic specialists believe impede military innovation in war and peace.

Constraints on Military Innovation

Military innovation, writes Adam Grissom, constitutes a marked change in the "scope and impact" of an armed service's performance, or "operational praxis." Innovation is said to advance "a significant increase in military effectiveness as measured by battlefield results."[1] Michael McNerney defines military innovation

as "newly applied doctrinal, organizational or technological change that has a definitive impact on combat effectiveness."[2]

Whether military organizations have the capacity to innovate in these ways has
been the subject of academic attention in security studies since the 1980s. That
literature has identified conditions that determine whether military organizations
are likely to innovate.

The initial inquiry into the subject pinpointed several factors obstructing military innovation in both war and peace. Those constraints made it difficult for
militaries to change, even in the face of necessity. Davidson observes that a "critical point of agreement among scholars is that if left alone, the military would be
unlikely to change."[3] Barry Posen and Jack Snyder both came to this conclusion
in early studies on the subject.[4]

What are the barriers that make military innovation problematic? Based on a
review of the literature, Janine Davidson identifies three principal obstacles.[5] The
first two have their roots in organizational behavior and bureaucratic behavior.[6]
With respect to the former, resistance is the result of formalized norms, standard
operating procedures, and the routine ways that large organizations in general,
and the military in particular, function. Those practices often serve as barriers to
innovation. One example can be seen in Posen's study of the years between the two
world wars in the twentieth century.[7] Customary organizational behavior throws
up Chinese walls—formidable and often insuperable barriers that constitute ob-
structions to military innovation.

Bureaucratic politics constitute a second impediment, notes Davidson: "Military leaders . . . seek to promote the importance of their organization and to preserve [its] distinctive organization essence," or central mission. Change in that
mission is resisted unless leaders believe it will "enhance the importance of the
organization."[8] More Chinese walls! Consider the US Army's commitment during
the Vietnam War to employing operational methods developed for conventional
warfare in Europe. For example, in his definitive study of *The Army and Vietnam*,
Andrew Krepinevich documents how the generals pushed on with conventional-
war methods developed for the NATO theater.[9] Although those methods proved
ill-suited for Vietnam, army leaders remained steadfast in their commitment to
them because they reflected the army's distinctive way of fighting.[10]

A third barrier is imposed by organizational culture, which Wilson describes
"as a persistent, patterned way of thinking about the central tasks of and human
relationships within an organization." The culture of an organization can result in
rigid adherence to operating principles and ways of doing things. When this happens, an organization "will change slowly, if at all." Moreover, new challenges are

met with "routinized rather than adaptive behavior."[11] Richard Downie finds that institutional memory and history, key factors that shape organizational culture, frequently impede an organization's capacity to change. "When the norms, SOPs, and doctrines" of an organization "become widely accepted and practiced," they will "form the organization's institutional memory." And that memory is then socialized into members, making the organization "resistant to change."[12] Yet more Chinese walls!

John Nagl finds this at play in his study of the British Army in the Malayan Emergency of 1948–60 and US ground forces in Vietnam. Each was initially committed to a core conventional warfighting mission despite facing a guerrilla force. However, "when conventional tactics . . . failed in Malaya the British army had few problems creating an internal consensus that change was needed," while the US Army remained unwavering in its commitment to "its core competency. . . . The organization never developed a consensus that change was required."[13] Why? The "critical independent variable" for these divergent approaches, concluded Nagl, was "organizational culture." It "determines whether innovation succeeds or fails."[14]

Determinants of Military Innovation

As the study of military innovation progressed, attention shifted to identifying factors that might allow a military organization to overcome these obstacles to innovation. Grissom, Davidson, Nagl, McNerney, Downie, and Theo Farrell have summarized the findings from those studies.[15]

The first determining factor, explains Davidson, is civilian intervention. Because militaries resist change, "the civil-military dynamic is critical, as civilian leaders must interact with their military counterparts to drive the organization to innovate." However, civilian success in doing so "depends on the delicate nature of civil-military relations."[16] Grissom highlights "empirical studies that buttress the civil-military model," including Kimberly Zisk's analysis of how civilian defense officials fostered change in Soviet military doctrine, particularly in the last decade of the Cold War. These studies found civilians driving innovation.[17]

A second trigger of military innovation is interservice or intraservice competition. The "core contention," according to Grissom, "posits that the services will compete to develop capabilities to address contested mission areas, believing that additional resources will accrue to the winner. The result is innovation."[18] Several case studies support this proposition. One example is how competition between

the US Army and the US Air Force during the 1950s over close air support resulted in the army developing attack helicopters to secure that mission.[19] Intraservice innovation, according to Rosen, involves "one of the primary combat arms of
a service" envisioning change in the way it fights.[20] With this vision as the starting
point, the particular part of the service undertakes a campaign within its branch
to convince midlevel officers to accept this new theory and to marshal the necessary resources to put it into practice.[21] Rosen draws his examples from US military
policy from 1905 to 1960.

The culture of an organization, although identified earlier as a barrier to military innovation, can also prompt innovation under certain circumstances. Those
conditions include, according to Farrell, an external shock such as losing a war.
He finds that, depending on the nature of an organization's culture, leaders of a
military service can steer it toward innovation.[22]

Yet other scholars find that "the growing body of organizational learning theory
provides a context for understanding why and how certain militaries are able to
learn and adapt."[23] Why are some able to innovate, while others are unable to do
so? The broader literature on organizational learning has sought to answer these
questions since the appearance of two studies: first, James March and Herbert
Simon's volume *Organizations* and then *A Behavioral Theory of the Firm* by March
and Richard Cyert.[24] Both works were concerned with the circumstances in which
an organization faces a major crisis that undermines its operational performance—
in other words, when the organization's capacity to accomplish core tasks has
fallen below minimum levels of effectiveness. As a result, the firm faces a crisis in
practice. It confronts the challenge of identifying and implementing change. To
do so, it must be able to learn, adapt, and innovate.

From this starting point, research has sought to identify practices and procedures that foster the attainment of such knowledge and to assess their impact
on organizational change. What various studies have found is that organizations
in the midst of a crisis can find knowledge acquisition, learning, and innovation
very challenging. However, those studies also identify behavioral and managerial
techniques that can equip an organization with the capacity to overcome crises in
operational performance.

This chapter examines the extent to which the presence of such characteristics
helps explain *why* the transformation of TF 714 took place. To do so, the chapter
utilizes elements of an analytic framework, described below, deduced from business and management studies concerned with organizational learning and adaptation. The construct is composed of characteristics that the literature suggests
enable organizations to learn and innovate when faced with an inability to execute
core tasks.

The Characteristics of Learning Organizations

Descriptions of what constitutes a learning organization abound in the business and management literature. For David Garvin, writing in the *Harvard Business Review*, a learning organization is "skilled at acquiring and transferring knowledge and at modifying its behavior to reflect this new knowledge and insights."[25] In a similar vein, Marlene Fiol and Marjorie Lyles note that "organizational learning means the process of improving actions through better knowledge and understanding."[26]

Although there may be a consensus that learning organizations are those with the capacity to acquire new knowledge about shortfalls in performance and that such knowledge becomes the basis for adapting institutional behavior to rectify performance shortfalls, what does not exist, observes Peter Pawlowsky, is a road map or blueprint for "organizational learning [that] is widely accepted."[27] This is due, Martin Schulz reflects, to the diverse nature of the field: "Is the main focus . . . exploring the sources of organizational learning, is it on different forms of learning, or is it on the outcomes of organizational learning? It appears that organizational learning is about all three."[28]

Since the appearance of *Organizations* and *A Behavioral Theory of the Firm*, business and management studies have endeavored to identify specific managerial characteristics that facilitate learning. Schulz notes that this research "has intensified considerably since the late 1980s. The number of publications increased dramatically . . . and new empirical research programs got off the ground." As a result, a "field of organizational learning [has emerged and] evolved into a diverse network of loosely interconnected clusters of ideas."[29]

No consensus has been reached in that literature over what constitutes those behavioral and managerial characteristics that enable learning to take place. Rather, this relatively new field encompasses wide-ranging ideas, propositions, and empirical findings. Nonetheless, based on a review of the literature, it is possible to identify the following six learning characteristics of organizations that have successfully adapted to crises in performance. These characteristics inform the subsequent exploration of why TF 714 was able to adapt and transform organizationally, technologically, and operationally.

Unforeseen Challenges Do Not Paralyze the Organization

Learning organizations are not paralyzed by surprise. They develop competences for responding to unforeseen challenges that undercut operational performance. Members learn roles, methods, and modes of behavior that prepare them for the unexpected. To do so, management specialists have identified ways of making organizations more agile by adopting methods that address surprise through team-based exercises.[30] Uncertainty is not feared. Rather, when surprise occurs, agile organizations are prepared to manage it.

Problem Solving Is a Core Organizational Competence

Learning organizations institutionalize problem-solving methods that foster the diagnosis of operational challenges. Problem solving is a shared responsibility for the organization as a whole, not just the leadership.[31] Well-ordered and systematic problem solving is a core part of the organization's disposition, a way of thinking and acting, a part of the organization's personality.[32]

Organizational Practices Are Challengeable

All organizations develop routines, or SOPs, to accomplish objectives. However, only a subset of organizations is capable of changing those routines when confronted with a sudden breakdown in performance.[33] To do so, SOPs must be challengeable. Members of the organization must be empowered to contest existing routines in order to foster changes in them.[34] Agency must be fostered. Individuals within an organization must be able to exercise the capacity to challenge existing routines.[35]

Knowledge Collection Sets in Motion Systemic Learning

Learning organizations discover the sources of failure in performance through a capacity to collect and analyze information about such shortcomings. They are "skilled at creating, acquiring, and transferring knowledge."[36] Through knowledge collection and analysis, the reasons for which existing practices have become ineffective can be determined.[37] Garvin notes that such information can be derived from two sources: "the experiences and past history" of the organization itself and "the experiences and best practices of others."[38] With respect to the former, learning organizations "review their successes and failures, assess them systematically, and record the lessons."[39] Learning organizations also recognize that "powerful insights can come from looking outside one's immediate environment to gain new perspectives [from others]. Enlightened managers know that others likewise can be fertile sources of ideas and catalysts for creative thinking."[40]

Leaders Nurture a Milieu Conducive to Learning

Leaders of learning organizations establish practices that encourage the cross-fertilization of new ideas and promote the dissemination of information and knowledge. They empower members of the organization through a participatory approach that encourages collective problem solving.[41] Organizations that function in this manner require a different style of leadership from that based on the assumption that only from the top can a crisis in practice be understood and turned around. Juxtaposed to this traditional view, Peter Senge and others propose that organizations that are able to learn and innovate to address declining practice have senior leaders who foster interplay and interaction between themselves and the rest of the organization's members.[42] They nurture the development of organizations in which the people who make up an organization expand their capacity to understand complex challenges and actively contribute to problem solving. In today's complex environment, leaders must decentralize authority to nurture initiative by subordinates at the operating level.[43]

Organizational Memory Captures and Retains Innovations but Not Rigidly

Once innovation takes place, learning organizations insert those changes into the organization's memory. New SOPs are embedded in memory and transformed into new operating routines.[44] However, in addressing today's complex problems, new solutions may remain suitable for only a transitory period.[45] In complex contexts, reconfiguring operating practices will require a resilient learning cycle.[46]

Why Task Force 714 Was Able to Transform

Three factors explain why TF 714 was able to innovate, transforming itself during the darkest days of the Iraq War. Each is an outgrowth of different aspects of organizational learning. First, TF 714 adopted characteristics that allow an organization facing a crisis in practice to learn through self-reflection and to transform based on such reassessments. TF 714 demonstrated features of a learning organization that foster introspection, adaptation, and change. Second, the task force's leadership facilitated learning and innovation by acting against the instincts of traditional military commanders. In other words, the leadership decentralized authority to nurture initiative at the operating level that did not have to wait for direction from the top to attack a new target. Third, TF 714 expanded its network to include other nations fighting al-Qaeda or movements associated with it. The task force did so to learn from the experiences of others who had faced similar challenges and innovated.

Learning through Organizational Self-Reflection

TF 714 was able to dismantle AQI's networks because the task force emulated several of the characteristics of a learning organization described above to carry out self-reflection and transform based on that introspection and reassessment. These included institutionalizing problem-solving methods from below, fostering empowerment and agency of those individuals and teams closest to the operational level, and collecting and analyzing knowledge that advanced systematic learning.

To adopt these characteristics necessitated, in the first place, structural change because TF 714 was constructed over two decades as a top-down military organization that was highly compartmentalized and semiautonomous. General McChrystal described it as a closed system in which problem solving was the responsibility of the leadership. Leaders were to break challenges down, think through puzzles, and select the most effective solutions. Those solutions, once identified, were to be implemented by the organization's rank and file. While TF 714 did not wholly conform to the top-down model in that there was flexibility in terms of problem solving at the tactical level, above that level it adhered to a traditional chain of command.[47]

This was the approach of TF 714 when it deployed to Iraq. The "organization was designed for a problem set that no longer existed," explained McChrystal. "We brought an industrial-age force to an information-age conflict."[48] Traditional methods of operating were too deliberate and too hierarchical to decipher the puzzle presented by Iraq's fast-paced, decentralized, and networked insurgency. TF 714 had to be redesigned and form partnerships with several US intelligence agencies to decipher and counter the unprecedented challenge confronting it in Iraq. The mission of degrading AQI could not be accomplished by a highly compartmentalized and top-down military organization. It came down to transform or lose.

Problem Solving

AQI was a new problem set. A new organizational approach was needed to make sense of AQI's fast-paced and networked insurgency. This meant changing roles, rules, and patterns of interaction within the counterterrorism organization. Moreover, the organization itself would have to expand and add new affiliates that were not part of its network. All members of the network were going to have to learn to work together as a team.

The far-reaching scope of that transformation was subsequently captured in the McChrystal maxim "To defeat a networked enemy we had to become a network." By this he meant that TF 714 "had to figure out a way to retain [its] traditional capabilities of professionalism, technology, and, when needed, overwhelming force, while achieving levels of knowledge, speed, precision, and unity of effort that only a network could provide."[49]

A new organizational mechanism was needed to help TF 714 unravel the AQI puzzle. To combat such complex and unconventional security challenges required the formation of an interagency networked team. According to James Orton and Christopher Lamb, the following factors contribute to the effectiveness of interagency teams facing complex challenges.[50] Each factor facilitates coordination and integration of the diverse functional expertise that each team member brings to the mission.

1. **A Clearly Defined Mission.** Successful interagency teams establish a strategic consensus on a discrete mission and how it is to be executed.
2. **A Single Organization Leads.** Successful interagency teams have one member leading an effort in which cooperation is voluntary. The lead organization must be able to convince interagency associates to join because there are rewards for engaging in the mission.
3. **Collaborative Partnerships.** To recruit collaborative partners, lead organizations must learn about those it seeks to partner with, understand their interests, and recognize what it would take to build a relationship of trust, transparency, and cooperation with them.
4. **Team Culture.** Successful interagency teams establish a cohesive and transparent team culture to foster adoption of shared values and to establish a high degree of trust.
5. **Learning and Adaptation.** Team learning is an ongoing process of self-reflection and change. Teams acquire, share, and embed new knowledge into team operating procedures.
6. **Leadership.** Team leaders are successful not because they are forceful, decisive, and charismatic. Rather, it is because they build team systems that achieve successful outcomes by decentralizing authority and by empowering those closest to the fight. Teams require leaders who can exercise authority without suffocating the creativity of the team, facilitating the team's adaptive and effective performance.[51]

An organizational mechanism for setting this transformation in motion was not immediately apparent to the task force's leadership. There was no blueprint for turning TF 714 into the kind of organization that could achieve the objectives envisaged by its commander. However, as discussed in previous chapters, when Admiral McRaven proposed that TF 714 adopt and adapt the concept of a JIATF, McChrystal was convinced to do so. It took until 2005 to construct the JIATF, and in the process its members instituted problem-solving methods capable of fostering effective diagnoses of AQI's operational practices and forging members of the IC and the counterterrorism task force into a union of trust and common purpose.

In sum, the operating environment dominated by AQI demanded change in the cultures of secrecy and autonomy of the intelligence agencies and the task force opposing AQI. The organizational mechanism to bring about that change was the JIATF. Through it, TF 714's leadership fostered a new operational approach of cooperation and trust.

Empowerment and Agency

Agency is a critical feature of learning organizations facing complex challenges.[52] It equips individual members with license to contest existing routines when operating practices break down and fail to deliver in the field. Members are empowered to appraise existing operational TTPs and to propose changes to them. For TF 714, after adopting the JIATF structure, the next step in the transformation process was to instill in new interagency partners an interdependent learning and problem-solving way of operating based on agency. That entailed empowering the JIATF's members, down to the lowest practical working level, with the capacity described in the third characteristic of a learning organization noted above (i.e., organizational practices are challengeable).

The leadership of TF 714 concluded that it had to shed its top-down approach to command and control, substituting for it decentralized authority and problem solving from below. If TF 714 was to outpace AQI, explained McChrystal, problem solving and decision-making in the task force could not wait for him to disseminate commands. "A big piece of why we lagged behind AQI lay in our need to relay decisions up and down the chain of command. The requirement to consult me for strikes was symptomatic of a bureaucracy . . . grown slower and more convoluted as the world around it had become faster." The old process was taking too long and its "effects were crippling." The solution, McChrystal asserted, was to decentralize authority—"individuals and teams closest to the problem . . . offered the best ability to decide and act decisively."[53]

As the JIATF began to take shape with the addition of the CIA, the NSA, the FBI, the DIA, the NGA, and others, personnel from each of those agencies deployed to TF 714's headquarters in Iraq. Once there, they found a different kind of work environment from that at their home institution. They learned, General Flynn explained, that "you've got voice [agency]. . . . Everybody had a voice and so rank didn't matter, age didn't matter—what mattered was the value you added. Did you have value to provide, and if you did, provide it! You have a responsibility to do that. It's not just the commander or the J2 [intelligence chief] or the J3 [operations chief]—it's everybody."[54]

He gave the following example of how agency and empowerment could manifest itself in junior personnel at the TF 714 headquarters. Most days, the joint operations center would schedule capture/kill operations to be executed that night. Earlier in the day, however, a junior interrogator might learn something during the interrogation of a prisoner captured on a mission the night before and realize "that's going to impact tonight's missions. So, he would step away from the interrogation and wouldn't go back through a layered hierarchy to report what he learned but would go straight to the officer running the [joint operations center] to explain, 'We just learned this, and we think it's going to affect tonight's operations.'"[55]

A member of the JIATF who served at the working level in 2007–9 gave the following description of how agency manifested itself:

> [It was] the only organization I have ever been in where as long as you're going toward mission accomplishment, there was no fear of speaking out. In some organizations, I've seen it be feared to do so, especially if the leader was going to bleed you white if you said something he didn't agree with. General McChrystal himself had a voracious thirst for knowledge. And if someone had a more accurate conception of what the truth was, what the right answer was, he would support him. It did not matter what rank they were. It could be an intel captain doing an update.[56]

Agency was a critical enabler if the JIATF and task force were to prevail over what their leadership came to describe as a "complex" AQI challenge. For those in the world of international business, Gökçe Sargut and Rita McGrath observe, coping with accelerating "levels of complexity" has posed an acute challenge: "Complexity affects almost everything we touch: the products we design, the jobs we do, and the organizations we oversee. Most of this increase has resulted from the information technology revolution. . . . Systems that used to be separate are now interconnected and interdependent, which means that they are, by definition, more complex."[57]

What the leadership of TF 714 discovered was that coping with complexity was a challenge facing not only the business world but also military organizations engaged in modern irregular warfare. AQI posed a complex challenge for TF 714. Understanding it, McChrystal recalled, was "not an easy insight to come by. It was only . . . with considerable difficulty that we came to understand how the emerging networks of Islamist insurgents and terrorists were fundamentally different from any enemy the United States has previously known or faced."[58]

Those differences were most apparent, David Knoke observed, in AQI's "organizational structures and strategies. In place of vertically integrated hierarchies, today's Jihadis assemble in continually shifting networks."[59] Their organization did not mirror a hierarchical organizational structure. Their strategy was "to drive out foreign occupying forces by inflicting such high levels of injury and death that a democratic government would be forced to withdraw."[60] This was AQI's method of fighting. It constituted a plethora of decentralized groupings that made effective use of information technologies to form into an array of dispersed networks able to conduct operations across Iraq.[61]

Information, Knowledge, Intelligence

To defeat a complex web of networks, Flynn told McChrystal in 2004, TF 714 had to become more of an intelligence organization than an operations organization: "I said to General McChrystal, 'Your intelligence operations are a small part of your organization and they need to be 80 percent of what you do as an organization. It needs to be the majority of what the task force does.'" Although TF 714 "was an exquisite capability, they did not have the intelligence that they needed. They weren't even considering it to the degree that they should have."[62] In sum, an important learning juncture for TF 714 was the realization that to be effective, its operational units had to be coordinated with a robust intelligence capability drawn from several of the three-letter agencies of the IC. Actionable intelligence had to lead the way in the fight against AQI.

Business and management studies have found that successful learning organizations are able to identify the causes of their ineffectiveness by developing the means to secure information and knowledge about those shortcomings. For a military organization at war, this is an essential capability, not least in the case of TF 714, which was embroiled in a fight with a clandestine and networked enemy. Intelligence—information and knowledge—had to lead the way. Amassing and disseminating timely and accurate intelligence about AQI was the sine qua non for success. The task force had to achieve (as explained in chapter 5) intelligence dominance.

As noted above, an essential characteristic of a learning organization is the capacity to discover the sources of failure in performance through the capacity to collect and analyze information about such shortcomings and to make the necessary changes in TTPs. Through knowledge collection and analysis, the reasons why existing practices have become ineffective can be determined. Effective knowledge collection—intelligence—was essential for TF 714. Recall that Garvin notes that such knowledge can be derived from two sources: "the experiences and past history" of an organization itself and "the experiences and best practices of others." With respect to the latter, TF 714 expanded its network to draw on the experiences of others fighting al-Qaeda and other extremist groups aligned with it. It understood, as Garvin remarks, that learning organizations recognize "powerful insights can come from looking outside one's immediate environment to gain new perspectives. Enlightened managers know that others likewise can be fertile sources of ideas and catalysts for creative thinking."[63]

But equally important for TF 714 was its own ability to amass and disseminate intelligence. It was able to do so, as Flynn explained, by flipping the targeting process. "Instead of 80 percent of the task force effort being focused on operations and 20 percent on intelligence, the opposite became the case." He argued that transforming F3 into F3EAD was essential: "If we were going to defeat this enemy, they had to have pressure applied to them constantly. And this was the only way to do so constantly."[64]

By itself, TF 714 could not execute F3EAD. It did not have the intelligence capacity to do so. That necessitated an interagency collaborative effort. Therefore, achieving the buy-in of the three-letter intelligence agencies was essential to achieve intelligence dominance. Without it, the process of analyzing and exploiting intelligence collected on operations to initiate more operations could never have achieved the tempo needed to degrade the insurgent underground and networked apparatus. As a highly compartmentalized and semiautonomous organization, TF 714 did not have the necessary intelligence capacity.

The JIATF brought together three critical ingredients—people, process, and systems—to employ F3EAD to achieve intelligence dominance. F3EAD enabled the task force "to plan and execute operations against the enemy faster than the enemy could react" to those operations. It provided the way for the task force to get inside AQI's networks to "simultaneously direct [multiple] operations against several parts of it."[65]

F3EAD transformed targeting. No longer was the focal point on seizing or destroying enemy personnel, equipment, and facilities. Rather, the main effort now concentrated on the intelligence elements of the process: exploit and analyze. This transformation set in motion a continuous cycle of learning that provided the task force with the capacity to dominate the operational tempo of the battle with AQI and to unmask its networks.

In sum, these three characteristics of learning organizations, when adopted by TF 714, constituted the first key factor in explaining why TF 714 was able to achieve an organizational, technological, and operational sea change to dismantle AQI's networks across Iraq.

Leadership Facilitated Learning

A second factor explaining why TF 714 and its JIATF partners were able to dismantle AQI's networks is that McChrystal instilled within both TF 714 and the joint task force an organizational culture conducive to learning and innovation. His leadership mattered. But to successfully drive organizational change, his own leadership style had to change.

Organizational experts argue that in today's complex, interdependent, and fast-changing world, leaders can no longer assume that a crisis in operational practice can be tackled only from the top. Instead, today's leaders are called on to decentralize authority and nurture initiative by subordinates at the operating level. They must empower members of their organization through a leadership approach that encourages collective learning, adaptation, and change from the bottom up. To this end, assert David Snowden and Mary Boone,

> leaders often will be called upon *to act against their instincts*. They will need to know when to share power and when to wield it alone, when to look to the wisdom of the group and when to take their own counsel. A deep understanding of context, the ability to embrace complexity . . . and a willingness to flexibly change leadership style will be required for leaders who want to make things happen in a time of increasing uncertainty.[66]

Snowden and Boone are writing here about the challenges of conducting business in today's complex world, but their observation, as the leadership of TF 714 discovered, was no less true for the conduct of war. If TF 714 was to increase its operational tempo to overwhelm AQI, the task force's decision-making had to be decentralized. Those down the chain of command had to be empowered, and the leaders of TF 714 had to learn to "act against their instincts."[67] With the establishment of the JIATF and its maturation, the stage was set for a showdown between TF 714's operational teams and AQI. But to reach the operational tempo needed to prevail, yet another hurdle had to be overcome—the problem of what then Colonel Sacolick characterized as "blinks" in the F3EAD targeting cycle.[68] A blink was a bottleneck that slowed the cycle down. The more blinks, the slower the process, the fewer the raids against AQI's networks.

To gain a better understanding of this problem, Sacolick conducted a reassessment of the cycle and discovered "that between each of the F3EAD elements there [could be] an unintended pause or 'blink' that resulted all too often in a missed opportunity to hit a target." If one could "remove the blinks from the process," said the commander of the army units of TF 714, the result would be a "dramatic increase in operational speed."[69] And the speed and frequency with which AQI targets were hit were the keys to degrading and dismantling its networks.

Sacolick found there were different sources of blinks. Early on, many were due to a lack of trust and cultural barriers among the agencies that constituted the JIATF. However, these blinks were reduced considerably as the JIATF took root and trust was established between, on the one side, the intelligence agencies that it comprised and, on the other side, TF 714's operational units. Technology shortfalls likewise slowed down the targeting cycle. But these, too, were reduced over time as the task force leadership was able to acquire what was needed in terms of technological solutions.

The final source of blinks was the chain-of-command system itself. It was a twentieth-century organizational structure—a top-down model in which authority and power in the organization were wielded from the top leadership down to those planning and executing operations. Decision-making at the top of the chain of command and the pace of TF 714's operational tempo were inversely related. The more traditional the nature of the command-and-control process, the slower the F3EAD cycle moved, and the stronger AQI remained.

To overcome this last source of blinks necessitated a change in the traditional approach to leadership exercised by military organizations, even special ones such as TF 714. Blinks in the command-and-control system could be removed, but that meant empowering the rank-and-file by delegating decision-making authority downward. License to plan and execute operations would have to be decentralized and pushed downward to the operating level if the number of raids were to be accelerated. Waiting for General McChrystal to make the call on missions delayed TF 714's capacity to win the fight against AQI. Recall what McChrystal said about the counterterrorism force that deployed to Iraq in 2003: The "organization was designed for a problem set that no longer existed. . . . We brought an industrial-age force to an information-age conflict."[70] Traditional methods of operating were too deliberate and too hierarchical to dismantle Iraq's fast-paced and networked insurgency. A highly compartmentalized and top-down military organization could not accomplish that mission. TF 714 had to be redesigned, and that included changing how its leadership approached command and control.

Empowerment of those at the operational level of the task force was necessary to accelerate the rate at which raids were carried out, explained General Votel, who replaced McRaven as commander of TF 714. To do so meant decentralizing authority and decision-making. "Officers leading raiding teams in the field had a great deal of decision-making authority to select and hit targets. There were standards that had to be met, but within them they made the call." Votel, as the commanding general, "had to be willing to accept risks, give up control, and trust those [we] were empowering."[71] Only in this way could the task force speed up the operational tempo to three hundred raids per month.

As a result of this fundamental change in the command system, the task force leadership became enablers rather than "hands-on leaders whose personal competence and force of will dominated battlefields . . . for generations." To defeat the AQI network, McChrystal concluded that he had to eschew "the temptation to lead as a chess master, controlling each move of the organization."[72] Rather, he would become an "eyes-on, hands-off enabler," a facilitator who established a context in which those down the chain of command were "not looking over their shoulder wondering what does the old man want done. The old man wants to win. That's it, and so a lot of them were ready to do it, to take the lead, particularly in the specialized units."[73]

The impact of this change on operational tempo was recounted by McChrystal in a *Foreign Affairs* interview in 2013: "In August 2004, in all of Iraq, our task force did 18 raids. And we thought that was breakneck speed. . . . Two years later, in August 2006, we were up to 300 raids a month—ten a night. This meant [our] network now had to operate at a speed that was not even considered before, not in our wildest dreams."[74]

The only way this tempo could be achieved, he added, was by changing TF 714's command-and-control system. "It had to have decentralized decision-making, because you can't centralize ten raids a night. You have to understand them all, but you have to allow your subordinate elements to operate very quickly." They had to be able to "understand who or what is a target, locate it, capture or kill it, take what intelligence you can from people or equipment or documents, analyze that, and then you go back and do the cycle again, smarter."[75]

The leadership lessons from five years in command of the counterterrorism forces in Iraq, Afghanistan, and elsewhere have been encapsulated by McChrystal in *Team of Teams: New Rules of Engagement for a Complex World*. That book helps answer the question posed at the beginning of this chapter: *Why* was TF 714 able to achieve an organizational, technological, and operational sea change to dismantle AQI? His answer, laid out in *Team of Teams*, is that TF 714 did so by turning the highly specialized and compartmentalized organization into a network of teams that dismantled AQIs networks across Iraq. The book also confirms what Snowden and Boone say about why today's leaders have to *act against their instincts*: they have to do so because "the velocity and volume of decisions needing to be made in today's complex environments exceeds the capabilities of even the most gifted leaders. Therefore, empowerment of those lower rungs is a simple necessity."[76]

The sheaf of reviews of *Team of Teams* reiterates the volume's central premise—namely, that teams can accomplish much more in today's complex world than individual leaders can. Review after review concurs that to be successful, today's leaders must hand decision-making authority over to teams empowered with the information they need to make successful decisions at the operational levels of the organization.

In the twenty-first century, establishing teams across an organization to improve performance is touted as the only way to overcome crises in practice caused by complex challenges. But for this to take place, leaders must engender trust among the teams they are empowering to ensure that they share a common understanding of the organization's goals, which in turn will generate an efficient and cooperative harmony across the entire organization. Trust is indispensable for teams to function together effectively. By empowering teams closest to the fight to accomplish their missions, TF 714's leadership enabled TF 714's operational units to innovate in ways they would not have been able to in a traditional top-down system of command. To confront a complex environment and compete against a networked enemy, TF 714's leadership enabled speed to act, and that meant it took an "eyes-on, hands-off" approach to command.

The new leadership model, McChrystal stresses in *Team of Teams*, "is anything but passive. The leader acts as an 'Eyes-On, Hands-Off' enabler who creates and maintains an ecosystem in which the organization operates."[77] The army had prepared McChrystal to lead like a chess player: "Our leaders, including me, had been trained as chess masters, and we hoped to display the talent and skill of masters."[78] But for the fight against enemies such as AQI, he adopted a different leadership style, that of "a gardener, enabling rather than directing."[79] What this meant, he explains, was not eschewing leadership but adopting a very different form of it that had the following features:

> Creating and maintaining the teamwork conditions we needed—tending the garden—became my primary responsibility. Without my constantly pruning and shaping our network, the delicate balance of information and empowerment that sustained our operations would atrophy, and our success would wither. I found that only the senior leader could drive the operating rhythm, transparency, and cross-functional cooperation we needed. I could shape the culture and demand the ongoing conversation that shared consciousness required. Leading as a gardener meant that I kept the Task Force focused on clearly articulated priorities by explicitly talking about them and by leading by example.[80]

Commanding by enabling was every bit as demanding as being the traditional leader he characterized as "a chess master." Creating and enabling a network of teams rather than directing and controlling every move of a hierarchal organization required employing different leadership techniques. Coming to this understanding necessitated realizing that much of what McChrystal had been taught about leadership was out of date. Accepting that fact took a leader who was open to the ideas of others as well as capable of his own innovative thinking. His tenet that it "takes a network to defeat a network" is illustrative of his ability to think outside the box.

Liam Collins notes several examples of McChrystal's peer commanders who in 2004 failed to grasp the true nature of the burgeoning insurgency in Iraq.[81] But McChrystal commanded a unit that "had been focused on the al Qaeda network since 9-11 so they had years of experience with this unconventional threat."[82] And as *Team of Teams* chronicles, the task force and its commander came to understand that AQI was a different kind of insurgent organization. It consisted of many decentralized units that employed Information Age technologies to form into dispersed networks to escalate attacks across Iraq. That understanding led McChrystal to conclude that TF 714 had to transform itself into a network that was augmented with a robust intelligence capability provided by the various intelligence agencies. That was his innovative solution for countering AQI: it "takes a network to defeat a network."

But other organizational and operational concepts that were necessary for his network conception to reach fruition and function were proposed by others. And McChrystal was open to embracing them. Three illustrations of this openness were the concepts of intelligence-driven operations, the JIATF, and F3EAD.

McChrystal understood the importance of intelligence. But the concept of how intelligence should drive operations and operations generate intelligence was not his. It came from his J2, Colonel Flynn, who convinced him to adopt it. As explained at other points in this book, an organizational mechanism for setting such a transformation in motion was also not immediately apparent to the task force leader as he grappled with the complex challenge of AQI and how to fight it. There was no blueprint for turning TF 714 into the kind of intelligence-driven organization that could achieve the objectives he hoped to achieve. However, there was a relatively unknown organizational concept—a joint interagency task force— that McRaven suggested could be adapted to TF 714's complex Iraqi battlespace and would bring all of the intelligence agencies inside the TF 714 tent, providing the robust intelligence capabilities that were needed. Amassing and disseminating operationally timely intelligence about AQI was essential for TF 714's success. McChrystal embraced the JIATF concept.

Setting up the JIATF brought into sharp focus the need to adopt a different targeting cycle to exploit the intelligence generated by TF 714 and its JIATF partners. Initially, the task force was focused on finding, fixing, and finishing targeting—F3. It did not exploit and analyze intelligence collected on raids or through other means to identify new targets to accelerate the number of raids against AQI. To increase operational tempo, the task force had to transform F3 into F3EAD. Collins explains that the idea for adopting F3EAD "came from Colonel Scott Miller in early 2004. At that time, he was commanding a TF 714 subordinate task force in Iraq."[83] Miller realized that "the task force lacked the internal capacity that was required for the exploitation and analysis part of the cycle," but Miller "understood the criticality of exploitation and analysis and hoped the term would help communicate what the task force was trying to do."[84] Eventually it did, as Collins elaborates:

> In the summer of 2004, Colonel Bennet Sacolick, the commander of TF 16, came into McChrystal's office and put a single PowerPoint slide on the monitor that read "FIND-FIX-FINISH-EXPLOIT-ANALYZE." The words represented the targeting cycle that Miller outlined in January 2004. Although Miller had developed the concept earlier in the year, this was the first time that it had been articulated in such a clear and concise manner. This provided McChrystal exactly what he needed to communicate the idea effectively with his interagency partners. It allowed him to explain what he needed and how it supported the war effort.[85]

There are several other important dimensions of McChrystal's approach to leadership through "enabling rather than directing" that contributed to the transformation of TF 714 into a network. These included the identification of innovative procedures and mechanisms that established a networked operating system based on cooperation, trust, and interdependence among its members. Those innovative procedures and mechanisms, described throughout this narrative, were adopted by TF 714 to augment its networked operating system. Each helped construct an environment that generated real-time interaction and problem solving across the task force to exponentially increase operational tempo. Those innovations enhanced the capacity of TF 714 to act decisively, with speed and precision, to maneuver inside AQI's networks fast enough to seriously degrade them from the inside out.

In sum, leadership made a difference and contributes to our understanding of *why* TF 714 was able to reconstruct itself organizationally, technologically, and operationally to eviscerate AQI. McChrystal facilitated learning, adaptation, and transformation. He did so by *acting against his instincts*, knowing when to share power and when to wield it.[86] By acting as an eyes-on, hands-off enabler, he created and maintained an ecosystem in which the task force could accomplish its mission.[87]

Learning from the Experiences of Others Fighting Terrorism

Garvin, as noted above, argues that learning organizations discover the sources of a failure in practice and the ways to address them either through an understanding of the "experiences and past history of their own organization" or through "the experiences and best practices of others."[88] With respect to the latter, he observes that learning organizations recognize that "powerful insights can come from looking outside one's immediate environment to gain new perspectives [from others]. Enlightened managers know that others likewise can be fertile sources of ideas and catalysts for creative thinking."[89]

In the case of TF 714, there were other national-level counterterrorism organizations whose experiences and best practices could be drawn upon. Indeed, several intelligence specialists concur with Jennifer Sims that "since the terrorist attacks of 11 September 2001, the role of foreign intelligence liaison has taken center stage in the global war on terror."[90] Daniel Byman, for instance, has observed that "perhaps more than any other policy instrument, foreign liaison relationships play a vital role in counterterrorism against global terrorist groups like the Islamic State and Al Qaeda."[91]

To take advantage of liaison opportunities, TF 714 had to expand its network to encompass other nations that could share their counterterrorism operational and programmatic experiences to help TF 714 think through how to deal with AQI. "We began as a network of people, then grew into a network of teams, then a network of organizations, and ultimately a network of nations," explained McChrystal.[92] Most notably, this network of nations included Israel, with which the United States has had one of its strongest intelligence liaison relationships, dating back to 1951, "when Prime Minister David Ben-Gurion . . . offered, and the CIA accepted, the concept of a liaison relationship between the U.S. and Israeli intelligence communities."[93] That was the beginning of intelligence exchanges and cooperation between the two nations that has, over the decades, taken the form of many formal memoranda, including ones with US counterterrorism forces.

In the early 2000s, Israel was embroiled in the Second Intifada, which began following the collapse of the Camp David Summit and Ariel Sharon's visit to the Temple Mount. Largely consisting of a campaign of escalating suicide attacks against civilian targets, the Second Intifada caught Israel's security establishment off guard.[94]

While terrorism was not a new challenge, during the late 1990s Israel found itself facing armed groups that were increasingly innovative and resolute (notably, Hezbollah and Hamas), against which its security services needed to adapt in order to maintain the upper hand. This challenge was particularly demanding for the intelligence services of Shin Bet, Aman, and Mossad. They were increasingly unable to collect real-time, actionable intelligence on their enemies' operational activities. Moreover, intelligence was not driving operations.

To adapt, Shin Bet put itself at the forefront of embracing advanced collection and analysis technologies from the Information Age revolution that could amass multidimensional, real-time, actionable intelligence on the activities of its irregular adversaries. New tools of analysis could be used to manage that intelligence data, which was increasingly voluminous. The goal was actionable intelligence assessments that operators could act on expeditiously. Organizationally, for these collection and analysis capabilities to be effective, they had to work together in the same facility. The force behind these changes was Shin Bet's chief in the late 1990s, Ami Ayalon.

At the same time, Gen. Moshe Ya'alon, the former director of Aman, who in the late 1990s had been appointed chief of the IDF's Central Command, likewise found his intelligence capabilities severely wanting. Israel had very sophisticated collection capabilities, but they existed in information silos with no synergy between them or with the operational units they could be integrated with and support. Along with Yuval Diskin, who at that time commanded Shin Bet's Jerusalem District, Ya'alon sought to construct an innovative organizational solution to the way intelligence was employed to fight terrorism, by bringing all the intelligence agencies and operational counterterrorism units together in one place in a joint interagency facility. This took the form of what came to be known as the Joint War Room (JWR).[95] What Diskin brought to this new arrangement was a keen understanding of the advantages that advanced technical collection methods and data-mining systems could contribute to the irregular warfare fight.

The first principle of the JWR concept was that all the collection agencies had to be present in one place and that the intelligence they gathered would be fused into common databases. The goal was for JWR analysts to have access to all relevant information. To achieve this, Shin Bet had to integrate the computer systems of the different collection agencies. The end result was that all relevant data could be displayed in a manner that would be digestible by analysts. The goal was for that intelligence to drive counterterrorism operations.

With the outbreak of the Second Intifada, the concepts of the JWR and intelligence-driven operations were adopted for counterterrorism operations across Israel and the Palestinian territories. It constituted a new organizational, technological, and operational system for fighting the terrorism offensive that was rapidly escalating in 2001. The JWR exploited the technological revolution taking place in intelligence and information and adopted several of the features identified by Orton and Lamb to advance effective interagency team building. These factors facilitated the coordination and integration of the functional expertise each Israeli intelligence and operational unit brought to the mission of preventing suicide operations.

The timing was fortuitous, given the strategic challenge the Second Intifada posed to Israel. In 2002, it was hit with fifty-three successful suicide bombings that killed 238 civilians, with many more failures; the number of volunteers seeking to take part in suicide operations was reportedly burgeoning. Yoram Schweitzer writes that the "massive use of suicide attacks . . . went far beyond merely being a tool for causing pain, destruction, and death to Israelis, and became a psychological weapon for fighting Israel because of its ability to leave its menacing imprint on the Israeli public's self confidence and morale." Major terrorist attacks, such as the 2002 Netanya Passover massacre,[96] caused "many Israelis despair." They came to see their government as unable to deal with "intolerable damage and disruption to every aspect of daily life."[97] The Israeli population was traumatized.

To de-escalate the suicide offensive, Israel needed to refocus its targeting strategy, so instead of trying to stop individual operatives dispatched against Israeli civilian targets, the goal became degrading the capacity of the terrorist organization to plan and execute operations. Ronen Bergman describes this new approach as focused on targeting "the ticking infrastructure behind the attacks." This included the "recruiters, couriers, and weapons procurers, as well as people who maintained safe houses and smuggled money—the entire organization overseen by commanders or regional cells." Also included were the organization's high-value targets, the "main military commanders" and "political leaders." The objective was to remove enough of them to bring the terrorism apparatus—the ticking infrastructure—to a standstill.[98]

A key architect of the new strategy, Shin Bet chief Avi Dichter, held that if the military had the appropriate capabilities and was supported by the intelligence agencies aligned together in the JWR (and managing high-quality signals, imagery, and human intelligence to drive operations), Israel had the means to degrade and dismantle the terrorism apparatus. These organizational, technological, and operational innovations provided the means to allow Israel's counterterrorism forces to dramatically increase their capacity to conduct operations. Rather than relying on periodic and discrete missions, Israel accelerated its operational tempo to be able to execute up to five missions per day. And instead of preempting individual operatives on the way to attack civilian targets, Israel focused on preventing operations from being planned and executed by the terrorism apparatus by degrading and dismantling that apparatus.[99]

By 2004, the number of successful suicide attacks was reduced to 17, with nearly 160 operations foiled. And in 2005, those numbers declined further to 9 successful attacks, with 46 thwarted.[100] The adaptations and innovations described above provided Israel with an offensive capability to attack and degrade the terrorism infrastructure through targeted killing of the midlevel planners, managers, and commanders who facilitated suicide operations. Political leaders were also targeted. According to Ophir Falk, "Israel's targeted killing policy, along with other less significant factors during the first decade of the 21st century, was effective in mitigating suicide terror attacks generated from the Territories in general and from Gaza most specifically. Israel's targeted killing policy achieved tactical and strategic success. From a tactical perspective, the operations accurately eliminated their targets. From a strategic perspective, the policy was the key factor in stopping or at least mitigating suicide bombing fatalities."[101] These developments, in conjunction with the "reoccupation of the Palestinian cities in Operation Defensive Shield" and "construction of the security barrier in areas vulnerable to infiltration from the territories to Israel," brought about a sharp reduction in suicide attacks.[102] Israel was able to prevail—at the operational level—over a terrorist challenge that observers in general believed to be insurmountable. By constructing an interagency task force—the JWR—comprising intelligence agencies and operational capabilities, Israel brought the terrorist organization to its knees in 2004 and 2005.

During those same two years, TF 714 began to confront the growing Iraqi insurgency described in this book. Interestingly, there are clear similarities between the ways in which Israel's security agencies responded to the Second Intifada and how TF 714 adapted itself to combat AQI in Iraq. To what extent was TF 714 aware of ongoing developments in Israel? Did the Israeli experience help it think through how to tackle the AQI challenge?

Ascertaining the answers to these questions is complicated because liaison arrangements between intelligence and security agencies are, in general, highly secret and difficult to pin down. This is certainly the case when the United States and Israel are involved. However, interviews conducted with retired senior Israeli military and security officials disclosed that a special liaison relationship existed between members of TF 714 and their Israeli counterparts from late 2003. According to General Ya'alon, who during 2002–5 served as chief of staff of the IDF, and Maj. Gen. Amos Yadlin, who during 2004–6 served as Israel's military attaché to the United States and during 2006–10 as head of Aman, TF 714 maintained an ongoing liaison presence in Israel from early 2004.[103]

As a result, explained Ya'alon, Israel shared with the task force its experiences and expertise in adapting and reorganizing to counter the challenges posed by the Second Intifada. Beginning in late 2003, this interaction included intensive meetings in Israel with senior leaders from TF 714. The Israelis shared all the organizational, technological, and operational details of the counterterrorism system they had constructed to reduce the onslaught of suicide operations. TF 714 leaders learned how Israel empowered individual commanders and teams closest to the fight with the authority to decide and act decisively without going back up the chain of command. Empowerment of those at the lower rungs of the chain of command was essential in Israel's fight against terrorist organizations, Ya'alon explained.[104]

Task force representatives were able to observe how Israel's counterterrorism system functioned operationally up close by watching how the JWR performed its tasks as well as by going into the field with IDF units on missions. Israel provided, said Ya'alon, a complete picture of its experience in employing new technologies to defuse the Second Intifada. Liaison was very intense and took many forms. Eventually it also went both ways, because by late 2006, TF 714 began sharing with its Israeli liaison partners the lessons it was drawing from the fight against AQI.[105]

General Yadlin, as the head of Aman, interacted directly with TF 714 leaders during their almost monthly visits to Israel. In a series of interviews in 2018, he explained how he sought to convey the details and nuances of the Israeli system for fighting terrorism. He provided briefings on different ways of conducting intelligence-driven operations by encouraging initiative at the fighting level, and his points were illustrated through operational case studies and by taking TF 714's representatives into the field with Israeli units. Yadlin spoke with TF 714's liaison representatives often, providing them with extensive access to the Israeli counterterrorism system, including showing them how it employed diverse technologies such as ISR platforms.[106] Collins reports that McChrystal, "after visiting Israel in February 2004, asked USSOCOM to bypass the slow acquisition process and buy [these] ready-made Israeli platforms." However, the US Air Force blocked those efforts because it contravened the formal process for acquiring foreign military equipment.[107]

Yadlin saw his role, and those of his subordinates, as giving TF 714 a comprehensive understanding of the conceptual and operational details of how Israel dismantled the terrorist organization that had traumatized its society. He told TF 714's leaders that "to fight terror you have to become more Israeli, adopting our model." Yadlin believes the leadership of TF 714 "was open to doing so."[108]

Other members of Israel's counterterrorism apparatus confirmed the nature of the liaison relationship with TF 714. Barak Ben-Zur had joined Shin Bet in 1996 and had held a variety of positions, including head of various departments and divisions. In 2000, he was appointed head of the research unit, and in 2003, he became special assistant to the director of Shin Bet, Avi Dichter. He also served as a member of the prime minister's steering committee for negotiations with the Palestinians. During his time with Shin Bet, and earlier in Aman, Ben-Zur observed intelligence liaison arrangements with the United States, which he characterized as a regularized process. He described it as close cooperation, a natural transfer of ideas, and noted that the innovations described above were shared with US counterparts.[109]

To summarize, Israel became an important liaison partner for TF 714, and in 2004, it essentially became a part of TF 714's network. This was accomplished through the assignment of liaison officers from TF 714 to Israel to generate trust and strengthen ties with it. Liaison officers were an important part of the counterterrorism network constructed by McChrystal. "The mission of the LNOs," he explained, was to establish a reciprocal rapport in which each partner shared and benefited. The role of the LNOs was to "lay a foundation for the trusting relationships we needed to develop between the nodes of our network."[110] LNOs were necessary because AQI did not exist in a vacuum. It was part of a global jihadist apparatus. Consequently, the sharing of information and knowledge was essential not just among US government agencies but also with allies. LNOs were handpicked, recalled McRaven. They were "always high performers," and each was expected to build relationships between their assigned location and the task force.[111]

The task force leadership first went to Israel in the fall of 2003. Shortly thereafter, a liaison team was assigned to stay in Israel to facilitate and deepen cooperation. The liaison team was given extensive access to learn how Israel adapted to fight the Second Intifada through organizational, technological, and operational innovations. LNOs gained an understanding of the concept of the JWR, the employment of different intelligence-collection platforms, and the process through which intelligence-driven operations degraded the terrorist infrastructure by targeting midlevel planners, managers, and commanders as well as their political leaders.

TF 714's network included other nations in addition to Israel. Intelligence and special operations cooperation between the United States and the United Kingdom dated back to World War II. Several decades later, newly established US counterterrorism forces had established liaison relationships with their British counterparts.[112] And in Iraq, British SAS (Special Air Service) and SBS (Special Boat Service) forces deployed units to join TF 714. As Mark Urban details in *Task Force Black: The Explosive True Story of the SAS and the Secret War in Iraq*, "they were part of the ruthless fight, night after night, to target and eliminate AQI's secret networks."[113] During 2005, Task Force Black, as the British forces were collectively known, was integrated into TF 714. This gave the SAS in particular an important role in the unremitting offensive against AQI, as Urban documents. According to an August 2008 report in the British newspaper the *Telegraph*, "More than 3,500 insurgents have been taken off the streets of Baghdad by the elite

British force in a series of audacious 'Black Ops' over the past two years. It is understood that while the majority of the terrorists were captured, several hundred, who were mainly members of the organization known as 'al-Qaeda in Iraq' have been killed by the SAS."[114]

Israel and the United Kingdom made the most extensive contributions to TF 714's network, but other nations were also members, including Saudi Arabia and Jordan. Each had experience with and unique capabilities for fighting terrorism. Beginning in 2003, Saudi Arabia came under attack from jihadist fighters who had been radicalized by al-Qaeda in Afghanistan and were returning home. They helped fuel a bloody internal war in Saudi Arabia that continued for several years.

One of the unique elements of Saudi Arabia's counterterrorism operations was a system established for prosecuting and rehabilitating captured terrorists. The effectiveness of this program has been scrutinized by various specialists. Jessica Stern finds that "although a number of other governments have made similar attempts, Saudi Arabia, perhaps surprisingly, is at the cutting edge. Some four thousand individuals have graduated from the rehabilitation program, and a comprehensive effort is now under way to dissuade youth from joining terrorist groups in the first place. The Saudi approach is an extremely important experiment that may have implications for counter-radicalization programs around the globe—not just for Muslim terrorist groups, but others as well."[115]

Christopher Boucek concurs with Stern,[116] although others are less sanguine.[117] The extent to which TF 714 introduced elements of the Saudi system into TF 714's own detention program is not known; what is not in doubt is that the Saudis shared with TF 714 the specifics of their deradicalization and rehabilitation program as part of liaison arrangements.[118]

From the Jordanians, the task force learned of their long experience in employing HUMINT operations to penetrate and disrupt terrorist cells.[119] Although those techniques could not be replicated by TF 714 itself, there were lessons from the Jordanian experience that their Iraqi counterparts embraced as they began in 2009 to play a more active role as TF 714's partner.[120]

In sum, TF 714 expanded its network to include other nations fighting terrorism. It did so because its leadership realized it could learn from the experiences of others who had faced similar challenges and had innovated. The leadership of TF 714 understood that learning organizations can and should look "outside one's immediate environment to gain new perspectives [from others]. Enlightened managers know that others likewise can be fertile sources of ideas and catalysts for creative thinking."[121] TF 714's leadership gained important insights about effective and inventive counterterrorism strategies from others, in particular the Israelis, through liaison arrangements.

EPILOGUE: MORE IRREGULAR WAR AND THE CHALLENGE OF REVISIONIST STATE POWERS

THIS BOOK HAS TOLD THE STORY OF JOINT SPECIAL OPERATIONS COMMAND'S counterterrorism force that deployed to Iraq in 2003 as Task Force 714. Once on the ground, it was assigned the mission of dismantling the al-Qaeda in Iraq–dominated insurgency whose violent attacks were escalating precipitously. But the task force found that AQI was different, a puzzle that baffled it. AQI's secret, decentralized, and networked organization was unlike that of any twentieth-century insurgency it was familiar with. Task force leaders quickly determined they faced an enemy they had never envisioned and one they could not fight through their preexisting ways of conducting counterterrorism operations. They confronted an enemy they did not understand and for which they had to fundamentally change their operational focus from a peacetime strategic scalpel designed to execute a small number of periodic missions to an industrial-strength counterterrorism machine constructed for a fast-paced, irregular wartime environment.

As the preceding chapters illustrate, TF 714 adapted and transformed in the midst of the Iraq War and, from 2006 to 2010, was able to dismantle AQI's clandestine networks to a degree that it could no longer function in a cohesive manner. It did so by increasing operational tempo from 18 to 300 night raids per month and eliminating a large number of the midlevel commanders and managers of AQI's networks, the linchpins of the organization. In doing so, the task force changed the paradigm for conducting twenty-first-century counterterrorism operations.

To achieve these results, TF 714 had to transform and partner with several US intelligence agencies to neutralize an unprecedented enemy. The mechanism for achieving that transformation was the joint interagency task force. The JIATF forged those intelligence agencies and TF 714 into a union, based on interdependence and cooperation, that established problem-solving methods capable of uncovering AQI's networks. Having adopted the JIATF, TF 714 shed its top-down style of command and control, substituting decentralized authority and problem solving from below. To outpace AQI, decision-making could not wait for senior leaders to disseminate commands. That took too long and was too slow.

TF 714 transformed into an intelligence-led organization. Its operational units, JSOC's counterterrorism teams, were coordinated with a robust intelligence capability drawn from the CIA, the NSA, the FBI, the DIA, and the NGA, among others. To learn and adapt, TF 714 amassed information and knowledge about a new problem set: a complex, clandestine, and networked enemy empowered by Information Age technology. The task force achieved intelligence dominance over AQI by adopting a new operational concept: find, fix, finish, exploit, analyze, and disseminate. F3EAD transformed targeting and provided the means to get inside AQI's networks to dominate the operational tempo of the fight against them.

Once inside, the JIATF helped identify central and peripheral figures, patterns of behavior, and clusters of nodes to degrade AQI's operating system. Doing this fast enough—hitting many targets each night—resulted in TF 714 outpacing AQI's capacity to adapt, causing its networks to collapse in upon themselves. Chapters 3 through 5 explained the impact that the transformation of intelligence collection, analysis, and covert paramilitary direct-action raids had on AQI's operational tempo and the extent to which it allowed TF 714 to eliminate a large number of the midlevel commanders and managers—those who made their networks function. As Admiral McRaven noted, during 2008, "the intelligence being collected during our raids and from the interrogations of the many members of AQI that we captured on those raids . . . [signaled that] a major decline was taking place in the capacity of different parts of their networks to carry out operations. Our kill/capture raids were considerably driving down their operational capacity. We were able to gauge and evaluate their decline."[1]

Those achievements explained *how* TF 714 was able by the end of 2009 to disrupt AQI's clandestine apparatus, operational timetable, and freedom of movement, putting the group on the defensive. The task force seriously degraded AQI's ability to conduct operations, and a large number of its operational cells, financial units, communications and media centers, bomb- and IED-production facilities, and arms acquisition networks were put out of business. Finally, the task force dismantled networks to the degree that AQI could no longer function in the cohesive manner it once had. In addition to discerning *how* TF 714 accomplished this mission, this volume also revealed three reasons *why* it was able to do so.

TF 714 changed the paradigm for conducting twenty-first-century counterterrorism operations against networked irregular enemies like AQI. But that transformed counterterrorism force was not employed only in Iraq. Variations of the task force were established elsewhere and became part of a transnational and networked counterterrorism campaign carried out against al-Qaeda and its associated movements, and later ISIS, in several other geographic locations. This became the embodiment of the often-cited McChrystal refrain: "To defeat a networked enemy we had to become a network."[2]

Counterterrorism Force Operations beyond Iraq: It Takes a Network

Operation Enduring Freedom was a major setback for al-Qaeda because it lost its Afghanistan sanctuary from which it had planned and executed attacks against the United States from 1996 to 2001, including 9/11. During those years, it had attracted as many as twenty thousand foreign fighters from more than fifty countries to training camps located there.[3] They were the second generation of transnational warriors attracted to al-Qaeda's global mission. The first wave had grown out of the Soviet invasion of Afghanistan. Many thousands from across the Muslim world joined that fight in the 1980s.

To reconstitute itself, al-Qaeda spawned new strategists who offered inventive ripostes to the setbacks imposed by Operation Enduring Freedom, proposing new ways of attacking. One example was Abdel Aziz al-Muqrin. In a *Practical Course for Guerrilla War*, which initially appeared incrementally in issues of an online al-Qaeda publication, he proposed adoption of insurgency strategy and provided a guide, cast in al-Qaeda's Islamist ideological framework, for local al-Qaeda affiliates to fight apostate Arab regimes. This dovetailed with bin Laden's exhortation in the early 2000s to al-Qaeda's emerging regional affiliates to attack locally, take territory, and create sanctuaries. And in 2003, with its invasion of Iraq, the United States became part of this strategy of fighting locally. Al-Muqrin himself helped lead one such effort in Saudi Arabia before he was killed by Saudi security forces in 2004.[4]

Some of these local affiliates, as well as al-Qaeda central in the Pakistan-Afghanistan border region, became targets for operations carried out by JSOC's counterterrorism forces during the 2000s. Iraq was not their only area of operations. JSOC was engaged in multiple geographic locations, with Iraq being far and away the main effort and the one we know the most about. As shown below, information about those other counterterrorism units fighting in other geographic locations is limited, affecting what can be said about them. Nevertheless, the network established in Iraq by TF 714 was broadened in the late 2000s to include counterterrorism units engaged in several other places.

Beginning in the fall of 2001, counterterrorism forces engaged in Operation Enduring Freedom. And while their role was limited, they contributed to the ouster of the Taliban and al-Qaeda from Afghanistan. They did so in late October through a campaign of deception and direct action across southern Afghanistan that sought to distract and tie down Taliban forces located there, preventing them from relocating north to take part in the defense of Kabul against an impending Northern Alliance attack enabled by US airpower and advisers. After the fall of the Taliban, the counterterrorism force downsized but continued to search for al-Qaeda leaders who had escaped into Pakistan.

Once the Iraq War began, Afghanistan became an ancillary mission for the counterterrorism force. Initially, this focused on al-Qaeda in Pakistan, trying to locate bin Laden and his senior associates. Direct-action raids against the Taliban were proscribed until 2006 when General McChrystal directed a counterterrorism task force to begin to target them.[5] But by the time it started to do so in the summer of that year, the Taliban insurgency was escalating. And the Taliban presented a different challenge from their Iraqi counterparts. The Taliban insurgency was rural and spread out over considerable territory. Also, the number of targets hit monthly in Afghanistan remained limited: less than 20 percent of TF 714's operational tempo of three hundred night raids a month. Not until 2011, after the United States withdrew from Iraq, did this accelerate.

Somalia became another location where a TF 714–like variant conducted counterterrorism operations, although not in the years immediately after 9/11 when Somalia was a CIA area of responsibility. In the first half of the 2000s, JSOC was in Somalia, but its mission was limited to employing its unique human and signals intelligence capabilities to track targets, but it did not mount strikes against them. However, when intelligence indicated there was a growing al-Qaeda presence in the Horn of Africa, this generated concern, especially when al-Qaeda gained traction with al-Shabaab, an Islamist insurgent group based in Somalia.

Al-Shabaab was a minor player in Somalia before Ethiopia intervened in 2006. An understanding of the reasons behind that intervention is not necessary here. However, grasping its impact on al-Shabaab is. It "transform[ed] the group from a small, relatively unimportant part of a more moderate Islamic movement into the most powerful and radical armed faction in the country."[6] By 2008, al-Shabaab's ranks had grown from "four hundred into the thousands." And "the group's ties to al-Qaeda [also] emerged during this period."[7]

These developments resulted in increased counterterrorism force attention. However, unlike in Iraq and to a much lesser extent Afghanistan, the details of what type of task force was established in the Horn is extremely limited. It appears that small elements were deployed to several locations, possibly including northeastern Kenya, Djibouti, Somaliland, off the Somali coast on a naval platform, and inside Somalia itself. However, the size of these units is not known, but the concept of operations appears to have been to strike from the periphery. The extent to which direct-action and other attacks took place remains secret.

Following 9/11, local al-Qaeda elements became active on the Arabian Peninsula, carrying out violent attacks in Yemen and Saudi Arabia. With respect to the latter, beginning in 2003, al-Qaeda forces executed a wave of terrorist strikes aimed at overthrowing the monarchy. According to Angela Gendron, this resulted in "more than 150 Saudis and foreigners . . . killed in a campaign which targeted Western establishments and Saudi oil installations." Saudi security forces responded forcefully. Gendron notes that "mass arrests, detentions, and . . . trials are evidence of a determination by Saudi authorities to confront the terrorists and gather intelligence to root out nascent cells. . . . A measure of the apparent success of the security forces in capturing or killing extremists within the Kingdom and foiling several terrorist plots is that the remaining elements of Saudi-based al-Qaeda cells seem to have been forced to regroup and launch attacks from . . . Yemen."[8] Still, this campaign of terrorism lasted into the late 2000s.

The extent to which the United States abetted Saudi Arabia in its fight against al-Qaeda could not be determined, but the results contributed to Yemen becoming of increasing concern to Washington in the late 2000s. It is important to note that Yemenis who fought against the Soviets in Afghanistan in the 1980s also returned home beginning in the mid-1990s to establish al-Qaeda in Yemen (AQY). In October 2000, AQY executed a major attack in the port of Aden by piloting a skiff alongside the USS *Cole* and detonating several hundred pounds of explosives. The result was a gaping hole in its hull and seventeen dead US Navy sailors. In 2002, another AQY suicide attack was carried out against a French oil tanker. In response, the United States sent Special Forces and intelligence personnel to assist the Yemeni governments counterterrorism forces. And in 2002, a US drone strike killed AQY's leader, Abu Ali al-Harithi. These efforts caused AQY to experience a serious decline in members by the end of 2003.

However, this changed in the late 2000s as AQY benefited from twenty-three of its incarcerated members escaping from a high-security prison in Sana'a in February 2006 through a tunnel dug from a neighboring mosque. Of the men who escaped, two became key leaders of AQY—Nasir al-Wuhayshi and Qasim al-Raymi. The latter had served as Osama bin Laden's secretary. Both men played a key role in rebuilding AQY and, in 2009, merging al-Qaeda's Saudi Arabian and Yemeni branches into al-Qaeda in the Arabian Peninsula. The Saudis also contributed to this union by continuing to drive more and more of its own extremists into Yemen.

The merger resulted in AQAP initiating attacks both inside Yemeni borders and well beyond them. According to an assessment by the Mapping Militant Organizations project at Stanford University, "in the region, AQAP targets foreigners

and security forces as part of their scheme to overthrow Saudi and Yemeni governments. . . . Abroad, the group targets the United States, as seen with the Christmas
day bomber who attempted to blow up a Detroit-bound flight." It also "targets
U.S. allies in Europe. For example, AQAP claimed responsibility for the 2015
Charlie Hebdo attack." And it "attacked British diplomats in Yemen . . . because
Britain is the main ally of America in the war against Islam" and "gave the Jews
control over the land of Palestine."[9]

These developments led President Obama to ramp up secret counterterrorism
operations against AQAP. His counterterrorism adviser, John Brennan, described
AQAP as "the most active operational franchise" of Al-Qaeda.[10] As a result, US
counterterrorism forces already deployed in the region, as noted above, began
to expand operations in the Horn of Africa and the Arabian Peninsula to attack
AQAP. Both direct-action and drone strikes increased.[11]

Finally, as TF 714's operational tempo in Iraq decreased in 2009 due to its effectiveness in dismantling AQI's networks, Admiral McRaven, now in command
of the counterterrorism force, began increasing operations in Afghanistan. And
the plan was to further escalate operations in 2010 as the Obama administration
reconsidered its strategy there.

Driving that reassessment was General McChrystal, who in June 2009 was appointed commander of the International Security Assistance Force in Afghanistan.
Based on a sixty-day review of the situation, he proposed a population-centric
counterinsurgency strategy empowered by a thirty-three-thousand-troop surge.
He also intended to ramp up counterterrorism operations. From firsthand experience in Iraq, recounted in this book, McChrystal concluded that effective COIN
requires a counterterrorism counterpart to dismantle the clandestine infrastructure of insurgent organizations. In Afghanistan, that was the Taliban.

According to one former regional counterterrorism task force commander who
served twice in that role in Afghanistan, that context was unlike Iraq. The latter
"was a nearly ideal operational environment with comparatively developed infrastructure, benign terrain, adequately enabled conventional forces, a more exploitable target set and a very different detention apparatus that housed a culturally
different type of detainee. These factors led to a more effective and efficient . . . CT
targeting process." Afghanistan was very different. It was "geographically larger,
with extreme terrain, limited and underdeveloped infrastructure, weather challenges, sanctuary that is exploited, a larger fragmented population, limited detention capacity and a lower density of U.S. troops."[12] But in terms of counterterrorism operations, he noted that "lessons from Iraq and more than ten years of
operating in Afghanistan yield[ed] a more capable and efficient CT force moving
into . . . [this] new phase of U.S. military engagement."[13]

One early example of effectiveness, he noted, was "in the summer of 2009 when a CT element was committed to an area" where a conventional US Army force "had experienced 19 U.S. casualties from improvised explosive devices (IEDs) in a period of three days. In 30 days of synchronized operations, the CT element helped reduce IED events by 90 percent, which dramatically increased the [conventional force's] freedom of action and thus its ability to conduct more effective population-centric COIN operations."[14]

This early example was illustrative of counterterrorism force targeting that, as in Iraq, eliminated many commanders and managers of Taliban networks across Afghanistan as well as leaders of al-Qaeda and of the Haqqani Network, which is affiliated with al-Qaeda. To do so, several regional counterterrorism task forces were established in Afghanistan that closely coordinated with conventional US Army units fighting in those assigned geographic locations. Over the next few years, counterterrorism forces persistently attacked the Taliban as part of a larger COIN campaign. Hundreds of individuals critical to enabling Taliban operations were taken off the battlefield.

Counterterrorism best practices refined by TF 714 proved transferable for operations against the Taliban. But unlike in Iraq, those counterterrorism methods did not dismantle the Taliban as they had AQI. Many Taliban were successfully targeted, but the insurgency continued. The reasons why this was the case have to do with the differences between these two insurgency contexts, some of which were identified above by the former regional counterterrorism task force commander. And then there was the Taliban and the Karzai government.

Counterterrorism targeting, in conjunction with the surge and population-centric COIN, exacted a high cost on the Taliban, driving them out of large parts of southern Afghanistan. This provided a window of opportunity to improve Afghan security forces, to distribute reconstruction aid, to facilitate local governance in places where it did not exist, and to tackle corruption.

But the COIN strategy in Afghanistan, once territory was secured and Taliban insurgent networks degraded, did not establish the conditions for postconflict transition, political reconciliation, and reconstruction, as had been the case in Iraq. Recall that in August 2010, the United States initiated Operation New Dawn in Iraq, which began the withdrawal of its forces while continuing to train Iraqi security forces to maintain the stability that had been accomplished and maintain a TF 714 residual force that, in conjunction with its Iraqi counterparts, kept AQI on its back, preventing a resurgence.

The COIN strategy in Iraq, expedited by the surge, and counterterrorism operations created an inflection point in the war. It produced change by considerably deescalating the violence. It was the crossover point from the kinetic fight to the beginning of the postconflict phase. Operation New Dawn sought to capitalize on that turning point, and it was to be followed by a US residual force considered essential if Iraqi stability was to be sustained, professionalization of the Iraqi security forces continued, and the long process of postconflict political reconciliation and reconstruction undertaken. Such inflection points can prove fleeting if not capitalized upon. Unfortunately, the residual force was not established, and, as discussed, dire consequences ensued.

The Afghanistan surge, together with COIN operations, and counterterrorism direct-action raids against Taliban commanders and managers never reached such an inflection point. The violence was reduced precipitously, and the Taliban was never degraded to the irreducible minimum. That was because the Taliban had embedded their insurgency in Afghan society. Since the early 2000s, they worked to establish an infrastructure of support, to recruit and expand the size of their force (estimated at thirty-five thousand in 2010), and to take advantage of sanctuary.

Also contributing to the limited success of these efforts was the commitment of the Karzai government to them. Recall that the goal was to establish the conditions for political reform as part of reconciliation and reconstruction. This would include institution building, establishment of rule of law, and an equitable redistribution of power and resources. Unfortunately, all of this was resisted because it would have upset the impropriety, malfeasance, and corruption of Karzai's administration. As a result, when the surge ended and Washington began to draw down its troops and resources, the Taliban regained the initiative and escalated the war.

The operations of the regional counterterrorism task forces in Afghanistan had proved effective but were not enough. And in 2014, that mission ended. Those counterterrorism forces that remained in Afghanistan were refocused solely on counterterrorism targets. These included al-Qaeda, the Haqqani Network, and the Islamic State of Iraq and the Levant–Khorasan Province. Whether other terrorist groups also in the Afghanistan-Pakistan region were included is unclear, even though ISAF commanders noted several others on the State Department's list of foreign terrorist organizations were located there.

Finally, there was a counterterrorism element from JSOC that supported Operation Inherent Resolve, the military intervention against the Islamic State of Iraq and Syria. In Syria it was an adjunct of the unconventional warfare strategy in which the United States and partner nations enabled an internal resistance group—the Syrian Democratic Forces—to help disrupt and topple ISIS, which included taking its capital in Raqqa. During this campaign, the counterterrorism forces executed their core tasks, including direct-action strikes against ISIS commanders and other key personnel. For example, they facilitated the targeting of

Abd al-Rahman Mustafa al-Qaduli, described as the top financier of ISIS, who was killed by helicopters that followed his vehicle in eastern Syria. He was just one of many being targeted to drain key ISIS personnel, including the group's "minister of war," Omar al-Shishani, and Abu Sarah, "believed to be the group's chief accountant and . . . in charge of paying the group's fighters."[15] In summation, these developments disclose the evolution of the US transnational counterterrorism network that grew out of TF 714. It evolved over time under the leadership of General McChrystal and later Admiral McRaven and General Votel. During its second decade, this network expanded further as the Obama administration established in the Washington area a "targeting center to oversee the growing use of special operations strikes against suspected militants in hot spots around the world." The concept had originated with Admiral McRaven, at the time the JSOC commander. In effect, the new center adopted the tracking and targeting system that TF 714 first created in Iraq and turned it into "a cloud-computing network tied into all elements of U.S. national security, from the eavesdropping capabilities of the National Security Agency to Homeland Security's border-monitoring databases." The network was "designed to sift through masses of information to track militant suspects across the globe."[16] A forward adjunct was established in the Middle East in 2016. The goal was to expand the counterterrorism forces' existing targeting center in the region and enhance its connections with the Washington-area platform.[17]

The evolution of this complex counterterrorism network was designed to respond to what had turned into a multigenerational and transnational fight against al-Qaeda, ISIS, and their affiliates. That global jihadist phenomenon was now in its fourth generation. The first grew out of the Soviet invasion of Afghanistan. Many thousands from across the Muslim world had joined to fight the infidel Red Army. In doing so, they established an ideological narrative that went beyond Afghanistan, and they became the initial members of a mission-oriented international movement for fighting a global religious war. In the 1990s, they began doing so in many places. And their ranks were reinforced by a second generation trained in Afghan camps during the period 1996–2001. The Taliban provided al-Qaeda with sanctuary from which they instructed an estimated twenty thousand fighters.[18] A third generation was spawned in Iraq following the US invasion in 2003. Al-Qaeda saw Iraq as an opportunity to produce a new corps of fighters, and many joined the fight there, becoming part of the international mission. Finally, the Arab Spring and subsequent civil war in Syria produced the fourth generation, an estimated thirty thousand from several regions.

This multigenerational and transnational jihadist movement and the ideology upon which it is based, while having suffered major setbacks in Syria and Iraq since

2016, and earlier due to Operation Neptune Spear, has not ended. An understanding of that reality was reflected in the steps taken to strengthen JSOC's global counterterrorism network. Triggering that development was an appreciation of the fact that those making up this multigenerational and transnational movement are committed to an existential struggle. Moreover, if the past is prologue, they will learn and adapt from their recent setbacks. Al-Qaeda did so after 2001 and 2011, and ISIS will do so in the future.

Moreover, the United States and its allies can expect future terrorist tactics and techniques to reflect the "rapid development of commercial technology . . . to improve their capabilities." One recent study has "identified eight [such] areas: drones, including armed drones; social media services; artificial intelligence; encrypted communications; virtual currencies; the Dark Web; offensive cyber capabilities; and weapons of mass destruction." And its authors note that "this list is not exhaustive but represents important emerging areas that Salafi-jihadist networks may attempt to leverage in the future."[19]

It is against this backdrop that the Trump administration's National Defense Strategy (NDS) declared that the principal security challenge confronting the United States now is the "re-emergence of long-term, strategic competition between nations."[20] In other words, "great power politics [and competition] is back," and the irregular war against al-Qaeda, ISIS, and their affiliates is no longer a principal security concern of the United States.[21]

The Trump Administration and the National Defense Strategy

This pronouncement not only declared that the "central challenge to U.S. prosperity and security is the reemergence of long-term, strategic competition by . . . revisionist powers" but also that against those states the US "competitive advantage has eroded in every domain of warfare . . . air, land, sea, space, and cyberspace." Today China and Russia are said to be "competing across all dimensions of power."[22] And those challenges necessitate "increased and sustained investment, because of the magnitude of the threats they pose to U.S. security and prosperity today, and the potential for those threats to increase in the future."[23]

This assessment calls for the United States to prioritize thwarting China and Russia across the spectrum of conflict and in each of the warfighting domains. To do so, "three distinct lines of effort" are singled out: "First, rebuilding military readiness as we build a more lethal Joint Force; Second, strengthening alliances as we attract new partners; and Third, reforming the [Defense] Department's business practices for greater performance and affordability."[24] This almost single-minded attention to strengthening the lethality, modernization, and readiness of US forces to "compete, deter, and win" against China and Russia prioritizes preparing for the conflicts of tomorrow. It takes precedence in the NDS over today's fight against post-9/11 irregular enemies. Indeed, "rogue regimes such as North Korea and Iran" are also given priority because "states are the principal actors on the global stage."[25]

Juxtaposed to the NDS, the 2019 Worldwide Threat Assessment of the US intelligence community is much less sanguine about downgrading the importance of the fight against violent extremism. It warns that "global jihadists in dozens of groups and countries threaten local and regional US interests, despite having experienced some significant setbacks in recent years, and some of these groups will remain intent on striking the US homeland. Prominent jihadist ideologues and media platforms continue to call for and justify efforts to attack the US."[26]

ISIS, the IC's assessment notes, "commands thousands of fighters in Iraq and Syria, and maintains eight branches, more than a dozen networks, and thousands of dispersed supporters around the world, despite significant [recent] leadership and territorial losses." Declaring it defeated would be ill-advised because ISIS "will exploit any reduction in CT pressure to strengthen its clandestine presence and accelerate rebuilding key capabilities, such as media production and external operations."[27]

Likewise, al-Qaeda and its "affiliates are involved in insurgencies and maintain safe havens, resources, and the intent to strike local and regional US interests in Africa, the Middle East, and South Asia." And its "senior leaders are strengthening the network's global command structure and continuing to encourage attacks against the West, including the United States." The IC's assessment concludes, "We expect al Qaeda's global network will remain a CT challenge for the United States and its allies."[28]

In reality, the United States enters the third decade of the twenty-first century facing both renewed strategic competition from China and Russia and a continuation of irregular and protracted war against a multigenerational and transnational jihadist movement. And while each president who has confronted the latter—Bush, Obama, and Trump—has declared victory over it, such victory laps have proved premature. After the loss of its sanctuary in Afghanistan, al-Qaeda was said by President Bush to be in decline. But it proved resilient, spawning new strategists who devised inventive solutions to overcome post-9/11 setbacks. Then Operation Neptune Spear eliminated bin Laden in 2011, and President Obama judged al-Qaeda "on the ropes" and called ISIS its "JV team." But again al-Qaeda innovated, recreating itself as a network of affiliated and associated groups able to fight on many fronts. And ISIS gained dominance over an area of Iraq and Syria that contained a population of seven to eight million people.

In late 2015, ISIS gains began to unravel. Then, in October 2017, with the fall of Raqqa, the caliphate fell. This led President Trump to declare victory. "We have defeated ISIS in Syria, my only reason for being there during the Trump Presidency." He ordered the withdrawal of US forces.[29] Others cautioned that a declaration of mission accomplished was premature, reflecting the warning of Gen. James Mattis that "no war is over until the enemy says it's over. We may think it over, we may declare it over, but in fact, the enemy gets a vote."[30]

What the above infers is that the United States requires a security architecture able to manage two very different challenges and contexts: one that is immediate and ongoing, the other on the horizon and indeterminate. On the one hand, the US will have to continue to engage in the post-9/11 irregular war against ISIS, al-Qaeda, and their networks of affiliated groups. That generational and ideological clash shows no sign of coming to an end. On the other hand, as the NDS proposes, the US must also rebuild and modernize its conventional forces to be able to compete with and deter China and Russia in tomorrow's contest against these revisionist state powers.

The forces needed for each of these challenges are different. One is a highly specialized and networked national counterterrorism force of warriors, described in this book, that has been engaged in a prolonged irregular war since 2001 and that has changed the paradigm for conducting twenty-first-century counterterrorism operations. The other will be a restructured conventional military force to compete with and deter China and Russia short of war, through superior capabilities. These are two distinct missions. Their differences are significant, and it is important to grasp these distinctions and the need of retaining each. The danger is that in the past US security institutions have resisted maintaining two such divergent forces and have been much more simpatico with the security context described in the NDS. Highly specialized and elite warriors for protracted irregular wars in the past fostered estrangement from and distrust by their conventional counterparts.

Earlier in this volume we recounted how before 9/11 such attitudes kept JSOC's counterterrorism units on the shelf in the 1990s. At that time, an impenetrable phalanx of obstacles could not be breached to employ counterterrorism capabilities offensively to preempt and disrupt al-Qaeda terrorists who struck at US targets abroad, culminating in 9/11. So dominant were those barriers that, when taken together, they successfully resisted initiatives to employ JSOC's special mission units to execute their core task—offensive measures to prevent, deter, and respond to terrorism. Since 9/11, the opposite has been the case. Those counterterrorism forces have been the tip of the spear, persistently and globally engaged in what has been described in this book as an irregular and protracted war against a multigenerational and transnational jihadist movement. They must remain so engaged in that fight for the foreseeable future.

NOTES

Acknowledgments

1. See William B. Ostlund, *Irregular Warfare: Counterterrorism Forces in Support of Counterinsurgency Operations*, Land Warfare Paper no. 91 (Arlington, VA: Institute of Land Warfare, Association of the United States Army [hereafter AUSA], 2012).

2. For a declassified version of this study, see Richard Shultz, "Showstoppers: Nine Reasons Why We Never Sent Our Special Operations Forces after Al Qaeda before 9/11," *Weekly Standard*, January 26, 2004, 25–33.

Introduction

1. Charles Krulak, "Marine Corps Future," National Press Club luncheon address, October 10, 1997, Washington, DC, https://www.c-span.org/video/?92628-1/marine-corps-future.

2. The speech by General Krulak, titled "Ne Cras," was first given to the Center for Naval Analysis's board of trustees on December 17, 1997, in Washington, DC. The essay, "Ne Cras: Not like Yesterday," was published in Richard Shultz and Robert Pfaltzgraff, eds., *The Role of Naval Forces in 21st Century Conflict* (Washington, DC: Brassey's, 2000). For a discussion of the essay, see Diane E. Davis and Anthony W. Pereira, *Irregular Armed Forces and Their Role in Politics and State Formation* (Cambridge: Cambridge University Press, 2003), 370–71.

3. The initial research on Task Force 714's operations was completed in 2014. I subsequently wrote about it in a monograph titled *Military Innovation in War: It Takes a Learning Organization; A Case Study of Task Force 714* (Tampa, FL: JSOU Press, 2016). I used this knowledge as the jumping-off point for addressing the larger questions and issues about intelligence theory and practice in two contexts, Cold War and post-9/11, and whether and how intelligence had to transform and did transform, which is the subject matter of this volume.

4. The manual "was downloaded more than 1.5 million times in the first month after its posting to the Fort Leavenworth and Marine Corps Web sites," according to John Nagl, a staff officer who worked for Gen. David Petraeus. And, he added, it was "widely reviewed, including by several Jihadi websites." See Sarah Sewall, ed., *The U.S. Army/Marine Corps Counterinsurgency Field Manual* (Chicago: University of Chicago Press, 2007), xxvii.

5. Sewall, 79, 118–19.

6. Department of Defense, *Irregular Warfare: Countering Irregular Threats; Joint Operating Concept* (Washington, DC: Department of Defense, July 2010), 28, http://www .au.af.mil/au/awc/awcgate/irregular/iw_joc2_0.pdf.

7. Gregory Treverton, *Intelligence for an Age of Terror* (Cambridge: Cambridge University Press, 2009), 15.

8. Neil Pollard, "On Counter-Terrorism Intelligence," in *National Intelligence Systems: Current Research and Future Prospects*, ed. Gregory F. Treverton and Wilhelm Agrell (Cambridge: Cambridge University Press, 2009), 117, 122, 127.

9. See, e.g., Paul Maddrell, "Failing Intelligence: U.S. Intelligence in the Age of Transnational Threats," *International Journal of Intelligence and Counterintelligence* 22, no. 2 (2009); and Roger Z. George, "Meeting 21st Century Transnational Challenges: Building a Global Intelligence Paradigm," *Studies in Intelligence* 51, no. 3 (2007).

10. Abram Shulsky, *Silent Warfare: Understanding the World of Intelligence*, 3rd ed. (Washington, DC: Potomac Books, 2002), 22.

11. Jeffrey Richelson, "Technical Collection in the Post-September 11 World," in Treverton and Agrell, *National Intelligence Systems*, 148–58. See also Jeffrey Richelson, "Intelligence: The Imagery Dimension," in *Strategic Intelligence*, vol. 2, *The Intelligence Cycle: The Flow of Secret Information from Overseas to the Highest Councils of Government,* ed. Loch Johnson (Westport, CT: Praeger Security International, 2007).

12. David Fulghum, "Hide and Seek," *Aviation Week and Space Technology*, February 28, 2005; Larry Greenemeier, "Pentagon Developing New Unmanned Spy Planes," *Scientific American*, September 17, 2007; Richard Best, *Intelligence, Surveillance, and Reconnaissance (ISR) Acquisition: Issues for Congress* (Washington, DC: Congressional Research Service, January 20, 2011), http://www.fas.org/sgp/crs/intel/R41284.pdf. See also the PBS program *Spies That Fly*, http://www.pbs.org/nova/spiesfly/.

13. Matthew M. Aid, "Prometheus Embattled: A Post-9/11 Report Card on the National Security Agency," *Intelligence and National Security* 21, no. 6 (2006); Joseph Fitsanakis and Ian Allen, *Cell Wars: The Changing Landscape of Communications Intelligence*, Research Paper no. 131 (Alimos, Greece: Research Institute for European and American Studies, May 2009).

14. See Roger George, "Fixing the Problem of Analytical Mind-Sets: Alternative Analysis," *International Journal of Intelligence and Counterintelligence* 17, no. 3 (Fall 2004); Roger George, "Beyond Analytic Tradecraft," *International Journal of Intelligence and Counterintelligence* 23, no. 2 (Summer 2010); and Gregory Treverton and C. Bryan Gabbard, *Assessing the Tradecraft of Intelligence Analysis* (Santa Monica, CA: Intelligence Policy Center, National Security Research Division, RAND Corp., 2008).

15. Richards Heuer, "Limits of Intelligence Analysis," *Orbis* 48, no. 1 (2004); Richards Heuer, "Computer-Aided Analysis of Competing Hypotheses," in *Analyzing Intelligence: Origins, Obstacles, and Innovations*, ed. Roger George and James Bruce (Washington, DC: Georgetown University Press, 2008).

16. For an early example, see Valdis Krebs, "Mapping Networks of Terrorist Cells,"

Connections 24, no. 3 (2001); Kathleen Carley, "Estimating Vulnerabilities in Large Covert Networks," *Proceedings of the 8th International Command and Control Research and Technology Symposium* (Washington, DC: National Defense University, 2003); Kathleen Carley, "Using Network Text Analysis to Detect the Organizational Structure of Cover Networks," *Proceedings of the North American Association for Computational Social and Organizational Science* (2004); Siddharth Kaza, Daning Hu, and Hsinchun Chen, "Identifying Significant Facilitators of Dark Network Evolution," *Journal of the American Society for Information Science and Technology* 60, no. 4 (2009); and Hsinchun Chen et al., "Analyzing Terror Campaigns on the Internet: Technical Sophistication, Content Richness, and Web Interactivity," *International Journal of Human-Computer Studies* 65, no. 1 (2007).

17. In the post–Cold War 1990s, serious reservations were raised in government and public policy circles about the use of covert action as an instrument of statecraft. Covert action was viewed as highly risky, with many more failures than successes, and out of step with US values. Those opposed to covert action equated it with morally dubious activities that should be eschewed. See Allan E. Goodman and Bruce D. Berkowitz, *The Need to Know: The Report of the Twentieth Century Fund Task Force on Covert Action and American Democracy* (New York: Twentieth Century Fund Press, 1992); Allan E. Goodman, *In from the Cold: The Report of the Twentieth Century Fund Task Force on the Future of U.S. Intelligence; Background Papers* (New York: Twentieth Century Fund Press, 1996); Arthur Hulnick, "U.S. Covert Action: Does It Have a Future?," *International Journal of Intelligence and Counterintelligence* 9, no. 2 (Summer 1996); and Loch Johnson, "On Drawing a Bright Line for Covert Operations," *American Journal of International Law* 86, no. 2 (April 1992).

18. National Commission on Terrorist Attacks upon the United States, *9/11 Commission Report* (New York: W. W. Norton, 2004), 350–52, https://www.9-11commission .gov/report/911Report.pdf (hereafter cited as *9/11 Commission Report*). For a pre-9/11 examination of reviving special operations forces, see Susan Marquis, *Unconventional Warfare: Rebuilding Special Operations Forces* (Washington, DC: Brookings Institution Press, 1997).

19. Andre Le Gallo, "Covert Action: A Vital Option on U.S. National Security Policy," *International Journal of Intelligence and Counterintelligence* 18, no. 2 (2005); Jennifer Gibbs, "Covert Action and the Pentagon," *Intelligence and National Security* 22, no. 1 (February 2007); Lawrence Cline, "Special Operations and the Intelligence System," *International Journal of Intelligence and Counterintelligence* 18, no. 4 (2005). For a summary of congressional attention, see Richard Best, *Special Operations Forces and CIA Paramilitary Operations: Issues for Congress* (Washington, DC: Congressional Research Service, August 3, 2009).

20. *9/11 Commission Report.*

21. Interview with Gen. Stanley McChrystal, USA (Ret.), July 2014, Arlington, VA. (Unless otherwise noted, the interviews for this book were conducted by the author.) See also Stanley McChrystal, "Lesson from Iraq: It Takes a Network to Defeat a Network,"

LinkedIn, June 21, 2013, https://www.linkedin.com/pulse/20130621110027-8614
5090-lesson-from-iraq-it-takes-a-network-to-defeat-a-network/.

22. Stanley McChrystal, *My Share of the Task: A Memoir* (New York: Penguin, 2013), 92.

23. Robert Scales, "The Quality of Command: The Wrong Way and the Right Way to Make Better Generals," *Foreign Affairs* 91, no. 6 (November/December 2012).

24. Interview with General McChrystal, July 2014.

25. "A Conversation with Stanley McChrystal," interview conducted by Gideon Rose, *Foreign Affairs* 92, no. 2 (March/April 2013).

26. Interview with Gen. Stanley McChrystal, USA (Ret.), May 2015, Alexandria, VA.

27. Interview with Adm. William McRaven, USN (Ret.), June 2015, Washington, DC.

28. Interview with Admiral McRaven, June 2015.

29. Interview with Admiral McRaven, June 2015.

30. To determine how and why TF 714 was able to learn and innovate, transforming itself in the midst of war, the author's research methods included a series of semistructured, in-depth interviews conducted with a range of experienced former practitioners and specialists who served in the unit. These included, most importantly, its senior leadership. To gain access to these individuals, the author drew on his long-standing and close association with the special operations community. Since the mid-1980s, he has maintained a close working relationship with various elements of that community. Currently, he is a senior fellow with SOCOM's Joint Special Operations University (JSOU). In addition to his ties with SOCOM, the author has worked closely with other parts of the special operations community, including the US Army's Special Warfare Center and School (SWCS). It was with the assistance of SWCS that he conducted research that led to his book *The Secret War against Hanoi: Kennedy's and Johnson's Use of Spies, Saboteurs, and Covert Warriors in North Vietnam*, which is the most comprehensive assessment of the Studies and Operations Group of the Military Assistance Command, Vietnam. Supplementing the information collected in the interviews for this study on TF 714 was information gleaned from interviews with other DOD officials knowledgeable about TF 714's operations in the Iraq War. Open-source literature on counterterrorism operations in Iraq and on the role of counterterrorism forces in those operations was also examined. There has been a noteworthy consideration of these issues in a number of open-source venues. The author collected and reviewed these materials.

31. At the graduation ceremony of the US Military Academy at West Point in June 2002, President George W. Bush told the cadets, "You graduate from this Academy in a time of war [in which] we face a threat with no precedent." See George W. Bush, "Graduation Speech at the United States Military Academy," June 1, 2002, https://georgewbush-whitehouse.archives.gov/news/releases/2002/06/20020601-3.html.

Chapter 1. Adapting Intelligence for Twenty-First-Century Irregular Warfare

1. Kurt Piehler, ed., *The Encyclopedia of Military Science* (Los Angeles: SAGE, 2013), 91.

2. Martin van Creveld, *The Transformation of War: The Most Radical Reinterpretation of Armed Conflict since Clausewitz* (New York: Free Press, 1991).

3. van Creveld, 224.

4. van Creveld, 224.

5. van Creveld, chap. 7. In the final chapter of *The Transformation of War*, van Creveld restates his arguments about how war is transforming in terms of who will fight, how they will fight, and why they will fight. This paragraph is based on that summation.

6. D. E. Showalter, "War Is a Thing in Itself," *Naval War College Review* 45, no. 3 (Summer 1992): 120–21.

7. James McDonough, "The Transformation of War," *Military Review* 71, no. 6 (June 1991): 93.

8. John Strawson, "The Transformation of War," *RUSI Journal* 136, no. 3 (Autumn 1991): 76–77.

9. Rupert Smith, *The Utility of Force: The Art of War in the Modern World* (New York: Random House, 2007), 19.

10. *Warfighting*, Marine Corps Doctrinal Publication 1 (Washington, DC: US Marine Corps, June 1997), 3.

11. See, e.g., Mary Kaldor, *New and Old Wars: Organizing Violence in a Global Era*, 2nd ed. (Stanford, CA: Stanford University Press, 2007); Robert I. Rotberg, ed., *When States Fail: Causes and Consequences* (Princeton, NJ: Princeton University Press, 2004); Keith Krause, ed., *Armed Groups and Contemporary Conflicts: Challenging the Weberian State* (New York: Routledge, 2010); Angel Rabasa and John E. Peters, *Ungoverned Territories: Understanding and Reducing Terrorism Risks* (Santa Monica, CA: RAND Corp., 2007); Stewart Patrick, *Weak Links: Fragile States, Global Threats, and International Security* (New York: Oxford University Press, 2011); Richard H. Shultz and Andrea J. Dew, *Insurgents, Terrorists, and Militias: The Warriors of Contemporary Combat* (New York: Columbia University Press, 2006); Troy S. Thomas, Stephen D. Kiser, and William D. Casebeer, *Warlords Rising: Confronting Violent Non-state Actors* (Lanham, MD: Lexington Books, 2005); Anthony Vinci, *Armed Groups and the Balance of Power: The International Relations of Terrorists, Warlords, and Insurgents* (New York: Routledge, 2008); Robert H. Dorff, "Failed States after 9/11: What Did We Know and What Have We Learned?," *International Studies Perspectives* 6, no. 1 (February 2005); Diane E. Davis, "Non-State Armed Actors, New Imagined Communities, and Shifting Patterns of Sovereignty and Insecurity in the Modern World," *Contemporary Security Policy* 30 (August 2009); and Roy Godson and Richard Shultz, *Adapting America's Security Paradigm and Security Agenda* (Washington, DC: National Strategy Information Center, 2011).

12. PRIO (in Norway), in association with the University of Uppsala's Conflict Data Program (in Sweden), records global armed conflicts annually. According to PRIO, in the 1950s, internal conflicts between states and armed groups represented between one-third and one-half of all conflicts, but by the 1990s they accounted for nearly all armed conflict. This trend has continued since 9/11. The Uppsala Conflict Data Program can be accessed at http://www.pcr.uu.se/research/ucdp/.

13. Lotta Harbom, Stina Högbladh, and Peter Wallensteen, "Armed Conflict and Peace Agreements," *Journal of Peace Research* 43, no. 5 (2006). According to the authors,

interstate armed conflict occurs between two or more states. Internationalized intrastate armed conflict occurs between the government of a state and internal armed opposition groups with outside intervention from another state. Intrastate armed conflict occurs between the government of a state and internal armed opposition groups without intervention from another state.

14. Human Security Research Group, *Human Security Report 2009/2010: The Causes of Peace and the Shrinking Costs of War* (Oxford: Oxford University Press, 2011), 159–60.

15. Mikael Eriksson, Peter Wallensteen, and Margareta Sollenberg, "Armed Conflict, 1989–2002," *Journal of Peace Research* 41, no. 5 (2003): 593.

16. *Human Security Report 2005* (Oxford: Oxford University Press, 2005).

17. As quoted in Richard Shultz, *Security Force Assistance and Security Sector Reform* (Tampa, FL: JSOU Press, 2013), 38.

18. Barbara Walter, "The New New Civil Wars," *Annual Review of Political Science* 20 (2017): 470.

19. Sebastian von Einsiedel, *Civil War Trends and the Changing Nature of Armed Conflict*, UNU-CPR Occasional Paper no. 10 (New York: United Nations University, Centre for Policy Research, March 2017). The origins of the Islamic State of Iraq and Syria, or ISIS, can be traced to Abu Musab al-Zarqawi, who first as the leader of Jama'at al-Tawhid wa'al-Jihad and then, after swearing allegiance to Osama bin Laden, of al-Qaeda in Iraq (AQI) was the driving force of the escalating insurgency in Iraq in 2003–6. On June 7, 2006, al-Zarqawi was killed in a Task Force 714 operation. In October 2006, AQI's shura council selected a new emir, Abu Bakr al-Baghdadi. A new operations chief likewise emerged in Haji Bakr, as well as a new war minister, Nu'man Salman Mansur al-Zaydi. This leadership began calling AQI the Islamic State of Iraq, or ISI, in an attempt gain a wider base of supporters. But in Iraq it continued to be known as AQI. During 2011–13, it took advantage of the opportunities provided by the US withdrawal and the political situations in Iraq and Syria due to the Arab Spring to begin a resurgence that would culminate in ISI taking control of significant territory in northern Iraq, including its second-largest city, Mosul, as well as gaining control of western Syria, including Aleppo and Raqqa. ISI continued to achieve remarkable territorial advances and in June 2014 declared the establishment of a caliphate, with al-Baghdadi named caliph. ISI now became known as the Islamic State Islamic of Iraq and Syria, or ISIS. It is also known as the Islamic State of Iraq and the Levant, or ISIL.

20. Erik Melander, Thérése Pettersson, and Lotta Themnér, "Organized Violence, 1989–2015," *Journal of Peace Research* 54, no. 4 (2016).

21. Melander, Pettersson, and Themnér, 728.

22. Melander, Pettersson, and Themnér, 729–30.

23. Melander, Pettersson, and Themnér, 730.

24. For an insightful discussion about the legitimacy challenge facing weak and fragile states, see K. J. Holsti, *The State, War, and the State of War* (Cambridge: Cambridge University Press, 2001).

25. Several research- and policy-oriented institutions have developed analytic

measurements for assessing the capacity and viability of nation-states. Their analyses have found that a large number of today's states can be classified as weak and fragile. See, e.g., the Fragile States Index produced annually by the Fund for Peace. The index consists of a ranking of 178 nations based on their levels of stability and the pressures they face. The assessment "is based on The Fund for Peace's proprietary Conflict Assessment Software Tool (CAST) analytical platform." CAST is a "comprehensive social science methodology." Data for the assessment is "from three primary sources [that] is triangulated and subjected to critical review to obtain final scores for each of 178 nations." See *Fragile States Index 2015* (Washington, DC: Fund for Peace, 2015). See also the Brookings Institution's Index of State Weakness in the Developing World, which ranks 141 developing states, and Susan Rice and Stewart Patrick, *Index of State Weakness in the Developing World* (Washington, DC: Brookings Institution, 2008).

26. Alyson J. K. Bailes, Keith Krause, and Theodor Winkler, *The Shifting Face of Violence*, Policy Paper no. 18 (Geneva Centre for the Democratic Control of Armed Forces, 2007), 18.

27. Richard Shultz, Roy Godson, and Querine Hanlon, *Armed Groups and Irregular Warfare: Adapting Professional Military Education* (Washington, DC: National Strategy Information Center, 2008), 38–41. See also Richard Shultz, Douglas Farah, and Itamara Lochard, *Armed Groups: A Tier-One Security Priority* (Colorado Springs, CO: Institute for National Security Studies, US Air Force Academy, 2004); Shultz and Dew, *Insurgents, Terrorists, and Militias*; and Peter Thompson, *Armed Groups: The 21st Century Threat* (New York: Rowman & Littlefield, 2014).

28. See the International Institute for Strategic Studies' Armed Conflict Database, www .iiss.org.

29. See Jane's, "Sentinel Security Assessment—North Africa," https://janes.ihs.com /NorthAfrica/Reference#.

30. Mapping Militants Project, Stanford University, http://web.stanford.edu/group /mappingmilitants/cgi-bin/.

31. Thompson, *Armed Groups*, 41. See also Querine H. Hanlon, "Globalization and the Transformation of Armed Groups," in *Armed Groups: Studies in National Security, Counterterrorism, and Counterinsurgency*, ed. Jeffrey Norwitz (Newport, RI: Naval War College Press, 2008), 137–47.

32. Michael Flynn, Rich Juergens, and Thomas Cantrell, "Employing ISR: SOF Best Practices," *Joint Forces Quarterly* 3, no. 50 (2008): 57.

33. Derek Jones, *Understanding the Form, Function, and Logic of Clandestine Insurgent and Terrorist Networks: The First Step in Effective Counternetwork Operations*, Report 12-3 (MacDill Air Force Base, FL: JSOU Press, April 2012), 39.

34. See, e.g., Eliot A. Cohen and John Gooch, *Military Misfortunes: The Anatomy of Failure in War* (New York: Free Press, 1990); Kelly Greenhill and Paul Staniland, "Ten Ways to Lose at Counterinsurgency," *Civil Wars* 9, no. 4 (2007): 402–19; David Kilcullen, "Counterinsurgency Redux," *Survival* 48, no. 4 (2006–7): 111–30; and Gregory Fremont-Barnes, ed., *A History of Counterinsurgency*, 2 vols. (New York: Praeger, 2015).

35. In the 2006 *QDR*, the DOD acknowledges that a meaningful gap exists between the changing nature of conflict and the available means to conduct conflict. The *QDR* goes on to stipulate that irregular warfare is now a vital mission area for the US military and stresses the need to prepare. The "long war," as the Pentagon describes the post-9/11 context, is characterized as "irregular in its nature." Enemies in that fight are depicted as "not traditional conventional military forces." Irregular warfare favors indirect and asymmetrical approaches and is inherently a protracted struggle, according to the *QDR*. See Department of Defense, *2006 Quadrennial Defense Review* (Washington, DC: Department of Defense, 2006), 1–19.

36. *Counterinsurgency*, US Army Field Manual No. 3-24, Marine Corps Warfighting Publication No. 3-33.5 (Washington, DC: Department of the Army, 2006); Department of Defense, *National Military Strategic Plan for the War on Terrorism* (Washington, DC: Department of Defense, 2006).

37. Department of Defense, *Irregular Warfare Joint Operating Concept*, version 1.0 (Washington, DC: Department of Defense, July 2007), 6, https://fas.org/irp/doddir/dod/iw-joc.pdf.

38. Department of Defense, 22.

39. *Irregular Warfare*, Department of Defense Directive 3000.07, December 2008, https://www.hsdl.org/?view&did=233338.

40. Secretary Gates warned that while "support for conventional modernization programs is deeply embedded in the Defense Department, my fundamental concern is that there is not commensurate institutional support for the capabilities needed to win today's irregular wars and their likely successors." See Robert Gates, "A Balanced Strategy: Reprogramming the Pentagon for a New Age," *Foreign Affairs* (January/February 2009).

41. *The Quadrennial Diplomacy and Development Review* (Washington, DC: Department of State 2009).

42. *The National Intelligence Strategy of the United States* (Washington, DC: Office of the Director of National Intelligence, August 2009), 1–3.

43. Department of Defense, *Irregular Warfare Joint Operating Concept*, 28.

44. Michael Flynn, *Fixing Intel: A Blueprint for Making Intelligence Relevant in Afghanistan* (Washington, DC: Center for a New American Security, 2010), 7.

45. Here is how McChrystal explained the process: "Operators and analysts from multiple units and agencies sat side by side as we sought to fuse our intelligence and operations efforts . . . into a unified effort. The idea was to combine analysts who found the enemy (through intelligence, surveillance, and reconnaissance); drone operators who fixed the target; combat teams who finished the target by capturing or killing him; specialists who exploited the intelligence the raid yielded, such as cell phones, maps, and detainees; and the intelligence analysts who turned this raw information into usable knowledge. By doing this, we speeded up the cycle for a counterterrorism operation, gleaning valuable insights in hours, not days." See Stanley A. McChrystal, "It Takes a Network: The New Front Line of Modern Warfare," *Foreign Policy* (March/April 2011). See also Stanley McChrystal, *My Share of the Task: A Memoir* (New York: Penguin, 2013), chap. 10.

46. National Commission on Terrorist Attacks upon the United States, *9/11 Commission Report* (New York: W. W. Norton, 2004), chap. 13.

47. Abram Shulsky, *Silent Warfare: Understanding the World of Intelligence*, 3rd ed. (Washington, DC: Potomac Books, 2002), 2–3.

48. Adapted from Mark Lowenthal, *From Secrets to Policy*, 4th ed. (Washington, DC: CQ Press, 2009), 8.

49. Jeffrey Richelson, *The U.S. Intelligence Community*, 3rd ed. (Boulder, CO: Westview, 1995), 3.

50. Roy Godson, *Dirty Tricks or Trump Cards: U.S. Covert Action and Counterintelligence* (Washington, DC: Brassey's, 1995), 1.

51. William Rosenau, "Understanding Insurgent Intelligence Operations," *Marine Corps University Journal* 2, no. 1 (Spring 2011): 1, 10.

52. See Aden C. Magee, "Countering Nontraditional HUMINT Collection Threats," *International Journal of Intelligence and Counterintelligence* 23, no. 3 (2010); Kevin O'Brien, "Assessing Hostile Reconnaissance and Terrorist Intelligence Activities," *RUSI Journal* 153, no. 5 (October 2008): 36–37; Gaetano Ilardi, "Al Qaeda's Operational Intelligence: A Key Prerequisite to Action," *Studies in Conflict and Terrorism* 31, no. 12 (2008): 1072–1102; Graham Tuberville, *Guerrilla Counterintelligence* (Tampa, FL: JSOU, 2009): 62–63; Carl Anthony Wege, "The Hizballah Security Apparatus," *Perspectives on Terrorism* 2, no. 7 (2008); and David Eshel, "Hezbollah's Intelligence War: Assessment of the Second Lebanon War," *Defense Update* 9, no. 1 (January 2007).

53. See Peter Finn and Joby Warrick, "In Afghanistan Attack, CIA Fell Victim to Series of Miscalculations about Informant," *Washington Post*, January 16, 2010; Zeeshan Haider, "CIA Bomber Video Calls for Attacks on U.S.," Reuters, January 10, 2010; Siobhan Gorman, Anand Gopal, and Yochi J. Dreazen, "CIA Blast Blamed on Double Agent," *Wall Street Journal*, January 5, 2010; and Joby Warrick, *The Triple Agent: The al-Qaeda Mole Who Infiltrated the CIA* (New York: Random House, 2011).

54. Godson, *Dirty Tricks or Trump Cards*, 251.

55. Roy Godson, "What Is Intelligence: Symbiotic Relationships among Discrete Functions," unpublished manuscript (September 1983), 34, 36.

56. Robert M. Clark, *Intelligence Analysis: A Target-Centric Approach*, 5th ed. (Los Angeles: CQ Press, 2017), 19–27.

57. Clark, 19–27.

58. Clark, 19–27; Richard L. Russell, *Sharpening Strategic Intelligence: Why the CIA Gets It Wrong and What Needs to Be Done to Get It Right* (Cambridge: Cambridge University Press, 2007), 3, 150; Richard L. Russell, "The Intelligence War against Global Terrorism," in *Strategic Intelligence*, vol. 4, ed. Loch K. Johnson (Westport, CT: Praeger Security International, 2007), 127–28, 136.

59. Mark Lowenthal's volume was the first published in 1984 as *U.S. Intelligence: Evolution and Anatomy* (New York: Praeger, 1984). The second edition would also be published by Praeger under the same title in 1992. In 2000, the third edition was

published by Congressional Quarterly Press under the new title *Intelligence: From Secrets to Policy* (Washington, DC: Congressional Quarterly Press, 2000). It is this edition that is being referenced in the text. Three subsequent editions appeared in 2004, 2008, and 2011.

60. Abram Shulsky's *Silent Warfare: Understanding the World of Intelligence* was first published by Brassey's in 1991, as the Cold War was ending. Subsequent revised editions appeared in 1995 and 2001 with the assistance of Gary Schmitt. In the text above, the reference is from Abram N. Shulsky and Gary J. Schmitt, *Silent Warfare: Understanding the World of Intelligence*, 2nd ed. (Washington, DC: Brassey's, 1995), xiii.

61. Jeffrey Richelson first published *The U.S. Intelligence Community* in 1985 with Ballinger Publishing Company and the second edition in 1989 with HarperCollins. The subsequent four editions in 1995, 1999, 2007, and 2011 were all published by Westview. Above we are referencing Richelson, *The U.S. Intelligence Community*, 3rd ed. (Boulder, CO: Westview, 1995), 476.

62. See Shultz, Farah, Lochard, *Armed Groups*; Shultz and Dew, *Insurgents, Terrorists, and Militias*; and Thompson, *Armed Groups*.

63. Treverton, *Intelligence for an Age of Terror*, 15.

64. Warren Fishbein and Gregory F. Treverton, "Making Sense of Transnational Threats," *Sherman Kent Center for Intelligence Analysis Occasional Papers* 3, no. 1 (October 2004); Neal Pollard, "On Counter-Terrorism and Intelligence," in *National Intelligence Systems: Current Research and Future Prospects*, ed. Gregory F. Treverton and Wilhelm Agrell (Cambridge: Cambridge University Press, 2009), 124–25.

65. Flynn, Juergens, and Cantrell, "Employing ISR," 57.

66. Fishbein and Treverton, "Making Sense of Transnational Threats"; Dan Byman, *The Five Front War: The Better Way to Fight Global Jihad* (New York: Wiley, 2007), 94.

67. Flynn, Juergens, and Cantrell, "Employing ISR," 57.

68. *National Strategy for Combating Terrorism* (February 2003), https://www.cia.gov /news-information/cia-the-war-on-terrorism/Counter_Terrorism_Strategy.pdf.

69. *National Strategy for Combating Terrorism*, 8–9.

70. See Mark Stout, "In Search of Salafi Jihadist Strategic Thought: Mining the Words of the Terrorists," *Studies in Conflict and Terrorism* 32, no. 10 (2009); Jim Lacey, *Deciphering Abu Musab Al-Suri's Islamic Jihad Manifesto* (Annapolis, MD: Naval Institute Press, 2008); Brynjar Lia, "Jihadi Strategists and Doctrinarians," in *Self-Inflicted Wounds: Debate and Divisions within Al-Qaeda and Its Periphery*, ed. Assaf Moghadam and Brian Fishman (West Point, NY: United States Military Academy, Combating Terrorism Center, 2011); Norman Cigar, *Al-Qaida's Doctrine for Insurgency: Abd Al-Aziz Al-Muqrin's Practical Course for Guerrilla War* (Washington, DC: Potomac Books, 2009); and Brynjar Lia, *Architect of Global Jihad: The Life of al Qaeda Strategist Abu Mus'ab al-Suri* (New York: Columbia University Press, 2008).

71. See the *9/11 Commission Report* for an in-depth look at how they did so.

72. Treverton, *Intelligence for an Age of Terror*, 32–33.

73. "Al Qaeda," accessed August 9, 2015, https://twitter.com/alqaeda.

74. Faisal Irshaid, "How ISIS Is Spreading Its Message Online," BBC, June 19, 2014, http://www.bbc.com/news/world-middle-east-27912569.

75. Pollard, "On Counter-Terrorism Intelligence," 117, 122, 127.

Chapter 2. Transforming from Hierarchy to Networks to Empower Armed Groups

1. Brian Jackson, "Groups, Networks, or Movements: A Command-and-Control-Driven Approach to Classifying Terrorist Organizations and Its Application to Al Qaeda," *Studies in Conflict and Terrorism* 29, no. 3 (2006): 224; Chris Dishman, "The Leaderless Nexus: When Crime and Terror Converge," *Studies in Conflict and Terrorism* 28, no. 3 (2005): 241.

2. Lindsay Heger, Danielle Jung, and Wendy H. Wong, "Organizing for Resistance: How Group Structure Impacts the Character of Violence," *Terrorism and Political Violence* 24, no. 5 (2012): 743–68; Chad Serena, *It Takes More than a Network: The Iraqi Insurgency and Organizational Adaptation* (Stanford, CA: Stanford University Press, 2014).

3. David Tucker, "Terrorism, Networks, and Strategy: Why the Conventional Wisdom Is Wrong," *Homeland Security Affairs* 4, no. 2 (2008).

4. Seth Jones, *Waging Insurgent Warfare: From the Viet Cong to the Islamic State* (Oxford: Oxford University Press, 2017), 94–97.

5. Tucker, "Terrorism, Networks, and Strategy."

6. On the effects of decapitation, see Bryan C. Price, "Targeting Top Terrorists: How Leadership Decapitation Contributes to Counterterrorism," *International Security* 36, no. 4 (2012): 9–46.

7. Vera Eccarius-Kelly, "Surreptitious Lifelines: A Structural Analysis of the FARC and the PKK," *Terrorism and Political Violence* 24, no. 2 (2012).

8. Eccarius-Kelly.

9. Daniel Byman, "Do Targeted Killings Work?," *Foreign Affairs* 85, no. 2 (March/April 2006): 95–111.

10. Byman, 102.

11. Elena Pokalova, *Chechnya's Terrorist Network: The Evolution of Terrorism in Russia's North Caucasus* (Santa Barbara, CA: ABC-CLIO, 2015), 52.

12. This adaptation paved the way for later remodeling the Chechen Republic of Ichkeria into a networked jihadist organization. See Pokalova, 35–38.

13. Pokalova, 41.

14. Pokalova, 49–52.

15. Pokalova, 57.

16. Ekaterina Stepanova, *Terrorism in Asymmetrical Conflict: Ideological and Structural Aspects* (Oxford: Oxford University Press, 2008), 119.

17. Richard H. Shultz and Andrea J. Dew, *Insurgents, Terrorists, and Militias: The Warriors of Contemporary Combat* (New York: Columbia University Press, 2009), 138–40.

18. John Arquilla and David Ronfeldt, "The Advent of Netwar: Analytic Background,"

Studies in Conflict and Terrorism 22, no. 3 (1999): 196. See also John Arquilla and David Ronfeldt, *Networks and Netwars: The Future of Terror, Crime, and Militancy* (Santa Monica, CA: RAND Corp., 2001).

19. Arquilla and Ronfeldt, "Advent of Netwar," 193.

20. Byman, "Do Targeted Killings Work?" See also Stephen T. Hosmer, *Operations against Enemy Leaders* (Santa Monica, CA: RAND Corp., 2002).

21. Assaf Moghadam, *Nexus of Global Jihad: Understanding Cooperation among Terrorist Actors* (New York: Columbia University Press, 2017).

22. Moghadam, 108.

23. Moghadam, 109.

24. Moghadam, 111.

25. Moghadam, 112.

26. Moghadam, 112.

27. Moghadam, 116.

28. Matthew Levitt, "Untangling the Terror Web: Identifying and Counteracting the Phenomenon of Crossover between Terrorist Groups," *SAIS Review of International Affairs* 24, no. 1 (2004): 33–48.

29. Moghadam, *Nexus of Global Jihad*, 130–32.

30. See Jackson, "Groups, Networks, or Movements," 250–52; and Bruce Hoffman, "The Changing Face of Al Qaeda and the Global War on Terrorism," *Studies in Conflict and Terrorism* 27, no. 6 (2004): 549–60.

31. See, for instance, Katherine Zimmerman, *The Al Qaeda Network: A New Framework for Defining the Enemy* (Washington, DC: American Enterprise Institute, 2013).

32. Hoffman, "Changing Face of Al Qaeda," 551; Levitt, "Untangling the Terror Web," 34.

33. *9/11 Commission Report: Final Report of the National Commission on Terrorist Attacks upon the United States* (New York: W.W. Norton, 2004), 66–67.

34. "Al-Qaeda Camps 'Trained 70,000,'" BBC News, January 4, 2005, http://news.bbc .co.uk/2/hi/europe/4146969.stm.

35. Rohan Gunaratna, *Inside Al Qaeda: A Global Network of Terror* (New York: Columbia University Press, 2002); Olivier Roy, *Globalized Islam: The Search for a New Ummah* (New York: Columbia University Press, 2004); and Fawaz Greges, *The Far Enemy: Why Jihad Went Global* (Cambridge: Cambridge University Press, 2004).

36. "Declaration of the World Islamic Front for Jihad against the Jews and the Crusaders," accessed at the Federation of American Scientists website, http://www.fas.org/irp /world/para/docs/980223-fatwa.htm.

37. For a discussion of these terms in al-Qaeda doctrine, see Greges, *Far Enemy*.

38. Levitt, "Untangling the Terror Web," 55.

39. Bill Braniff and Assaf Moghadam, "Towards Global Jihadism," *Perspectives on Terrorism* 5, no. 2 (May 2011): 36–49.

40. For a discussion of the concept of virtual sanctuary, see Steve Coll and Susan Glasser, "Terrorists Turn to the Web as Base of Operations," *Washington Post*, August 7, 2005;

Gabriel Weimann, *How Modern Terrorism Uses the Internet*, Special Report no. 116 (Washington, DC: United States Institute of Peace, March 2004); and Rita Katz and Josh Devon, "The Online Jihadist Threat," testimony before the House Armed Services Committee Terrorism, Unconventional Threats and Capabilities Subcommittee, US House of Representative, February 14, 2007, 4.

41. Ryan Evans, "From Iraq to Yemen: Al-Qaida's Shifting Strategies," *CTC Sentinel* 3, no. 10 (2010): 11–15.

42. Brian Fishman, "After Zarqawi: The Dilemmas and Future of al Qaeda in Iraq," *Washington Quarterly* 29, no. 4 (2006): 19–32.

43. George Michael, "The Legend and Legacy of Abu Musab al-Zarqawi," *Defence Studies* 7, no. 3 (2007): 338–57.

44. Kenneth Katzman, *Al Qaeda in Iraq: Assessment and outside Links* (Washington, DC: Congressional Research Service, 2008), 10; Fishman, "After Zarqawi," 25.

45. Katzman, *Al Qaeda in Iraq*, 11.

46. Stanley McChrystal, "It Takes a Network: The New Frontline of Modern Warfare," *Foreign Policy* 90, no. 1 (March/April 2011).

47. David Knoke, "It Takes a Network: The Rise and Fall of Social Network Analysis in U.S. Army Counterinsurgency Doctrine," *Connections* 33, no. 1 (July 2013): 2.

48. Martin Muckian, "Structural Vulnerabilities of Networked Insurgencies: Adapting to the New Adversary," *Parameters* 36 (Winter 2006–7): 15.

49. See Richard Shultz, *Global Insurgency Strategy and the Salafi Jihad Movement* (Boulder, CO: Institute for National Security Studies, 2008), 47–86.

50. David Galula, *Counterinsurgency Warfare: Theory and Practice* (Westport, CT: Greenwood, 2006).

51. On the effects of superpower involvement in insurgency, see Jones, *Waging Insurgent Warfare*.

52. Itai Brun, "'While You're Busy Making Other Plans': The 'Other RMA,'" *Journal of Strategic Studies* 33, no. 4 (2010): 535–65.

53. Brun.

54. Brun.

55. Avi Kober, "The Israel Defense Forces in the Second Lebanon War: Why the Poor Performance?," *Journal of Strategic Studies* 31, no. 1 (2008): 3–40.

56. Kober.

57. Kober.

58. See, e.g., Efrain Inbar, "How Israel Bungled the Second Lebanon War," *Middle East Quarterly* 19, no. 3 (2007); Giora Eiland, "The IDF: Addressing the Failures of the Second Lebanon War," in *The Middle East Strategic Balance 2007–2008*, ed. Mark Heller (Tel Aviv: Institute for National Security Studies, 2008), 31–37; and Matt Matthews, *We Were Caught Unprepared: The 2006 Hezbollah-Israeli War* (Collingdale, PA: Diane Publishing, 2011).

59. Marc Sageman, *Understanding Terror Networks* (Philadelphia: University of Pennsylvania Press, 2004), 165.

60. Sageman, 166.
61. Richard Shultz, "US Counterterrorism Operations during the Iraq War: A Case Study of Task Force 714," *Studies in Conflict and Terrorism* 40, no. 10 (2016): 1–29.
62. Shultz.
63. On the role of the midlevel commanders, see Peter Neumann, Ryan Evans, and Raffaello Pantucci, "Locating Al Qaeda's Center of Gravity: The Role of Middle Managers," *Studies in Conflict and Terrorism* 34, no. 11 (2011): 825–42.
64. Shultz, "US Counterterrorism Operations during the Iraq War."
65. Sageman, *Understanding Terror Networks*, 123.
66. Sageman, 99–135.
67. See Marc Sageman, *Leaderless Jihad: Terror Networks in the Twenty-First Century* (Philadelphia: University of Pennsylvania Press, 2011), 84.
68. Eliot Cohen, "A Revolution in Warfare," *Foreign Affairs* 75, no. 2 (March/April 1996): 37–54; Laszlo Solymar, "The Effect of the Telegraph on Law and Order, War, Diplomacy, and Power Politics," *Interdisciplinary Science Review* 25, no. 3 (2000): 203–10.
69. George Michael, "Counterinsurgency and Lone Wolf Terrorism," *Terrorism and Political Violence* 26, no. 1 (2014): 45–57.
70. John Curtis Amble, "Combating Terrorism in the New Media Environment," *Studies in Conflict and Terrorism* 35, no. 5 (2012): 339–53.
71. Jonathan Kennedy and Gabriel Weimann, "The Strength of Weak Terrorist Ties," *Terrorism and Political Violence* 23, no. 2 (2011): 201–12.
72. Gabriel Weimann, "Terrorist Dot Com: Using the Internet for Terrorist Recruitment and Mobilization," in *The Making of a Terrorist*, ed. James Forest (Westport, CT: Praeger, 2005).
73. Sageman, *Leaderless Jihad*, 109–23.
74. Arquilla and Ronfeldt, "Advent of Netwar," 195.
75. Brad McAllister, "Al Qaeda and the Innovative Firm: Demythologizing the Network," *Studies in Conflict and Terrorism* 27, no. 4 (2004): 297–319.
76. Arquilla and Ronfeldt, "Advent of Netwar," 197.
77. Richard Shultz, *Strategic Culture and Strategic Studies: An Alternative Framework for Assessing al-Qaeda and the Global Jihad Movement* (Tampa, FL: JSOU Press, 2012).
78. Shultz.
79. Mohammed M. Hafez, "Jihad after Iraq: Lessons from the Arab Afghans," *Studies in Conflict and Terrorism* 32, no. 2 (2009): 73–94; Thomas Hegghammer, "The Rise of Muslim Foreign Fighters: Islam and the Globalization of Jihad," *International Security* 35, no. 3 (2010): 53–94.
80. Hafez.
81. Arquilla and Ronfeldt, *Networks and Netwars*, 8.
82. Arquilla and Ronfeldt, 8.
83. Arquilla and Ronfeldt, 197.
84. Serena, *It Takes More than a Network*.
85. Serena.

86. Gökçe Sargut and Rita Gunther McGrath, "Learning to Live with Complexity," *Harvard Business Review* 89, no. 9 (2011): 68–76.

87. Sargut and McGrath. See also Shultz, "US Counterterrorism Operations during the Iraq War."

88. Sargut and McGrath, "Learning to Live with Complexity."

89. David Snowden and Mary Boone, "A Leader's Framework for Decision Making," *Harvard Business Review* 85, no. 11 (November 2007): 3.

90. See Moghadam, *Nexus of Global Jihad*.

91. Shultz, "US Counterterrorism Operations during the Iraq War."

92. Serena, *It Takes More than a Network*, 20.

93. Serena, 10–11.

94. Bernard Burnes, "Complexity Theories and Organizational Change," *International Journal of Management Reviews* 7, no. 2 (2005): 73–90.

Chapter 3. Transforming Intelligence Collection for Irregular War

1. The phrase "disciplines of intelligence collection" is borrowed from the title of the book by Mark Lowenthal and Robert Clark, *The Five Disciplines of Intelligence Collection* (Washington, DC: Congressional Quarterly Press, 2016).

2. Mark Lowenthal, *Intelligence: From Secrets to Policy*, 4th ed. (Washington, DC: Congressional Quarterly Press, 2009), 69.

3. Lowenthal, 79–80.

4. Lowenthal and Clark, Five Disciplines, 69.

5. For a discussion of the Soviet use of this terminology, see Herbert Romerstein and Stanislav Levchenko, *The KGB against the Main Enemy: How the Soviet Intelligence Service Operates against the United States* (Lexington, MA: Lexington Books, 1989).

6. David A. Deptula and R. Greg Brown, "A House Divided: The Indivisibility of Intelligence, Surveillance, and Reconnaissance," *Air & Space Power Journal* 22, no. 2 (Summer 2008).

7. Association of the United States Army, Institute of Land Warfare, *2006 Quadrennial Defense Review: Shifting Emphasis*, March 2006, 1–18, http://www.comw.org/qdr/fulltext/06ausa.pdf.

8. David Deptula and Mike Francisco, "Air Force ISR Operations: Hunting versus Gathering," *Air & Space Power Journal* 24, no. 4 (Winter 2010): 13–17.

9. Deptula and Mike Francisco.

10. Deptula and Mike Francisco.

11. Jeffrey Richelson, *The US Intelligence Community*, 6th ed. (Boulder, CO: Westview, 2012).

12. Lowenthal and Clark, *Five Disciplines*.

13. Lowenthal and Clark, 45.

14. Richelson, *US Intelligence Community*, 203.

15. Richelson, 205.

16. William Nolte, "Signals Intelligence," in Lowenthal and Clark, *Five Disciplines*, 81.

17. Richelson, *US Intelligence Community*, 203.

18. Richelson, 205.

19. Richelson, 169–70.

20. *DOD Dictionary of Military Terms* (2018), http://www.jcs.mil/Portals/36/Documents /Doctrine/pubs/dictionary.pdf?ver=2018-09-28-100314-687.

21. Richelson, *US Intelligence Community*, 241.

22. Abram Shulsky and Gary Schmitt, *Silent Warfare: Understanding the World of Intelligence*, 3rd ed. (Dulles, VA: Potomac Books, 2002), 31–32.

23. Michael Althoff, "Human Intelligence," in Lowenthal and Clark, *Five Disciplines*, 53.

24. Richelson, *US Intelligence Community*, 297.

25. Richelson, 307.

26. Eliot Jardines, "Open Source Intelligence," in Lowenthal and Clark, *Five Disciplines*, 5.

27. Lowenthal, *Intelligence: From Secrets to Policy*, 12.

28. This aversion can be seen in the often-told story of US code-breaking activities following World War I. Prior to the Great War, the United States had shown little interest in cryptography. However, thanks to an enterprising young cryptologist named Herbert Yardley, a code and cipher decryption detachment was established as part of the army's Intelligence Branch as war approached. It was designated MI-8 and assigned the task of both creating codes and ciphers for the United States and breaking those of other countries. After the war, MI-8 was officially disbanded but sub rosa relocated from Washington to New York City, where it continued its cryptographic operations under cover as a commercial enterprise. Funding was jointly shared by the army and the State Department. With Yardley as its director, for nearly a decade it successfully broke the codes of foreign governments. However, when Henry L. Stimson became secretary of state and learned of Yardley's activities, Stimson stopped State Department funding, arguing that "gentlemen do not read each other's mail." See David Kahn, *The Reader of Gentlemen's Mail: Herbert O. Yardley and the Birth of American Codebreaking* (New Haven, CT: Yale University Press, 2004), 98. For Yardley's own account, see Herbert Yardley, *The American Black Chamber* (Indianapolis, IN: Bobbs-Merrill, 1931).

29. The OSS consisted of the following branches: "The Research and Analysis (R&A) branch provided economic, social, and political analyses, sifting information from foreign newspapers and international business and labor publications. The Secret Intelligence branch (SI) engaged in clandestine collection from within enemy and neutral territory. The Special Operations (SO) branch conducted sabotage and worked with resistance forces. The Counterespionage (X-2) branch engaged in protecting U.S. and Allied intelligence operations from enemy penetrations. The Morale Operations (MO) branch was responsible for covert or 'black' propaganda. Operational Groups (OG) conducted guerrilla operations in enemy territory. Finally, the Maritime Unit (MU) carried out maritime sabotage." See the Senate Select Committee to Study Governmental Operations with Respect to Intelligence Activities, *Supplementary Detailed Staff Reports on Foreign and Military Intelligence*, book 4 (Washington, DC:

U.S. Government Printing Office, 1976), 5, http://www.intelligence.senate.gov/sites /default/files/94755_IV.pdf.

30. Stephen Budiansky, *Battle of Wits: The Complete Story of Codebreaking in World War II* (New York: Free Press, 2002).

31. Richelson, *US Intelligence Community*, 169–70.

32. Michael Warner, *Central Intelligence: Origin and Evolution* (Washington, DC: Center for the Study of Intelligence, CIA, 2001), 2–3.

33. Lowenthal, *Intelligence*, 19–20.

34. Paul Redmond, explains that a "denied area" is an "intelligence term . . . describing an extremely hostile operational environment with heavy surveillance." See Redmond, "The Challenges of Counterintelligence," in *The Oxford Handbook of National Security Intelligence*, ed. Loch Johnson (Oxford: Oxford University Press, 2010), 545.

35. Aid explains how the USSR's borders were under the control of the KGB, which "made it extremely difficult to sneak in or out of the Soviet Union." Additionally, "the Russian government limited travel visas," and for those foreigners granted entry, "their phones were tapped, their mail read, their apartments and cars were bugged, and those 'normal' Russians that they spoke to were closely questioned by the KGB." See Matthew Aid, "The National Security Agency and the Cold War," *Intelligence and National Security* 16, no. 1 (2001): 30.

36. Moscow was able to do so, notes Michael Sulick, a former director of the CIA's National Clandestine Service, because "the Soviets had thoroughly penetrated the US government in the 1930–40s and their acquisition of America's atom bomb secrets leveled the superpower playing field at the outset of the Cold War." Sulick notes that documents from the KGB archives include a "list of about 1,000 KGB agents in the U.S. over several decades." See Sulick, "Intelligence in the Cold War," *The Intelligencer Journal of U.S. Intelligence Studies* 21, no. 1 (Winter 2014–15): 47. The Mitrokhin archive, to which Sulick is referring, consists of handwritten notes that the KGB's archivist, Vasili Mitrokhin, made during his three decades of service in the KGB and which he brought with him when he defected. See Christopher Andrew and Vasili Mitrokhin, *The Sword and the Shield: The Mitrokhin Archive and the Secret History of the KGB* (New York: Basic Books, 1999).

37. Oleg Bukharin, "The Cold War Atomic Intelligence Game, 1945–70: From the Russian Perspective," *Studies in Intelligence* 48, no. 2 (2004), https://www.cia.gov/library /center-for-the-study-of-intelligence/csi-publications/csi-studies/studies/vol48no2 /article01.html.

38. Aid, "National Security Agency and the Cold War," 33.

39. Post–World War II demobilization had made deep cuts in army and navy communications intelligence. And while the air force created its own COMINT capability, it likewise was underresourced.

40. Richelson notes that the AFSA "had little power" or effectiveness, which became clear during the Korean War. A year into the conflict, "American military and civilian officials had become extremely unhappy about the performance of AFSA. . . . For

example, in mid-1951 the commander of US forces in the Far East, General Matthew B. Ridgway, was furious about the poor quality of the COMINT support his forces were receiving." See Richelson, *US Intelligence Community*, 32. See also Aid, "National Security Agency and the Cold War," 35.

41. Douglas Keane and Michael Warner, eds., *Foreign Relations of the United States, 1950–1955: The Intelligence Community, 1950–1955* (Washington, DC: US Government Printing Office, 2007), 262.

42. Cited in Aid, "National Security Agency and the Cold War," 28, 53.

43. Nolte, "Signals Intelligence," in Lowenthal and Clark, *Five Disciplines*, 81.

44. Aid, "National Security Agency and the Cold War," 38.

45. James Risen and Eric Lichtblau, "How the U.S. Uses Technology to Mine More Data More Quickly," *New York Times*, June 8, 2013.

46. Richelson, *US Intelligence Community*, 212.

47. Matthew Aid, "The Crisis Years: SIGINT and the Kennedy Administration: 1961–1963," chap. 5 in *Secret Sentry: The Untold Story of the National Security Agency* (New York: Bloomsbury, 2009).

48. Stephen Budiansky, *Code Warriors: NSA's Codebreakers and the Secret Intelligence War against the Soviet Union* (New York: Vintage, 2016).

49. For example, in the mid-1980s, intercepted messages made clear that Libya was behind the terrorist bombing of the La Belle discotheque in West Berlin, as President Ronald Reagan alluded to on national television on April 7, 1986. See Aid, *Secret Sentry*, chap. 10.

50. Nolte, "Signals Intelligence," in Lowenthal and Clark, *Five Disciplines*, 98.

51. Robert Clark, *Intelligence Collection* (Los Angeles: CQ Press, 2014), 500.

52. Richelson, *US Intelligence Community*, 206.

53. Clark, *Intelligence Collection*, 488.

54. Aid, "National Security Agency and the Cold War," 36.

55. The three military services each operated fleets of aircraft for this purpose. In the case of the air force, the aircraft used included its RC-135 reconnaissance fleet. As the RC-135 evolved through several models, it acquired the capacity to collect both electronic and communications signals and to transmit them in real time to ground stations to be analyzed.

56. Richelson, *US Intelligence Community*, 207–8.

57. These included Vortex, first launched in the early 1980s, and Orin at the end of the decade. They were targeted primarily on "Soviet missile and nuclear RDT&E [research, development, test, and evaluation] sites, defense related ministries, and defense industries." See Richelson, 211–12.

58. Gregory W. Pedlow and Donald E. Welzenbach, *The Central Intelligence Agency and Overhead Reconnaissance: The U-2 and Oxcart Programs* (Langley, VA: History Staff, CIA, 1992), 316, http://nsarchive.gwu.edu/NSAEBB/NSAEBB434/.

59. Pedlow and Welzenbach, 316.

60. Chris Pocock, *The U-2 Spyplane: Toward the Unknown; A New History of the Early Years* (Atglen, PA: Schiffer, 2000); Phil Taubman, *Secret Empire: Eisenhower, the CIA, and*

the Hidden Story of America's Space Espionage (New York: Simon & Schuster, 2003). Even though flights stopped over the USSR in 1960, in 1962 U-2s played an important role in the Cuban Missile Crisis and elsewhere during the Cold War.

61. Jeffrey Richelson, "The Technical Collection of Intelligence," in *Handbook of Intelligence Studies*, ed. Loch Johnson (London: Routledge, 2007), 106.

62. The National Aeronautics and Space Administration (NASA) defines the electromagnetic (EM) spectrum as the range of all types of EM radiation. Radiation is energy that travels and spreads out as it goes—the visible light that comes from a lamp in a house and the radio waves that come from a radio station are two types of electromagnetic radiation. The other types of EM radiation that make up the electromagnetic spectrum are microwaves, infrared light, ultraviolet light, X-rays, and gamma-rays. See NASA, Goddard Space Flight Center, "The Electromagnetic Spectrum," http://imagine.gsfc .nasa.gov/science/toolbox/emspectrum1.html.

63. Clark, *Intelligence Collection*, chaps. 9–12.

64. Jeffrey T. Richelson, *U.S. Satellite Imagery, 1960–1999*, National Security Archive Electronic Briefing Book no. 13 (Washington, DC: National Security Archive, 1999), https://nsarchive.gwu.edu/NSAEBB/NSAEBB13/.

65. Richelson. The first Gambit camera could produce photos with about an eighteen-inch resolution, while the last model produced photographs with resolution under six inches.

66. Richelson.

67. Richelson.

68. Clark describes them as "a passive sensor that receives and records the electromagnetic energy that is naturally emitted from objects." In doing so, it "creates an image and measures the intensity of the received energy" collected by the sensor. See Clark, *Intelligence Collection*, 495.

69. Radiometric images, Clark notes, can detect these military systems because they show up as images that "are hotter than their surroundings." See Clark, 247.

70. Clark, 498.

71. Clark, 247.

72. In the field of imagery intelligence, this is more often referred to as "camouflage, concealment, and deception," or CC&D. See Hampton P. Conley, *A History of Camouflage: Concealment and Deception* (Montgomery, AL: Air War College, 1988), http:// www.dtic.mil/dtic/tr/fulltext/u2/a216593.pdf.

73. For a detailed examination of these activities, see Brian Dailey and Patrick Parker, eds., *Soviet Strategic Deception* (Lexington, MA: Lexington Books, 1987); and Michael Mihalka, "Soviet Strategic Deception, 1955–1981," *Journal of Strategic Studies* 5, no. 1 (1982): 40–93.

74. Jeffrey Richelson, *U.S. Satellite Imagery, 1960–1999*, https://nsarchive2.gwu.edu /NSAEBB/NSAEBB13/.

75. Clark describes each of these radar collection missions in *Intelligence Collection*, 283–85, 303–4.

76. Richelson, *US Intelligence Community*, 37.

77. Jack O'Connor, *NPIC: Seeing the Secrets and Growing the Leaders; A Cultural History of the National Photographic Interpretation Center* (Alexandria, VA: Acumensa Solutions, 2015).

78. Darryl Murdock and Robert Clark, "Geospatial Intelligence," in Lowenthal and Clark, *Five Disciplines*, 111.

79. In 1986, the IC formally classified MASINT as an intelligence-collection discipline. For a discussion of its evolution, see John Morris and Robert Clark, "Measurement and Signature Intelligence," in Lowenthal and Clark, *Five Disciplines*, 161.

80. Theodore Shackley and Richard Finny, *Spymaster: My Life in the CIA* (Dulles, VA: Potomac Books, 2005), 1.

81. For details, see John Dziak, *Chekisty: A History of the KGB* (Lexington, MA: Lexington Books, 1988).

82. Sulick, "Intelligence in the Cold War," 47.

83. Richard Helms and William Hood, *A Look over My Shoulder: A Life in the Central Intelligence Agency* (New York: Random House, 2003), 127.

84. Allen Dulles, *The Craft of Intelligence* (New York: Harper & Row, 1963), 133–44.

85. Against Soviet officials working in overseas assignments, the classic recruiting method was more able to be employed by US intelligence. This was because the KGB could not keep them all under twenty-four-hour control. Once recruited, they were also more accessible to their CIA handlers, who could establish a system for remaining in contact when the agent returned for an assignment back in the USSR.

86. Penkovsky was severely disillusioned with the Soviet system. One reason given was that he "feared Khrushchev was leading the Soviet Union down the path to destruction. . . . Penkovsky wanted to help prevent a nuclear war between the superpowers, so he volunteered to spy." Adding to his disaffection was the fact that his career progression had stalled at the rank of colonel. See Central Intelligence Agency, "The Capture and Execution of Colonel Penkovsky, 1963" (historical document posted on the CIA website, March 15, 2010), https://www.cia.gov/news-information/featured -story-archive/2010-featured-story-archive/colonel-penkovsky.html.

87. Central Intelligence Agency.

88. David E. Hoffman, *The Billion Dollar Spy: A True Story of Cold War Espionage and Betrayal* (New York: Anchor, 2016), 13.

89. In conjunction with imagery, Penkovsky's information put Kennedy in the position of knowing that the Soviet ICBM force was considerably inferior to that possessed by the United States. Additionally, his information "gave the Kennedy Administration technical insights about the Soviet nuclear missiles deployed to Cuba. . . . Because of Penkovsky, Kennedy knew that he had three days before the Soviet missiles were fully functional to negotiate a diplomatic solution." See Central Intelligence Agency, "Capture and Execution of Colonel Penkovsky, 1963."

90. Central Intelligence Agency.

91. Tolkachev is said to have fumed with antagonism for the Soviet system and wanted

to inflict damage on it. His anger was stoked by the persecution suffered by his wife's family during the Stalinist purges of the 1930s. He also despised the treatment of famous Soviet dissidents Andrei Sakharov and Alexander Solzhenitsyn. For Tolkachev, they were "voices of conscience that waged a titanic struggle against Soviet totalitarianism." See Hoffman, *Billion Dollar Spy*, chap. 13.

92. Central Intelligence Agency, "A Look Back . . . The Execution of a 'Great Spy': Adolf Tolkachev" (historical document posted on the CIA website, September 25, 2008), https://www.cia.gov/news-information/featured-story-archive/2008-featured-story -archive/adolf-tolkachev.html.

93. Barry Royden, "Tolkachev, a Worthy Successor to Penkovsky: An Exceptional Espionage Operation," *Studies in Intelligence* 47, no. 3 (2003): 22. See also Milton Bearden and James Risen, *The Main Enemy: The CIA's Battle with the Soviet Union* (London: Century, 2003).

94. Benjamin Fischer, a former CIA analyst, operations officer, and chief historian of the agency, has proposed that Tolkachev was a fake, a KGB double agent who was dangled before the CIA, which took the bait. See Fischer, "The Spy Who Came in for the Gold: A Skeptical View of the GTVANQUISH Case," *Journal of Intelligence History* 8, no. 1 (Summer 2008): 39–54; and "The Man Who Wasn't There," *International Journal of Intelligence and CounterIntelligence* 30, no. 1 (2017): 30–52.

95. Jardines, "Open Source Intelligence," 14.

96. Jardines, 2.

97. Kalev Leetaru, "The Scope of FBIS and BBC Open-Source Media Coverage, 1979–2008," *Studies in Intelligence* 54, no. 1 (2010): 19.

98. Jardines, "Open Source Intelligence," 16.

99. Jardines, 16.

100. John Diamond, "Re-examining Problems and Prospects in U.S. Imagery Intelligence," *International Journal of Intelligence and CounterIntelligence* 14, no. 1 (2001): 1.

101. For assessments of the commission, see Loch Johnson, *The Threat on the Horizon: An Inside Account of America's Search for Security after the Cold War* (Oxford: Oxford University Press, 2011); Brit Snider, "Commentary: A Different Angle on the Aspin-Brown Commission," *Studies in Intelligence* 49, no. 1 (2005); and "A Roundtable Discussion: Brown Commission and the Future of Intelligence," *Studies in Intelligence*, no. 5, 1996.

102. Permanent Select Committee on Intelligence, *IC21: The Intelligence Community in the 21st Century* (Washington, DC: US Government Printing Office, April 1996), http:// www.gpo.gov/fdsys/pkg/GPO-IC21/content-detail.html.

103. Diamond, "Re-examining U.S. Imagery Intelligence," 3.

104. Diamond, 2.

105. Diamond, 4.

106. Cited in Diamond, 5.

107. Richard Shultz, Douglas Farah, and Itamara Lochard, *Armed Groups: A Tier-One Security Priority* (USAF Academy, CO: INSS Occasional Paper 57, September 2004).

108. National Commission for the Review of the National Reconnaissance Office, *Report of the National Commission to Review the National Reconnaissance Office: The NRO at the Crossroads*, "Executive Summary," 2, https://fas.org/irp/nro/commission/toc.htm.

109. National Commission for Review, 2.

110. National Commission for Review, 2.

111. Cited in Richard Best, *The National Security Agency: Issues for Congress* (Washington, DC: Congressional Research Service, 2001), 7.

112. Best, 7.

113. Best, 14.

114. David Ensor, "Biggest U.S. Spy Agency Choking on Too Much Data," CNN, November 25, 1999, http://www.cnn.com/US/9911/25/nsa.woes/.

115. Seymour Hersh, "The Intelligence Gap: How the Digital Age Left Our Spies out in the Cold," *New Yorker*, December 6, 1999, https://cryptome.org/nsa-hersh.htm.

116. For a discussion of the decisions to treat terrorism as a crime and law enforcement responsibility, see Richard Shultz, "Showstoppers: Nine Reasons Why We Never Sent Our Special Operations Forces after Al Qaeda before 9/11," *Weekly Standard*, January 26, 2004, 26–27.

117. National Commission on Terrorist Attacks upon the United States, *9/11 Commission Report* (New York: W. W. Norton, 2004), "The Performance of the Intelligence Community," staff statement no. 11, 10.

118. *9/11 Commission Report*, 10–11.

119. *9/11 Commission Report*, 12.

120. *9/11 Commission Report*, 9.

121. *9/11 Commission Report*, "Executive Summary," 12, http://govinfo.library.unt.edu/911/report/ 911Report_Exec.pdf.

122. George W. Bush, "State of the Union Address," January 29, 2002, https://georgewbush-whitehouse.archives.gov/news/releases/2002/01/20020129-11.html.

123. George W. Bush, "Graduation Speech at the United States Military Academy," June 1, 2002, https://georgewbush-whitehouse.archives.gov/news/releases/2002/06/200206 01-3.html.

124. As quoted at the start of the introduction to this book. See also discussion of Krulak's speech in Richard Shultz and Andrea Dew, *Insurgents, Terrorists, and Militias* (New York: Columbia University Press, 2006), 9–10.

125. Deptula and Brown, "House Divided," 5–16.

126. Dennis D. Fitzgerald divides the evolution of NRO imagery collection into four phases, the last of which is "Risk Management and National Reconnaissance from the Cold War up to the Global War on Terrorism." An article by that title appeared in the classified edition of *National Reconnaissance: Journal of the Discipline and Practice*, no. C1 (2003). An unclassified version is available at https://fas.org/irp/nro/journal/fitz.pdf.

127. Stephen Price, *Close ISR Support: Re-Organizing the Combined Forces Air Component Commander's Intelligence, Surveillance and Reconnaissance Processes and Agencies* (Monterey, CA: Naval Postgraduate School, 2009), 415.

128. Michael Sirak, "ISR Revolution," *Air Force Magazine*, June 2010.

129. Marshall Curtis Erwin, *Intelligence, Surveillance, and Reconnaissance (ISR) Acquisition: Issues for Congress* (Washington, DC: Congressional Research Service, April 16, 2013), 8.

130. Richelson, *US Intelligence Community*, 181.

131. According to Thompson, these included "31 E-3 Sentry Airborne Warning and Control System (AWACS) radar planes, 16 E-8 Joint Surveillance and Target Attack Radar System (JSTARS) aircraft, and 17 RC-135 Rivet Joint signals-intelligence planes." See Loren Thompson, *Intelligence, Surveillance, and Reconnaissance* (Washington, DC: Lexington Institute, 2013), 4.

132. Richelson, *US Intelligence Community*, 184.

133. Rebecca Grant, "The All-Seeing Air Force," *Air Force Magazine*, September 2008, 35.

134. Erwin, *Intelligence, Surveillance, and Reconnaissance (ISR) Acquisition*, 10–12. The United States also has a very large number of smaller UAVs, including Ravens, Wasps, Pumas, and T-Hawks.

135. See the MQ-1B Predator fact sheet, Military.com, http://www.military.com/equipment/mq-1b-predator.

136. MQ-9 Reaper fact sheet, Military.com, http://www.military.com/equipment/mq-9-reaper.

137. "Shadow 200 RQ-7 Tactical Unmanned Aircraft System, United States of America," Army Technology, http://www.army-technology.com/projects/shadow200uav/.

138. RQ-4 Global Hawk fact sheet, Military.com, http://www.military.com/equipment/rq-4-global-hawk.

139. Michael T. Flynn, Rich Juergens, and Thomas L. Cantrell, "Employing ISR: SOF Best Practices," *Joint Force Quarterly* (July 2008), 58.

140. Daniel Gouré, *Wide Area Persistent Surveillance Revolutionizes Tactical ISR* (Washington, DC: Lexington Institute, 2012), http://lexingtoninstitute.org/wide-area-persistent-surveillance-revolutionizes -tactical-isr/.

141. Loren Thompson, "Air Force's Secret 'Gorgon Stare' Program Leaves Terrorists Nowhere to Hide," *Forbes*, April 10, 2015, http://www.forbes.com/sites/lorenthompson/2015/04/10/air-forces-secret-gorgon-stare-program-leaves-terrorists-nowhere-to-hide/#2165c0eb5271.

142. Thompson.

143. Thompson.

144. Grant, "All-Seeing Air Force," 38.

145. Interview with Lt. Gen. Michael Flynn, USA (Ret.), October 2014, Alexandria, VA.

146. Follow-up interview with Gen. Stanley McChrystal, USA (Ret.), May 2015, Alexandria, VA.

147. Clark, *Intelligence Collection*, 90–91.

148. Clark, 90.

149. Matthew Aid, "All Glory Is Fleeting: Sigint and the Fight against International Terrorism," *Intelligence and National Security* 18, no. 4 (Winter 2003): 96.

150. Deptula and Francisco, "Air Force ISR Operations."

151. "Statement for the Record by Lieutenant General Michael V. Hayden, USAF, Director, National Security Agency/Chief, Central Security Service before the Joint Inquiry of the Senate Select Committee on Intelligence and the House Permanent Select Committee on Intelligence, 17 October 2002," http://nsarchive.gwu.edu/NSAEBB/NSAEBB24/nsa27.pdf.

152. "Statement for the Record by General Hayden."

153. Clark, *Intelligence Collection*, 115.

154. Clark, 89.

155. Clark, 89.

156. Clark, 116.

157. Clark, 117.

158. "Statement for the Record by General Hayden."

159. Matthew Aid, "The Troubled Inheritance: The National Security Agency and the Obama Administration," in *Oxford Handbook of National Security Intelligence*, ed. Loch Johnson (Oxford: Oxford University Press, 2010), 244.

160. "Snowden Leaks Intelligence 'Black Budget' to Washington Post," Al Jazeera America, August 29, 2013, http://america.aljazeera.com/articles/2013/8/29/nsa-snowden-leaks blackbudgettowashingtonpost.html.

161. Aid, "Troubled Inheritance," 244.

162. Dana Priest, "NSA Growth Fueled by Need to Target Terrorists, *Washington Post*, July 22, 2013, https://www.washingtonpost.com/world/national-security/nsa-growth-fueled -by-need-to-target-terrorists/2013/07/21/24c93cf4-f0b1-11e2-bed3-b9b6fe264871 _story.html?utm_term=.5450a669d3bf.

163. "Statement for the Record by General Hayden."

164. Danial Byman, "The Intelligence War on Terrorism," *Intelligence and National Security* 29, no. 6 (2014): 848.

165. Department of Defense Directive 5100.20, January 26, 2010, 3, http://www.dtic.mil /whs/ directives/corres/pdf/510020p.pdf.

166. See the NSA/CSS Georgia mission statement at https://www.nsa.gov/about/crypto logic-centers/georgia/.

167. "NSA/CSS Opens Newest Facility in Georgia," *Government Security News*, March 6, 2012, https://www.gsnmagazine.com/article/25772/nsacss_opens_newest_facility _georgia.

168. Aid, *Secret Sentry*, 300–301.

169. Aid, 301.

170. Aid, 301.

171. Aid, 301.

172. Yannick LeJacq, "How the NSA's XKeyscore Program Works," NBC News, July 31, 2013, http://www. nbcnews. com/technology/how-nsas-xkeyscore-program-works -6c10812168.

173. Glenn Greenwald, "XKeyscore: NSA Tool Collects Nearly Everything a User Does on the Internet," *Guardian*, July 31, 2013, https://www.theguardian.com/world/2013 /jul/31/nsa-top-secret-program-online-data.

174. Greenwald.

175. Greenwald.

176. Richelson, *US Intelligence Community*, 224.

177. Richelson, 225.

178. Aid, "Troubled Inheritance," 247.

179. "Inside the NSA's Real Time Regional Gateway," Fox News, http://video.foxnews
.com/v/ 4898263371001/?#sp=show-clips; "Bob Woodward Talks to ABC's Diane
Sawyer about Obama's Wars," ABC News, http://abcnews. go.com/WN/bob-wood
ward-tells-diane-sawyer-book-obamas-wars/story?id=11738879; and Shane Harris,
@War, The Rise of the Military-Internet Complex (New York: Houghton Mifflin Har-
court, 2014).

180. Ellen Nakashima and Joby Warrick, "For NSA Chief, Terrorist Threat Drives Passion
to 'Collect It All,'" *Washington Post*, July 14, 2013, https://www.washingtonpost.com
/world/national-security/for-nsa-chief-terrorist-threat-drives-passion-to-collect-it-all
/2013/07/14/3d26ef80-ea49-11e2-a301-ea5a8116d211_story.html? utm_term=. cbd
ab48c7b2d.

181. Nakashima and Warrick.

182. Harris, *@War*, 47.

183. Harris, *@War*, 50.

184. Sean Naylor, *Relentless Strike: The Secret History of Joint Special Operations Command*
(New York: St. Martin's, 2015), 258.

185. Morris and Clark, "Measurement and Signature Intelligence," 204.

186. James Risen and Judith Miller, "A Nation Challenged: Chemical Weapons; Al Qaeda
Sites Point to Tests of Chemicals," *New York Times*, November 11, 2001.

187. Mohammed M. Hafez and Maria Rasmussen, *Terrorist Innovations in Weapons of Mass
Effect, Phase II* (Monterey, CA: Naval Postgraduate School, Center on Contemporary
Conflict, 2012).

188. Department of State, Office of the Coordinator for Counterterrorism, "The Global
Challenge of WMD Terrorism," 179, https://www.state.gov/documents/organiza
tion/65477.pdf.

189. Amanda Vicinanzo, "Biological Terrorist Attack on US an 'Urgent and Serious
Threat,'" *Homeland Security Today*, May 2015, http://www.hstoday.us/single-article
/biological-terrorist-attack-on-us-an-urgent-and-serious-threat/0ce6ebf3524d83c537
b1f4f0cc578547.html.

190. Morris and Clark, "Measurement and Signature Intelligence," 202.

191. M. Kalacska and L. S. Bell, "Remote Sensing as a Tool for the Detection of Clandestine Mass Graves," *Canadian Society of Forensic Science Journal* 39, no. 1 (March
2006): 1–13.

192. "Measurement and Signatures Intelligence Find 'Fingerprints' on Earth," *Army Space
Journal* (Spring 2005), https://apps.dtic.mil/dtic/tr/fulltext/u2/a524898.pdf.

193. Arthur Herman, "Notes from the Underground: The Long History of Tunnel Warfare," *Foreign Affairs*, August 26, 2014, https://hudson.org/research/10570-notes-from
-the-underground-the-long-history-of-tunnel-warfare.

194. Jeffrey Richelson, "Underground Facilities: Intelligence and Targeting Issues," *National Security Archive*, September 23, 2013, http://nsarchive.gwu.edu/NSAEBB /NSAEBB439/.

195. Éric Denécé, "The Revolution in Intelligence Affairs: 1989–2003," *International Journal of Intelligence and Counterintelligence* 27, no. 1 (2014): 31.

196. Denécé, 31.

197. Frederick Hitz, "The Myths and Current Reality of Espionage," *International Journal of Intelligence and Counterintelligence* 18, no. 4 (2005–6): 730–33; Frederick Hitz, *Why Spy? Espionage in an Age of Uncertainty* (New York: Thomas Dunne, 2008); John McGaffin, "Clandestine Human Intelligence," in *Transforming U.S. Intelligence*, ed. Jennifer Sims and Burton Gerber (Washington, DC: Georgetown University Press, 2005); Richard Best, *Intelligence Issues for Congress* (Washington, DC: Congressional Research Service, September 18, 2009); Michael J. Sulick, "Human Intelligence," incidental paper, Seminar on Intelligence, Command, and Control, Cambridge, MA, March 22, 2007, http://pirp.harvard.edu/pubs_pdf/sulick/sulick-i07-1.pdf; Ishmael Jones [pseud.], *The Human Factor: Inside the CIA's Dysfunctional Intelligence Culture* (New York: Encounter, 2008); T. J. Waters, *Class 11: Inside the CIA's First Post-9/11 Spy Class* (New York: Dutton, 2006); and Amy Zegart, *Spying Blind: The CIA, the FBI, and the Origins of 9/11* (Princeton, NJ: Princeton University Press, 2007).

198. Charles Faddis, *Beyond Repair: The Decline and Fall of the CIA* (Guilford, CT: Lyons, 2010).

199. Gary Berntsen, *Human Intelligence, Counterterrorism, and National Leadership* (Washington, DC: Potomac Books, 2008).

200. Reuel Marc Gerecht, "A New Clandestine Service," in *The Future of American Intelligence*, ed. Peter Berkowitz (Stanford, CA: Hoover Institution Press, 2005), 103–38.

201. Linda Robinson, Kevin Whitelaw, "Why the CIA Is Having Such a Hard Time Keeping Its Best," *U.S. News & World Report*, February 13, 2006. See also Bill Gertz, "Intelligence Intransigence: Bureaucratic Process, Culture Resist Overhaul Effort," *Washington Times*, February 5, 2006; and Jeff Stein, "CIA's Loss of Top Spies Catastrophic, Says Agency Veteran," *Congressional Quarterly Homeland Security*, October 17, 2008.

202. Byman, "Intelligence War on Terrorism," 849.

203. Jennifer Sims, "Foreign Intelligence Liaison: Devils, Deals, and Details," *International Journal of Intelligence and Counterintelligence* 19, no. 2 (2006): 195–217.

204. Byman, "Intelligence War on Terrorism," 850.

205. Lawrence MacDonald, "Not Too Late to Fix U.S. Development Strategy in Pakistan: Molly Kinder and Wren Elhai," blog entry, Center for Global Development, April 25, 2011, https://www.cgdev.org/blog/not-too-late-fix-us-development-strategy-pakistan-molly-kinder-and-wren-elhai.

206. Dana Priest, "Foreign Network at Front of CIA's Terror Fight," *Washington Post*, November 15, 2005.

207. See Richard J. Aldrich, "Dangerous Liaison: Post-September 11 Intelligence Alliances," *Harvard International Review* 24, no. 3 (2002): 50–54; Sims, "Foreign

Intelligence Liaison"; Andrew Koch, "Counter-Terrorism Co-operation Is Endan-
gered by US Renditions," *Jane's Intelligence Review* (October 2005); Kevin M. Cieply,
"Rendition: The Beast and the Man," *Joint Force Quarterly* 48, no. 1 (January 2008):
19–21; and Stéphane Lefebvre, "The Difficulties and Dilemmas of International Intelligence Cooperation," *International Journal of Intelligence and Counterintelligence* 16,
no. 4 (2005–6): 537.

208. Mark Mazzetti, "Panel Faults CIA over Brutality and Deceit in Terrorism Interrogations," *New York Times*, December 9, 2014, 1; Senate Select Committee on Intelligence, *Committee Study of the CIA's Detention and Interrogation Program*, "Executive
Summary," April 3, 2014, https://www.intelligence.senate.gov/sites/default/files/pub
lications/CRPT-113srpt288.pdf.

209. "Ex-CIA Directors: Interrogations Saved Lives," *Wall Street Journal*, December 10,
2014.

210. The composition of the TF 714 teams that conducted night raids could vary depending on the complexity of the mission, the enemy situation, and the location of the
target, among other factors. The teams mainly comprised either US Army or US
Navy SOF, also known as elite tier-one forces. Navy teams based their mission profiles
around the sixteen-man SEAL platoon, adding commandos and/or other support personnel, known as "enablers," in order to accomplish specific tasks. The basic building
block of the army SOF were twelve-man teams that would be combined under their
troop-level headquarters to address more complex objectives. During the most dangerous phases of the war, raids could involve forty to one hundred men supported by a
vast intelligence infrastructure located at TF 714's headquarters. Those forces would
usually be divided into several groups: One would conduct the assault on a building
or series of buildings while another group provided overwatch to the first group in
case the situation deteriorated. A final group would provide security by isolating the
objective and preventing interference by enemy reinforcements, curious civilians, or
Iraqi government forces. More often than not, helicopters from the army's 160th
Special Operations Aviation Regiment ferried the teams to and from their objectives.
On occasion, the operators would travel by armored vehicles. Most of the men were
armed with upgraded M4 carbines and a backup pistol, but some would be equipped
with shotguns to assist in breaching doors and in clearing rooms, while others would
be equipped with sniper rifles to provide precision fire. Each would be equipped with
a short-range radio that provided intrateam communication, while leaders carried a
second, longer-ranged radio to maintain contact with their headquarters and aviation
support.

211. Interview with General Flynn, October 2014.

212. Michael Bond, "Interview: Michael Koubi, Israeli Interrogator," *New Scientist*, November 20, 2004. For a thorough treatment on how the Israelis approach interrogations, see Robert Coulam, "Skill versus Brutality in Interrogation: Lessons from Israel
for American Policy," *Intelligence and National Security* 28, no. 4 (2013): 566–90.

213. Interview with General McChrystal, Alexandria, VA, July 2014.

214. Shultz and Godson, "Intelligence Dominance," *Weekly Standard*, July 2006, 25, https://www.weeklystandard.com/richard-h-shultz-jr-and-roy-godson/intelligence -dominance.

215. Interview by telephone with Adm. William McRaven, USN (Ret.), May 3, 2015.

216. Matthew Alexander, *How to Break a Terrorist: The U.S. Interrogators Who Used Brains, Not Brutality, to Take Down the Deadliest Man in Iraq* (New York: St. Martin's Griffin, 2008).

217. Byman, "Intelligence War on Terrorism," 845.

218. Byman, 845.

219. *Tactical Site Exploitation and Cache Search Operations Handbook* (Ft. Leavenworth, KS: Center for Army Lessons Learned, 2007), 3.

220. *Tactical Site Exploitation*, 3.

221. Stanley McChrystal, *My Share of the Task: A Memoir* (New York: Penguin, 2013), 105.

222. Interview with General McChrystal, July 2014. The issues cited from interviews with General McChrystal are also discussed in several places in his *My Share of the Task*: 105–7, 138–40, 153–57, 199.

223. Interview with General McChrystal, July 2014.

224. Interview with General Flynn, October 2014.

225. Jardines, "Open Source Intelligence," 17.

226. Jardines, 26.

227. Hanna Rogan, "Jihadism Online: A Study of How al-Qaeda and Radical Islamist Groups Use the Internet for Terrorist Purposes," prepared under the auspices of Transnational Radical Islamism Project, Norwegian Defence Research Establishment, Kjeller, Norway, March 2006, 8.

228. This section is drawn from Richard Shultz, *Strategic Culture and Strategic Studies: An Alternative Framework for Assessing Al Qaeda and the Global Jihadi Movement* (Tampa, FL: JSOU Press, 2012).

229. Brynjar Lia and Thomas Hegghammer, "Jihadi Strategic Studies: The Alleged Al Qa-ida Policy Study Preceding the Madrid Bombings," *Studies in Conflict & Terrorism* 27, no. 5 (September/October 2004): 355.

230. Lia and Hegghammer, 371.

231. Thomas Hegghammer, "Strategic Studies in Jihadist Literature," presentation to the Middle East Institute, Washington, DC, May 17, 2006.

232. Mark Stout, "In Search of Salafi Jihadist Strategic Thought: Mining the Words of the Terrorists," *Studies in Conflict & Terrorism* 32, no. 10 (October 2009): 876.

233. Brynjar Lia, "Doctrines for Jihadi Terrorist Training," *Terrorism and Political Violence* 20, no. 4 (2008): 518. See also Shultz, *Strategic Culture and Strategic Studies*.

234. Clark, *Intelligence Collection*, 492.

Chapter 4. Transforming Intelligence Analysis for Irregular War

1. *9/11 Commission Report*, "Executive Summary," http://govinfo.library.unt.edu/911 /report/911Report_Exec.htm.

2. Carmen Medina, "The New Analysis," in *Analyzing Intelligence: Origins, Obstacles, and Innovations*, ed. Roger Z. George and James B. Bruce (Washington, DC: Georgetown University Press, 2008), 240.

3. Medina, 240.

4. Medina, 241.

5. Letitia Long, "Activity Based Intelligence: Understanding the Unknown," *Intelligencer: Journal of U.S. Intelligence Studies* 20, no. 2 (Fall/Winter 2013): 7–16.

6. Parts of this chapter were published by the author in an article titled "Post-9/11 Wartime Intelligence Analysis," in *Intelligence and National Security* 33, no. 7 (Fall 2018).

7. US Senate, *Final Report of the Select Committee to Study Governmental Operations with Respect to Intelligence*, book 4 (Washington, DC: US Government Printing Office, April 29, 1976), 16.

8. US Senate, 16.

9. US Senate, 9.

10. John Hollister Hedley "The DI: A History of Service," in *The Directorate of Intelligence: Fifty Years of Informing Policy, 1952–2002* (Washington, DC: CIA, Center for the Study of Intelligence, 2002), 9. For an assessment of the Office of Reports and Estimates, see Woodrow Kuhns, "The Beginning of Intelligence Analysis in CIA—The Office of Reports and Estimates: CIA's First Center for Analysis," *Studies in Intelligence* 51, no. 2 (2007): 27–45.

11. Hedley "The DI," 10–11. It comprised the following divisions: the Office of Intelligence Coordination, to handle interagency coordination for the director; the Office of Collection and Dissemination, to collect intelligence materials from the Department of State and the Department of Defense as the director's liaison element; the Office of Current Intelligence, to prepare the daily intelligence brief for the president and senior policymakers; the Office of National Estimates, to draft and coordinate national estimates with the other intelligence services; the Office of Scientific Intelligence, to conduct weapons-related research; the Office of Research and Reports, to initially conduct basic economic and subsequently political research; and the Office of Operations, to monitor foreign radio broadcasts.

12. Sherman Kent, *Strategic Intelligence for American World Policy* (Princeton, NJ: Princeton University Press, 1949).

13. Jack Davis, "Sherman Kent and the Profession of Intelligence Analysis," *Sherman Kent Center for Intelligence Analysis: Occasional Papers* 1, no. 5 (November 2002), https://www.cia.gov/library/kent-center-occasional-papers/vol1no5.htm.

14. Kent, *Strategic Intelligence*.

15. Arthur Hulnick, "What's Wrong with the Intelligence Cycle," *Intelligence and National Security* 21, no. 6 (December 2006): 959.

16. Robert M. Clark, *Intelligence Analysis: A Target-Centric Approach* (Los Angeles, CA: CQ Press, 2017), 31.

17. Clark, 31.

18. Hulnick writes, "Intelligence managers to learn what policy makers are up to . . .

often have to take the initiative to obtain the information. If intelligence managers at various levels are in touch with their policy counterparts, this sharing of information may work quite well. Over the years, intelligence managers have tried to systematize this process by asking policy officials to provide specifics on their concerns. In the Carter administration, for example, a system of National Intelligence Topics (NITs) was created as a way of soliciting guidance for intelligence. Later they were called Key Intelligence Questions (KIQs). In some cases, when policy consumers failed to submit NITs or KIQs, managers had to resort to sending policy officials a list of topics, asking them to cross out the ones they thought were not necessary or adding those they wanted to the list. Even then the lists were sometimes ignored. In the end, intelligence managers have to make decisions about the subjects that ought to be covered. See Hulnick, "What's Wrong with the Intelligence Cycle," 960.

19. Hulnick, 961.
20. Clark, *Intelligence Analysis*, 31.
21. Hulnick, "What's Wrong with the Intelligence Cycle," 961.
22. Hulnick.
23. Jeffrey Richelson, *US Intelligence Community*, 6th ed. (Boulder, CO: Westview, 2011), 376.
24. Harold Ford, *Estimative Intelligence* (McLean, VA: Association of Former Intelligence Officers, 1993), 3.
25. Richelson, *US Intelligence Community*, 383.
26. See, e.g., *National Intelligence Estimate: Soviet Capabilities for Strategic Nuclear Conflict, 1983–1993* (Washington, DC: CIA, 1983), https://www.cia.gov/library/reading room/docs/DOC_0000268226.pdf. See also *National Intelligence Estimate: Soviet Forces and Capabilities for Strategic Nuclear Conflict through the Late 1990s* (Washington, DC: CIA, July 1987), https://www.cia.gov/library/readingroom/docs/DOC_0000 802749.pdf.
27. Ford, *Estimative Intelligence*, 38.
28. Richelson, *US Intelligence Community*, 376–77.
29. Jack Davis, "Strategic Warning: If Surprise Is Inevitable, What Role for Analysis?," *Sherman Kent Center for Intelligence Analysis: Occasional Papers* 2, no. 1 (January 2003), https://www.cia.gov/library/kent-center-occasional-papers/vol2no1.htm.
30. Illustrative is the *Strategic Warning Committee's Watchlist*, "a weekly report that tracks and assigns probabilities to potential threats to U.S. security or policy interests within the following six months." It is produced by the Interagency Strategic Warning Committee. See Richelson, *US Intelligence Community*, 382.
31. Richard Kerr, "The Track Record: CIA Analysis from 1950 to 2000," in George and Bruce, *Analyzing Intelligence*, 37.
32. To understand Soviet military power, it was necessary to assess the capacity of the Soviet economy to support the burden of the defense sector. Studies on all important aspects of Soviet economic performance began to be produced by the DI. While those assessments generated their share of controversy, especially with respect to the burden

that defense spending placed on the Soviet economy, Kerr writes that by the "early 1970s, the CIA reliably reported on the failings of that economy and its implications for Soviet military spending." Although much of that analysis was highly classified, beginning in the mid-1970s major assessments of it were made public by the CIA through the Joint Economic Committee of the US Congress. They revealed the methodology that the DI had developed for assessing planned economies like that of the USSR, which pointed to steady decline and deep structural weaknesses. Kerr, 39.

33. Donald Steury, ed., *Intentions and Capabilities: Estimates of Soviet Strategic Forces, 1950–1983* (Washington, DC: CIA, Center for the Study of Intelligence, 1996), xxi.

34. Steury, ix.

35. Steury, ix.

36. See Douglas F. Garthoff, "Assessing the Soviet Challenge," in *Directorate of Intelligence*, 28.

37. Garthoff, 28.

38. An evaluation of the overall accuracy of Soviet NIEs is beyond the scope of this brief look back at the evolution of the analytic process, but the issue is discussed in Garthoff, 28–31. See also Kerr, "Track Record," 37–42; John Prados, *The Soviet Estimate: U.S. Intelligence Analysis and Soviet Strategic Forces* (New York: Dial, 1986); Richard Smoke, *National Security and the Nuclear Dilemma*, 3rd ed. (New York: McGraw-Hill, 1993); Lawrence Freedman, *The Evolution of Nuclear Strategy*, 3rd ed. (New York: Palgrave, 2003); Joseph D. Douglass Jr. and Amoretta M. Hoeber, *Soviet Strategy for Nuclear War* (Stanford, CA: Hoover Institution Press, 1979); Raymond L. Garthoff, *Deterrence and the Revolution in Soviet Military Doctrine* (Washington, DC: Brookings Institution Press, 1990); and Roy Godson, ed., *Intelligence Requirements for the 1980s: Analysis and Estimates* (Brunswick, NJ: Transaction Publishers, 1980).

39. Kerr, "Track Record," 42.

40. Kerr, 44.

41. See Daniel Wagner, "Analysis of the Vietnam War," in *Directorate of Intelligence*, 39–45.

42. James B. Bruce and Roger Z. George, "Intelligence Analysis: The Emergence of a Discipline," in George and Bruce, *Analyzing Intelligence*, 1.

43. Carmen Medina, "The New Analysis," in George and Bruce, *Analyzing Intelligence*, 241–42.

44. Richards Heuer and Randolph Pherson, *Structured Analytic Techniques* (Washington, DC: CQ Press, 2001), 3.

45. Heuer and Pherson, 23.

46. Heuer and Pherson, 22.

47. Jim Marchio, "Analytic Tradecraft and the Intelligence Community: Enduring Value, Intermittent Emphasis," *Intelligence and National Security* 29, no. 2 (2014): 172.

48. These were (1) describes the quality and reliability of sources, (2) provides caveats, uncertainties, or confidence in the analyst's judgments, (3) distinguishes between underlying intelligence and assumptions and judgments of an analyst, (4) incorporates

alternative analysis where appropriate, (5) sets out relevance to US national security, (6) specifies logic of argumentation, (7) highlights change or consistency, and (8) specifies accuracy of judgments and assessments. See Marchio, 160.

49. Richards Heuer, *The Psychology of Intelligence Analysis* (McLean, VA: CIA, Center for the Study of Intelligence, 1999), 4.

50. Heuer, xx.

51. Heuer and Pherson, *Structured Analytic Techniques*, 23.

52. US Government, *A Tradecraft Primer: Structured Analytic Techniques for Improving Intelligence Analysis* (McLean, VA: CIA, Center for the Study of Intelligence, 2009), https://www.cia.gov/library/publications/publications-rss-updates/tradecraft-primer -may-4-2009.html.

53. Heuer and Pherson, *Structured Analytic Techniques*, 9.

54. Garthoff, "Assessing the Soviet Challenge," 30.

55. Kerr, "Track Record," 42–49. These included the challenges posed by the rise of Communist China to the status of a world power. During the Vietnam War, Kerr notes, that conflict "occupied CIA analysts' attention for over 15 years." And North Korea, nuclear proliferation and conventional conflict in South Asia, wars in the Middle East, and Central American revolutions and insurgencies of the 1980s were all subjects that DI analysts covered.

56. Garthoff, "Assessing the Soviet Challenge," 30.

57. Allan Goodman, "The Future of US Intelligence," *Intelligence and National Security* 11, no. 4 (1996): 646.

58. Goodman, 652.

59. "Presidential Security Directive 35: Intelligence Requirements" (Washington, DC: Office of the President, March 1995), https://fas.org/irp/offdocs/pdd35.htm.

60. "Presidential Security Directive 35."

61. House of Representatives, Permanent Select Committee on Intelligence, *Staff Study XI: Intelligence Support to Military Operation*, prepared for *IC21: The Intelligence Community in the 21st Century* (June 5, 1996), 3.

62. House of Representatives, 6.

63. John W., "Supporting Military Operations," in *Directorate of Intelligence*, 65.

64. Paul Pillar, "Dealing with Transnational Threats," in *Directorate of Intelligence*, 53.

65. Pillar, 53.

66. Pillar, 56–57.

67. Paula Scalingi, "Proliferation and Arms Control," *Intelligence and National Security* 10, no. 4 (1995): 150.

68. US House of Representatives, Permanent Select Committee on Intelligence, *Staff Study XII: Intelligence Centers*, prepared for *IC21: The Intelligence Community in the 21st Century* (June 5, 1996), 3.

69. Of course, there was always a small cadre of analysts who during the Cold War focused on internal low-intensity conflicts and who in the 1990s concentrated on what were called "military operations other than war" or "peace operations" as well as on international organized crime and terrorism.

70. Thomas Doherty, "Should There Be a Human Warfighting Domain (HWD)?," *Small Wars Journal*, December 3, 2015, http://smallwarsjournal.com/jrnl/art/should-there-be-a-human-warfighting-domain.

71. Rupert Smith, *Utility of Force: The Art of War in the Modern World* (New York: Vintage Books, 2008), 19.

72. *Counterinsurgency*, US Army Field Manual 3-24, http://usacac.army.mil/cac2/Repository/Materials/COIN-FM3-24.pdf.

73. For an assessment of counterinsurgency in Iraq, see Gökçe Sargut and Rita Gunther McGrath, "Learning to Live with Complexity," *Harvard Business Review* 89, no. 9 (2011): 68–76. See also Richard Shultz, *The Marines Take Anbar: The Four-Year Fight against al Qaeda* (Annapolis, MD: Naval Institute Press, 2013).

74. The Sunni Awakening was a movement in which Sunni tribesmen and their leadership who had formerly fought against US troops realigned themselves to help counter groups affiliated with al-Qaeda. These Sunni fighters added a great deal of manpower to the counterinsurgency effort.

75. Stanley McChrystal, *My Share of the Task: A Memoir* (New York: Penguin, 2013), 153–54.

76. Gregory Treverton, "Creatively Disrupting the Intelligence Paradigm," *International Relations and Security Network* (August 2014), http://www.css.ethz.ch/content/specialinterest/gess/cis/center-for-securities-studies/en/services/digital-library/articles/article.html/182698.

77. Clark, *Intelligence Analysis*, 45.

78. The concept "pattern-of-life" is a key part of activity-based intelligence (ABI), an analysis methodology that emerged toward the end of the first decade of twenty-first-century irregular wars. "ABI practitioners have advanced the concept of large-scale data filtering of events, entities, and transactions to develop understanding through spatial and temporal correlation across multiple data sets." In Iraq, TF 714 adopted the idea of accessing the pattern-of-life found in AQI networks. It did so by focusing on "the specific set of behaviors and movements associated with a particular entity over a given period of time. The focus on the individual is the fundamental uniqueness of the ABI method and drives the need for a new set of techniques and approaches to intelligence analysis." Although ABI as a formal approach to intelligence analysis appears to have emerged toward the end of TF 714's operations in Iraq, the way that TF 714 approached intelligence-driven operations has much in common with ABI. See Patrick Biltgen, Todd S. Bacastow, Thom Kaye, and Jeffrey M. Young, "Activity-Based Intelligence: Understanding Patterns-of-Life," in United States Geospatial Intelligence Foundation, *The State and Future of GEOINT* (Washington, DC: United States Geospatial Intelligence Foundation, 2017), 24–27, https://usgif.org/system/uploads/4897/original/2017_SoG.pdf.

79. *The Targeting Process*, US Army Field Manual 3-60 (Washington, DC: Department of the Army, 2010), B-6.

80. Patrick Biltgen and Stephen Ryan, *Activity-Based Intelligence: Principles and Applications* (Boston: Artech House, 2016), 139–40.

81. David Pendall, "Persistent Surveillance and Its Implications for the Common Operating Picture," *Military Review* 85, no. 6 (November/December 2005): 42.

82. Ellen Nakashima and Joby Warrick, "For NSA Chief, Terrorist Threat Drives Passion to 'Collect It All,'" *Washington Post*, July 14, 2013.

83. Chandler Atwood, "Activity-Based Intelligence: Revolutionizing Military Intelligence Analysis," *Joint Forces Quarterly* 77 (Second Quarter 2015): 26.

84. Kenneth Cukier and Viktor Mayer-Schönberger "The Rise of Big Data: How It's Changing the Way We Think about the World," *Foreign Affairs* (May/June 2013), https://www.foreignaffairs.com/articles/2013-04-03/rise-big-data.

85. Biltgen and Ryan, *Activity-Based Intelligence*, 140.

86. Biltgen and Ryan, 140.

87. Biltgen and Ryan, 12–13.

88. Clark, *Intelligence Collection*, 497.

89. Biltgen and Ryan, *Activity-Based Intelligence*, 12–13.

90. See Bruce Berkowitz, "The Soviet Target: Highlights in the Intelligence Value of Gambit and Hexagon, 1963–1984," *National Reconnaissance: Journal of the Discipline and Practice*, no. 2012-U1 (Spring 2012), http://www.nro.gov/history/csnr/articles/docs/gh%20journal_web.pdf.

91. Biltgen and Ryan, *Activity-Based Intelligence*, 140.

92. Biltgen and Ryan, 140.

93. Atwood, "Activity-Based Intelligence," 27.

94. Cited in Kristin Quinn, "A Better Toolbox," *Trajectory* (Winter 2012): 13, http://trajectorymagazine.com/wp-content/uploads/2017/04/USG-008-Winter-2012_Final.pdf.

95. Quinn, 13.

96. Biltgen and Ryan, *Activity-Based Intelligence*, 41.

97. Atwood, "Activity-Based Intelligence," 26.

98. Biltgen and Ryan, *Activity-Based Intelligence*, 257.

99. The entry for "algorithm" on the Techterms.com website explains, "An algorithm is a set of [mathematical] instructions designed to perform a specific task. . . . Search engines use proprietary algorithms to display the most relevant results from their search index for specific queries. In computer programming, algorithms are often created as functions. . . . For example, an image viewing application may include a library of functions that each use a custom algorithm . . . designed to process image data." Very complex and sophisticated versions of such algorithms are employed by the NGA as well as the NSA. See https://techterms.com/definition/algorithm.

100. Michael T. Flynn, Rich Juergens, and Thomas L. Cantrell, "Employing ISR: SOF Best Practices," *Joint Force Quarterly* (July 2008), 57.

101. Biltgen and Ryan, *Activity-Based Intelligence*, 140.

102. Clark, *Intelligence Analysis*, 41.

103. Clark, 45.

104. Mary DeRosa, *Data Mining and Data Analysis for Counterterrorism* (Washington, DC: CSIS, 2004), 3.

105. Christopher Clifton, "Data Mining," *Encyclopedia Britannica* (2009), https://www
.britannica.com/technology /data-mining.

106. Lei-da Chen, Toru Sakaguchi, and Mark N. Frolick, "Data Mining Methods, Applications, and Tools," *Information Systems Management* (Winter 2000), https://vdocu
ments.site/data-mining-methods-applications-and-tools.html.

107. Clifton, "Data Mining."

108. Clark, *Intelligence Analysis*, 177.

109. Steve Ressler, "Social Network Analysis as an Approach to Combat Terrorism: Past,
Present, and Future Research," *Homeland Security Affairs* 14 (2018), https://www.hsaj
.org/articles/171.

110. Ressler.

111. Clark, *Intelligence Analysis*, 177.

112. In Analyst's Notebook's latest iteration, IBM describes it as "a visual analysis tool that
helps you turn data into intelligence. The solution provides innovative features such as
connected network visualizations, social network analysis, and geospatial or temporal
views to help you uncover hidden connections and patterns in data." See "IBM i2
Analyst's Notebook," https://www.ibm.com/us-en/marketplace/analysts-notebook.

113. "IBM i2 Analyst's Notebook."

114. Clark, *Intelligence Analysis*, 179.

115. For a review of these studies, see Bernard Burnes, "Complexity Theories and Organizational Change," *International Journal of Management Reviews* 7, no. 2 (2005): 73–90.

116. Sargut and McGrath, "Learning to Live with Complexity," 68.

117. David Snowden and Mary Boone, "A Leader's Framework for Decision Making,"
Harvard Business Review (November 2007): 4, https://hbr.org/archive-toc/BR0711.
See also David Snowden, "Strategy in the Context of Uncertainty," *Handbook of Busi-
ness Strategy* 6, no. 1 (2005): 47–54.

118. Sargut and McGrath, "Learning to Live with Complexity," 68.

119. Sargut and McGrath, 4.

120. Clark, *Intelligence Analysis*, 185.

121. Clark, 185.

122. Sudhanshu Chauhan and Nutan Kumar Panda, *Hacking Web Intelligence: Open Source
Intelligence and Web Reconnaissance Concepts and Techniques* (Amsterdam: Elsevier,
2015).

123. Chauhan and Panda, 217.

124. Clark, *Intelligence Analysis*, 192.

125. Chauhan and Panda, *Hacking Web Intelligence*, 217.

126. Chauhan and Panda, 218.

127. Chauhan and Panda, 221.

128. Chauhan and Panda, 221.

129. Ernesto Dal Bó, Pedro Dal Bó, and Rafael Di Tella, "Plata o Plomo? Bribe and Punishment in a Theory of Political Influence," *American Political Science Review* 100, no. 1
(February 2006): 41.

130. Chauhan and Panda, *Hacking Web Intelligence*, 222.

131. Chauhan and Panda.

132. Chauhan and Panda.

133. Chauhan and Panda.

134. Clark, *Intelligence Analysis*, 176, 182.

135. Clark, 191.

136. US Joint Forces Command, Joint Warfighting Center, *Commander's Handbook for Attack the Network* (2011), http://www.jcs.mil/Portals/36/Documents/Doctrine/pams _hands/atn_hbk.pdf.

137. US Joint Forces Command, III-1.

138. US Joint Forces Command, III-6.

139. US Joint Forces Command, III-6.

140. McChrystal, *My Share of the Task*, 92.

141. Interview with Lt. Gen. Michael Flynn, USA (Ret.), October 2014, Alexandria, VA.

142. Interview with General Flynn, October 2014.

143. Interview with Adm. William McRaven, USN (Ret.), November 2014, Washington, DC.

144. McChrystal, *My Share of the Task*, 105.

145. Daniel Byman, "Intelligence War on Terrorism," *Intelligence and National Security* 29, no. 6 (2014): 845.

146. Interview with Gen. Stanley McChrystal, USA (Ret.), July 2014, Alexandria, VA. The issues cited from interviews with General McChrystal are also discussed in several places in McChrystal's *My Share of the Task*, 105–7, 138–40, 153–57, and 199.

147. Flynn, Juergens, and Cantrell, "Employing ISR," 58–59.

148. McChrystal, *My Share of the Task*, 157–58.

149. Interview with a former senior intelligence officer who was a leader in the synchronization of analysis, intelligence targeting, and operational fusion in TF 714 and similar organizations, December 2017.

150. Follow-up telephone interview with Adm. William McRaven, USN (Ret.), May 15, 2015.

151. Interview with General Flynn, October 2014.

152. Interview with General Flynn, October 2014.

153. McChrystal, *My Share of the Task*, 155.

154. Interview with a former senior intelligence officer, December 2017.

155. Flynn, Juergens, and Cantrell, "Employing ISR," 58–59.

156. Interview with a former senior intelligence officer, December 2017.

157. McChrystal, *My Share of the Task*, 153.

158. Follow-up interview with Gen. Stanley McChrystal, USA (Ret.), May 2015, Alexandria, VA.

159. Interview with General McChrystal, May 2015.

160. Interview with a former senior intelligence officer, December 2017.

161. Stanley McChrystal with Tantum Collins, David Silverman, and Chris Fussell, *Team*

of Teams: The New Rules of Engagement for a Complex World (New York: Portfolio, 2015), 25.

162. Interview with General McChrystal, July 2014.
163. Interview with General McChrystal, July 2014.

Chapter 5. Transforming Covert Paramilitary Operations for Irregular War

1. Loch Johnson, *A Season of Inquiry: The Senate Intelligence Investigation* (Lexington: University Press of Kentucky, 2014).

2. Roy Godson, ed., *Intelligence Requirements for the 1980s: Elements of Intelligence* (Washington, DC: National Strategy Information Service, 1979), 67.

3. Among the leading voices to first make this argument was George Kennan in his article "Morality and Foreign Policy," *Foreign Affairs* (Winter 1985/86), https://www.foreignaffairs.com/articles/united-states/1985-12-01/morality-and-foreign-policy.

4. Parts of this chapter were published by the author in an article titled "U.S. Counterterrorism Operations during the Iraq War: A Case Study of Task Force 714," *Studies in Conflict and Terrorism* 40, no. 10 (Fall 2017).

5. Roy Godson, *Dirty Tricks or Trump Cards: U.S. Covert Action and Counterintelligence* (Washington, DC: Brassey's, 1995), 2.

6. Godson, 2.

7. William Daugherty, *Executive Secrets: Covert Action and the Presidency* (Lexington: University Press of Kentucky, 2006), 12.

8. Intelligence Authorization Act, Fiscal Year 1991, L. 102-88, www.govtrack.us/congress/bills/102/hr1455/text.

9. Godson, *Dirty Tricks or Trump Cards*, 3.

10. Daugherty, *Executive Secrets,* 72.

11. Godson, *Dirty Tricks or Trump Cards*, 3.

12. Mark Lowenthal, *From Secrets to Policy*, 4th ed. (Washington, DC: CQ Press, 2009), 170.

13. This is discussed by Godson in different sections of *Dirty Tricks or Trump Cards*, e.g., 21–22, 125, 136. See also Arthur Willert, *The Road to Safety: A Study in Anglo-American Relations* (New York: Praeger, 1953).

14. White was positively identified by the FBI, through evidence gathered by the Venona project, as a Soviet source code-named "Jurist." See Robert Louis Benson and Michael Warner, eds., *Venona: Soviet Espionage and the American Response, 1939–1957* (Washington, DC: NSA/CIA, 1996). White, "in preparation for the Yalta conference," advanced the Soviet position that "Germany's chemical, electrical, and metallurgical industrial capacity be completely dismantled." He argued to the president that "there is nothing I can think of that can do more at this moment to engender trust or distrust between the United States and Russia than the position this Government takes on the German problem." Ultimately, the United States took a different position toward post–World War II West Germany. See Abram Shulsky, *Silent Warfare: Understanding the World of Intelligence*, 3rd ed. (Washington, DC: Potomac Books, 2002), 80.

15. Daugherty, *Executive Secrets*, 82.
16. According to Schweizer, this included money, communications equipment, computers, fax machines, and related items. See Peter Schweizer, *Victory: The Reagan Administration's Secret Strategy That Hastened the Collapse of the Soviet Union* (New York: Atlantic Monthly Press, 1996), chap. 3.
17. Kenneth Osgood, "Propaganda," Encyclopedia.com, https://www.encyclopedia.com /social-sciences-and-law/political-science-and-government/political-science-terms -and-concepts/propaganda.
18. Godson, *Dirty Tricks or Trump Cards*, 151.
19. Godson, 151.
20. Richard Shultz, *The Secret War against Hanoi: The Untold Story of Spies, Saboteurs, and Covert Warriors in North Vietnam* (New York: HarperCollins, 1999), chap. 4. Was this believable? Maybe to the uninitiated public, but North Vietnamese security services probably saw through it even though the United States carried out other covert operations in the north to make it seem as if there were secret resistance cells operating there. In general, such radio operations are classified as gray propaganda.
21. Shultz and Godson explain that "while purporting to be independent nongovernmental organizations," Soviet fronts were "directed by the CPSU [Communist Party of the Soviet Union] to promote its foreign policy objectives." See Richard Shultz and Roy Godson, *Dezinformatsia: Active Measures in Soviet Strategy* (McLean, VA: Pergamon-Brassey's, 1984), 196.
22. Shultz and Godson, 117.
23. Godson, *Dirty Tricks or Trump Cards*, 154.
24. Daugherty, *Executive Secrets*, 78.
25. Shulsky, *Silent Warfare*, 89.
26. See Stephen Hosmer and Thomas Wolfe, *Soviet Policy and Practice in the Third World* (Lexington, MA: Lexington Books, 1983); Mark Katz, *The Third World in Soviet Military Thought* (Baltimore: Johns Hopkins University Press, 1982); and Richard Shultz, *The Soviet Union and Revolutionary Warfare* (Stanford, CA: Hoover Institution Press, 1988).
27. Mark P. Lagon, *The Reagan Doctrine: Sources of American Conduct in the Cold War's Last Chapter* (Westport, CT: Greenwood Publishing Group, 1994).
28. Daniel Byman, *Deadly Connections: States That Sponsor Terrorism* (New York: Cambridge University Press, 2005).
29. William Rosenau and Austin Long, *The Phoenix Program and Contemporary Counterinsurgency* (Santa Monica, CA: RAND Corp., 2009), vii–viii.
30. Rosenau and Long, 24.
31. Graham Turbiville, *Hunting Leadership Targets in Counterinsurgency and Counterterrorist Operations* (Hurlburt Field, FL: JSOU Press, 2007), 74–75.
32. US Congress, 94th Congress, 2nd session, Senate, April 26, 1976 (hereafter cited as Church Committee Report), 141.
33. Church Committee Report, 142.

34. Since they were revealed, each has received wide attention in the literature on intelligence that has burgeoned since the 1980s. For the single best compilation of this vast amount of books, reports, articles, and other items, see *The Literature of Intelligence*, a bibliography compiled over the past seventeen years by J. Ransom Clark. He notes that the bibliography contains "most major, many minor, and some obscure books dealing in some fashion with intelligence matters. . . . As often as possible, these are accompanied by comments or reviews from myself, Alec Chambers, published reviews, bibliographers, authors who have chosen to comment on other writers' works, or some other source." All items are organized into the major substantive categories of intelligence, including covert action. A review of the materials in that part of the bibliography will lend support to this observation. See J. Ransom Clark, *The Literature of Intelligence: A Bibliography of Materials, with Essays, Reviews, and Comments*, http://intellit.muskingum.edu/maintoc.htm.

35. This included the creation of special units for these activities. OSS operational groups and Jedburgh teams, for example, fought behind enemy lines in Europe with existing resistance organizations. These operations, in today's parlance, would be classified as unconventional warfare. See Richard Smith, *OSS: The Secret History of America's First Central Intelligence Agency* (Guilford, CT: Rowman & Littlefield, 2005). See also Bradley Smith, *The Shadow Warriors: O.S.S. and the Origins of the C.I.A.* (New York: Basic Books, 1983); and Colin Beavan, *Operation Jedburgh: D-Day and America's First Shadow War* (New York: Penguin, 2007).

36. Church Committee Report, 154.

37. Church Committee Report, 152–53.

38. Following World War II, President Truman scaled back the size and scope of wartime intelligence capabilities. However, massive Soviet clandestine funding and support for communist parties and fronts in Europe and the real possibility that they could come to power through elections created a crisis for Washington.

39. The Italian election provided a case study of how Moscow intended to use a strategy of subversion to threaten European stability. This was stated as such in National Security Council Directive 10/2, which characterized these activities as Moscow's "vicious covert activities," necessitating that the United States develop the capacity to counter them. Cited in Daugherty, *Executive Secrets*, 122.

40. In addition to political action, in the late 1940s and early 1950s the United States also sponsored covert paramilitary programs that sought to foster resistance movements inside the Soviet bloc. But to do so against the kinds of dictatorial states that the USSR established once it was in control of Eastern Europe proved fruitless. Soviet security forces and their counterparts in Albania, Poland, the Baltic states, and in other places where the United States sought to nurture resistance movements came to naught. These came to be referred to as "denied areas." See Godson, *Dirty Tricks or Trump Cards*, 46–49; and Shultz, *Secret War against Hanoi*, 11–12.

41. In his "X Article," Kennan called for a strategy of "patient but firm and vigilant containment of Russian expansive tendencies" through the "adroit application of

counterforce at a series of constantly shifting geographical and political points." See Mr. X, "The Sources of Soviet Conduct," *Foreign Affairs* (July 1947).

42. Richard Best, *Covert Action: An Effective Instrument of U.S. Foreign Policy?* (Washington, DC: Congressional Research Service, 1998), 15–16. See also Wilson D. Miscamble, *George F. Kennan and the Making of American Foreign Policy, 1947–1950* (Princeton, NJ: Princeton University Press, 1992).

43. Church Committee Report, 146.

44. Church Committee Report, 145–47.

45. Best, *Covert Action*, 33. An illustrative example was Ramón Magsaysay in the Philippines. With the assistance of the CIA, he fostered democratic change through anticorruption and political reform measures, eventually winning the presidency of the Philippines in 1953. See Edward Lansdale, *In the Midst of Wars: An American's Mission to Southeast Asia*, 2nd ed. (New York: Fordham University Press, 1991); and Cecil B. Currey, *Edward Lansdale: The Unquiet American* (Boston: Houghton Mifflin, 1988). For an alternative view, see Jonathan Nashel, *Edward Lansdale's Cold War* (Boston: University of Massachusetts Press, 2005).

46. Daugherty, *Executive Secrets*, 133.

47. Best, *Covert Action*, 33.

48. Paramilitary operations reflected a view of the Cold War consistent with the counsel provided to the administration in the 1954 Doolittle Report on covert activities and the CIA. The report characterized the Soviet Union as a much more dire threat than that perceived by the Truman administration. The United States was "facing an implacable enemy whose avowed objective is world domination by whatever means." To meet this ominous challenge necessitated "learning to subvert, sabotage and destroy our enemies" by using tactics "more clever, more sophisticated, more effective . . . [and] more ruthless than those employed by the enemy." See James Doolittle, "Report on the Covert Activities of the Central Intelligence Agency," July 26, 1954, 2–3, 20, http://cryptome.org/cia-doolittle.pdf.

49. Howard Jones, *The Bay of Pigs* (Oxford: Oxford University Press, 2008).

50. Cited in Daugherty, *Executive Secrets*, 156.

51. Church Committee Report, 153. The details of a number of those programs—secret support to labor, student, and media organizations—became public knowledge through exposés published in the *Saturday Evening Post* and the New Left magazine *Ramparts*. See Thomas Braden, "Speaking Out: I'm Glad the CIA Is Immoral," *Saturday Evening Post*, May 20, 1967; and Marcus Raskin, "A Short Account of International Student Politics and the Cold War with Particular Reference to the NSA, CIA, Etc.," *Ramparts*, March 1967.

52. See Thomas Ahern, *Undercover Armies: CIA and Surrogate Warfare in Laos, 1961–1973* (Washington, DC: CIA, Center for the Study of Intelligence, 2006).

53. Shultz, *Secret War against Hanoi*, 3, 23–30. Kennedy quickly became disenchanted with the CIA's direction of the program, which he assessed as "too little and not fast enough." In 1963, he reassigned it to the US Army Special Forces with the order to

escalate. It included agent networks, a notional resistance movement, deception, psychological warfare, maritime activities, and cross-border clandestine reconnaissance operations in Laos. Most of these activities came to an end in the final years of the Johnson administration with the exception of cross-border raids, which lingered until Nixon ended the war.

54. Rosenau and Long, *Phoenix Program*, vii. See also Mark Moyar, *Phoenix and the Birds of Prey: The CIA's Secret Campaign to Destroy the Viet Cong* (Annapolis, MD: Naval Institute Press, 1997).

55. William Colby and James McCargar, *Lost Victory: A Firsthand Account of America's Sixteen-Year Involvement in Vietnam* (New York: Contemporary Books, 1989).

56. See David Galula, *Counterinsurgency Warfare: Theory and Practice* (Westport, CT: Praeger Security International, 1964); John McCuen, *The Art of Counter-Revolutionary War* (Harrisburg, PA: Stackpole, 1966); and Robert Thompson, *Defeating Communist Insurgency: The Lessons of Malaya and Vietnam* (New York: Praeger, 1966).

57. Church Committee Report, 148.

58. Godson, *Dirty Tricks or Trump Cards*, 52.

59. Best, *Covert Action*, 40.

60. Covert assistance to Solidarity in Poland by the administration was undertaken in conjunction with the Vatican and Pope John Paul II. The extent of this program has been described by Carl Bernstein in his biography of John Paul II and summarized by Daugherty. See Carl Bernstein and Marco Politi, *His Holiness: John Paul II and the History of Our Time* (New York: Penguin Books, 1997); and Daugherty, *Executive Secrets*, 197–203. See also Robert Gates, "American Paralysis," chap. 3, in his *From the Shadows: The Ultimate Insider's Story of Five Presidents and How They Won the Cold War* (New York: Simon & Schuster, 1996), 53–63.

61. According to a study by Alan J. Kuperman, while there is debate over the effectiveness of the Stingers, "rigorous U.S. Army analysis conducted in early 1989 by a team sent to 'go sit with the Mujahedin' in Pakistan for several weeks . . . concluded that by war's end the rebels had scored approximately 269 kills [downed aircraft] in about 340 engagements . . . for a remarkable 79 percent kill ratio." See Alan J. Kuperman, "The Stinger Missile and U.S. Intervention in Afghanistan," *Political Science Quarterly* 114, no. 2 (Summer 1999): 246.

62. Daugherty, *Executive Secrets*, 206.

63. These actions took the form of various congressional restrictions that limited assistance to the Contras, including a complete cutoff that was meant to last from October 1984 through December 1985. However, due to extensive White House pressure, this stoppage was ended in October 1985, and $100 million in assistance to the Contras was appropriated by Congress. The legislation also removed restrictions on CIA engagement with the Contras in executing the program.

64. See Richard Shultz, "Covert Action and Executive-Legislative Relations: The Iran-Contra Crisis and Its Aftermath," *Harvard Journal of Law and Public Policy* 12, no. 2 (Spring 1989): 479–81.

65. Robert Chesney, "Military-Intelligence Convergence and the Law of the Title 10 / Title 50 Debate," *Journal of National Security Law and Policy* 5, no. 2 (2012): 593.

66. Chesney, 593–94.

67. Chesney, 595.

68. Chesney, 593–94.

69. Chesney, 599.

70. Chesney, 600.

71. See Intelligence Authorization Act, Fiscal Year 1991, https://www.govtrack.us/congress/bills/102/hr1455/text.

72. Richard Shultz, "Low-Intensity Conflict," *Survival* 31, no. 4 (July/August 1989): 359.

73. Susan Marquis, *Unconventional Warfare: Rebuilding U.S. Special Operation Forces* (Washington, DC: Brookings Institution Press), 62.

74. Chesney, "Military-Intelligence Convergence," 546.

75. Marquis, *Unconventional Warfare,* 73.

76. Mark Bowden, *Guests of the Ayatollah: The First Battle in America's War with Militant Islam* (New York: Grove, 2007).

77. See Marquis, *Unconventional Warfare*; David Tucker and Chris Lamb, *United States Special Operations Forces* (New York: Columbia University Press, 2007); Linda Robinson, *Masters of Chaos: The Secret History of the Special Forces* (New York: PublicAffairs, 2004); and Thomas Adams, *US Special Operations Forces in Action: The Challenge of Unconventional Warfare* (London: Routledge, 1998).

78. William B. Ostlund, *Irregular Warfare: Counterterrorism Forces in Support of Counterinsurgency Operations*, Land Warfare Paper no. 91 (Arlington, VA: Institute of Land Warfare, AUSA, September 2012), https://www.ausa.org/sites/default/files/LWP-91-Irregular-Warfare-Counter-Terrorism-Forces-in-Support-of-Counterinsurgency-Operations.pdf.

79. Roger Hilsman, "Does the CIA Still Have a Role?," *Foreign Affairs* (September/October 1995): 104–16.

80. Walter Pincus, "Ex-CIA Chief Backs Smaller Spy Agency: Gates Plan Would Transfer Some Intelligence and Paramilitary Operations to Pentagon," *Washington Post*, December 10, 1994.

81. Daugherty, *Executive Secrets*, 219.

82. Daugherty, 219.

83. Presidential Decision Directive-39 (June 21, 1995), https://fas.org/irp/offdocs/pdd/pdd-39.pdf.

84. Presidential Decision Directive-62 (May 22, 1998), http://clinton.presidentiallibraries.us/items/show/16200.

85. Quoted in Richard Shultz, "Showstoppers: Nine Reasons Why We Never Sent Our Special Operations Forces after Al Qaeda before 9/11," *Weekly Standard*, January 26, 2004, 26.

86. Shultz, 26.

87. During 2002, I had the opportunity to conduct research for the DOD into why, prior to 9/11, US counterterrorism forces were never used to hunt down al-Qaeda terrorists who had taken American lives. Putting the units to their intended use proved

impossible—even after al-Qaeda bombed the World Trade Center in 1993, bombed two US embassies in East Africa in 1998, and nearly sank the USS *Cole* in Yemen in 2000. I conducted the research in a classified setting. But subsequently a declassified version was published in the *Weekly Standard* as "Showstoppers: Nine Reasons Why We Never Sent Our Special Operations Forces after Al Qaeda Before 9/11." I identified nine self-imposed constraints that kept the special-mission units sidelined, even as al-Qaeda struck at American targets around the globe. In this chapter, I highlight the most important of the nine.

88. Shultz, "Showstoppers," 28.

89. Shultz.

90. Shultz, 27.

91. Shultz.

92. Shultz, 29.

93. Shultz, 30.

94. Shultz, 31.

95. Shultz, 31. Richard Clarke, for instance, pushed hard for the use of the counterterrorism force against al-Qaeda. According to several officials who served on the Joint Staff in the Pentagon, the senior brass characterized Clarke as "a madman, out of control, power hungry, wanted to be a hero, all that kind of stuff." And when Clarke persisted, they added, "wild, irresponsible, abrasive" and "intolerant."

96. Shultz, 31.

97. President George W. Bush, graduation speech at the United States Military Academy, West Point, New York, June 1, 2002, https://georgewbush-whitehouse.archives.gov/news/releases/2002/06/20020601-3.html.

98. *Special Operations*, Joint Publication 3-05, July 16, 2014, http://www.jcs.mil/Portals/36/Documents/Doctrine/pubs/jp3_05.pdf.

99. US Special Operations Command, *United States Special Operations Command History: 1987–2007* (Tampa, FL: SOCOM, 2007), 90.

100. Leigh Neville, *Special Operations Forces in Afghanistan* (Oxford: Osprey, 2008), 44–45.

101. *9/11 Commission Report*, 66–67.

102. Rohan Gunaratna, in his 2001 book *Inside Al Qaeda*, identified elements in Pakistan, Saudi Arabia, Yemen, Sudan, Uzbekistan, Egypt, Syria, Lebanon, Jordan, the Palestinian territories, Algeria, Libya, Eritrea, Somalia, Bosnia, Chechnya, Indonesia, the Philippines, Malaysia, Germany, the United Kingdom, and the United States. See Gunaratna, *Inside Al Qaeda*.

103. Quoted in Sean Naylor, "Inside the Pentagon's Manhunting Machine," *Atlantic*, August 28, 2015, https://www.theatlantic.com/international/archive/2015/08/jsoc-manhunt-special-operations-pentagon/402652/. See also Sean Naylor, *Relentless Strike: The Secret History of Joint Special Operations Command* (New York: St. Martin's, 2016).

104. Seymour Hersh, "Manhunt: The Bush Administration's New Strategy in the War against Terrorism," *New Yorker*, December 23, 2002.

105. Mark Mazzetti, *The Way of the Knife: The CIA, a Secret Army, and a War at the Ends of the Earth* (New York: Penguin, 2013), 129.

106. *Special Operations*, Joint Publication 3-05.
107. See Mark Bowden, *Killing Pablo: The Hunt for the World's Greatest Outlaw* (New York: Penguin, 2001).
108. See Mark Bowdoin, *Black Hawk Down: A Story of Modern War* (New York: Grove, 1999).
109. See Naylor, *Relentless Strike*, 63–69.
110. *Department of Defense Dictionary of Military and Associated Terms*, Joint Publication 1-02 (as amended through June 15, 2015), https://ratical.org/radiation/NuclearEx tinction/jp1_02.pdf.
111. AUSA, *Key Issues Relevant to Actionable Intelligence*, Torchbearer National Security Report (Arlington, VA: Institute of Land Warfare, AUSA, June 2005), https://www .ausa.org /sites/default/files/TBNSR-2005-Actionable-Intelligence.pdf.
112. Liam Collins, "Military Innovation in War: The Criticality of the Senior Military Leader" (PhD dissertation, Princeton University, 2014), 208.
113. Joel Christie, "Dead Hand: Deck of 52 Most-Wanted Iraqi Playing Cards Given to Soldiers at the Start of the War," *Daily Mail*, October 18, 2014, http://www.dailymail .co.uk/news/article-2798050/dead-hand-deck-52-wanted-iraqi-playing-cards-given -soldiers-start-war-shows-fall-saddam-ace-spades-hussein-s-army.html.
114. "Uday and Qusay: An Obituary," Al Jazeera, July 23, 2003, https://www.aljazeera .com/archive/2003/07/ 2008491535854416.html.
115. After the 2001 operations in Afghanistan, followed by Operation Iraqi Freedom, JSOC forces went through several changes in nomenclature. For the specifics, see Neville, *Special Operations Forces in Afghanistan*; Stanley McChrystal, *My Share of the Task: A Memoir* (New York: Porfolio/Penguin, 2013); Naylor, *Relentless Strike*; and Mark Urban, *Task Force Black: The Explosive True Story of the Secret Special Forces War in Iraq* (New York: St. Martin's, 2012).
116. For a good examination of Operation Iraqi Freedom planning, see the epilogue in Michael R. Gordon and Bernard E. Trainor, *Cobra II: The Inside Story of the Invasion and Occupation of Iraq* (New York: Vintage, 2007).
117. These data, which were compiled weekly by the DOD from January 2004 to April 2009, are contained in Anthony Cordesman, *The Uncertain Security Situation in Iraq: Trends in Violence, Casualties, and Iraqi Perceptions* (Washington, DC: Center for Strategic and International Studies, 2010).
118. Cordesman.
119. This was the result, for example, of HVT operations against the National Liberation Front, the Revolutionary Armed Forces of Colombia, the Shining Path, the Kurdistan Worker's Party, and the Irish Republican Army—all hierarchical organizations. To varying degrees, each of these armed groups was demoralized when its top leadership was eliminated. See Turbiville, *Hunting Leadership Targets*, 74–75.
120. For an insightful discussion of what constitutes al-Qaeda's center of gravity, see Peter Neumann, Ryan Evans, and Rajfaello Pantucci, "Locating Al Qaeda's Center of Gravity: The Role of Middle Managers," *Studies in Conflict and Terrorism* 34, no. 11 (2011). The authors argue that "the ongoing debate about the structure and dynam-

ics of Al Qaeda has failed to appreciate an organization layer that is situated between the top leadership and the grass-roots. Rather than being 'leaderless' or 'leader-led,' it is the group's middle management that holds Al Qaeda together . . . that facilitates the grass-roots' integration into the organization and provides the leadership with the global reach it needs in order to carry out its terrorist campaign. They are, in other words, the connective tissue that makes Al Qaeda work." While focused not on Iraq but on al-Qaeda's regional components, Neumann, Evans, and Pantucci's argument parallels what TF 714 discovered in Iraq in 2004 about the need to target midlevel commanders and operators.

121. Interview with Lt. Gen. Michael Flynn, USA (Ret.), October 2014, Alexandria, VA.
122. Interview with Lt. Gen. Bennet Sacolick, USA (Ret.), September 2014, McLean, VA.
123. Interview with Gen. Stanley McChrystal, USA (Ret.), July 2014, Alexandria, VA.
124. Interview with Maj. Gen. David Scott, USAF (Ret.), June 2014, Tampa, FL.
125. Interview with General McChrystal, July 2014.
126. Interview with General McChrystal, July 2014.
127. Robert Scales, "The Quality of Command: The Wrong Way and the Right Way to Make Better Generals," *Foreign Affairs* (November/December 2012), https://www.foreignaffairs.com/reviews/review-essay/quality-command.
128. Interview with Adm. William McRaven, USN (Ret.), November 2014, Washington, DC.
129. Interview with Admiral McRaven, November 2014.
130. Interview with General McChrystal, July 2014.
131. Interview with General McChrystal, July 2014.
132. Interview with General McChrystal, July 2014.
133. Interview with Admiral McRaven, November 2014.
134. Michael Flynn, Rich Juergens, and Thomas Cantrell, "Employing ISR: SOF Best Practices," *Joint Forces Quarterly*, no. 50 (Third Quarter 2008): 57.
135. Interview with General Flynn, October 2014.
136. Roy Godson, "Intelligence Dominance Consistent with Rule of Law Principles," in *Adapting America's Security Paradigm and Security Agenda*, ed. Roy Godson and Richard Shultz (Washington, DC: National Strategy Information Center, 2010), 134, https://apps.dtic.mil/dtic/tr/fulltext/u2/a516785.pdf. See also Richard Shultz and Roy Godson, "Intelligence Dominance," *Weekly Standard*, July 31, 2006, 23.
137. Figures cited in Daniel Byman, "Curious Victory: Explaining Israel's Suppression of the Second Intifada," *Terrorism and Political Violence* 24, no. 5 (November 2012), https://www.tandfonline.com/doi/pdf/10.1080/09546553.2011.652317?needAccess=true.
138. Shultz and Godson, "Intelligence Dominance," 23.
139. Shultz and Godson, 23.
140. Interview with General McChrystal, July 2014.
141. Stanley McChrystal et al., *Team of Teams: The New Rules of Engagement for an Interconnected World* (New York: Portfolio, 2015). For a discussion of this point, see pp. 208–10.

142. Stanley McChrystal, "Lesson from Iraq: It Takes a Network to Defeat a Network," June 21, 2013, https://www.linkedin.com/pulse/20130621110027-86145090-lesson-from-iraq-it-takes-a-network-to-defeat-a-network/.

143. Stanley McChrystal, "It Takes a Network: The New Frontline of Modern Warfare," *Foreign Policy*, March/April 2011, 83.

144. Evan Munsing and Christopher J. Lamb, *Joint Interagency Task Force–South: The Best Known, Least Understood Interagency Success* (Washington, DC: National Defense University Press, June 2011), 1, 83.

145. Interview with Admiral McRaven, November 2014.

146. Interview with General Flynn, October 2014.

147. Interview with General McChrystal, July 2014.

148. McChrystal, *My Share of the Task*, 119.

149. Charles Faint and Michael Harris, "F3EAD: Ops/Intel Fusion Feeds the SOF Targeting Process," *Small Wars Journal* (January 31, 2012): 1, http://smallwarsjournal.com/jrnl/art/f3ead-opsintel-fusion-%E2%80%9Cfeeds%E2%80%9D-the-sof-targeting-process.

150. Interview with Lt. Gen. Eric Fiel, USAF (Ret.), May 28, 2015, Tampa, FL.

151. Follow-up interview with Gen. Stanley McChrystal, USA (Ret.), May 2015, Alexandria, VA.

152. Interview with Admiral McRaven, November 2014.

153. Collins, "Military Innovation in War," 227–78.

154. McChrystal, *My Share of the Task*, 168.

155. McChrystal, *My Share of the Task*, 168. See also Richard Shultz, *Military Innovation in War: It Takes a Learning Organization; A Case Study of Task Force 714 in Iraq* (Tampa, FL: JSOU Press, 2016); and Collins, "Military Innovation in War."

156. Interview with Admiral McRaven, November 2014.

157. McChrystal et al., *Team of Teams*, 177.

158. Authorization for Use of Military Force, Public Law 107-40 (September 18, 2001), https://www.gpo.gov/fdsys/pkg/PLAW-107publ40/pdf/PLAW-107publ40.pdf.

159. Jennifer K. Elsea and Matthew C. Weed, *Declarations of War and Authorizations for the Use of Military Force: Historical Background and Legal Implications* (Washington, DC: Congressional Research Service, April 18, 2014), 15.

160. Eric Schmitt and Mark Mazzetti, "Secret Order Lets U.S. Raid Al Qaeda," *New York Times*, November 9, 2008.

161. Schmitt and Mazzetti.

162. Chesney, "Military-Intelligence Convergence," 574.

163. *2006 Quadrennial Defense Review*, February 6, 2006, https://archive.defense.gov/pubs/pdfs/QDR20060203.pdf.

164. Shultz, "Showstoppers," 25.

165. Jennifer Kibbe, "Conducting Shadow Wars," *Journal of National Security Law and Policy* 5, no. 2 (2012): 379.

166. Andru Wall, "Demystifying the Title 10-Title 50 Debate: Distinguishing Military

Operations, Intelligence Activities and Covert Action," *Harvard National Security Journal* 3, no. 1 (2012): 128.

167. Wall, 140.

168. Wall, 85.

169. Kibbe, "Conducting Shadow Wars," 389.

170. Kibbe, 379.

171. This section of the chapter relies on two previous publications by the author. First and foremost is Richard Shultz, "The Irreducible Minimum: An Evaluation of Counterterrorism Operations in Iraq," *Prism: The Journal of Complex Operations* 7, no. 3 (2018): 102–17, http://cco.ndu.edu/News/Article/1507636/the-irreducible-minimum-an -evaluation-of-counterterrorism-operations-in-iraq/. The second is Shultz, "U.S. Counterterrorism Operations during the Iraq War: A Case Study of Task Force 714," *Studies in Conflict and Terrorism* 40, no. 10 (2017), https://www.tandfonline.com/doi/ full/10.1080/1057610X.2016.1239990.

172. Department of Defense, *Measuring Stability and Security in Iraq*, Report to Congress in Accordance with the Department of Defense Supplemental Appropriations Act 2008, Section 9204, Public Law 110-252 (Washington, DC: Department of Defense, June 2010), https://dod.defense.gov/Portals/1/Documents/pubs/Master_9204_29Jan10 _FINAL_SIGNED.pdf.

173. Consider the December 2006 report of the Iraq Study Group, cochaired by former secretary of state James Baker and former Indiana congressman Lee Hamilton. The report painted a grim picture: "The challenges in Iraq are complex. . . . Violence is increasing in scope and lethality. . . . If the situation continues to deteriorate, the consequences could be severe." The report made seventy-nine recommendations, but the key issue was security and the role of US forces. With respect to that, it asserted, "There is no action the American military can take that, by itself, can bring about success in Iraq." See James Baker, Lee Hamilton, and Lawrence S. Eagleburger, *The Iraq Study Group Report: The Way Forward; A New Approach* (New York: Vintage Books, 2006), 7, 48, 51.

174. Department of Defense, *Measuring Stability and Security in Iraq*.

175. Frank Hoffman and Alexander Crowther, "The Surge in Iraq and Afghanistan," in *Lessons Encountered: Learning from the Long War*, ed. Richard Hooker and Joseph Collins (Washington, DC: National Defense University Press, 2015), 124–25.

176. See, e.g., Thomas Ricks, "Situation Called Dire in West Iraq," *Washington Post*, September 11, 2006.

177. Richard Shultz, *The Marines Take Anbar: The Four-Year Fight against Al Qaeda* (Annapolis, MD: Naval Institute Press, 2013), chap. 5.

178. Shultz, chap. 6.

179. Shultz, 231–32.

180. Stephen Biddle, Jeffrey A. Friedman, and Jacob N. Shapiro, "Testing the Surge: Why Did Violence Decline in Iraq in 2007," *International Security* 37, no. 1 (Summer 2012): 37.

181. For assessments of the impact of the surge, see Kimberly Kim Kagan, *The Surge: A Military History* (New York: Encounter Books, 2009); Michael Gordon and Bernard Trainor, *The Endgame: The Inside Story of the Struggle for Iraq, from George W. Bush to Barack Obama* (New York: Vintage, 2013); and Peter Mansoor, *Surge: My Journey with General David Petraeus and the Remaking of the Iraq War* (New Haven, CT: Yale University Press, 2013).

182. Galula, *Counterinsurgency Warfare*; Thompson, *Defeating Communist Insurgency*; Richard Clutterbuck, *The Long Long War: Counterinsurgency in Malaya and Vietnam* (New York: Praeger, 1966); Frank Kitson, *Low Intensity Operations: Subversion, Insurgency and Peacekeeping* (Harrisburg, PA: Stackpole Books, 1971); McCuen, *Art of Counter-Revolutionary War*; and Sarah Sewall et al., *U.S. Army/Marine Corps Counterinsurgency FM* (Chicago, IL: University of Chicago Press, 2008).

183. Interview with General McChrystal, May 2015.

184. Interview with General McChrystal, July 2014.

185. Interview with General McChrystal, July 2014.

186. Bill Roggio, "Targeting al Qaeda in Iraq's Network," *Long War Journal* (November 13, 2007), https://www.longwarjournal.org/archives/2007/11/targeting_al_qaeda_i_1.php.

187. Follow-up interview with Lt. Gen. Bennet Sacolick, USA (Ret.), June 15, 2015, McLean, VA.

188. Follow-up telephone interview with Adm. William McRaven, USN (Ret.), May 2015.

189. Interview with Admiral McRaven, May 2015.

190. Interview with General McChrystal, May 2015.

191. Interview with General McChrystal, May 2015.

192. Interview with General Fiel, May 2015.

193. Interview with General Fiel, May 2015.

194. Interview with Gen. Joseph Votel, USA (Ret.), May 2015, Tampa, FL.

195. Interview with General McChrystal, May 2015.

196. Interview with Admiral McRaven, May 2015.

197. Interview with General Sacolick, June 2015.

198. David Strachan-Morris, "The 'Irreducible Minimum': Al-Qa'ida in Iraq and the Effectiveness of Leadership Decapitation," *RUSI Journal* 155, no. 4 (August/September 2010): 32.

199. Interview with General McChrystal, July 2014.

200. Interview with General Sacolick, June 2015.

201. Interview with General McChrystal, May 2015.

202. Strachan-Morris, "Irreducible Minimum," 35.

203. Interview with Admiral McRaven, May 2015.

204. Interview with Admiral McRaven, May 2015.

205. For a review and evaluation of Operation New Dawn, see Richard R. Brennan Jr. et. al, "Transition Management," chap. 4 in *Ending the U.S. War in Iraq* (Santa Monica, CA: RAND Corp., 2013).

206. For the details, see Shultz, "Irreducible Minimum."

207. Florence Gaub, *An Unhappy Marriage: Civil-Military Relations in Post-Saddam Iraq* (Beirut: Carnegie Middle East Center, January 2016), http://carnegie-mec.org/2016/01/13/unhappy-marriage-civil-military-relations-in-post-saddam-iraq-pub-61955.

208. T. X. Hammes, "Raising and Mentoring Security Forces in Afghanistan and Iraq," in *Lessons Encountered*, ed. Richard Hooker and Joseph Collins (Washington, DC: National Defense University Press, 2015), 311.

Chapter 6. Task Force 714 and the Sources of Transformation

1. Adam Grissom, "The Future of Military Innovation Studies," *Journal of Strategic Studies* 29, no. 5 (October 2006): 907.

2. Michael McNerney, "Military Innovation during War: Paradox or Paradigm?," *Defense & Security Analysis* 21, no. 2 (June 2005): 202.

3. Janine Davidson, *Lifting the Fog of Peace* (Ann Arbor: University of Michigan Press, 2010), 10.

4. Barry Posen, *The Sources of Military Doctrine: France, Great Britain, and Germany between the World Wars* (Ithaca, NY: Cornell University Press, 1984); Jack Snyder, *Ideology of the Offensive: Military Decision-Making and the Disasters of 1914* (Ithaca, NY: Cornell University Press, 1984).

5. Davidson summarizes the organizational theory explanation as follows: "In this model, even when actors within a military organization desire a change in strategy or doctrine, structural mechanisms would likely mitigate against it." See Davidson, *Lifting the Fog of Peace*, chap. 1.

6. These have their origins in Graham Allison's classic study of decision-making and his utilization of the texts on organizational behavior to explain the Cuban Missile Crisis. See Graham Allison, *Essence of Decision: Explaining the Cuban Missile Crisis*, 2nd ed. (New York: Longman, 1999).

7. Posen found that the development of the Royal Air Force Fighter Command, which played a critical role in defeating the Luftwaffe in 1940's Battle of Britain, and of the German Army's blitzkrieg tactics of speed and surprise, which resulted in the spectacular German conquest of France, also in 1940, were opposed by the leadership of the Royal Air Force and the Wehrmacht, respectively. In each case, the leadership supported existing operating procedures, as organization theory posits. See Posen, *Sources of Military Doctrine*, chaps. 5–6.

8. Posen, 13. See also Anthony Downs, *Inside Bureaucracy* (Boston: Little, Brown, 1967); and James Q. Wilson, *Bureaucracy* (New York: Basic Books, 1989). The concept of organizational essence is attributed to Morton Halperin; see his *Bureaucratic Politics and Foreign Policy* (Washington, DC: Brookings Institution, 1974). See also Gary Miller, "Sources of Bureaucratic Influence," *Journal of Conflict Resolution* 28, no. 4 (1984).

9. Andrew Krepinevich, *The Army and Vietnam* (Baltimore, MD: Johns Hopkins University Press, 1988).

10. Andrew Krepinevich, *The Army and Vietnam*; Richard Shultz, "Breaking the Will of the Enemy during the Vietnam War: The Operationalization of the Cost-

Benefit Model of Counterinsurgency," *Journal of Peace Research* 15, no. 2 (1978). This commitment remained so even when new capabilities were introduced to address a rapidly deteriorating situation. Consider attack helicopters and the development of the First Cavalry Division (Airborne). Even though the division was deployed to Vietnam, it had been developed and oriented for the conventional firepower-intensive operations favored by the US Army. This proved incongruous for the Vietnam contingency but consistent with the army's commitment to a conventional operational approach.

11. Wilson, *Bureaucracy*, 91.

12. Richard Downie, *Learning from Conflict: The U.S. Military in Vietnam, El Salvador, and the Drug War* (Westport, CT: Praeger, 1998), 23–24.

13. John Nagl, *Learning to Eat Soup with a Knife* (Chicago: University of Chicago Press, 2002), 215–17.

14. Nagl, 215.

15. Grissom, "Future of Military Innovation Studies"; Davidson, *Lifting the Fog of Peace*; Nagl, *Learning to Eat Soup with a Knife*; McNerney, "Military Innovation during War"; Theo Farrell, "Figuring Out Fighting Organizations: New Organizational Analysis in Strategic Studies," *Journal of Strategic Studies* 19, no. 1 (March 1996): 122–35; and Downie, *Learning from Conflict*.

16. Davidson, *Lifting the Fog of Peace*, 16.

17. Grissom, "Future of Military Innovation Studies," 909–10; Kimberly Zisk, *Engaging the Enemy: Organization Theory and Soviet Military Innovation, 1955–1991* (Princeton, NJ: Princeton University Press, 1993).

18. Grissom, "Future of Military Innovation Studies," 910–13.

19. James Bradin, *From Hot Air to Hellfire: The History of Army Attack Aviation* (Novato, CA: Presidio, 1994); Frederic Bergerson, *The Army Gets an Air Force* (Baltimore, MD: Johns Hopkins University Press, 1980).

20. Stephen Rosen, *Winning the Next War: Innovation and the Modern Military* (Ithaca, NY: Cornell University Press, 1991), 7.

21. Rosen.

22. See Theo Farrell and Terry Terriff, *The Sources of Military Change: Culture, Politics, Technology* (Boulder, CO: Lynne Rienner, 2002); and Theo Farrell, *The Norms of War: Cultural Beliefs and Modern Conflict* (Boulder, CO: Lynne Rienner, 2005).

23. Davidson, *Lifting the Fog of Peace*, 19.

24. James March and Herbert Simon, *Organizations* (New York: Wiley, 1958); Richard Cyert and James March, *A Behavioral Theory of the Firm* (Englewood Cliffs, NJ: Prentice Hall, 1963).

25. David Garvin, "Building a Learning Organization," *Harvard Business Review* (July/August 1993): 4.

26. Marlene Fiol and Marjorie Lyles, "Organizational Learning," *Academy of Management Review* 10, no. 4 (1985): 803.

27. Peter Pawlowsky, "Management Science and Organizational Learning," in *Handbook*

of Organizational Learning and Knowledge, ed. M. Dierkes et al. (Oxford: Oxford University Press, 2001), 64.

28. Martin Schulz, "Organizational Learning," in Joel A. C. Baum, ed., *Blackwell Companion to Organizations* (Malden, MA: Blackwell, 2002), 423.

29. Schulz, 418.

30. See Nirmal Pal and Daniel Pantaleo, *The Agile Enterprise: Reinventing Your Organization for Success in an On-Demand World* (New York: Springer, 2005); and Emmanuel Gobillot, *The Connected Leader: Creating Agile Organizations for People, Performance and Profit* (London: Kogan, 2008). Nagl found this was true of the British Army in the colonial period. It was structured "precisely to deal with the unexpected" and was "actively expected to innovate." See Nagl, *Learning to Eat Soup with a Knife*, 215.

31. J. C. Spender and P. H. Grinyer, "Organizational Renewal: Top Management's Role in a Loosely Coupled System," *Human Relations* 48, no. 8 (1995): 913.

32. The organization as a body applies a method of analysis that weighs contending facts and data with a view to the resolution of those differences through a process that engages all members in problem solving. See Peter Senge, *The Fifth Discipline: The Art and Practice of the Learning Organization* (New York: Doubleday, 1990), part 3.

33. March and Levitt describe routines as "rules, procedures, conventions, strategies, and technologies around which organizations are constructed and through which they operate." Routines "guide their behavior." See Barbara Levitt and James March, "Organizational Learning," *Annual Review of Sociology* 14 (1988): 320.

34. Organizational routines can be either resistant or open to change. Those resisting change do so because they are "bound by rules and customs." See M. Feldman, "Organizational Routines as Sources of Continuous Change," *Organizational Science* (November/December 2000): 622, and Neil Costello, *Stability and Change in High-Tech Enterprise: Organizational Practices and Routines* (London: Routledge, 2000).

35. Feldman found that implanting agency in organizations will allow those executing routines to foster change if needed. If agency exists within an organization's culture, it will allow for change when routines do not result in the intended outcomes. See Feldman, "Organizational Routines," 622–23.

36. Garvin, "Building a Learning Organization," 3.

37. J. C. Spender, "Organizational Knowledge, Learning, and Memory: Three Concepts in Search of a Theory," *Journal of Organizational Change Management* 9, no. 1 (1996): 73, 75.

38. Garvin, "Building a Learning Organization," 4.

39. Garvin, 7.

40. Garvin, 9.

41. Spender describes such organizations as ones "re-conceptualized as a community of practice." Leaders empower, motivate, and build the trust of members through a participatory approach that embodies collective problem-solving and adaptation. See Spender, "Organizational Knowledge," 72–75.

42. See Senge, *Fifth Discipline*; and Peter Senge, "The Practice of Innovation," *Leader to*

Leader (Summer 1998). See also Peter Drucker, *Management*, rev. ed. (New York: HarperCollins, 2008); Douglas McGregor, *The Human Side of Enterprise*, annotated ed. (New York: McGraw-Hill, 2006); and Amy Edmondson and Bertand Moingeon, "Learning, Trust and Organizational Change," in *Organizational Learning and the Learning Organization*, ed. Mark Easterby-Smith, Luis Araujo, and John Burgoyne (London: SAGE, 1999).

43. Stanley McChrystal et al., *Team of Teams: The New Rules of Engagement for an Interconnected World* (New York: Portfolio, 2015), chaps. 10–12; J. Richard Hackman, *Leading Teams: Setting the Stage for Great Performances* (Cambridge, MA: Harvard Business School Publishing Corporation, 2002); Morton Hanson, *Collaboration: How Leaders Avoid the Traps, Build Common Ground, and Reap Big Results* (Cambridge, MA: Harvard Business School Publishing Corp., 2009).

44. Once innovation and adaptation take place, explains Downie, learning organizations "institutionalize those lessons in organizational memory." See Downie, *Learning from Conflict*, 23.

45. F. A. Hayek, "The Theory of Complex Phenomena," in *Readings in the Philosophy of Social Science*, ed. Michael Martin and Lee McIntyre (Cambridge, MA: MIT Press, 1994); Ben Ramalingam et al., *Exploring the Science of Complexity: Ideas and Implications for Development and Humanitarian Efforts* (London: Overseas Development Institute, 2008).

46. Andrew Zolli and Ann Marie Healy, *Resilience: Why Things Bounce Back* (New York: Simon & Schuster, 2012); Brian Walker, *Resilience Thinking: Sustaining Ecosystems and People in a Changing World* (Washington, DC: Island Press, 2006).

47. McChrystal et al., *Team of Teams*. For a discussion of this point, see chap. 2 and pp. 208–10.

48. Stanley McChrystal, "Lesson from Iraq: It Takes a Network to Defeat a Network," June 21, 2013, https://www.linkedin.com/pulse/20130621110027-86145090-lesson-from-iraq-it-takes-a-network-to-defeat-a-network/.

49. Stanley McChrystal, "It Takes a Network: The New Frontline of Modern Warfare," *Foreign Policy*, March/April 2011, 83.

50. James Orton with Christopher Lamb, "Interagency National Security Teams," *Prism*, no. 2 (2014), https://cco.ndu.edu/Portals/96/Documents/prism/prism_2-2/Prism_47-64_Orton-Lamb.pdf.

51. Orton and Lamb.

52. In the social sciences, an "agent" refers to an individual engaging with the structure of the social system. "Human agency" in the context of this discussion of learning organizations is about how individuals and groups can, if empowered, exercise their capacity for acting freely to question the operating procedures and processes of the larger organization of which they are a part. Individuals can take part in a range of activities in doing so. Human agency challenges the hierarchical structures of traditional organizations. Albert Bandura describes agency as "people's beliefs about their capabilities to exercise control over events that affect their lives. Self-efficacy beliefs function as

an important set of proximal determinants of human motivation, affect, and action. They operate on action through motivational, cognitive, and affective intervening processes." See Albert Bandura, "Human Agency in Social Cognitive Theory," *American Psychologist* 44, no. 9 (September 1989): 1175. See also Erasmus Mayr, *Understanding Human Agency* (Oxford: Oxford University Press, 2011).

53. McChrystal et al., *Team of Teams*, 219.

54. Interview with Lt. Gen. Michael Flynn, October 2014, Alexandria, VA.

55. Interview with General Flynn, October 2014.

56. Interview with a midlevel member of TF 714 who served in 2007–9, August 2014. Interviewee requested his name be withheld and the location of the interview not be disclosed.

57. Sargut and McGrath, "Learning to Live with Complexity," 68.

58. McChrystal, "New Frontline of Modern Warfare," 2.

59. David Knoke, "It Takes a Network: The Rise and Fall of Social Network Analysis in U.S. Army Counterinsurgency Doctrine," *Connections* 33, no. 1 (July 2013): 2.

60. Knoke, 2.

61. Martin Muckian, "Structural Vulnerabilities of Networked Insurgencies: Adapting to the New Adversary," *Parameters*, Winter 2006–7, 15.

62. Interview with General Flynn, October 2014.

63. Garvin, "Building a Learning Organization," 9.

64. Interview with General Flynn, October 2014.

65. Charles Faint and Michael Harris, "F3EAD: Ops/Intel Fusion Feeds the SOF Targeting Process," *Small Wars Journal*, January 2012, https://smallwarsjournal.com/jrnl/art/f3ead-opsintel-fusion-"feeds"-the-sof-targeting-process.

66. David Snowden and May Boone, "Leader's Framework for Decision Making," *Harvard Business Review* 85, no. 11 (December 2007): 6.

67. Snowden and Boone, 6.

68. Interview with Lt. Gen. Bennet Sacolick, September 2014, McLean, VA.

69. Interview with General Sacolick, September 2014.

70. McChrystal, "Lesson from Iraq."

71. Interview with Gen. Joseph L. Votel, USA (Ret.), May 2015, Tampa, FL.

72. McChrystal et al., *Team of Teams*, 231.

73. Interview with Gen. Stanley McChrystal, USA (Ret.), July 2014, Alexandria, VA.

74. Gideon Rose, "Generation Kill: A Conversation with Stanley McChrystal," *Foreign Affairs* 92, no. 2 (March/April 2013): 2–3.

75. Rose, 3.

76. McChrystal et al., *Team of Teams*, 209.

77. McChrystal et al., 232.

78. McChrystal et al., 224.

79. McChrystal et al.

80. McChrystal et al., 226.

81. Collins, "Military Innovation in War," 242.

82. Collins, 242.

83. Collins, 211.

84. Collins, 212.

85. Collins, 214–15.

86. Snowden and Boone, "Leader's Framework for Decision Making," 6.

87. McChrystal et al., *Team of Teams*, 232.

88. Garvin, "Building a Learning Organization," 4.

89. Garvin, 4.

90. Jennifer Sims, "Foreign Intelligence Liaison: Devils, Deals, and Details," *International Journal of Intelligence and CounterIntelligence* 19, no. 2 (2006): 195.

91. Daniel Byman, "Intelligence Liaison and Counterterrorism: A Quick Primer," *Lawfare* (blog), May 16, 2017, https://www.lawfareblog.com/intelligence-liaison-and-counter terrorism-quick-primer.

92. McChrystal, "Lesson from Iraq."

93. Jeffrey Richelson, *The US Intelligence Community*, 6th ed. (Boulder, CO: Westview, 2012), 286.

94. The account that follows, detailing how Israel adapted organizationally, technologically, and operationally to respond to the Second Intifada, is based on both secondary sources and field research in Israel during the summer of 2018. With respect to secondary sources, these include Ronen Bergman, *Rise and Kill First: The Secret History of Israel's Targeted Assassinations* (New York: Random House, 2018); Jason Gewirtz, *Israel's Edge: The Story of the IDF's Most Elite Unit—Talpiot* (Springfield, NJ: Gefen, 2016); James Carmichael, *Israeli Special Forces and Intelligence Services* (Amazon Digital Services, 2017); Gal Hirsch, *Defensive Shield: An Israeli Special Forces Commander on the Front Line of Counterterrorism* (Springfield, NJ: Gefen, 2016); Daniel Byman, *A High Price: The Triumphs and Failures of Israeli Counterterrorism* (Oxford: Oxford University Press, 2011); and Samuel Katz, *The Ghost Warriors: Inside Israel's Undercover War against Suicide Terrorism* (New York: Berkley Caliber, 2016). The author also consulted the publications of two of Israel's leading security institutes, the Institute for National Security Studies at Tel Aviv University (http://www.inss.org.il) and the International Institute for Counter-Terrorism at the Interdisciplinary Center, Herzliya (https://www.ict.org.il). Field research involved semistructured interviews with several former senior military and security officers who commanded during the Second Intifada.

95. For an insightful discussion of these developments see Bergman, *Rise and Kill First*, chap. 27.

96. "Thirty people were killed and 140 injured—20 seriously—in a suicide bombing in the Park Hotel in the coastal city of Netanya, in the midst of the Passover holiday Seder with 250 guests. Hamas claimed responsibility for the attack. The terrorist walked into the dining room of the hotel, in the center of the city, and detonated an explosive device. The terrorist was identified as Abdel-Basset Odeh, a member of the Hamas Iz a Din al-Kassam Brigades, from the West Bank city of Tulkarem, which is just 10 kilometers (six miles) east of Netanya." Israel Ministry of Foreign Affairs,

March 27, 2002, https://mfa.gov.il/MFA/MFA-Archive/2002/Pages/Passover%20 suicide%20bombing%20at%20Park%20Hotel%20in%20Netanya.aspx.

97. Yoram Schweitzer, "The Rise and Fall of Suicide Bombings in the Second Intifada," *Strategic Assessment* 13, no. 3 (2010): 43–44. See also Jonathan Schachter, "The End of the Second Intifada," *Strategic Assessment* 13, no. 3 (October 2010); and Zaki Shalom and Yoaz Hendel, "The Unique Features of the Second Intifada," *Military and Strategic Affairs* 3, no. 1 (May 2011).

98. Bergman, *Rise and Kill First*, 499.

99. Bergman, chaps. 27–30.

100. Schweitzer, "Rise and Fall of Suicide Bombings," 46.

101. Ophir Falk, "Measuring the Effectiveness of Israel's 'Targeted Killing' Campaign," *Perspectives on Terrorism* 9, no. 1 (2015): 21.

102. Falk, 45.

103. Interviews with Gen. Moshe Ya'alon and Maj. Gen. Amos Yadlin, July 2018, Institute for National Security Studies, Tel Aviv University.

104. Interview with General Ya'alon, July 2018.

105. Interview with General Ya'alon, July 2018.

106. Interviews with General Yadlin, July 2018.

107. Liam Collins, "Military Innovation in War: The Criticality of the Senior Military Leader" (PhD diss., Princeton University, 2014), 225.

108. Interviews with General Yadlin, July 2018.

109. Interview with Barak Ben Zur, July 2008, Interdisciplinary Center, Herzliya, Israel.

110. Richard Shultz, *Military Innovation in War: It Takes a Learning Organization; A Case Study of Task Force 714 in Iraq* (MacDill Air Force Base, FL: JSOU Press, 2016), 55.

111. Cited in Shultz, 56.

112. Sean Naylor, *Relentless Strike: The Secret History of Joint Special Operations Command* (New York: St. Martin's Griffin, 2016); David Tucker and Christopher Lamb, *United States Special Operations Forces* (New York: Columbia University Press, 2007); Tom Clancy and Carl Steiner, *Shadow Warriors: Inside the Special Forces* (New York: Berkley, 2003); Susan Marquis, *Unconventional Warfare: Rebuilding U.S. Special Operation Forces* (Washington, DC: Brookings Institution Press, 1997); and Thomas Adams, *US Special Operations Forces in Action* (London: Routledge, 1997).

113. Mark Urban, *Task Force Black: The Explosive True Story of the Secret Special Forces War in Iraq* (New York: St. Martin's Griffin, 2012).

114. Sean Rayment, "SAS Kills Hundreds of Terrorists in 'Secret War' against al-Qaeda in Iraq," *Telegraph*, August 30, 2008, https://www.telegraph.co.uk/news/newstopics /onthefrontline/2652496/SAS-kill-hundreds-of-terrorists-in-secret-war-against-al -Qaeda-in-Iraq.html.

115. Jessica Stern, "Deradicalization or Disengagement of Terrorists: Is It Possible?," Koret-Taube Task Force on National Security and Law, 2010, Hoover Institution, Stanford University, https://www.hoover.org/sites/default/files/research/docs/futurechallenges stern.pdf.

116. Christopher Boucek, "Counter-Terrorism from Within: Assessing Saudi Arabia's Religious Rehabilitation and Disengagement Program," *RUSI Journal* 153, no. 6 (2008): 60–65, https://carnegieendowment.org/files/boucek_rusi.pdf.

117. Roel Meijer, "Saudi Arabia's Religious Counter-Terrorist Discourse," Middle East Institute, February 15, 2012, http://www.mei.edu/content/saudi-arabia's-religious-counter-terrorist-discourse.

118. Interview with a former member of TF 714 with knowledge of the liaison relationships with other nations, July 2018. Interviewee requested his name be withheld and the location of the interview not be disclosed.

119. Interview with former member of TF 714, July 2018.

120. Follow-up telephone interview with Adm. William McRaven, USN (Ret.), May 2015.

121. Garvin, "Building a Learning Organization," 4.

Epilogue

1. Follow-up telephone interview with Adm. William McRaven, USN (Ret.), May 2015.

2. Stanley A. McChrystal, "It Takes a Network: The New Front Line of Modern Warfare," *Foreign Policy* (March/April 2011), https://foreignpolicy.com/2011/02/21/it-takes-a-network/.

3. *The 9/11 Commission Report* (New York: W. W. Norton, 2004), 66–67.

4. See Norman Cigar, *Al-Qa'ida's Doctrine for Insurgency: Abd Al-Aziz Al-Muqrin's "A Practical Course for Guerrilla War"* (Washington, DC: Potomac Books, 2008); and Jonathan Schanzer, *Al-Qaeda's Armies: Middle East Affiliate Groups and the Next Generation of Terror* (New York: Specialist Press International, 2005).

5. They also supported a CIA program that trained and directed what were known as counterterrorism pursuit teams. Operating from several locations in Afghanistan, these teams focused on targeting terrorist suspects, insurgents, and criminal elements in the Afghanistan-Pakistan border region. However, this was largely a CIA effort that grew into a substantial force of three thousand indigenous fighters. For a description of their evolution, see Thomas Gibbons-Neff, Eric Schmitt, and Adam Goldman, "A Newly Assertive C.I.A. Expands Its Taliban Hunt in Afghanistan," *New York Times*, October 22, 2017, https://www.nytimes.com/2017/10/22/world/asia/cia-expanding-taliban-fight-afghanistan.html. See also Bob Woodward, *Obama's Wars* (New York: Simon & Schuster, 2010).

6. Claire Felter, Jonathan Masters, and Mohammed Aly Sergie, "Al-Shabab," Council on Foreign Relations Backgrounder, updated January 31, 2019, https://www.cfr.org/backgrounder/al-shabab. See also International Crisis Group, "Al-Shabaab Five Years after Westgate: Still a Menace in East Africa," report no. 265, September 21, 2018, https://www.crisisgroup.org/africa/horn-africa/kenya/265-al-shabaab-five-years-after-westgate-still-menace-east-africa.

7. Felter, Masters, and Sergie, "Al-Shabab."

8. Angela Gendron, "Confronting Terrorism in Saudi Arabia," *International Journal of Intelligence and CounterIntelligence* 23, no. 3 (2010): 487–89.

9. "Al Qaeda in the Arabian Peninsula," Mapping Militant Organizations, https://cisac

.fsi.stanford.edu/mappingmilitants/profiles/al-qaeda-arabian-peninsula?high light=April+19.

10. "Al Qaeda in the Arabian Peninsula," Mapping Militant Organizations.

11. "Al Qaeda in the Arabian Peninsula," Council on Foreign Relations Backgrounder. For an overview of how this evolved, see Thomas Gibbons-Neff and Dan Lamothe, "Obama Administration Expands Elite Military Unit's Powers to Hunt Foreign Fighters Globally," *Washington Post*, November 25, 2016, https://www.washingtonpost .com/news/checkpoint/wp/2016/11/25/obama-administration-expands-elite-mili tary-units-powers-to-hunt-foreign-fighters-globally/?utm_term=.5343e7fedbee.

12. William B. Ostlund, *Irregular Warfare: Counterterrorism Forces in Support of Counterinsurgency Operations*, Land Warfare Paper no. 91 (Arlington, VA: Institute of Land Warfare, AUSA, September 2012), 8–9, https://www.ausa.org/sites/default/files /LWP-91-Irregular-Warfare-Counter-Terrorism-Forces-in-Support-of-Counterinsur gency-Operations.pdf.

13. Ostlund, 9.

14. Ostlund, 5.

15. Michael S. Schmidt and Mark Mazzetti, "A Top ISIS Leader Is Killed in an Airstrike, the Pentagon Says," *New York Times*, March 25, 2016, https://www.nytimes .com/2016/03/26/world/middleeast/abd-al-rahman-mustafa-al-qaduli-isis-reported -killed-in-syria.html.

16. Kimberly Dozier, "U.S. Building a Network to Hit Militants," Associated Press, January 5, 2011, http://www. nbcnews.com/id/40930584/ns/us_news-security/t/us -building-network-hit-militants/#.XGcW_OhKiUk.

17. Kimberly Dozier, "Elite U.S. Special Operators Build Center for Perpetual War on Terror," Daily Beast, November 28, 2016, https://www.thedailybeast.com/trump -just-put-his-own-emergency-declaration-in-legal-jeopardy?ref=scroll.

18. *9/11 Commission Report*, 66–67.

19. Seth G. Jones et al., *The Evolution of the Salafi-Jihadist Threat* (Washington, DC: Center for Strategic and International Studies, 2018), https://www. csis.org/analysis /evolution-salafi-jihadist-threat.

20. *National Defense Strategy of the United States of America*, https://dod.defense.gov/Por tals/1/Documents /pubs/2018-National-Defense-Strategy-Summary.pdf.

21. Micah Zenko, "America's Military Is Nostalgic for World Wars," *Foreign Policy* (March 13, 2018), https:// foreignpolicy.com/2018/03/13/americas-military-is-nostalgic-for -great-power-wars/.

22. *National Defense Strategy of the United States of America*, 2–3.

23. *National Defense Strategy of the United States of America*, 2–3.

24. *National Defense Strategy of the United States of America*, 2–3.

25. *National Defense Strategy of the United States of America*, 2–3.

26. Daniel R. Coats, *Worldwide Threat Assessment of the US Intelligence Community*, Statement for the Record, January 29, 2019, 10, https://www.dni.gov/files/ODNI /documents/2019-ATA-SFR---SSCI.pdf.

27. Coats, 11.

28. Coats, 12.

29. "Trump Pulling All U.S. Troops from Syria, Declaring ISIS Defeated," PBS News Hour, December 19, 2018, https://www.pbs.org/newshour/world/trump-pulling-all -u-s-troops-from-syria-declaring-isis-defeated.

30. "Gen. James Mattis Q&A," *Small Wars Journal*, https://smallwarsjournal.com/blog /gen-james-mattis-qa.

INDEX

Abdul-Rahman, Sheikh, 88

actionable intelligence, 111, 151, 156

activity-based intelligence (ABI), 247n78

Afghanistan: al-Qaeda camps in, 37, 209; CIA in, 149, 270n5; Karzai government in, 150, 208; Soviet war in, 45, 209; use of satellites in, 73; US military operations in, 25–26, 148–51, 203–4, 206–7, 208; US support to Mujahideen in, 137, 141, 255n61

agency, 184–86, 266–67n52

Aid, Matthew, 56, 58, 76, 78, 79–80, 231n34

Aideed, Mohammed, 151

Air Force Directorate of Intelligence, 56

Alexander, Keith B., 81–82, 112

Alexander, Matthew, 88

algorithms, 117, 248n99

all-channel networks, 45–46

al-Qaeda, 41, 70, 148, 211–12; Afghanistan camps of, 37, 209; attack on CIA by, 24; bombing of US embassies by, 67, 69, 76, 146; Bush on, 10, 211; as global network, 29–30, 37, 38, 150; in Horn of Africa, 75, 204; Information Age technologies used by, 38–39, 70, 91; and 9/11 attacks, 30, 38, 49, 203; Operation Enduring Freedom fight against, 148–51; relationship between core and affiliates of, 36, 45; strategy and ideology of, 37–38, 39–40, 45; USS *Cole* attacked by, 67; US threat assessments of, 146, 211, 256–57n87; war on US declared by, 146, 163; in Yemen and Saudi Arabia, 75, 205

al-Qaeda core (AQC), 37, 38

al-Qaeda in Iraq (AQI): clandestine apparatus of, 152–53; commanders and managers killed or captured, 168–69, 171, 175; as complex challenge, 2, 31, 37, 39, 48, 155; critical nodes of, 129–30, 160–61, 202; as decentralized network, 2, 153, 155, 186, 192, 258–59n120; escalation of attacks by, 10, 42; espionage employed by, 24; foreign jihadists joining, 38–39; IED factories of, 83; impact of TF 714 raids on, 7, 169–70, 202; interrogation of detainees from, 87–88; ISIS emergence from, 174, 220n19; network analysis of, 117–18; as network of networks, 8, 37, 39, 48, 131, 155, 186; operational tempo of, 6, 31, 40, 125, 154, 161, 166, 171, 172, 202; as strategic surprise, 31, 153, 154; strategy of, 38, 39, 186; structure of, 42, 153, 155, 186; as unlike other enemies, 2, 31, 152–53, 185–86, 192, 201. *See also* Iraq

al-Qaeda in the Arabian Peninsula (AQAP), 38, 205–6

Al-Qaeda in Yemen (AQY), 205

Al Qaeda Network Exord (AQN Exord), 163, 165

al-Shabaab, 76, 204

Althoff, Michael, 53

Aman, 156, 194–95, 198

analysis. *See* intelligence analysis

Analyst's Notebook, 120, 249n112

analytic standards, 102, 245–46n48

Andrews, Robert, 150

Ansar al-Sunna (later Ansar al-Islam), 39

Arab-Israeli conflict, 100

Armed Conflict Database, 18

Armed Forces Security Agency (AFSA), 57, 231–32n40

armed groups. *See* nonstate armed groups
The Army and Vietnam (Krepinevich), 176
Arquilla, John, 36, 44
Atwood, Chandler, 112, 116–17
Azzam, Abdullah Yusuf, 43, 45

al-Baghdadi, Abu Abdullah Al-Rashid, 171
al-Baghdadi, Abu Bakr, 174, 220n19
Bailes, Alyson, 17
Baker, James, 261n173
Bakr, Haji, 220n19
al-Balawi, Humam, 24, 86
Balkans, 67, 83
Bandura, Albert, 266–67n52
Basayev, Shamil, 34
Basque Homeland and Liberty (ETA), 33
Battle of Wits: The Complete Story of Codebreaking in World War II (Budiansky), 55
A Behavioral Theory of the Firm (March and Cyert), 178, 179
behaviors and signatures, 113–14
Ben-Gurion, David, 194
Ben-Zur, Barak, 198–99
Bergman, Ronen, 196
Berntsen, Gary, 85
Best, Richard, 140
Biddle, Stephen, 168
big data: as concept, 111–13; and network analysis, 117–24, 125
Biltgen, Patrick, 111, 113–15, 117, 118
bin Laden, Osama, 45, 69; strategy of, 37–38, 39, 203; at Tora Bora, 26, 150; US killing of, 49–50, 132; war on US declared by, 146, 163
black propaganda, 136–37
blinks, 188–89
Boone, Mary, 47, 121, 188
Boren, David, 66
Bosnia, 151
Boucek, Christopher, 200
Brennan, John, 206
Brown, Harold, 144
Bruce, James B., 101
Brun, Itai, 41
Budiansky, Stephen, 55

Bukharin, Oleg, 56
Bush, George H. W., 142–43
Bush, George W., 85, 98; on al-Qaeda, 10, 211; and US war measures, 70, 148–49, 162–63, 218n31
Byman, Daniel, 78, 85, 88, 126, 194

Cano, Alfonso, 33
Cantrell, Thomas, 19
Carter, Jimmy, 98, 141, 244n18
Castro, Fidel, 100, 138
Central Intelligence Agency (CIA): in Afghanistan, 149, 270n5; al-Qaeda attack on, 24; covert actions by, 138–40, 145, 147, 254n48; creation of, 56, 95; HUMINT by, 54, 62–64, 86–87, 234n85; intelligence analysis by, 95, 99–100, 104, 119–20, 146, 245n32, 246n55; intelligence collection on Soviets by, 57, 62–64, 234n85; Office of Military Affairs of, 105; paramilitary operations of, 5, 164; as part of Iraq joint task force, 31, 159, 184, 202; SIGINT by, 61, 81; in Somalia, 204; view of al-Qaeda by, 70, 146
Central Intelligence Group (CIG), 55–56
Central Security Service (CSS), 78–79
chain network, 45
Chauhan, Sudhanshu, 122–23
Chechens, 34–35
Chen, Lei-da, 119
Chesney, Robert, 142–43
China, 27, 210, 211, 212, 246n55
Church Committee (Senate Select Committee to Study Governmental Operations with Respect to Intelligence), 138–40, 141
civilian deaths, 17
civilian intervention, 177
Clark, Peter, 94
Clark, Robert: on intelligence analysis, 96, 109, 118–19, 120, 121–22, 124; on intelligence collection, 52, 61, 76, 77, 83, 233nn68–69
Clarke, Richard, 146, 257n95
Clausewitz, Carl von, 2
Clifton, Christopher, 119
Clinton, Bill, 67, 69, 104, 145, 147

Cobra Focus, 79

Cold War: COMINT during, 59, 76; covert action during, 136, 139–41, 253n40; HUMINT during, 54, 56, 57, 62–64; IMIT during, 59–60; information collection during, 50, 51; intelligence analysis during, 95–103, 109, 246n60; intelligence collection during, 52, 53, 54, 56–57; MASINT during, 61–62; paramilitary operations during, 137, 138–44, 253n40, 254n48; SIGINT during, 57–59, 76; Soviet Union as intelligence focus during, 26–27

collection. *See* intelligence collection

Collins, Liam, 161, 192, 193, 198

Colombia, 151

command-and-control systems: of centralized armed groups, 33, 34–35, 137–38; of decentralized armed groups, 33, 36, 41–42; of TF 714, 182, 184, 189–90, 201–2

Commander's Handbook for Attack the Network, 124

Commission on Roles and Capabilities of the US Intelligence Community, 66

communications intelligence (COMINT), 52, 232n40; during Cold War, 59, 76; in post-9/11 period, 76, 77, 78, 80–81

complexity: of challenges, 120–21; of networks, 46–47

Conflict Assessment Software Tool (CAST), 221n25

Conflict Data Program, 15

Congressional Research Service (CRS), 68

Contras, Nicaraguan, 100–101, 137, 141, 142, 255n63

Corona program, 59–60

Counterinsurgency (Field Manual 3-24), 3, 20, 21, 107, 168

counterintelligence, 30, 134; importance of, 23–24; by Soviet Union, 63, 102

Counternarcotics Center (CNC), 101, 105–6

Counterterrorism Center (CTC), 70, 101, 105

counterterrorism intelligence centers (CTICs), 86

covert action, 9–10, 132–74; Carter administration's limitations on, 141; Church

Committee investigations into, 138–40, 141; during Cold War, 136, 139–41, 253n40; as component of intelligence, 5, 23, 24; congressional oversight of, 142–43; controversial nature of, 132, 133; definitions of, 134, 164; downsizing of in 1990s, 145–48; 9/11 changing terms of debate over, 5, 10, 133; presidential authority for, 162–66; in propaganda, 136–37; under Reagan, 141–42; subdisciplines of, 135–38; during World War II, 135, 138, 253n35

covert political action, 135, 138–39, 140, 254n48

covert propaganda, 136–37

Creveld, Martin van, 13–14

Crime and Narcotics Center, 106

Cuba, 100, 138, 140

Cuban Missile Crisis, 58, 64, 233n60, 234n89

Cukier, Kenneth, 112–13

current intelligence, 25, 95, 98

Cyert, Richard, 178

Dailey, Dell, 151–52

data: big data, 111–13, 117–24, 125; known and unknown, 114–15; preparation of, 115–17. *See also* intelligence collection

databases, 18, 96, 209; multi-INT, 94, 116, 117, 118–20, 128, 129, 195; XKeyscore, 80

Daugherty, William, 134, 136–37, 140, 145–46

Davidson, Janine, 176, 177, 263n5

decentralization, 35–40; of AQI, 2, 153, 155, 186, 192, 258–59n120; benefits and advantages of, 42–43; of TF 714, 188, 189–90, 201–2

Defense Intelligence Agency (DIA), 31, 128, 159, 184, 202

Defense Threat Reduction Agency, 84

Denécé, Éric, 84–85

Department of Defense (DOD): and adaptation to irregular war, 19–20, 222n35; and imagery-collection systems, 61; and paramilitary operations, 5, 164; unconventional warfare defined by, 149; *Weekly Security Incidents Trends* of, 166–67

Deptula, David, 50, 51, 76
Diamond, John, 67
Dichter, Avi, 196, 198
Directorate of Intelligence (DI): Cold War
    intelligence analysis by, 95, 96, 98, 99, 101–
    6; creation of, 95; divisions of, 243n11
Diskin, Yuval, 195
Distributed Common Ground Systems
    (DCGS), 72
DNI Presenter, 80
Doherty, Thomas, 107
Donovan, William, 55
Doolittle Report, 254n48
Downie, Richard, 177, 266n44
Downing, Wayne, 146
Dudayev, Dzhokhar, 34, 35
Dulles, Allen, 59, 63

edges (in network analysis), 122–23
Einsiedel, Sebastian von, 16
Eisenhower, Dwight, 140
electromagnetic spectrum, 60, 233n62
electronic intelligence (ELINT), 52, 58, 76
Ensor, David, 68
Eriksson, Mikael, 15
Escobar, Pablo, 123, 151

F3 cycle, 108, 125–26, 192–93
F3EAD cycle, 74, 125–31; adoption of concept,
    159–62, 192–93; and analysis process, 109–
    11, 129–30; "blinks" in, 188; contributors
    to, 78, 81–82; exploit and analyze phase of,
    108, 125–28, 129, 159, 160, 187; F3 shift
    to, 108, 125–26, 192–93; fix phase of, 71,
    118, 127; targeting process transformed by,
    168–69, 187, 202
Faddis, Sam, 85
Faint, Charles, 160
Falk, Ophir, 197
Farrell, Theo, 178
Federal Bureau of Investigation (FBI), 31, 56,
    158, 159, 184, 202
Feinstein, Dianne, 87
Feith, Douglas, 150
Feldman, M., 265n35

Fiel, Eric, 160, 170
Fiol, Marlene, 179
Fischer, Benjamin, 235n94
Fitzgerald, Dennis, 71
The Five Disciplines of Intelligence Collection
    (Lowenthal and Clark), 52
Flynn, Michael, 19, 128, 153, 187; on agency,
    184–85; on interagency partnership, 125–26,
    159; and interrogations, 87, 89–90; on ISR,
    74, 76; on need for intelligence, 21, 82, 186
Ford, Gerald, 100
Ford, Harold, 99
Foreign Broadcast Intelligence Service (FBIS), 65
foreign instrumentation and signals (FISINT),
    52, 58, 76
Fort Gordon, 79
Fragile States Index, 221n25
Friedman, Jeffrey, 168
Frolick, Mark, 119
Fund for Peace, 221n25
The Future of American Intelligence (Gerecht), 85

Gambit cameras, 60, 233n65
Garthoff, Douglas, 103
Garvin, David, 179, 180, 186–87, 194
Gates, Robert, 20, 145, 222n40
Gauthier, Dave, 116
Gendron, Angela, 205
georeferencing, 116, 117
George, Roger Z., 101
geospatial analysis, 79, 130. See also imagery
    intelligence; National Geospatial Intelligence
    Agency (NGA)
Gerecht, Reuel Marc, 85
Godson, Roy, 17–18, 252n21; on covert action,
    134, 135; on elements of intelligence, 22–23,
    24; on intelligence dominance, 156
Goodman, Allan, 104
Gorbachev, Mikhail, 143
Gorgon Stare system, 75
Gouré, Daniel, 75
Grant, Rebecca, 73
Grissom, Adam, 175, 177
Guardian, 80
Guatemala, 140

Hacking Web Intelligence (Chauhan and Panda), 122–23

Hamas, 34, 41, 84, 194

Hamilton, Lee, 261n173

Hanlon, Querine, 17–18

Haqqani Network, 207, 208

Harbom, Lotta, 15, 219–20n13

Hard Target Research and Analysis Center, 84

al-Harithi, Abu Ali, 205

Harris, Michael, 160

Harris, Shane, 81, 82

Hayden, Michael, 77, 78

Hegghammer, Thomas, 91, 92

Helms, Richard, 63

Herman, Arthur, 84

Hersh, Seymour, 68–69

Heuer, Richards, 5, 101–3

Hezbollah, 24, 36, 41–42, 194

hierarchical organizations, 33–35, 42, 137–38

high-value targets (HVTs), 35, 42, 152–53, 258n119

Hilsman, Roger, 145

Högbladh, Stina, 15, 219–20n13

Holland, Charles, 150–51

Homeland Security, 83

House Permanent Select Committee on Intelligence (HPSCI), 66, 104, 143

Hull, Cordell, 65

Hulnick, Arthur, 96, 243–44n18

human intelligence (HUMINT), 70, 97; characteristics of, 53–54; during Cold War, 54, 56, 57, 62–64; and foreign intelligence services, 85–86; in post-9/11 wars, 84–90

Human Security Report Project, 15–16

human warfighting domains, 106–9

imagery intelligence (IMINT): characteristics of, 52–53; during Cold War, 59–60; in post-9/11 period, 71–76; post–Cold War shift in, 67; and signals, 21, 222n45; strategic importance of, 59–61

Information Age technologies: armed groups' use of, 19, 38–39, 43–44, 48, 54, 70; and big data, 111–12; and propaganda, 136. *See also* Internet; social media

intelligence, 12–31; actionable, 111, 151, 156; activity-based, 247n78; armed groups as challenge for, 27–31; current, 25, 95, 98; defined, 22–26; failures in, 25–26, 70, 93; and irregular war, 3–6, 21; and IRS systems, 71–72; as leading the way, 3, 12; McChrystal on need for, 131, 155–56, 168, 192; and operations, 25, 111, 130; primary instruments of, 4–5; state-centric approach to, 26–27; strategic and tactical, 25, 67; TF 714 based on, 10, 155–56, 186, 192, 202; warning, 98–99

intelligence, surveillance, and reconnaissance (ISR) systems: components of, 71–72; TF 714 use of, 73–76, 118, 127

intelligence analysis, 9, 93–131; alternative, 102, 103; analysts' qualities, 101–3; of big data, 111–15; during Cold War, 95–103, 109, 246n60; as component of intelligence, 5, 23; and detainee interrogations, 87–88; establishment of standards for, 102, 245–46n48; in F3EAD cycle, 109–11, 129–30; four domains of, 113–15; and intelligence cycle, 96–98; network analysis, 117–24, 130; post-9/11, 93–94, 106–25; in post–Cold War 1990s, 103–6; traffic and signature, 77–78

Intelligence Analysis (Clark), 109, 118–19, 120, 121–22, 124

Intelligence Authorization Act: for fiscal year 1991, 134, 164, 165; for fiscal year 2001, 68

intelligence collection, 8–9, 49–92; in aftermath of 9/11, 69–92; during and after World War II, 55–56; during Cold War, 50, 51, 53, 54, 56–57; as component of intelligence, 4–5, 22, 23, 24; disciplines of, 51–54; from HUMINT, 53–54, 56, 57, 62–63, 70, 84–90, 97; from IMINT, 52–53, 59–61, 67, 71–76; from MASINT, 61–62, 63, 82–84; from OSINT, 54, 64–65, 90–92; and Operation Neptune Spear, 49–50; and post-9/11 wars, 70–92; post–Cold War 1990s reassessments of, 50–51, 65–69; from SIGINT, 52, 55, 57–59, 76–82

intelligence cycle, 96–98, 106–9

intelligence dominance, 6, 156–57, 159–60, 187, 202
Intelligence: From Secrets to Policy (Lowenthal), 27, 50
Intelligence in the Age of Terror (Treverton), 3–4, 27
Intelligence Oversight Act of 1980, 142, 143
intelligence sharing, 161–62
International Institute for Strategic Studies, 18
Internet: armed groups' use of, 44, 54, 90, 91; and NSA, 77, 79–80
interrogations, 54, 87–88, 127
intrastate conflicts, 15–19
Iran, 98, 100, 140, 142, 144
Iran-Contra affair, 142
Iraq, 151–72; Anbar Province COIN campaign in, 167–68; Baathist-jihadist cooperation in, 36–37; consequences of withdrawal from, 172–74; declining violence in, 7, 167, 168, 169–70, 202; Maliki government in, 173–74; onset of insurgency in, 19, 42, 152, 166–67, 261n173; and Operation Desert Storm, 1, 12–13, 60, 71, 104–5; Operation New Dawn in, 172–73, 207–8; Sunni Awakening movement in, 107, 167, 172, 247n74; TF 714 raids in, 7, 81–82, 87, 89, 90–92, 126–27, 169–70, 175, 190, 201, 202, 204, 241n210; toppling of Saddam Hussein in, 151–52; and transnational jihadists, 39–40, 44–45, 105, 209–10; US intelligence failures in, 25, 70, 93. *See also* al-Qaeda in Iraq; Task Force 714
Irish Republican Army, 24, 33, 120, 137, 258n119
Irregular Warfare (DOD Directive 3000.07), 20
Irregular Warfare Joint Operating Concept (JOC), 3, 20, 21
Islamic Jihad, 34
Islamic State of Iraq, 174
Islamic State of Iraq and Syria (ISIS), 16, 211, 212; counterterrorism operations against, 208–9; formation of, 39, 220n19; use of social media by, 31
Israel: Netanya Passover massacre in, 196,

268–69n96; and Second Intifada, 156, 194, 195–96, 268n94; and Second Lebanon War, 41–42; targeted killings by, 34, 197; TF 714 learning from, 10–11, 156–57, 194–99
Italy, 139, 253n39

Jane's Information Group, 18
Japan, 135
Jardines, Eliot, 54, 64–65, 90
Jihadi Iraq, 91
joint interagency task force (JIATF): adopting concept of, 156–59, 184, 192; agency within, 184–85; components of, 31, 159, 184, 202; and F3EAD cycle, 160, 187; formation of, 31, 158–59; importance of, 126, 187, 189; and liaison officers, 162; McChrystal on, 158, 159, 184, 192; McRaven and, 158, 184, 192
Joint Special Operations Command (JSOC), 145, 202, 204, 210, 212–13; in Afghanistan, 149–51, 203; campaign against ISIS by, 208–9; establishment of, 144; in Iraq, 151–52, 159, 162, 163–64; manhunts by, 151; in Somalia, 204
Joint Special Operations University (JSOU), 218n30
Joint War Room (JWR) concept, 195–96, 197, 198, 199
Jones, Seth, 33
Jordan, 86, 200
Juergens, Rich, 19

Karzai, Hamid, 150, 208
Kelly, John, 167
Kennan, George, 139, 253–54n41
Kennedy, John, 64, 140, 254–55n53
Kent, Sherman, 95–96
Kenya, 69, 76, 146
Kerr, Richard, 99, 104, 245n32
Key Intelligence Questions (KIQs), 244n18
KGB, 63, 137, 231nn35–36, 234n85
Kibbe, Jennifer, 165
King, James C., 67
Knoke, David, 39, 186
known knowns, 114

known unknowns, 114–15
Korean War, 95
Koubi, Michael, 87
Krause, Keith, 17
Krepinevich, Andrew, 176
Krulak, Charles, 1, 70
Kuperman, Alan J., 255n61
Kurdistan Workers' Party, 33, 137, 258n119
al-Kuwaiti, Abu Ahmed, 49–50

labor unions, 135, 252n16
Lamb, Christopher, 158, 183, 195
Laos, 140–41, 254–55n53
leadership: and acting against instincts, 10, 181,
     188, 190, 193; TF 714 model of, 183, 188–
     93. See also command-and-control systems
learning organizations: challenging
     organizational practices in, 180; and
     knowledge collection, 180; leaders of, 181,
     264n41; and organizational culture, 181;
     and organizational learning theory, 178; and
     problem solving, 180; TF 714 as, 181, 182,
     185, 186–87; and unforeseen challenges,
     179–80
Levitt, Barbara, 265n33
Lia, Brynjar, 91, 92
liaison officers (LNOs), 162, 199
Libya, 232n49
link analysis, 119–20, 130
lone wolf analysts, 101–2
Long, Austin, 137, 140–41
Long, Letitia, 94
Lowenthal, Mark, 22, 27, 56, 135; on
     intelligence collection, 50, 52, 55
Lyles, Marjorie, 179
Lynch, Jessica, 152

Magsaysay, Ramón, 254n45
Malaya, 177
al-Maliki, Nuri, 173, 174
Mapping Militants Project, 18
March, James, 178, 265n33
Marchio, Jim, 102
Marquis, Susan, 144

al-Masri, Abu Ayyub, 171
Mattis, James, 212
Mayer-Schönberger, Viktor, 112–13
Mazzetti, Mark, 151
McChrystal, Stanley, 152, 153, 171, 209; on
     AQI as different challenge, 39, 125, 131,
     154, 157, 185–86; brought Industrial Age
     force to Information Age war, 6, 11, 189;
     on capturing material and documents, 89,
     126; as commander in Afghanistan, 206;
     on destroying AQI, 130, 161, 168, 175;
     and F3EAD concept, 108, 129, 168–69; on
     fusion of signals and imagery, 21, 222n45; on
     interrogations, 87; on ISR, 76, 127; on joint
     task force, 158, 159, 184, 192; on leadership
     and command, 182, 184, 185, 188, 190,
     191–92, 193; on liaison officers, 162, 199;
     My Share of the Task, 21, 126, 159; on need
     for intelligence, 131, 155–56, 168, 192; on
     need for TF 714 adaptation, 6, 125, 154,
     157; on need to become network, 6, 158,
     183, 194; on O&I briefings, 162; Team of
     Teams, 190–93; and TF 714 raids, 169–70,
     190, 204; visit to Israel by, 198
McConnell, John Michael, 57
McCurdy, David, 66
McGrath, Rita, 120–21, 185
McNerney, Michael, 175–76
McRaven, William, 154, 161, 162, 173; in
     Afghanistan, 206; on AQI's evolution,
     155; on importance of intelligence, 7,
     202; and intelligence analysis, 126, 128;
     on interrogations, 88; and joint task force
     concept, 158, 184, 192; on liaison partners,
     199; on raids against AQI, 7, 169, 170, 171,
     202; and transnational targeting center, 209
measurement and signatures intelligence
     (MASINT): characteristics of, 53; during
     Cold War, 61–62; in post-9/11 period, 82–84
Medina, Carmen, 93–94, 101, 106
Mekhtab al-Khidemat, 43
Melander, Erik, 16–17
Meyer, Edward, 144
MI5 (UK), 120

MI-8, 230n28

military innovation: civilian intervention as driver for, 177; constraints on, 175–77; definition of, 175–76; determinants of, 177–78; organizational culture and behavior as barriers to, 176–77, 263n5, 263–64n10; service competition as trigger for, 177–78

Military Review, 14

Miller, Scott, 193

Mitrokhin, Vasili, 231n36

Mladić, Ratko, 151

Mohammed, Khalid Sheikh, 49, 86, 88

Morris, John, 83

Mossad, 156, 194–95

MQ-1 Predator, 73

MQ-9 Reaper, 73

Mujahideen Shura Council, 39, 174

multi-INT data fusion, 115–17, 119, 125

Munsing, Evan, 158

al-Muqrin, Abdel Aziz, 203

Murdock, Darryl, 61

My Share of the Task (McChrystal), 21, 126, 159

Nagl, John, 177

National Commission for the Review of the National Reconnaissance Office, 68

National Defense Strategy (NDS), 210–11, 212

National Geospatial-Intelligence Agency (NGA), 61, 84, 184

National Imagery and Mapping Agency (NIMA), 61, 67

national intelligence estimates (NIEs), 95, 98; of Soviet economy, 99, 244–45n32; of Soviet military, 99–100, 107

National Intelligence Strategy of the United States (2003), 29–30

National Intelligence Strategy of the United States (2009), 20

National Intelligence Topics (NITs), 244n18

National Liberation Front (FLN, Algeria), 33

National Media Exploitation Center (NMEC), 128–29

National Military Strategic Plan for the War on Terrorism, 20

National Photographic Interpretation Center, 61

National Reconnaissance Office (NRO), 56, 69; congressional reviews of, 66, 67–68; creation of, 61; in post-9/11 period, 71, 84; satellites of, 59, 60, 61, 73

National Security Act of 1947, 56, 95

National Security Agency (NSA), 56, 58, 66, 68, 112; establishment of, 140; and fight against al-Qaeda, 49, 76–77, 78–82, 184

National Security Council Directive 68 (NSC-68), 139

Naval War College Review, 13–14

Netanya Passover massacre, 196, 268–69n96

network analysis, 117–24; as indispensable tool, 121–22; key elements of, 122–24; TF 714 use of, 130; threat network analysis, 124–25

networks: all-channel, 45–46; al-Qaeda as global, 29–30, 37, 38, 150; AQI as network of, 8, 37, 39, 48, 131, 155, 186; benefits and advantages of, 42–43; complex, 46–47; and nodes, 36, 46, 122–23; nonstate armed groups as, 2, 35–48; TF 714 as, 6, 157–58, 183, 192; variants of, 45–47

Nicaragua, 100–101, 137, 141, 142, 255n63

9/11 attacks: al-Qaeda conduct of, 30, 38, 49, 203; changed terms of covert action debate, 5, 10, 133; intelligence failures in, 25, 70, 93

9/11 Commission Report, 5, 21, 69, 70, 93, 150

nodes: within AQI, 129–30, 160–61, 202; and links, 118; and networks, 36, 46, 122–23

Nolte, William, 58

Nonproliferation Center (NPC), 106

nonstate armed groups, 32–48; adoption of term, 17–18; alliances and partnerships of, 36–37; camouflage and concealment by, 84; command-and-control of, 32, 33, 34–35, 36, 41–42, 137; as complex threat, 45–48; Creveld anticipation of, 13; decentralized, 2, 19, 35–40; growth of, 18, 144; hierarchical and centralized, 33–35, 42, 137–38; HUMINT efforts against, 84–85; as intelligence challenge, 27–31; intentions of, 30–31; irregular warfare conducted by, 2, 8, 12, 17, 32, 37, 50–51,

164; location characteristic of, 30; mergers by, 36; networked, 2, 35–48; organizational restructuring of, 40–45; post–Cold War, 12–14; and power asymmetries, 40–41; recruitment by, 43, 48; shape of, 29; size and structure of, 29; strategies of, 30, 36–37; transnational nature of, 39–40, 44–45, 105, 209–10; use of Internet and social media by, 19, 43–44, 48, 54; visibility characteristic of, 27–29. *See also* al-Qaeda; al-Qaeda in Iraq

Northern Alliance, 149, 204

North Korea, 100, 246n55

Obama, Barack, 172, 206, 209, 211–12; and Operation Neptune Spear, 49, 132

Al-Obeidi, Ahmed, 171

Odierno, Raymond, 171

Office of Coordinator of Information (COI), 55

Office of Current Intelligence (OCI), 95

Office of Intelligence Research, 56

Office of Military Affairs, 105

Office of National Estimates (ONE), 95, 99

Office of Naval Intelligence, 56

Office of Research and Reports (ORR), 95

Office of Soviet Analysis, 103

Office of Strategic Services (OSS), 55, 138, 230n29, 253n35

Office of the Director of Central Intelligence, 66

Oliver, Kay, 99

Omar, Mohammed, 149

Open Source Center (Reston, VA), 90

open-source intelligence (OSINT): characteristics of, 54; in post-9/11 period, 90–92; during World War II, 64–65

Operation Desert Storm, 1, 12–13, 60, 71, 104–5

Operation Eagle Claw, 144

Operation Enduring Freedom, 148–51, 203–4

Operation Inherent Resolve, 208–9

Operation Iraqi Freedom: fight against insurgency, 153–62, 166–72; legal authority for, 162–66; and toppling of Saddam Hussein, 151–52. *See also* Iraq

Operation Neptune Spear, 49–50, 132, 210, 211

Operation New Dawn, 172–73, 207–8

operations and intelligence (O&I) briefings, 161–62

Operation Zapata, 140

organizational culture, 176–77, 180, 188, 265n35

organizational memory, 181, 266n44

organizational routines, 180, 265n34

Organizations (March and Simon), 178, 179

Orton, James, 183, 195

Pahlavi, Mohammad Reza, 98

Pakistan, 86

Panda, Nutan Kumar, 122–23

paramilitary operations: during Cold War, 137, 138–44, 253n40, 254n48; as component of covert action, 23, 137–38; debate over responsibility for, 5, 164; by US special operations forces, 23, 137; during Vietnam War, 140–41, 254–55n53

pattern-of-life concept, 110, 247n78

Pawlowsky, Peter, 179

Peace Research Institute (PRIO), 15

Pendall, David, 112

Penkovsky, Oleg, 63–64, 234n85, 234n89

Petraeus, David, 168

Pettersson, Thérèse, 16–17

Philippines, 254n45

Phoenix Program, 140–41

photographic intelligence (PHOTOINT), 60

Pillar, Paul, 105–6

Poland, 135, 141, 252n16, 255n60

political action, covert, 135, 138–39, 140, 254n48

Pollard, Neal, 4

Posen, Barry, 176, 263n7

Practical Course for Guerrilla War (al-Muqrin), 203

Presidential Decision Directive 35, 104, 106

Presidential Decision Directive 39, 146

Presidential Decision Directive 62, 146

President's Daily Brief (PDB), 98

Price, Stephen, 71–72

problem solving: as core organizational competence, 180, 265n32; by TF 714, 182–84

propaganda, 136–37, 138–39
Psychology of Intelligence Analysis (Heuer), 102–3

al-Qaduli, Abd al-Rahman Mustafa, 208–9
Quadrennial Defense Review (2006), 19–20, 222n35
Quadrennial Diplomacy and Development Review (2009), 20
Qutb, Sayyed, 45

radar imagery, 61
radio broadcasts, 64–65, 136
radiometers, 60, 233nn68–69
Raduyev, Salman, 34, 35
al-Raymi, Qasim, 205
Reagan, Ronald, 105, 137, 141–42, 232n49
Real Time Regional Gateway (RTRG), 81–82
reconnaissance aircraft, 59, 232n55. *See also* U-2 spyplanes
Red Army Faction (Germany), 33
Red Brigades (Italy), 33
Remote Operations Center (ROC), 79–80
Ressler, Steve, 119–20
Revolutionary Armed Forces of Colombia (FARC), 33–34, 137, 258n119
Rhyolite satellites, 59, 232n57
Richelson, Jeffrey, 22, 27, 231–32n40; on intelligence collection, 4, 51–52, 53, 54, 59, 61, 80
Ridgway, Matthew B., 232n40
Rogan, Hanna, 90
Ronfeldt, David, 36, 44
Roosevelt, Franklin D., 55, 65
Rosen, Stephen, 178
Rosenau, William, 24, 137, 140–41
Royden, Barry, 64
RQ-4 Global Hawk, 74
RQ-7 Shadow, 73–74
Rumsfeld, Donald, 150–51, 163, 164
RUSI Journal, 14
Russia, 210, 211, 212
Ryan, Stephen, 111, 113–15, 117, 118

Sacolick, Bennet, 153, 169, 170, 171, 188–89
Saddam Hussein, 81, 152

Sageman, Marc, 42, 43
Sakaguchi, Toru, 119
Sarah, Abu, 209
Sargut, Gökçe, 120–21, 185
Saudi Arabia, 200, 205
Scalingi, Paula, 106
Schmitt, Gary, 53
Schoomaker Peter, 146
Schulz, Martin, 179
Schweitzer, Yoram, 196
Scott, David J., 153–54
Second Intifada, 156, 194, 195–96, 268n94
Second Lebanon War (2006), 41–42
Senate Select Committee on Intelligence (SSCI), 68, 142–43
Senate Select Committee to Study Governmental Operations with Respect to Intelligence (Church Committee), 138–40, 141
Senge, Peter, 181
Sentinel Security Assessments, 18
Shackley, Ted, 62–63
Shapiro, Jacob, 168
Sharon, Ariel, 194
Shikaki, Fathi, 34
Shin Bet, 156–57, 194–96
Shining Path (Peru), 137, 258n119
al-Shishani, Omar, 209
Shulsky, Abram, 22, 27, 53, 137
Shultz, Richard, 252n21
signals intelligence (SIGINT), 4–5, 68, 70; characteristics of, 52; during Cold War, 57–59, 76; and imagery, 21, 222n45; and post-9/11 wars, 76–82; during World War II, 55
Silent Warfare (Shulsky), 27
Simon, Herbert, 178
Sims, Jennifer, 85, 86, 194
site exploitation, 88–90, 127
Slocombe, Walter, 147
Smith, Rupert, 14, 15, 107
Smith, Walter Bedell, 95
Snowden, David, 47, 121, 188
Snyder, Jack, 16, 176
social media, 31, 48, 54, 90
social network analysis (SNA), 122
Solidarity (Poland), 135, 141, 252n16, 255n60

Sollenberg, Margareta, 15

Somalia, 76, 151, 204

Somoza, Anastasio, 142

Soviet Forces for Intercontinental Conflict (Steury), 99

Sovietology, 192

Soviet Union: and Afghanistan, 45, 209; atomic bomb of, 56, 231n36; border control by, 56, 231n35; and Communist parties, 253nn38–39; covert operations by, 135, 137; economy of, 99, 244–45n32; information collection on, 26–27, 50, 56–58; international front groups of, 136, 252n21; military power of, 56–57, 62, 99–100, 103, 234n89

Special Collection Service (SCS), 81

Special Operations (Joint Publication 3-05), 151

Special Operations Command (SOCOM), 5, 6, 7, 157; in Afghanistan, 149–50; establishment of, 144; and fight against al-Qaeda, 165–66; Joint Special Operations University of, 218n30; legal authority for, 164–66; limits put on, 146–47, 148. *See also* Task Force 714

Special Warfare Center and School (SWCS), 218n30

speech recognition, 77

Spender, J. C., 265n41

standard operating procedures (SOPs), 3, 132, 153–54, 176

star or hub network, 45

State Department, 20, 56, 208, 230n28

Stern, Jessica, 200

Steury, Donald, 99

Stimson, Henry L., 230n28

Stout, Mark, 91

strategic intelligence, 25, 67

Strategic Intelligence (Kent), 95–96

strategic surprise, 31, 153, 154, 179–80

strategic warning, 99, 244n30

Sulick, Michael, 63, 231n36

Sunni Awakening movement, 107, 167, 172, 247n74

Sun Tzu: *The Art of War,* 32

Support to Military Operations (SMO), 104–5

surveillance satellites, 72–73

Syria, 208–9, 212

tactical warning, 98–99

Tailored Access Operations (TAO), 79–80

Taliban: and al-Qaeda, 37, 209; insurgency by, 204, 206–7, 208; US ouster of, 25–26, 71, 148, 149–50, 203–4

Tanzania, 69, 76, 146

The Targeting Process (US Army Field Manual 3-60), 111

Task Force 20, 151–52

Task Force 714: and activity-based intelligence, 247n78; AQI as complex challenge for, 39, 48, 155; AQI as strategic surprise for, 31, 153, 154; AQI commanders and mangers taken out by, 168–69, 171, 175; Balad head-quarters of, 81, 87, 117–18, 126, 129, 131, 159, 161; command-and-control system of, 182, 184, 189–90, 201–2; creation of, 152; decentralization of, 188, 189–90, 201–2; detainees captured by, 54, 87–88, 127; and evolution of US counterterrorism operations, 173, 202–3, 209; and F3EAD targeting cycle, 109–10, 125–31, 159–62; imagery collection by, 71–76; impact of raids by, 7, 169–70, 202; as industrial-scale killing machine, 154, 168–69; initial response to AQI by, 153–54; intelligence dominance achieved by, 6, 156–57, 159–60, 187, 202; as intelligence-driven organization, 10, 126–27, 155–56, 186, 192, 202; Israel's lessons for, 10–11, 156–57, 194–99; ISR systems used by, 73–76, 118, 127; and joint task force, 125, 126, 156–59, 184, 187; leadership model of, 183, 188–93; as learning organization, 181, 182, 183, 188–93, 194, 197–99; and links between intel-ligence disciplines, 24–25; mission of, 108, 152–53, 168, 172, 183; network analysis by, 117–18; number of raids by, 7, 126–27, 175, 190, 201; operational authority of, 166; operational tempo of, 7, 10, 126, 127, 130, 131, 133, 160, 168, 169, 175, 187, 188–90, 193, 196, 201, 204, 206; opera-tional victory by, 166–72; partnerships of,

Task Force 714 (*continued*)
125, 126, 158–59, 183, 187, 199; problem
solving by, 182–84; reasons for transformation by, 181–200; SIGINT and COMINT
used by, 81–82; site exploitation by, 88–90,
127; team culture and organization of, 183,
191, 241n210; transformed into network, 6,
157–58, 183, 192; United Kingdom as network partner for, 199–200; video teleconferencing used by, 128, 161–62
Task Force Black, 199–200
Task Force Black (Urban), 199
Task Force Dagger, 149
Task Force Sword, 149–50
*Team of Teams: New Rules of Engagement for a
Complex World* (McChrystal), 190–93
Technical Advisory Group (TAG), 68–69
telephone surveillance, 77
Tenet, George, 69–70, 86
Thailand, 120
Themnér, Lotta, 16–17
Thompson, Peter, 18
threat network analysis, 124–25
"threshold doctrine," 141
Tolkachev, Adolf, 64, 234–35n91, 235n94
Tora Bora, 25–26, 150
traffic and signature analysis, 77–78
The Transformation of War (Creveld), 13–14
Treverton, Gregory, 3–4, 27, 109
Truman, Harry, 55, 253n38
Trump, Donald, 210–12

U-2 spyplanes, 59, 72, 73, 233n50
unconventional warfare, 34; DOD definition
of, 149; tactics, techniques, and procedures
of, 14; US adopts methods of, 51, 144,
148–50, 208
Unconventional Warfare (Marquis), 144
underground facilities, 84
United Kingdom, 94, 135, 177, 199–200, 263n7
unknown unknowns, 115
unmanned aerial vehicles (UAVs), 4, 53, 73–75,
80, 237n134
Urban, Mark, 199

US Central Command (CENTCOM), 149–50
US Code of Federal Regulations: Titles 10 and
50 of, 147, 164
US embassies: al-Qaeda bombing of, 67, 69, 76,
146; and signals collection, 80–81
The U.S. Intelligence Community (Richelson),
27, 51–52
U.S. News & World Report, 85
USS *Cole*, 67
US special operations forces (SOF). *See* Joint
Special Operations Command (JSOC);
paramilitary operations; Task Force 714
The Utility of Force (Smith), 14, 15, 107

vehicle-borne IEDs (VBIEDs), 83
video teleconferencing (VTC), 128, 161–62
Vietnam War, 101, 177, 263–64n10; US
covert propaganda during, 136, 252n20;
US paramilitary efforts during, 140–41,
254–55n53
visibility, armed group, 27–29
Votel, Joseph L., 170, 189, 209

Wall, Andru, 164–65
Wallensteen, Peter, 15, 219–20n13
Walter, Barbara, 16
warning intelligence, 98–99
War Powers Resolution, 162–63
@War: The Rise of the Military-Internet Complex
(Harris), 81, 82
Washington Post, 81
weapons of mass destruction (WMDs),
34, 106
Weekly Security Incidents Trends, 166–67
weight, armed group, 123
White, Harry Dexter, 135, 251n14
wide-area persistence surveillance
(WQAPS), 75
Wilson, James Q., 176–77
Wilson, Woodrow, 135
Winkler, Theodor, 17
word spotting, 77
World Peace Council (WPC), 136
World War I, 135, 230n28

World War II, 55, 64–65, 263n7; US covert actions during, 135, 138, 253n35
Worldwide Threat Assessment (2019), 211
al-Wuhayshi, Nasir, 205

XKeyscore, 80

Ya'alon, Moshe, 195, 197, 198
Yadlin, Amos, 197, 198

Yardley, Herbert, 230n28
Yassin, Ahmed, 34
Yemen, 76, 205–6

al-Zarqawi, Abu Musab, 38–39, 40, 42, 45, 88, 220n19
al-Zaydi, Nu'man Salman Mansur, 220n19
Zero Dark Thirty, 132
Zisk, Kimberly, 177

ABOUT THE AUTHOR

Richard H. Shultz Jr. is the Lee E. Dirks Professor of International Politics and director of the International Security Studies Program at the Fletcher School of Law and Diplomacy at Tufts University. He has held three chairs: Olin Distinguished Professor of National Security, US Military Academy; Secretary of the Navy Senior Research Fellow, Naval War College; and Brigadier General Oppenheimer Chair of Warfighting Strategy, US Marine Corps. Presently, he is senior fellow at the US Special Operations Command's Joint Special Operations University. Since the mid-1980s, he has served as a security consultant to various US government agencies concerned with national security.

He is the author of several books, including most recently *The Marines Take Anbar: The Four-Year Fight against Al Qaeda*; *Insurgents, Terrorists, and Militias: The Warriors of Contemporary Combat* (coauthored with Andrea J. Dew); and *The Secret War against Hanoi: The Untold Story of Spies, Saboteurs, and Covert Warriors in North Vietnam*.